American Culture, Canons, and the Case of Elizabeth Stoddard

American Culture, Canons, and the Case of Elizabeth Stoddard

Edited by Robert McClure Smith
and Ellen Weinauer

THE UNIVERSITY OF ALABAMA PRESS
Tuscaloosa and London

Typeface is Bembo

∞
The paper on which this book is printed meets the minimum requirements of
American National Standard for Information Science–Permanence of Paper for
Printed Library Materials, ANSI Z39.48-1984.

Library of Congress Cataloging-in-Publication Data

American culture, canons, and the case of Elizabeth Stoddard / edited by
Robert McClure Smith and Ellen Weinauer.
p.   cm.
Includes bibliographical references and index.
ISBN 0-8173-1313-3 (alk. paper)
1. Stoddard, Elizabeth, 1823–1902—Criticism and interpretation—History.
2. Women and literature—United States—History—19th century. 3. Canon
(Literature) I. Smith, Robert McClure. II. Weinauer, Ellen M.

PS2934.S3 Z55 2003
813'.4—dc21

2002155303

British Library Cataloguing-in-Publication Data available

To Barbara, Andrew, and Ian
                    —RMS

To Jonathan, Liana, and Raphael
                    —EMW

Contents

Acknowledgments

This project owes a special debt to those who pioneered scholarship on Elizabeth Stoddard and worked to make her texts available to contemporary audiences. In particular, we wish to thank James H. Matlack, whose exhaustive 1968 dissertation on Stoddard's life and writing provides the groundwork for virtually every essay in this volume and who has graciously granted us permission to quote from his work. We also extend our appreciation to Lawrence Buell and Sandra A. Zagarell, whose critical edition of Elizabeth Stoddard's writings first put her on the American literary map and brought her to our attention. We are grateful for their pioneering work of literary recovery and for their contributions to this volume. We wish, too, to thank the many individuals who responded to our call for papers for this collection and those others who have offered their support to this project, especially Anne Boyd, Ann-Marie Ford, and Abbie Sprague of the National Gallery.

The anonymous readers for the University of Alabama Press provided thoughtful responses to this collection from its earliest stages and offered invaluable suggestions for its improvement. The staff at the University of Alabama Press provided timely advice and help along the way. Finally, we are grateful to our contributors for their scholarly insight, their diligence, and their unflagging commitment to this project.

We both received generous support from our respective academic institutions, to which we owe our thanks. The John and Elaine Fellowes fund of Knox College and the University of Southern Mississippi provided financial assistance for costs incurred acquiring permissions for this volume. Knox College and the University of Southern Mississippi both provided sabbatical grants that allowed us to complete the majority of the work that this collection has entailed. We are grateful for such tangible forms of institutional support and for the more intangible intellectual support offered by our colleagues and friends at our home institutions.

A lively electronic correspondence and a commitment to genuine, mutually supportive collaborative work has enhanced our work on this volume over the last several years, and we are grateful to the American Literature Association Convention that brought us together back in 1999. Our academic labors—and our non-academic lives—have been greatly enriched by the love, encouragement, generosity, and patience of our spouses, Barbara Tannert and Jonathan Barron, and our children, Andrew and Ian Smith and Liana and Raphael Barron. It is to them that we owe our greatest debts, and to them that this book is dedicated.

For permission to publish Stoddard manuscripts in their possession we are indebted to the Special Collections of Houghton Library, Harvard University, Columbia University, Boston Public Library, and the Addison-Shelley Collection of the Pennsylvania State University Libraries.

An earlier version of Sandra A. Zagarell's essay titled "Profile: Elizabeth Drew Barstow Stoddard (1823–1902)" was published in *Legacy* 8.1 (1991): 39–49. We thank the University of Nebraska Press for permission to reprint.

Emily Dickinson's poetry is reprinted by permission of the publishers and the Trustees of Amherst College from *The Poems of Emily Dickinson,* ed. Thomas H. Johnson, Cambridge, MA: Belknap Press of Harvard University Press, Copyright © 1951, 1955, 1979 by the President and Fellows of Harvard College.

*American Culture, Canons, and the
Case of Elizabeth Stoddard*

Introduction

Crossing Can(n)on Street

Ellen Weinauer and Robert McClure Smith

> Mrs Stoddard was beginning to make her distinct and special quality
> felt in the magazines, in verse and fiction. In both it seems to me
> that she has failed of the recognition that her work merits. Her tales
> and novels have in them a foretaste of realism, which was too strong
> for the palate of their day, and is now too familiar, perhaps. It is a
> peculiar fate, and would form the scheme of a pretty study in the
> history of literature.
>
> William Dean Howells, *Literary Friends and Acquaintances*

Mattapoisett is a very different place today from the town where
Elizabeth Drew Barstow Stoddard was born and raised and where she
returned as a summer vacationer for thirty-five years. During her childhood, the town was a major shipbuilding center whose prosperity was
inextricably tied to the vagaries of the whaling industry. The *Acushnet,*
the whaler on which Herman Melville shipped in 1841 and which he
later immortalized as the *Pequod,* was launched in 1840 from a Barstow
yard in Mattapoisett. Later, with the financial collapse of the whaling
industry after the Civil War, the town emerged from economic depres-
sion as a fashionable summer resort for vacationing Bostonians. Now,
only a plaque on Shipyard Park commemorates the founders' trade, and
the main tourist highway bypasses Mattapoisett, looping south across the
Sagamore Bridge to Cape Cod and Martha's Vineyard. The town is
sleepy and pretty, a place where Boston professionals buy second homes
and sail white yachts on Buzzard's Bay. On a Friday night by the Ned's
Point lighthouse, you can watch windsurfers unpack their SUVs. The
Shipyard Gallery, once a rigging loft, is now a quaint deli/bookstore. By
the old wharf, not far from the town gazebo, where you can hear a local
orchestra perform on summer evenings, is a refreshment kiosk called

the Ice-Cream Slip. Walking downtown to the Slip for early-morning coffee, you might well see a Porsche parked on the jetty.

The Mattapoisett Inn on Water Street is a white three-story building overlooking the harbor. It is the oldest operating seaside inn in the nation, and its small restaurant and bar must be among the most crowded. Clustered around the inn are silver-shingled colonials and capes from Mattapoisett's prosperous years that today look much as they must have looked to Elizabeth Stoddard—the Josiah Holmes House (1805), the Dr. Vernon Southworth House (1839), and the Benjamin Barstow House (1797). On the wall of the Elihu Sherman House (1797) is a memorial plaque: "Here was born, November 3, 1846, Francis Davis Millet— drummer-boy—war-correspondent—author—illustrator—artist—He went down with the Titanic, April 15, 1912." There are some things the town wants to remember.

Unlike the ill-fated and well-memorialized Millet, Elizabeth Barstow Stoddard seems to have been largely effaced from and forgotten in the history of Mattapoisett. To get to the gray, cedar-shingled Barstow house where the Stoddard family stayed when they summered in Mattapoisett, you need to cross Cannon Street. A view that was once unobstructed is today obscured by bushes that front the seawall project and an expanse of sand and gorse belonging to the Mattapoisett Land Trust. But from the window of Stoddard's room you can see almost all of the bay and harbor, a deep tree line on the opposite shore flattening to a long peninsula and then disappearing in an expanse of blue breaking away to the horizon. A local real-estate agent now owns the old Barstow house. Like all the longtime residents of Mattapoisett, the owner is familiar with the Barstow name (there are other Barstow houses and a Barstow Street along the shorefront). In 1967, James Matlack observed that Mattapoisett was a small town with a long memory, a place that "holds all outsiders at a distance and gossips vigorously about its own kin." He noted that Stoddard's "often satiric portraits of the town and its people also generated a legacy of ill-will which was long harbored and is not yet entirely dissipated" ("Literary Career" 21). If just thirty-five years ago Stoddard still held a place (albeit one gained by "ill-will") in Mattapoisett's "long memory," today she is all but forgotten. Currently, the only itemized holding in the Mattapoisett Historical Society concerning Stoddard is a grainy photocopy of Matlack's dissertation. Stoddard's erasure from the local historical record is almost complete. In a historical reminiscence titled *Old Mattapoisett: A Summer Portrait,* Edward Wood, interested primarily in the Stoddards' role as returning summer visitors, writes, "By

1992 [Stoddard's] best-known novel, *The Morgesons,* had long since disappeared from the shelves of the Mattapoisett Public Library, and was represented there only by a yellowed entry in the card catalogue" (61). Wood was not himself engaged in the local-author-recovery business: while admitting that the novel is "an almost perfect mirror of the town," he notes that Stoddard's realistic representation of the local populace "brought pain to the delicate social covenant that undergirded village life" (66). In a *Daily Alta California* column of 1856, Stoddard indicated her awareness of the discomfiting effect her work had on her native village: "I am, in fact, looked upon as a vampire here; for sustenance I write about them, and ridicule them" (8 June 1856). Writing so many years later, Wood turns the tables on Stoddard, "ridiculing" her in order, apparently, to finish her off: he observes that "the record of [Stoddard's] repeated outrageous—indeed, often devastating—behavior, even toward her closest friends, is appalling" and, as a curious capstone, remarks that "in photographs taken in her younger years, [she] looks the part: rather unattractive in appearance, spare, gaunt and shrewd" (61). In just this way, perhaps, the local vampire is finally staked.[1]

But that conclusion is, perhaps, unfair. When the locals construct their own edited versions of town history, it is often more convenient to forget the difficult resident. The coherent historical narrative sometimes demands the erasure of the occasional misfit, the one who unsettles the "delicate social covenants" of local life. In this regard, the residents of small coastal New England towns are not so different from the makers and re-makers of our American literary canons—selective narrative historians, cliquish protectors of decorous boundaries, well-intentioned eliminators of the awkward case. Pierre Bourdieu notes that the literary field is "a veritable social universe where, in accordance with its particular laws, there accumulates a particular form of capital and where relations of force of a particular type are exerted" and that those relations ultimately determine "who is part of the universe, who is a real writer and who is not" (164). Stoddard fits as neatly into the memory of idyllic village life as she does into our various master narratives of American literary history—which is to say that she fits not at all. That Stoddard should have vanished simultaneously from the history of Mattapoisett and from the American literary universe is hardly coincidental—identical desires motivate and sustain the two exclusionary processes, and they exert very similar "relations of force."

In this volume, we wish to insist on the importance of "crossing can(n)on street," of crossing over to look more closely at this "vanished" writer and, further, at the challenges she poses to our own critical narratives and the canonical categories that underwrite them. Not only is Stoddard a crucially important figure in the literature of the antebellum and postbellum periods (and a writer who seriously complicates that often convenient historical demarcation), but critical neglect of her work has had serious ramifications for our understanding of American literary history. By reconsidering Stoddard's fiction, poetry, and journalism and analyzing her current marginal status in the evolving canon of American literary studies, this volume raises important questions about women's writing in the nineteenth century and literary canon formation in the twentieth. Stoddard is a compelling example of the contingency of critical values and the instability of literary history. Drawing on a range of theoretical approaches and cultural materials, the essays in this volume, therefore, seek to elevate the reputation of this still neglected but important writer and to intervene in the ongoing debates about the development of a literary canon and the relationship between literature and the culture in which it is embedded.

William Dean Howells once observed of Elizabeth Stoddard that "in whatever she did she left the stamp of a talent like no other" (*Literary Friends* 87). That unique talent expressed itself in a remarkable range of literary venues. From 1854 to 1858, Stoddard wrote regular columns for the *Daily Alta California,* a San Francisco newspaper. As the paper's "Lady Correspondent," Stoddard delivered news of the East Coast world to the growing new West, commenting—incisively, often ironically—on everything from contemporary political and cultural events (newly published writers, women's rights conventions) to summers spent in coastal New England. Beginning in 1853, Stoddard—influenced by her husband and the circle of "genteel poets" of which he was a part—began writing verse, much of which was well received and published in such venues as the *Atlantic Monthly, Harper's,* and *Putnam's.* Between 1860 and the early 1890s, Stoddard would write highly acclaimed short fiction for those same magazines. Most significantly, between 1862 and 1867 she would publish her three immensely innovative novels. This extraordinary fiction, complex, elliptical, and evocative, is a remarkable and unique achievement in nineteenth-century American literature. As Sandra Zagarell and others have noted, Stoddard was at the epicenter of New York's literary salon culture, where she encountered such influential figures as William Cullen Bryant, Thomas Bailey Aldrich, Alice and Phoebe Cary, Caroline Kirkland, George Ripley, and Horace

Greeley. Despite this fact, she—to quote Howells once again—"never would write like anyone but herself." Her uniqueness was at once a gift and a burden. Although, for example, Stoddard's novels were reprinted twice in her lifetime (first in 1888–89 and then in 1901), and although she received the acclaim of such esteemed writers as Nathaniel Hawthorne and Howells, her fiction never sold, and her work never received the large-scale public attention for which she hoped.[2] It is apparently true that Stoddard was, as critic Richard Foster asserted in 1972, "writing for audiences not yet born" ("Fiction" 162).

Given Stoddard's varied and original literary achievements, it is not surprising that her work became part of the "recovery" effort pioneered by reconstructionist literary critics in the 1980s. Following the lead of Matlack and Foster, Lawrence Buell and Sandra Zagarell introduced Stoddard to a new generation of readers in their 1984 collection *The Morgesons and Other Writings, Published and Unpublished*. Buell and Zagarell's effort to help "birth" an audience for Stoddard—an effort manifested not only in their collaborative critical collection but also in their important individual treatments of Stoddard's work[3]—appears to have had an almost immediate effect. A flurry of articles about and treatment of Stoddard and her work appeared in academic journals and in book-length studies of nineteenth-century American writing by such influential critics as David Reynolds, David Leverenz, and Susan K. Harris. Responding to this "revival" of interest in Stoddard—and indicating the increasing perception of Stoddard's "teachability"—Sandra Gilbert and Susan Gubar printed Stoddard's "Lemorne *versus* Huell" in their *Norton Anthology of Literature by Women* (1988); and both the *Norton Anthology of American Literature* (1989) and the *Heath Anthology of American Literature* (1990) followed Gilbert and Gubar's lead, including "Lemorne *versus* Huell" in new editions. Finally, as perhaps the strongest indicator of Stoddard's canonical acceptance, Penguin picked up *The Morgesons* for their "Penguin Classics" series in 1997.

Despite these efforts—and what they seem to indicate about her canonical status—Stoddard remains curiously absent from the contemporary critical consciousness. Important feminist studies of the period often neglect to mention Stoddard altogether (Mary Kelley's *Private Woman, Public Stage: Literary Domesticity in Nineteenth Century America* [1984], Jane Tompkins's *Sensational Designs* [1986], and Susan Coultrap-McQuin's *Doing Literary Business: American Women Writers in the Nineteenth Century* [1990], for example, have nothing to say about Stoddard). While other critical studies do examine Stoddard's work, their treatments do not always enhance its reputation. In *Beneath the American Renaissance* (1988), for example, David Reynolds gives Stoddard a fair amount of attention; but his (scantily evidenced) argument turns on the notion that Stoddard's work is actually strikingly ordinary, her best-known novel being "a *typical example* of the dark genre of women's writings" and "*typical* of the broken narrative patterns of the literature of misery" (409, emphasis added).[4] Such critical gaps and negative assessments perhaps help explain why the one full-length biographical study of Stoddard, Matlack's "The Literary Career of Elizabeth Barstow Stoddard," is, while an extraordinarily detailed text that indicates Stoddard's centrality to nineteenth-century literary culture, an unpublished dissertation now twenty-five years old; why there has been, as yet, no single critical monograph focused on Stoddard's fiction; why a search of the *MLA Bibliography* turns up a total of only thirty-four citations for Stoddard; why there has been no significant, defining article about her in a major journal in the field such as *American Literature* or *American Literary History*. It is little wonder, therefore, that such "mainstream" publications as the *Columbia Literary History of the United States* (1988) and the *Columbia Literary History of the American Novel* (1991) offer Stoddard only the most cursory mention, often in passing. Indeed, the former summarizes Stoddard's entire oeuvre in two sentences, describing *The Morgesons* as a "striking work of gloomy local color" (303). Descriptive evaluations such as these serve only to validate a comment made by Stoddard in a letter to Edmund Stedman shortly after the novel's publication in 1862: "Indications are that it will be misunderstood."[5] It would appear that Stoddard's assessment was prescient with regard not only to *The Morgesons* but also to her later novels, her short fiction, and her poetry. Despite the excellent recovery work of Buell and Zagarell, the later valiant effort by Susan K. Harris to locate Stoddard in the larger critical narrative of nineteenth-century women's literature,[6] and the small but committed number of articles and dissertations written about her work in recent years, Elizabeth Stoddard remains strangely anomalous, a historical curiosity and, always, a seriously overlooked American writer of significance.

In attempting to make sense of the ongoing neglect of Stoddard and her work, Zagarell has argued that "Stoddard's place in American literature has remained negligible primarily because readers have never known how to place her" ("Repossession" 45). Zagarell's assessment is borne out in the existing criticism: variously identified as a domestic novelist, an antisentimentalist, a local-color precursor of realism, a Brontë-inspired gothicist, a provincial gothicist, and a proto-modernist, Stoddard seems to have fallen through the critical cracks. Thus, for example, while Buell and Zagarell claim *The Morgesons* as an important precursor of twenti-eth-century narrative experimentation, Reynolds identifies the same text as "typical" of and in conformity with nineteenth-century generic formations. Such diametrically opposed readings give validity to Dawn Henwood's assertion that Stoddard's works "defy hairsplitting categori-cal analysis because they consistently disturb the limits conventionally imposed on the categories themselves" ("First-Person Storytelling" 43). Stoddard's writing, in other words, continually abjures the definitions critics seek to impose upon it—a fact that has had considerable rami-fications for the later reception of Stoddard's work by the overarching critical narratives of literary history. In retrospect, and for the under-standable purpose of maintaining thematic and formal consistency, it has been judicious for scholars to ignore Stoddard's disturbing of neat bound-aries and to slight her writing's fraying of established generic categories.

While the primary concern of this collection is to establish Stod-dard's literary significance, then, our analysis necessarily extends to the critical history of Stoddard's reception and, thus, to the problematic process of canon formation. The very existence of competing nine-teenth-century literary anthologies like the *Heath* and the *Norton,* with their ever-evolving and ever more diversified representations of texts, indicates the extent to which canon formation has become perhaps *the* key issue for scholars of this particular literary period. The influential work of feminist scholars like Jane Tompkins, Nina Baym, and Judith Fetterley has immensely complicated our understanding of the estab-lished canon of nineteenth-century American literature. The most im-mediate consequence of their feminist critique has been the dramatic reinclusion of women writers, often the same writers implicitly referred to by Hawthorne, in that memorable offhand remark to his publisher, as that "d——d mob of scribbling women" (*Letters* 304). Thus, previously forgotten or, at least, neglected writers like Caroline Kirkland, Fanny Fern, Louisa May Alcott, Susan Warner, E. D. E. N. Southworth, and Alice Cary have been reevaluated in recent years. The publication of new bi-ographies and critical monographs has sustained this important work of recovery. Crucial to this ongoing revisionary impulse has been the prin-ciple that canon formation—that is, the actual process of selection and evaluation—is always significantly related to, if not a function of, critical technique. A reader who finds "sentimental power" where others have found mere "sentimentality" is a reader who provides a rather different analysis of the "sentimental" text.

Given the recent resurrection of so many forgotten women writers, Stoddard's continued difficult placement in the canon of nineteenth-century literature makes her an especially revelatory case. While other American women writers of the era identified more as professionals than as artists, Stoddard embraced a male-derived Romantic model of self-as-artist, and although drawn to the subject matter and narrative structures favored by her female contemporaries, she continually evidences a stylistic affinity with experimental Romantic gothicists like Edgar Allan Poe and Hawthorne while usually employing a cryptic, elliptically imploded prose style quite unlike that of any other writer of the era. The fact that recent theoretical constructions of nineteenth-century women's literature have not made narrative experimentation a defining characteristic of women's fiction of this period suggests that Stoddard's continued elision from the developing canon of American literature and her bold stylistic experimentation may be related phenomena. A marginal figure in the earlier male-centered canon, Stoddard has had the misfortune of maintaining her marginal status—in part, due to the radical nature of her fictional experiment—in the new and evolving canon of the period. The essays in this volume make the case that Stoddard's status as perpetual misfit provides a significant insight into the problematic process of canon formation and reformation and, most disturbingly, show how the act of critical revaluation and reconstruction may fall prey to the techniques of the exclusionary practice it exposes. While the collection's inquiry into the politics of literary reputation takes Stoddard's literary texts as its point of departure, each of the essays offers a more extensive understanding of ante- and postbellum American culture. Individual essays locate Stoddard in the context of her contemporaries, be they canonical figures like Hawthorne and Dickinson or marginalized authors such as Fern, Alcott, Woolson, or the genteel poets in whose circle Stoddard (probably to her detriment) consistently moved. Other analyses offer more insistently cultural investigations, situating Stoddard in the context of the major discursive formations of nineteenth-century American culture: the discourses of sentimentalism and domesticity; race and ethnicity; incest and masochism; anorexia and female invalidism; nationalism and localism; the Civil War and Reconstruction. Through these multifaceted investigations, the essays provide a complex view of both Stoddard's literary texts and the texts of the culture and milieu that contour her fiction, poetry, and journalism.

Fittingly, we begin our query into Elizabeth Stoddard's peculiar and illuminating literary case with an overview of her life and career written by Sandra Zagarell—one of the two critics to whom we are indebted for introducing Stoddard to contemporary academic audiences. In her biographical foreword, "Elizabeth Drew Barstow Stoddard (1823–1902)," Zagarell traces Stoddard's path from her often troubled youth and family circumstances in a whaling and shipbuilding town to the genteel literary circles of New York City and her later friendships with Caroline Kirkland, Horace Greeley, William Cullen Bryant, George Ripley, Alice Cary, and other notable peers. Commenting on the triumphs and failures of the fiction, and its incredibly convoluted reception in Stoddard's own lifetime, and quoting liberally from the writer's correspondence and early journalism, Zagarell maintains that Stoddard's work complicates considerably our sense of nineteenth-century literature by women. Echoing Howells's view that "[Stoddard] never could write like anyone but herself," Zagarell ponders the uniqueness of Stoddard's compelling project to articulate the nature and dynamics of a woman's subjectivity. Zagarell concludes that her "philosophic and stylistic originality, her conflicts, her accomplishments and her failures render Elizabeth Stoddard's work, and her life, of great interest. In both, she not only challenges our models of nineteenth-century American women writers . . . she pursues questions that continue to speak across the distance of time."

Zagarell's articulation of the "challenges" that Stoddard's work and life pose to our critical models lays the groundwork for the analysis of literary identity and canon formation undertaken in this volume's first set of essays, "The Writer, the Canon, and the Protocols of Print." In "'Among a Crowd, I Find Myself Alone': Elizabeth Stoddard and the Canon of Nineteenth-Century American Women's Poetry," Robert McClure Smith takes up one such critical challenge directly in an analysis of Stoddard's poetry—poetry that has gone all but unmentioned in the work of contemporary critics. For Smith, it is precisely this absence that makes Stoddard's poetry such an effective test case for the categories by which nineteenth-century American women's poetry is understood. In recent years, the New Historicist–inflected argument that women's poetry of the era, although adhering to mainstream sentimental conventions and the expressive limitations of traditional forms, performs significant "cultural work" has challenged the New Critical celebration of a poetic complexity inhering in paradox and irony—a critical model that facilitated the earlier canonization of Emily Dickinson. Reminding us that judgments with canonical force are institutionally located, Smith observes that Stoddard, who had little sympathy for the formal experimentation of Dickinson and who was equally temperamentally averse to any sustained celebration of sentimental experience in her poetry, offers a useful complication of the dual critical models. Noting that Stoddard was a poet only too aware of her "difficult self-location in the gap between residual and emergent nineteenth-century poetic categories," Smith argues that a study of the liminal position of Stoddard's poetry (and, by implication, of Stoddard's fiction) between the polar dimensions of the dominant categories may permit nothing less than the inscription of an alternative understanding of literary gender representation in the nineteenth century.

Like Smith, Margaret Amstutz focuses on texts that have been largely marginalized in Stoddard scholarship in order to analyze, from a different perspective, the genesis of this writer's unusual literary project. In "Elizabeth Stoddard as Returned Californian: A Reading of the *Daily Alta California* Columns," Amstutz argues that Stoddard's early journalism as a correspondent from New York City for the *Daily Alta California* significantly contoured the distinctive grain of her literary voice. Examining particular columns, most significantly Stoddard's report on the New York Crystal Palace exhibition of 1854, Amstutz claims that the journalistic genre with which Stoddard commenced her career and, in particular, the imaginative journey undertaken by Stoddard-as-narrator to California originally enabled the later movement of the narrative self in her fiction beyond the dual legacies of British and American (especially Hawthornian) influence. In the *Daily Alta* columns, Amstutz finds a public forum for testing both Hawthorne's presentation of the moral imagination and his legacy of self-questioning, a forum framed and informed by the bicoastal landscape of Stoddard's embryonic literary imagination. In Amstutz's reading, Stoddard's journalism thus afforded her an apprenticeship both intertextual and interstitial; locating her own voice as a writer in relation to the sketches of her distant cousin Hawthorne in particular, Stoddard also found the means—through the situated triangulation of landscape for her immediate audience—to begin charting an alternate cartography of the self. Attuned by her early journalism to the chasm between storyteller and audience, between experienced and envisioned environment, Stoddard discovered an imaginative space from within which she could, ultimately, assert her own literary ambition, relocate herself squarely in her native New England culture, and engage, in an act of "arachnid revisionism," the legacy left her by deeply influential precursors.

While Smith and Amstutz are concerned with the genesis and early formation of Stoddard's distinctive literary voice, Paul Crumbley chooses to locate that voice very much within the larger culture of postbellum women writers. In "Haunting the House of Print: The Circulation of Disembodied Texts in 'Collected by a Valetudinarian' and 'Miss Grief,'" Crumbley considers two short stories that provide evidence of their female writers' awareness of their problematic positioning within contemporary print culture. For Crumbley, both Stoddard's "Valetudinarian" and Constance Fenimore Woolson's "Miss Grief" show that print culture in nineteenth-century America was so resistant to the original contributions of female writers that the more dedicated among them were deprived of the cultural support that would have enabled them to live healthy lives and produce works that would have reached a public readership. Both stories are, in essence, constructed around texts (a diary in the case of "Valetudinarian," a novel in the case of "Miss Grief") that never appear. These disembodied, "missing" texts haunt the stories in which they figure so prominently through the lingering effect they have on those who read, write, and hear them. By pointing to manuscript compositions that have great power but are incapable of print publication, Crumbley argues, these stories achieve two objectives of particular importance to nineteenth-century American women writers: they illuminate the extent to which print conventions constrain literary representation, and they draw attention to human experiences—in these instances, female—that lie outside the protocols of print culture. That the female authors described in these stories are from the beginning sickly, and eventually die unpublished, further magnifies the degree to which Stoddard and Woolson saw a correlation between female health and the establishment of an official print record that would acknowledge and, therefore, give cultural life to the actual experiences of real women. Woolson provocatively identified Stoddard as an example of the effect writing can have on female health: upon hearing that the latter was ill in 1876, Woolson asked Edmund Stedman, "Why do literary women break down so?" What these short stories demonstrate is that for both authors this was an important question, but one that proved most productive when left unanswered. Indeed, it enables both writers to make mind-body/text-body oppositions central to the evocation of heteroglossia unique to the female writer's contemplation of public utterance. In both works, ailing female authors inhabit an unstable ground between individual artistic integrity and the belief that historical change depends on public utterance; in this way, each story identifies a correspondence between personal health and publication that mirrors larger concerns with the health of a culture that impedes the circulation of texts generated by half its members.

Crumbley's analysis of the correlation in Stoddard's work between female health and textual circulation, between (sickly) "deviant" women and silenced texts, suggests that, for Stoddard, women's bodies and women's writing can never be separated. His analysis thus provides a fitting entrance into the more specific investigations of ideologies of gender and domesticity offered by Julia Stern, Susanna Ryan, and Jaime Osterman Alves. Indeed, both Stern and Ryan expand on Crumbley's inquiry into notions of "female health" in their somewhat divergent readings of Stoddard's best-known novel, *The Morgesons*. For these writers, Stoddard's virtual obsession with appetite—the ingestion and consumption of food, starvation and hunger—signals her ongoing concerns with female agency, power, and voice.

In "'I Am Cruel Hungry': Dramas of Twisted Appetite and Rejected Identification in Elizabeth Stoddard's *The Morgesons*," Julia Stern examines the ways in which domesticity functions perversely and parasitically in Stoddard's best-known novel. Recognizing the novel's unflinching display of sadistic and masochistic behaviors in domestic settings, Stern argues that Stoddard uses sadism and masochism—and their related co-morbid phenomena, hysteria and the twisting of appetite—as a means of countering the domestic discourse central to white, middle-class culture. Stern notes that virtually every character in *The Morgesons*, whether major or minor, "maintains a troubled relation to desire." Framing these renditions of "troubled" desire with psychoanalytic studies of "identificatory disturbances," Stern argues that by "understanding the ways in which Stoddard's characters do not identify with—or fail to internalize—the people and things populating their emotional landscapes, the perverse ways in which they relate to their own desires," we can begin to understand Stoddard's challenge to the discourse with which nineteenth-century women (writers) have come to be most fully associated: sentimentalism. Examining Stoddard's perverse depiction of maternal nurturance and mother-child relations in particular, Stern argues that through "variations on the motif of perverse consumption, Stoddard's book offers a dialectical rebuttal to the women's tradition inaugurated" by such writers as Susan Warner and Harriet Beecher Stowe and "allows us to reimagine a postsentimental genealogy" for American women's fiction of the Civil War and post–Civil War eras.

Susanna Ryan's "'Perversions of Volition': Self-Starvation and Self-Possession in Dickinson and Stoddard" also examines Stoddard's rendition of appetite and desire in order to recognize the place of her work in a literary genealogy—a genealogy that in this case extends from the other major New England experimentalist of the era, Emily Dickinson. Beginning with T. W. Higginson's observation that the Dickinson household in Amherst reminded him of nothing so much as Stoddard's novels, and noting some remarkable biographical similarities between the two writers, Ryan traces the connection between the writers' relation to hunger and their understanding of their own agency. In particular, Ryan demonstrates how both writers, through tropes of starvation and appetite, and by inversion of the teleology of conventionally masculine narratives of experience and self-development, imagine alternative possibilities for female growth and self-possession. Moving from Dickinson's anorexic poetics, which "posits an autoerotics of growth through emaciation," to *The Morgesons,* in which self-possession is desired but elusive, Ryan frames the works of both writers with historically situated, self-starving or self-pleasuring "perversions of volition," thereby exposing the numerous and often conflicted ways in which mid-nineteenth-century culture expressed anxieties regarding any means of female agency. For Dickinson and Stoddard, the acceptance or refusal of food serves as a way to represent the negotiation of a female process of self-growth that relies on neither a bildungsromanesque drive toward self-understanding nor the conventions of heterosexual domesticity. But while Dickinson can imagine a "sublimely unified, autoerotic self," Stoddard —writing in the arguably more constrained form of the "realistic" novel —would seem to suggest that the "enclosed satisfactions of the lyric self are complicated by an appetitive imbrication with things external," a habitation within the social and relational world. Read in conjunction, the works of both authors represent a complicated and contrasting effort by women to manipulate both cultural limitations and their own bodies to achieve a self ultimately both appetitive and volitional.

While it is true that Stoddard's challenging treatment of female appetite and will seems to have compromised her bid for a wide audience, both in her own day and in ours, it is also true that Stoddard was a visible presence to her contemporaries, publishing a surprising number of stories—some seventy short pieces—in some of the most widely read and respected periodicals of her day. In "Home Coming and Home Leaving: Interrogations of Domesticity in Elizabeth Stoddard's *Harper's* Fiction, 1859–1891," Jaime Osterman Alves shows that a broader look at Stoddard's periodical publications will add new dimensions to our understanding of her depiction of female identity and the domestic stage on which that identity was largely enacted. Between 1859 and 1891, Stoddard published eighteen short stories in *Harper's New Monthly Magazine,* thus establishing a literary home for her work and creating a substantial complement to her longer fiction, poetry, and journalistic writings. While a few of the *Harper's* stories have garnered scholarly attention, the majority have been consigned to obscurity. Yet within these stories, Alves maintains, Stoddard records—in a manifestly middle-class and largely conservative print venue—the complex and often ambivalent relationships that white, middle-class women had toward their domestic spaces. Indeed, like Julia Stern, Alves suggests that neglecting the challenges Stoddard's fiction poses to the twinned discourses of domesticity and sentimentalism impoverishes current (re)considerations of nineteenth-century women's writing. Specifically, Alves explores how Stoddard contests domestic discourse by manipulating two of its primary tenets. First, Stoddard rejects the (middle-class) assumption that the external structures of domestic space provide accurate mirrors into the intimate emotional lives of its inhabitants. Unlike that imagined by such "home advice" writers as Catherine Beecher and Harriet Beecher Stowe, Stoddard's "whole domesticity" shows not just "delicate, beautifully colored papers" and tidy kitchens but also the "rough beams" and the difficult labor by which middle-class homes, and the women who inhabit and construct them, are truly constituted. Second, and related, Stoddard contests "her culture's divisions between public and private spheres," showing instead that "public" and "private" function as "modes of behavior" that both describe and circumscribe "the self that a character presents to the world, or withholds from it." Ultimately, by undermining the notion that the home is a transparent haven separate from the "public" world, and suggesting that the home is as prone to chaos, conflict, and secrecy as the world "beyond" it, Stoddard seeks to show how women might gain greater degrees of agency and self-control over both the "private" and the "public" aspects of their lives. In examining a variety of stories that have gone virtually unread by Stoddard scholars—not to mention by Americanist critics at large—Alves reminds us, as does Smith in his essay on Stoddard's poetry, that "forgotten" texts can often complicate and challenge critical paradigms.

By turning their attention to Stoddard's widely neglected second and third novels, the essays by Lisa Radinovsky, Jennifer Putzi, and Ellen Weinauer continue the complicating recovery work initiated by Alves and Smith. These essays aim, both explicitly and implicitly, not only to illustrate the importance of some of the unexamined texts in the Stoddard "canon" but also to illuminate, via Stoddard, some of the alternative (and perhaps critically unacknowledged) ways in which women writers engaged in the debates and discursive formations of nineteenth-century America. As the essays in this volume demonstrate, Stoddard's work, when it is read at all, is typically viewed through the lens of gender ideologies and the discourse of domesticity. Rarely, however, has her work been seen in the context of, or as a direct response to, the explicit political debates of her day. Most strikingly, despite having described her first novel in terms of the Civil War ("The Morgesons was my Bull Run," she once told Edmund Stedman [qtd. in Buell and Zagarell xix]), Stoddard is almost never linked to the "war decade" during which she published her three full-length works of fiction. In the final section of this volume, "Race, Reconstruction, and American Citizenship," we include essays that seek at once to situate Stoddard's work in terms of the issues of the Civil War—in particular, to understand her complex navigation of the issues of race, American race relations, and citizenship—and to explore some of the alternative ways in which (women) writers of the period entered what Lyde Cullen Sizer has called the "terrain of national concern" (5) in the wartime and postwar periods.

In "(Un)Natural Attractions? Incest and Miscegenation in *Two Men*," Lisa Radinovsky offers a reading of Stoddard's overlooked second novel, published in 1865, when the twin specters of slavery and emancipation were creating increased opposition to interracial coupling and concerns about incest. These two violations of taboos, linked under the slave system, were similarly described as "unnatural" in the antebellum period. Yet Stoddard chooses to attack conventional beliefs about relationships, manhood, womanhood, racial difference, and desire with unusually realistic representations of both interracial and incestuous relationships. Radinovsky acknowledges that in *Two Men* Stoddard provides a remarkably complex representation of both black and white women and an unidealized perspective on racism. However, in refusing to allow her primary African American female character to live, let alone marry a white man, Stoddard proves to be less comfortable—and less radical—in her treatment of racism than in her related analysis of incest. Thus, while the interracial relationship in the novel is represented as destructive, the incestuous relationship is represented as the novel's most successful family formation and the most rational course toward emotional regeneration. Indeed, the paternal incest in this novel embodies the story's return to comparative tranquillity after the scandal of interracial liaison. Although incest was a popular subject in early American gothic and seduction novels and mid-nineteenth-century American domestic best-sellers, recent scholars have argued that American literature of this period indicates a powerful fear of the consequences of incest. In her representation of incest, Stoddard has less in common with American authors than with the European Romantic poets who may, in fact, have inspired her deployment of transgressive sexuality. Like Shelley in *Laon and Cythna,* Stoddard uses incest to critique institutional structures and the established conventions on which they depend. Differing from the American Romantics and sentimentalists, who tended to portray incest as coercive and destructive, Stoddard's radical experiment with psychological realism permits her characters to wrestle with their understandings of their relationships and negotiate their incestuous desires. The extent of Stoddard's radicalism in this regard raises interesting questions about what Radinovsky sees as the limitations in Stoddard's perception of American race relations.

Like Radinovsky, Jennifer Putzi offers a reading of *Two Men* that situates Stoddard's novel in terms of the politics of race brought to the cultural forefront during the Civil War. Specifically, in "The 'American Sphinx' and the Riddle of National Identity in Elizabeth Stoddard's *Two Men,*" Putzi examines the novel's treatment of interracial relationships and racial "otherness" in the context of the issues of national identity and citizenship that the war and the emancipation of the millions of men, women, and children once held as slaves had rendered so pressing. As does Radinovsky, Putzi reads Stoddard's depiction of African American characters as instrumental in this regard. But, Putzi notes, those characters are not the only ones whose citizenship is called into question in the course of the novel. Following Donald Pease and Amy Kaplan, Putzi insists on the importance of reading American nationality in an international framework; to that end, Putzi notes and discusses at length Stoddard's use of Venezuela as a site in the novel of (male) adventure and cultural membership. Situating the novel's repeated (and often quite specific) references to Venezuela in terms of its romanticization in American periodical literature and its political history, Putzi argues that the battletorn nation becomes, for Stoddard, a manifestation of the dangers of excess passion and, more important, of voluntary expatriation. In her survival and her ultimate integration into the American family, Stoddard's white female protagonist, Philippa—perceived throughout the novel as a "foreigner"—serves as a foil both for the men who escape to Venezuela and for Charlotte, the African American protagonist who can claim "citizenship" only in death. By complicating notions of "foreignness," creating characters whose racial categorization is problematic, and exploring the contours of racial identity in an international frame, Stoddard attempts to write a novel that challenges binary thinking about race and identity. Her effort to do so, however, founders on the rock of what Toni Morrison has identified as white Americans' need for the "Africanist presence." Ultimately, Putzi suggests, Stoddard cannot imagine any (white) American citizenship that does not require the abjection of the racialized "other."

Turning her attention to a text that is even more neglected than *Two Men* (and often viewed as Stoddard's weakest fictional production), Ellen Weinauer extends some of Putzi's inquiries into notions of national identity and membership through a reading of Stoddard's third and final novel, *Temple House* (1867). In "Reconstructing *Temple House,*" Weinauer notes and seeks to amend Stoddard's erasure from the critical record that accounts for writing, by both men and women, about the Civil War and Reconstruction eras. Written in the wake of the passage of the Thirteenth Amendment and the Civil Rights Act, and amidst debates about the Fourteenth Amendment, *Temple House* engages in Reconstruction America's urgent debates about the content and meaning of nationhood, freedom, and citizenship. It does so, Weinauer suggests, through a deployment of gothic tropes—doubling and inversion, fusion and reversal—that exposes what Teresa Goddu has called, in her interrogation of American gothic literature, the "historical horrors that make national identity possible yet must be repressed in order to sustain it" (10). Stoddard's exploration of these "historical horrors" operates around the contrast between *Temple House,* an apparently gothic "haunted house" that is, in fact, a site of liberation and autonomy, and "the Forge," an apparently anti-gothic site of comfort, class privilege, and social membership that is, in fact, a "haunted house." In the novel, Temple House becomes a site of refuge for and a community of a diverse group of "others"— laboring men and upper-class women, "foreigners" and the native-born, Native Americans and African Americans. But if Stoddard can be said to hold out Temple House as a nearly utopian community, the novel stages ongoing racialist dramas that compromise this "model nation" and that suggest the author's own embeddedness in the very (gothic) national structures she would have her narrative critique.

By putting Stoddard's work in the context of postbellum discourses of race, ethnicity, and citizenship, Radinovsky, Putzi, and Weinauer argue implicitly for her abiding relevance to many of the issues with which contemporary critics are concerned. Such an argument does not deny Stoddard's uniqueness among her contemporaries so much as it reminds us—as do virtually all of the essays collected here—that we must always understand the particularity and peculiarity of Stoddard's literary projects in terms of the cultural structures in which they were undertaken. In his afterword to this volume, Lawrence Buell centers the question of Stoddard's "endurance" on our ability to recognize at once her exceptionality and her embeddedness within ante- and postbellum America's aesthetic and social discourses. Buell, who is as appropriate a figure to bring this volume to a conclusion as Sandra Zagarell is to initiate its investigations, reminds us that, for all the vicissitudes of Stoddard's reputation, both in her own day and in ours, her work is still with us, exciting scholars, teachers, and students to pursue what Zagarell calls the "questions that . . . speak across the distance of time." For Buell, Stoddard's ongoing ability to inspire such forms of inquiry can assure us of her endurance; provided that we are willing to take up the challenges her work poses to us as readers, teachers, and writers, Buell insists, Stoddard's "critical future" is not a "question of whether" so much as it is "of when, and in precisely what directions."

Like Buell, we feel certain that Stoddard has a critical future—indeed, we might well attribute this volume to our desire to play a role in ensuring that future and shaping its direction. We can trace the genesis of our collection to an earlier American Literature Association conference in Baltimore where, baffled and frustrated by Stoddard's continued neglect, and sharing a mutual interest in her work, the editors organized a panel that brought together scholars especially interested in Stoddard's reception in the nineteenth century and continued marginal status in American literary studies in the twentieth century. With the enthusiasm of the young and untenured, we shared our deep conviction, grounded in our own pedagogical experience, that students responded not merely with enthusiasm to Stoddard but with a visceral reaction elicited by no other female writer of the era with the exception of Dickinson. In his reminiscences, Richard Stoddard observed of his wife, "Elizabeth Barstow was one of those irrepressible girls who are sometimes born in staid

Puritan families, to puzzle their parents and to be misunderstood. Her spirits were high, and her disposition willful" (108). A high-spirited and willful aesthetic disposition has, in our eyes, similarly puzzled a staid American literary scholarship to the degree that it has found Stoddard all too conveniently *repressible.* Consequently, an attempt to establish Stoddard as one of the pivotal American writers of the nineteenth century, a veritable *return of the repressed,* necessarily complicates our understanding of women's literature in this period. In seeking to effect that complication, this volume makes an initial gesture toward a more comprehensively gendered reading of nineteenth-century women's literature and the literary history it has made. The measure of its success will be its provocation to future inquiry. Taken together (and occasionally in sharp juxtaposition), these essays open new areas of study and map the territorial space of future debate. But while charting these areas of further exploration, this volume and the particular challenge it offers to literary history scarcely exhaust the opportunities for revisionary readings of Stoddard. A brief perusal of our table of contents reveals that none of the essays included provide sustained readings of, for example, such key Stoddard short stories as "Lemorne *versus* Huell" or "The Prescription," or of her bizarre children's book *Lolly Dinks's Doings.* As Lawrence Buell observes in his afterword, this will be the necessary work of other scholars whom we hope to inspire to study a literary career of "balked originality to set beside Dickinson's and Melville's." As Howells expressed it, Stoddard's work has had—both in her own day and in ours—a "peculiar fate, and would form the scheme of a pretty study in the history of literature." It is our wish that this "scheme of a pretty study" will serve to guide others toward a more comprehensive reading of Stoddard and her literary productions and, at the very least, will give some indication that this is a writer now—finally—being understood.

NOTES

1. The sexism implicit in Wood's description of Stoddard recalls comments made by Bayard Taylor about his "friend" in the 1860s, remarks that also associated Stoddard's difficult nature with her gender. In a letter of 20 May 1865 to George Curtis, Taylor observed of Stoddard, "She is very clever, and has fine qualities, but there is a disagreeable morbid streak running through her, and she is absurdly proud and suspicious." On 16 March 1866 he informed Thomas Aldrich that Stoddard "is hopelessly diseased, mentally and morally." But what

really disturbed Taylor, one can't help feeling, was revealed in this letter to Edmund Stedman of 9 September 1875: "She has read nothing of mine for a long while, and probably never will again. Apart from this—which is of light consequence—she is, intellectually, hopelessly demoralized, far beyond what you have suspected. There is no salvation for her." To a degree, and Taylor's parenthetical disclaimer notwithstanding, Stoddard's damnation would appear to be directly related to her failure to respond adequately to Taylor's own literary efforts (qtd. in Matlack, "Literary Career" 239, 271, 437).

2. In a letter of 26 January 1863, Nathaniel Hawthorne, a distant relative of Stoddard, commented that *The Morgesons* "seemed to me as genuine and lifelike as anything that pen and ink can do. The latter part showed much power, but struck me as neither so new or so true. . . . There are very few books of which I take the trouble to have any opinion at all, or of which I could retain any memory so long after reading them, as I do of The Morgesons" (qtd. in Matlack, "Literary Career" 275). In Richard Stoddard's *Recollections,* the author recalls Hawthorne's adding in his letter, "I hope you will not trouble yourself too much about the morals of your next book; they may be safely left to take care of themselves" (131). Hawthorne would also tell Stoddard: "I read The Morgesons at the time of publication, and thought it a remarkable and powerful book, though not without a painful element mixed up in it" (letter of 8 Jan. 1863, qtd. in Matlack, "Literary Career" 267). Contrarily, Hawthorne's literary descendant Henry James would critically eviscerate *The Morgesons* as "a thoroughly bad novel . . . totally destitute of form," possessing "not even the slightest mechanical coherency." For James, Stoddard's fiction was merely a recording of "disjointed, pointless repartee" (*Literary Criticism* 614).

3. Buell published a chapter on Stoddard in his *New England Literary Culture,* and Zagarell published her important study of *The Morgesons,* "The Repossession of a Heritage," in *Studies in American Fiction.*

4. Throughout *Beneath the American Renaissance,* Reynolds is drawn into a series of almost symptomatic gender distinctions. His assessment of Stoddard partakes of a systematic inversion of typical gender stereotypes that, paradoxically, diminishes the potency of women's art: "The style of the male subversive writers from Neal through Lippard was experimental in an eruptive, highly emotional way; that of woman writers like Cary and Stoddard was experimental in a muted, withdrawn way" (409).

5. Stoddard to Stedman, 22 June 1862, qtd. in Matlack, "Hawthorne and Elizabeth Barstow Stoddard" 285.

6. See Susan K. Harris, *Nineteenth-Century American Women's Novels.*

Biographical Foreword

Elizabeth Drew Barstow Stoddard (1823–1902)

Sandra A. Zagarell

Elizabeth Drew Barstow Stoddard is a challenging figure for students of nineteenth-century American literature. A strong individualist, she has always been cited for the uniqueness of her personality and her work. William Dean Howells said that "in whatever she did she left the stamp of a talent like no other, and of a personality disdainful of literary environment" (*Literary Friends* 77). She wrote like none of her male contemporaries, although, implicitly making her an honorary male, Howells continued, "In a time when most of us had to write like Tennyson, or Longfellow, or Browning, she never would write like anyone but herself." And she was at odds with the prevailing women's literary traditions, though her work bears the traces of several. In a period when the voices of most American women writers were raised publicly about subjects like the cultivation of religious and familial feeling, education, domesticity, the representation of communities, and public reform, her most compelling project was to articulate the nature and dynamics of a woman's subjectivity. Her medium, which was equally intense, was nevertheless distinctly American—an idiosyncratic and highly charged New England regionalism.

Gender and culture significantly complicated Stoddard's situation. She had few models for the type of expression she craved. Though an indigenous American discourse for exploring subjectivity was being created during her time, it was generally unavailable to her. Not only was it predominantly male, but in the judgment of the literary circle on which she relied for guidance and support—that of her husband, the poet Richard Henry Stoddard, and his friends, who fancied themselves the founders of a genteel American poetic tradition—the vernacular and personal character of the work of writers like Walt Whitman was hopelessly vulgar. She was familiar with British and Continental Romantic literature, but this, too, did not provide her with models: the subjectivity in question was decidedly masculine, and the culture not American—and in any case, Richard Stoddard and his associates deemed the importance of Romantic poetry to lie not in its articulation of the self but in its creation of a highly wrought aesthetic. The few writers whose concern with subjectivity seemed to Stoddard directly akin to hers were women—George Sand, Charlotte and Emily Brontë—but they were also culturally removed and appeared more as individual instances than as forgers of discourses also accessible to her.

As Howells's comment about the stamp of her talent indicates, Stoddard's intense commitment to herself fueled her writing, and this commitment also helped differentiate between her sense of vocation and that of virtually every other middle-class woman writer of her era. Whereas contemporary American women writers of fiction and journalism almost uniformly identified more as professionals than as artists,[1] she embraced a male-derived Romantic model of self-as-artist in which passion and language, desire and creativity, fused. Her sense of herself as a woman was essential to her, and while her conception of that womanhood included, uneasily, a yearning for ties with other women, it was grounded fundamentally in a Romantic commitment to the primacy of individual experience that was deeply at odds with the domestic, religious, and communitarian tenets of Victorian American womanhood. In her writing and in her life (at least as constructed in her letters), the cornerstones of the subjectivity to whose pursuit Stoddard committed herself were sexuality, self-expression, and a quest for agency. These convictions have an almost contemporary ring, and they inform the powerful depictions of the social and literary obstacles to women's self-realization that occur frequently in her published writing. But they also underlie a position that appears, to a present-day commentator, as constricting in some ways as it was liberating in others. Elizabeth Stoddard was daring and original; she was outspoken on behalf of women's right to self-realization, if sometimes personally quite unsisterly; but she was also profoundly narcissistic and often handicapped by a deep need for personal and literary admiration.

Born Elizabeth Drew Barstow in the whaling and shipbuilding town of Mattapoisett at the base of Cape Cod, Stoddard came from an old if undistinguished New England family. Her immediate family was well off and, though not part of the town aristocracy, enjoyed local prominence. Her father, Wilson Barstow Sr., was a successful shipbuilder who encouraged family members to enjoy their affluence. Yet Elizabeth's early experience of prosperity was tempered by a sense of its precariousness: her father went bankrupt three times, the first instance in 1843. She was also stung by the family's exclusion from Mattapoisett's "best" society and would satirize the parochialism of New England's elite families frequently in her writing. Though she felt the pinch of provincial life, her family allowed her a freedom to follow her own impulses that might surprise twenty-first-century readers familiar with such literary models of self-control as Ellen Montgomery of Susan Warner's *The Wide, Wide World* (1850) or Gertrude Flint of Maria Cummins's *The Lamplighter* (1854). Though her formal schooling was brief (and willful: she apparently resisted a wave of evangelical conversion during one of two terms at Wheaton), she had the run of the well-stocked library of Mattapoisett's minister, Thomas Robbins, and read widely in eighteenth-century literature, including drama, even though such reading was off limits for most girls of her era. According to Richard Stoddard, she "had a passion for reading, but a great disinclination for study," and the many books she read in Robbins's library constituted "the only education she ever had" (*Recollections* 108, 110).

The Barstow family appears to have consisted of intense and willful individuals deeply involved with one another yet committed to following their separate courses: many readers have detected an autobiographical ring in *The Morgesons*'s description of the Morgeson family as "a stirring, cheerful family, independent of each other, but spite of our desultory tastes" forming "mutual habits."[2] Cassandra Morgeson probably embodies some of Elizabeth's personal traits, particularly her self-absorption, tempestuousness, outspokenness (Elizabeth's father, she reported, "once said he never saw any human being with such a talent for the disagreeable"),[3] and preoccupation with her immediate family. For Elizabeth, family life underwent a radical change in the late 1840s: the deaths of her sister Jane in 1848 and her mother in 1849 left her feeling abandoned, unsettled, and restless. From 1849 to 1852 she cemented her relationship with her favorite brother, Wilson, and traveled a good deal under the protection of an older woman friend. She also formed an extremely intense bond with another woman, Margaret Sweat, of Providence, Maine (to whom she wrote, "All of my aim is to live intensely, and were calmness promised me, my heart would die out in its coldness and silence" [4 May 1852]—and with whom, in what would become the pattern of many of her friendships, she broke after some years).[4] Finally, she became increasingly interested in literature. In 1851 she attended the literary soirees of hostess Anne Lynch in New York, where she made acquaintances among New York's literati, among them the poet Richard Henry Stoddard.

The romantic attachment that quickly developed between Elizabeth Barstow and Richard Stoddard initially deepened Elizabeth's crisis of identity, however. Even eight months after their marriage in December 1852, her letters to Margaret Sweat express a conflict between being absorbed by romantic love and pursuing a (Romantic) quest for individual experience: "The *me* would live and die for him," she writes, "yet another part would go through all worlds scrutinizing and pondering on whatever is. This dual life is painful" (24 Aug. 1853).[5] The conventional restriction of self to the marriage relationship was obviously disturbing for her. During the months of her courtship, her attachments to Wilson and to Margaret Sweat intensified. Two weeks after she and Stoddard had secretly married, she tried to express her diverse allegiances in a letter to Margaret Sweat, and her phrasing, while cryptic and posturing, suggests that she felt the self to whose pursuit she was dedicated to be at least as inchoate as it was unorthodox. She opens by comparing her capacity for feeling with Margaret's, then declares: "I was in love fifteen years with my father—Now I am in love with Wilson. Happily with the latter I am more independent than with the former—all my life nearly comes of these loves." She next dissects her feelings about Stoddard, concluding, "You must think how rare is an intellectual marriage between two wonderfully sensuous persons!" After further proclamations about romantic love, she returns to Wilson, with whom, despite her marriage, she contemplates going to California, and concludes with the subject of herself and Margaret Sweat. "A remote spark of a prophet shows up that I shall be in the midst of just such life as I am made for [that is, marriage]—If it comes to pass[,] this prospect[,] you and me will be enabled to *exchange* each other—I hope you will have no children. I have signified my intention to that effect—and [we] will walk the world together two *single* married women" (23 Dec. 1852).[6]

Eventually, Elizabeth Stoddard came to feel that her marriage could fulfill her in many ways. She moved to New York with Richard, writing lyrically to Margaret Sweat that "we have paradisal nights, last night a great yellow moon shone down on our beds, our eyes, our bodies. Yes we have Eden, only better cooking than Adam had" (4 June 1853).[7] The marriage soon became the intense bond it would remain all their lives, despite family tragedy and some periods of estrangement;[8] it also proved a support for Elizabeth's creativity. She had already become interested in writing, publishing a brief sketch in the Duyckinck brothers' *Literary*

World in 1852. In 1853, with Richard as her tutor, she started writing poetry, and in some of her early efforts she evokes heightened psychic states effectively. Still, the metric constraints on which Richard insisted, the slenderness of her own poetic gift, and a sense that she would have greater freedom in a medium in which Richard did not constitute himself an authority probably soon helped direct her main interest to prose. From 1854 to 1858, she was the "Lady Correspondent" of a San Francisco newspaper, the *Daily Alta California,* work she probably took on partly as a way of communicating with her brother Wilson, who had finally gone to California in 1853. Writing semimonthly columns, she expressed herself exuberantly on a range of subjects, from books, authors, and political conflicts through impressions of New York City to women's rights; as she later said, the position served as an important apprenticeship in prose writing and an introduction to remunerative work.

Elizabeth Stoddard's first two decades in New York formed a period of relative happiness and of personal and creative growth, though they also saw the beginnings of the setbacks and tragedies that would make her later life almost unrelentingly grim. The Stoddards moved in literary circles that included Alice and Phoebe Cary and Caroline Kirkland as well as William Cullen Bryant, Horace Greeley, George Ripley, Kate Field, and Thomas Bailey Aldrich. Their home became the center for the evening gatherings of Richard and his poet friends, among them writer Bayard Taylor and poet and future anthologizer Edmund Clarence Stedman, who became Elizabeth's close, lifelong friend and confidant. The Stoddards' marriage included an intellectual companionship that both would cherish throughout their lives. In 1855, their son Willy was born. Elizabeth Stoddard also apparently achieved some of the personal admiration she sought. In the early 1860s, she appeared to be without "prototype" to one young woman observer, who saw her as a "singular woman, who possessed . . . strongly the ability to sway all men who came within her influence. Brilliant and fascinating, she needed neither beauty nor youth, her power was so much beyond such aids. On every variety of subject she talked with originality and ready wit; with impassioned speech expressing an individuality and insight most unusual and rare" (Woodman, *Crowding Memories* 14).[9]

For a time, Elizabeth also seemed able to pursue her own kind of writing while achieving recognition and commercial success. Soon after the *Alta* association ended, she began to write short stories, and in this medium she was quickly energized by a determination to reveal her protagonists' subjectivity while making enough of a show of conforming to conventions to place her work successfully in popular magazines. In 1860, the *Atlantic Monthly* printed "My Own Story," but only after she followed editor James Russell Lowell's request that she tone down the piece's eroticism. After this experience, an exploration of the disjunction between representing a woman's desire and adhering to the cultural codes that shaped such desire became the focus of some of her most interesting work. Throughout the decade, however, she also published more conventional sentimental tales and regional sketches.

Still, personal loss marked this period of professional accomplishment. In 1859, Elizabeth gave birth to a deformed child who soon died, and in 1861, Willy, too, died. Neither Richard nor Elizabeth enjoyed the heights of literary success both craved, nor did they achieve the financial security they needed. With Hawthorne's assistance, Richard Stoddard had become inspector of customs in 1853 (a position he would lose in 1870), but his salary barely covered household expenses, and neither could rely on writing as a steady source of income. Elizabeth was particularly bitter at the triumphs of other members of the Stoddard circle—Taylor, playwright George Boker—and jealousy and frustration began to give her outspokenness a nearly pathological dimension. She quarreled with Boker and Taylor over imagined slights, and probably some real ones, and began to exhibit a contempt for the wives of her male friends—especially for the wives of very close friends, like Marie Taylor and Laura Stedman—that would persist all her life. She sometimes half-regretted her outbursts, but she typically convinced herself that she was right. Venting her hostility seems to have given her a form, albeit a negative one, of the audience she deeply needed. After one quarrel with the Taylors, she wrote to Richard: "My heart is most ungodly towards those people and I have no doubt but that I am most ungenerous and mean, but *I love* to be as I am."[10]

Despite tragedies and disappointments, until the end of the 1860s Elizabeth Stoddard entertained the belief that she could invest, and realize, herself in writing marketable fiction about matters critical to her. She wrote each of the three novels she published during the decade with high hopes, only to receive little public response. In *The Morgesons* (written during 1860–61, published in 1862) she depicted her heroine's unwavering quest for self-determination while reflecting on the conventions that shaped her own construction of this unorthodox subject. Reviews were generally good, and her distant cousin Nathaniel Hawthorne, to whom a complimentary copy had been sent, wrote her a very flattering reply. Still, *The Morgesons* did not sell. Stoddard later accounted for this by blaming its publication ten days after the North's defeat at Bull Run, but the book's philosophic bleakness and what Bayard Taylor, among others, termed its "subjectiveness," as well as its cryptic dialogue, terse style, and economy of exposition, made it unappealing to the general reader.[11] In her next novel, *Two Men* (1865)—written while she was pregnant with her son Lorimer—she tried to make her writing more accessible, but the result was an uneasy compromise. While the protagonists, Jason Argus and Phillipa Luce, are as self-pursuing as the main characters of *The Morgesons,* the regionalism as stark, the exploration of family systems even more extensive, she is less formally creative in *Two Men,* relying heavily on tritely melodramatic plotting and on narrative cliché at points adopted from *Jane Eyre.* Though reviews were again good, *Two Men* was a greater market failure than *The Morgesons,* partly because the publishers, Bunce and Huntington, went bankrupt shortly after it was published. Stoddard made one more try for success with *Temple House.* This even more melodramatic production was published in 1867 to few reviews and very low sales.

Although Stoddard continued to write for the rest of her life, lack of recognition and the press of poverty contributed to the market-driven, ephemeral character of most of her subsequent writing: she never attempted another novel, specializing in reviews, slight regional sketches and tales, and, eventually, reminiscences. By 1874, she explained bitterly to the writer Elizabeth Akers Allen, "I am full of venality. I'll sell my grandmother's high temper, my uncle's drunkenness in articles" (28 Mar. 1874).[12] Most notable among her later productions was a children's book, *Lolly Dinks's Doings.* The stories in this collection are half fairy tale, half anti–fairy tale, sometimes quite macabre, and the book, which probably grew out of the stories she told her son Lorry, also features the interplay between mother-narrator and son-listener.[13] After Richard lost his Custom House position in 1870, the Stoddards' financial situation deteriorated further, and in 1880 they had to remove Lorry from school and send him to work (money would remain a worry, but Richard was able to secure more regular work shortly thereafter). Her family and friends provided Elizabeth intermittent support. She maintained relationships with several younger women writers—editor and journalist Elizabeth Akers Allen, journalist Lilian Whiting, author Louise Chandler Moulton, poet Julia Dorr—but her jealousy and egotism disrupted these friendships. A letter to Dorr suggests that, as in the days of Margaret Sweat, she thought of friendship primarily as a forum for her self-articulation, and of a friend as an audience as absorbed in her as she was in herself: "I wonder if you are so dreadfully alone so far as womanly friendship and sympathy go. . . . I wished for you and wondered if I could confide to you my complex nature and life . . . I am sometimes so driven by circumstances that I feel at bay. I stamp my feet, shake my mane at anybody who looks at me through my bars" (31 Mar. 1879).[14] During the 1870s she also had an association, about which little is known, with a younger man named Edward Smith, who escorted her to cultural events and gave her expensive gifts—and with whom she denied having an affair. Her most important friendship was with Edmund Clarence Stedman, who remained personally devoted to her and committed to her work all her life: the frank and expressive relationship she had with him gave her some of the appreciation she found so rarely.

Genuine literary recognition never came to Elizabeth Stoddard during her lifetime, but as realism came to dominate American letters, her early writing received sporadic attention. In 1888–89, Stedman was able to persuade the New York firm of Cassell to publish revised editions of all three novels. Once more, despite a flurry of interest, they sold poorly, yet even the promise of success provided Elizabeth with renewed incentive to write, and she produced a good number of essays, poems, and stories over the next several years. In 1895, Houghton Mifflin issued her selected *Poems;* in 1897, at a congratulatory dinner given in Richard's honor in which he was commemorated by Howells, Arthur Conan Doyle, Edmund Gosse, and others, she, too, received frequent praise. The brightest development of her last years was the growing success of her son Lorry as an actor and playwright, but even this good fortune was cut short, for Lorry, whose health had always been frail, died in 1901 of tuberculosis of the throat. In the same year, her novels were reissued one last time, when an admirer bought the Cassell plates at an auction and Stedman was able to arrange for their republication by Henry T. Coates & Co.; she wrote a new preface for the occasion, but the results were predictably disappointing. Overtaken by suffering, age, and poor health, Elizabeth Stoddard died of double pneumonia in August 1902. Richard died the next year. She is buried next to Richard and Lorimer in Sag Harbor, New York.

Among Elizabeth Stoddard's most intriguing writings are the *Alta* columns, *The Morgesons,* some of the short stories of the 1860s, and her correspondence. In an era in which literary journalism, as exemplified by the musings of Ik Marvell (Donald Grant Mitchell), was often diffuse, hers was pointed, opinionated, and often quite humorous, though less directly concerned with gender politics than were the even sharper essays of Fanny Fern. Her columns were very popular, and more than one admiring reader paid her a visit on returning East. An appreciative audience proved a great stimulus, and she took obvious pleasure in expressing herself freely in print. "Owning" unabashedly that she was an "egoist," she developed a public voice in which the first-person singular figured largely, and she experimented with diverse tones, including the satiric and the culturally analytic.[15] "What a civilized individualism runs through the political speeches; Did you ever read one that did not have a political quotation in it?" she notes in one letter (20 July 1856); in another, opposing the newly passed Maine Liquor Law, she likens to her "doubt whether law can keep a man sober" her "doubt whether purity can be legislated into men by the imprisonment of lewd women" (19 May 1855). She also seems to have seen the masculine makeup of her readership as an opportunity for positioning herself as a unique woman—and a unique writer. Remaining virtually silent about domestic matters, she is especially critical of popular women writers. Indeed, she maintains that men are responsible for the success of women's fiction, for "no criticism assails [women novelists]. Men are polite to the woman, and contemptuous to the intellect. They do not allow woman to enter their intellectual arena to do battle with them" (22 Oct. 1854). Still, she betrays considerable uneasiness about the contradiction between establishing her superiority to other women and forging an identity within prevailing ideas about gender. While she mocks the "excessive prudery of American women . . . [who] seem to be on the alert for something improper in conversation or manners" and complains that "our women emasculate the Saxon language in order to attain what they call 'a refined phraseology,'" her equation of feminine refinement with linguistic castration forced her into the position of man manqué, and she adopts an awkward pseudo-swaggering pose: "I confess that I am something of a horror to such persons [refined women], for I knock down my ideas with Substantial English" (21 Sept. 1856). In the final analysis, it is only the "female genius"—women like Sand, the Brontës, and Elizabeth Barrett Browning, who achieved artistic success in a man's world despite obstacles of sex and gender—for whom she has respect (and whose ranks she clearly hopes to join). Her praise of painter Rosa Bonheur applies to them all: "I like to chronicle the success of a woman. If there be any so valiant as to trench on the domain appropriated by men to themselves, I hasten to do them honor. And I say—O courageous woman! What you have done for song, or art, under the disadvantage of crying, teething babies, the contemptuous silence of your husband, the incredulity of all your male acquaintances, shows that a parity of circumstances would bring about a parity of intelligence between you and our good lords and patrons" (18 Nov. 1855).

Such attention to the interplay between a woman's drive for creative self-realization and the impediments she faced is also characteristic of much of Stoddard's best fiction. In what is generally considered her most successful short story, "Lemorne *versus* Huell" (1861), narrative terseness intensifies the depiction of the ways in which class and gender force the protagonist, Margaret Huell, to hold her passion and anger in check. The plot doubles back on its apparently neutral mirroring of Margaret's self-suppression, revealing that the marriage into which it leads her is erotically charged but personally demeaning. Several other stories of the 1860s—among them "Tuberoses" (1864), "The Prescription" (1864), "The Chimneys" (1865)—also feature the contradictions between their heroines' desires for personal autonomy and romantic fulfillment and the structures of gender (and sometimes class) that stand between them and their goals.

All these stories call attention to the conventional ending of marriage as a constraint or partial restraint for heroine and author alike, and this is also true of *The Morgesons.* In this novel, Stoddard's concern with her heroine's self-development links her narrative with the conventional domestic novel. Like the works of Caroline Chesebro', Ann Stephens, and others reviewed in the *Alta, The Morgesons* centers around a young, maturing protagonist's increasing awareness of the world around her and of her relation to that world. The destiny of the significantly named Cassandra Morgeson, like those of the heroines of works of domestic woman's fiction, finally includes marriage and home management. Yet, in contrast to writers like Chesebro' or Susan Warner, Stoddard is deeply concerned with her heroine's sexuality and desire for spiritual and economic autonomy. In exploring Cassandra's subjectivity and the barriers to its full expression, she draws heavily on the kind of female gothic of which the Brontës made successful use (and that many writers of conventional domestic woman's novels avoided), suggesting extensive connections between Cassandra's psychic and sexual development and her social circumstances. After a series of symbolic encounters—which include a confrontation with a Byronic cousin whose smoldering sexuality figures her own sexual potential, with the confining domestic world of her mother and women relatives, and with a fiendish matriarch who reflects on the compromised nature of the social success Cassandra, too, craves—Cassandra eventually attains the self-possession she has sought.

Completing the picture, she makes a marriage that combines sexuality and gender parity. As in her short stories, however, Stoddard emphasizes the fictive character of the happy ending. Here, the exceptional nature of the heroine's experiences contrasts with the spectacle of her women relatives' stultified lives and the incapacities that shackle most of the novel's men, while the religious skepticism and general sense of existential precariousness that pervade the novel shadow the possibility of any lasting happiness.

One of the earmarks of *The Morgesons* is the disjuncture between its plot and its commitment to expressing subjectivity. Although the plot seemingly follows a conventional bildungsroman formula, many individual scenes are compelling because of an intensity of desire and expression that has no direct bearing on narrative line and often exceeds the narrative economy of bildungsroman. The incommensurability between plot and subject may have contributed to the difficulties Stoddard had with her second and third novels, and it is significant that the one form in which she sustained her commitment to expressing the self through her entire life was one in which plot—and public approbation—were irrelevant: the letter. Her intimate correspondence includes some of the most forceful examples on record of a nineteenth-century American woman's determination to delineate all of her emotions, compel her reader's allegiance, and, often, inscribe her life as a physical, sexual being. The letters to Margaret Sweat, of which forty-five out of the original fifty-five are extant, belong to this category. Equally powerful are her letters to Edmund Clarence Stedman, which span more than four decades. Her trust in Stedman's devotion and his obvious attraction to her give her particular liberty of expression: while relying heavily on romanticism, she combines other registers, including the vernacular, as she seeks to articulate (and incite) desire and to express grief, disappointment, and her increasingly complex sense of her own body. In an early letter, reporting Lowell's disapproval of her "tendency towards *the edge of things*," she mingles the intellectual and the physical in trying to account for her sensibility: "Alas. I am coarse and literal of nature, what shall I do? My sensual perceptions react on my brain and I am a meek[,] small, well disposed woman!" (4 May 1860). Commenting on her artistry as she writes *Two Men,* she mingles apprehensions about her literary reputation with boasts about her personal impact: "Your review of the Morgeson's [*sic*] was terrific. I felt myself a monster when I read it. [H]ow is it that I inspire love as a woman Edmund, with those terrific qualities—men and woman *still* love me with a headlong feeling that sends them into an exaltation" (12 July 1863). In 1891, when she is sixty-nine years old, she is still determined to elicit Stedman's response to her strongly felt sexuality, yet she also gropes to voice the discrepancy between that sexuality and the sexual invisibility imposed by age. "Since all women look handsome to you," she writes, "may I lie in your road-way soon, never will the brands of passion die out in my nature, through their blackness, the red fire will suddenly appear, and run like a serpant [sic]—I have constantly to struggle between the feeling of others, that I am an old woman to be set aside, while the young bachantes [sic] whirl by with uplifted arms in the dance of life—and my own feeling of my inward power of life, and achievement. I remind myself of that celebrated Irish gentleman who died lately, he was without arms and legs, but he left eight children!" (21 Aug. 1891).[16]

Elizabeth Stoddard's work has always eluded prevailing paradigms. The postbellum construction of romanticism and realism as opposites, which persisted throughout much of the twentieth century, called attention to her as an early realist, a label to which she strenuously objected.[17] Recent scholarly attention to her work, particularly *The Morgesons,* raises similar questions. Although commentators have pointed to several traditions that illuminate aspects of her writing, including domestic woman's fiction, feminist bildungsroman, female gothic, and New England gothic, no single tradition can account for it fully, as many scholars also acknowledge. Indeed, some of the memorable parts of *The Morgesons,* such as the year Cassandra spends at the home of her maternal grandfather while attending a snobbish girl's school, do not fit fully within any recognizable narrative conventions. Stoddard's example also contributes to our understanding of the diversity of the writing of antebellum women fictionalists. Further, she complicates our sense of these writers' allegiances to other women and to the culture of middle-class white women. She also urges us to think about the situation of a nineteenth-century woman with considerable talent and a deep need for affirmation—a woman who, while lacking the genius of Margaret Fuller or Emily Dickinson, was nonetheless impelled by a desire, radical for her day, to express subjectivity. Her philosophic and stylistic originality, her conflicts, her accomplishments, and her failures render Elizabeth Stoddard's work, and her life, of great interest. In both, she not only complicates our models of nineteenth-century American women writers but also, like many in her cohort, pursues questions that continue to speak across the distance of time.

NOTES

1. See Nina Baym's well-known formulation of literary women's conception of authorship, before 1870, as "a profession rather than a calling, as work and not art" (*Woman's Fiction* [1978] 32). In the introduction to the second edition of *Woman's Fiction* (1993) Baym suggests that she had earlier used the concept of "literary artist" somewhat anachronistically and proposes the term "genius" as more historically apt.

2. Elizabeth Stoddard, *The Morgesons and Other Writings* 24. All further citations of *The Morgesons* will refer to this edition and will appear parenthetically.

3. Letter from Elizabeth Stoddard to Elizabeth Akers Allen, 27 December 1873. Qtd. in Stoddard, *The Morgesons and Other Writings* 340.

4. Letter from Elizabeth Stoddard to Margaret Sweat, 4 May 1852. Allison-Shelley Collection, Pennsylvania State U Libraries. By permission.

5. Letter from Elizabeth Stoddard to Margaret Sweat, 24 August 1853. Allison-Shelley Collection, Pennsylvania State U Libraries. By permission.

6. Letter from Elizabeth Stoddard to Margaret Sweat, 23 December 1852. Allison-Shelley Collection, Pennsylvania State U Libraries. By permission.

7. Letter from Elizabeth Stoddard to Margaret Sweat, 4 June 1853. Allison-Shelley Collection, Pennsylvania State U Libraries. By permission.

8. Their close friend Edmund Clarence Stedman described it thus: "Their loves and hates were, without exception, the same—right or wrong, and often although they were wrong, each espoused the other's cause, and favoritisms. . . . Each could say of the other: I do not love Heathcliff, I *am* Heathcliff" (qtd. in Stedman and Gould 533).

9. As Woodman and others also attest, Stoddard also had a powerful effect on women. See Marie Hansen Taylor, *On Two Continents* 59, and Ruggles, *Prince of Players: Edwin Booth* 132.

10. Characteristically, she was more charitable toward Bayard than toward Marie, for she added: "I still think Bayard is a good fellow but she is a nasty woman, and her spite dirtied me all over, damn them too" (letter from Elizabeth Stoddard to Richard Henry Stoddard, 7 July 1865. Edmund Clarence Stedman Papers, Rare Book and Manuscript Collection, Columbia University Library, New York. By permission).

11. Letter from Bayard Taylor to Elizabeth Stoddard, 21 November 1862, Taylor, *Selected Letters of Bayard Taylor* 194.

12. Letter from Elizabeth Stoddard to Elizabeth Akers Allen, 28 March 1874. Colby College Special Collections, Waterville, ME. By permission.

13. See Matlack, "Literary Career" 501–8, and Buell and Zagarell, "Biographical and Critical Introduction" xx, for a fuller discussion of *Lolly Dinks's Doings.* Parts of this discussion of Stoddard's writing are adapted from the latter, as are parts of the more detailed discussion later of *The Morgesons.*

14. Letter from Elizabeth Stoddard to Julia Dorr, 31 March 1879. Abernathy Library of American Culture, Middlebury College, Middlebury, VT. By permission.

15. Elizabeth Stoddard, *Daily Alta California* 7 February 1856. Subsequent references to Stoddard's columns will be cited parenthetically by date of publication.

16. Letters from Elizabeth Stoddard to Edmund Clarence Stedman, 4 May 1860, 12 July 1863, 21 August 1891. Qtd. in Stoddard, *The Morgesons and Other Writings.*

17. Although she could not formulate alternatives to the prevailing concepts of realism and romanticism, she foundered when she tried to explain her work within this framework, insisting to Stedman, when a commentator credited her with the rise of realism, "I am *not* realistic—I am *romantic,* the very bareness and simplicity of my work is a trap for its romance—alas my characters are gilded" (letter from Elizabeth Stoddard to Edmund Clarence Stedman, 21 Aug. 1891. Qtd. in Stoddard, *The Morgesons and Other Writings*).

I

THE WRITER, THE CANON,
AND THE PROTOCOLS OF PRINT

"Among a Crowd, I Find Myself Alone"

Elizabeth Stoddard and the Canon of Nineteenth-Century American Women's Poetry

Robert McClure Smith

> The Poets light but Lamps—
> Themselves—go out—
> The Wicks they stimulate—
> If vital Light
>
> Inhere as do the Suns—
> Each Age a Lens
> Disseminating their
> Circumference—
> > Emily Dickinson
>
> > I would go free, and change
> Into a star above the multitude,
> To shine afar, and penetrate where those
> Who in the darkling boughs are prisoned close,
> But when they catch my rays, will borrow light,
> Believing it their own, and it will serve.
> > Elizabeth Stoddard, "Above the Tree"

An analysis of the marginal canonical status of Elizabeth Stoddard's poetry can, to a degree, elucidate the question of her equally problematic placement in the new canon of nineteenth-century American women's fiction. Moreover, the reception and evaluation of that poetry offers a convenient and revelatory case study in the larger dynamics of canon formation. In particular, the example of Stoddard's poetry and its marginal status, in American literary canons past and present, provides a useful demonstration of why nineteenth-century American women's poetry presents for contemporary scholars intent on historical revision such immense problems of categorization. The modernist notion that oppositional writing takes disjunctive forms—the critical model that facilitated the canonization of Emily Dickinson in the 1950s—has in recent years been complicated by the assertion that women's poetry of the era, although rigidly adhering to mainstream sentimental conventions and the expressive limitations of traditional forms, performs significant "cultural work" that foregrounds, and occasionally complicates, our understanding of gender formation in the nineteenth century.[1] These two categories (which inscribe the position that gendered subjectivity in this era is best understood *either* through the socially disengaged formal experimentation of the Dickinson lyric *or* through the cultural performativity of the sentimental poetic conventions of a Lydia Sigourney or Helen Hunt Jackson) are dangerously monolithic. Stoddard, who had no sympathy for the formal experimentation of Dickinson (or Walt Whitman) and who was temperamentally incapable of completely valorizing the "affectional connection and commitment" that constituted the "generative core of sentimental experience" (Dobson, "Reclaiming" 267), offers a useful complication of the dual paradigm.[2] Indeed, a study of the liminal position of Stoddard's poetry might facilitate an alternative understanding of literary gender representation in the nineteenth century.

If it has been difficult for previous scholars to take Stoddard seriously as a poet, this may be because her own remarks about her published poetry are often self-deprecating and, at times, airily dismissive. On 3 August 1856, she notes in her *Daily Alta California* column, "The day I send my last letter to California will be a sad day; I shall cry, and howl, and refuse to be comforted by the other little children of my brain, that have a feeble existence in the corners of news-papers, and spaces that 'must be filled up' in magazines." Stoddard's description of her poems and stories as diminutive in scale, as "little" and "feeble" offspring, is consistent throughout her correspondence. Indeed, in 1895 she responds to an inquiry about her newly released *Poems* with "[I] am lost in astonishment to hear that someone has *bought* my little book. I have seen no blaze on the river as yet" (qtd. in Matlack, "Literary Career" 604). Since Stoddard's remarks indicate that she did not hold her own poetic efforts in high regard, her biographers, following her lead, have found little to say about her verse. James Matlack observes that Stoddard's 1895 collection is a "worthy cumulative performance but, as Elizabeth herself said, for a first volume by a young poet it would have been a promising start; as the collected verse of a lifetime, it was a slender, almost sad offering." For Matlack, Stoddard's poetry is useful only for its potential biographical revelations: "At their best, the emotional intensity, elegiac reflection, and morbid self-revelation of the poetry help to illuminate her personality and her fiction" (607). Following Matlack's lead, Sandra Zagarell argues that "the metric constraints on which [her husband] insisted, the slenderness of her own poetic gift and a sense that she would have greater freedom in a medium in which [he] did not constitute himself an authority probably soon directed her main interest to prose" ("Profile" 43). Like Thoreau, so the argument might proceed, Stoddard became a poet only in prose. Curiously, Stoddard's biographers do not merely echo the sentiments in her letters regarding the limitations of her own poetic talent: they uncannily repeat her image of stunted growth. Stoddard's "little" and "feeble" offspring become "slender, almost sad," the product of a "slender gift." But it is worth considering whether Stoddard's assessment of her poetry is actually genuine or at all deeply felt. For any writer dealing with commercial failure, the self-deprecating diminution of the art may serve as a necessary defense mechanism. And for Stoddard, commercial success—as much as, if not more than, critical respect—represented a tangible validation of worth. Her volume's commercial failure may have affirmed her sense of her poems' "feeble existence," but there is little indication that she considered her poems, the work of a lifetime, to have a "feeble" worth. "I have seen no blaze on the river *as yet,*" she informs her sympathetic reader. The final two words are telling in their implication that Stoddard was as ambitious for the success of her poetry as for her fiction. By the end of the century, after all, Stoddard had seen many of her female contemporaries find a place in the canon of American poetry, or so it must have seemed.

When Stoddard's friend (and, later, her most significant correspondent) Edmund Clarence Stedman published *An American Anthology* in 1900, he would, in fact, include the work of more than 150 women poets. Fifty years later, one of the most notable consequences of the triumph of formalist criticism, and in particular of the technique of close reading cultivated and championed by the American New Critics, was the succinct erasure of the majority of these female poets from the historical record. Moreover, as Paula Bennett remarks, perhaps no other group of writers in American literary history has "been subject to more consistent denigration than nineteenth-century women, especially the poets," their work being "damned for its conventionality, its simplistic Christianity, its addiction to morbidity, its excessive reliance on tears" (*Anthology* xxxvi). By the 1980s, however, a feminist scholarly enterprise of critical salvage and reassessment was well under way. A nascent cultural criticism, with a proclivity for resituating women's literature in a web of class, race, gender, and economic affiliations, soon complicated and redefined our understanding of sentimental conventions and the subversive rhetoric of what Jane Tompkins, in her provocative and influential reassessment of antebellum literature, would dub "sentimental power." Moving from the modernist-inspired focus on the literary text as a self-contained artifact, a "well-wrought urn" of paradoxical tensions, toward a more complex theorization of how an artwork performs cultural work in particular historical and social contexts, the new scholarship advocated the recovery of nineteenth-century women's literature as a means of understanding the cultural and psychological contours of women's lives in the period. Ann Douglass's earlier argument that American women's literature in the mid–nineteenth century evidenced the decay of community-oriented Calvinism into rancid individualism and the beginnings of a death-inflected and debased mass culture met increasing opposition from scholars who now found in the literature of the period a subtle and often rhetorically complex textual affirmation of female power.[3] These were literary texts best evaluated by their social and moral objectives, comprehended in the context of their political intent and outcomes rather than by any possibly invidious comparisons with the work of male writers of the so-called American Renaissance, comparisons inevitably grounded in the ideologically suspect realm of aesthetics.

There are problems with this New Historical paradigm of nineteenth-century American women's literature. These problems are significant enough to have prevented the reception model from completely reifying into a critical orthodoxy. Identifying one of the key limitations, Judith Fetterley observes that a primary emphasis on the context in which these texts were originally read diminishes their potential significance for today's readers unless they are to be given a thorough critical education in the horizon of expectations of their nineteenth-century predecessors ("Commentary"). Inevitably, a focus on the cultural work of the literary text eschews (even necessarily disregards) difficult questions of aesthetic value that inhere in its formal structure. And yet—perhaps to state the obvious—the frisson of literary works, their power of reader seduction, is often a feature of their rhetorical and linguistic complexity, the consequence of a stylistic sophistication (and occasional jolt of innovation) that offers to the reader those fleeting moments of identification and self-loss we call, for lack of a better word, pleasure. The cultural-studies-centered interpretation of nineteenth-century women's literature has, thus, been better able to offer compelling readings of fiction than it has of compressed and linguistically charged poetry. As a result, although the contours of a new canon of nineteenth-century fiction have assumed preliminary, if still contestable, shape, in her editor's introduction to *Nineteenth-Century American Women Poets: An Anthology,* Bennett can still pointedly observe that to claim that "the canon which, for better or worse, will sort this material out has yet to be established is a mammoth understatement" (xxxix).

That Stoddard presents a particular problem of "sorting" is immediately evident from her quite different, although equally problematic, status in two of the most widely used anthologies of nineteenth-century women's verse. In *Anthology,* Bennett selects poets primarily on the basis of their formal, aesthetic achievement. Although one of the founding principles of the volume is that the "heart" of American women's verse lay "not in the poet but in the poem" (xl), that "nineteenth-century women's poetry was most accurately thought of as, figuratively if not literally, an 'anonymous' art . . . where making—not being—was the dominant mode, and where moments of substantive creativity could be discovered . . . scattered diffusely through a population of unknowns" (xl), Bennett also divides her anthology into two sections whose organizing principles are author-centered and, ultimately, contoured by decidedly hierarchical value distinctions made on the basis of formal merit. The first section, "Principal Poets," offers substantial and varied selections from the work of Lydia Sigourney, Elizabeth Oakes Smith, Frances Osgood, Alice Cary, Phoebe Cary, Lucy Larcom, Rose Terry Cooke, Helen Hunt Jackson, and other key "principals." It is in the second section, "Poems from Regional, National, and Special Interest Newspapers and Periodicals, arranged chronologically," that we find Stoddard represented by two poems identified by periodical publication and date— "Mercedes" (*Atlantic,* 1858) and "Before the Mirror" (*Harper's New Monthly Magazine,* 1860). Obviously, the brief and selective sampling from poets identified by Bennett as having "non-principal" status could never hope to represent fully the range and power of an idiosyncratic poetic voice. This is the necessary limitation of any literary anthology. However, given the power of the anthology to institutionalize evolving literary canons, a brief selection may also prove quite sufficient to *misrepresent* a poetic voice. In fact, neither of the poems chosen by Bennett is entirely typical of Stoddard's work. Indeed, the poet herself, in an 1882 letter to E. A. Allan, complains of her husband's decision to represent her poetry, in his editorial revision of the standard Griswold anthology, with one of the poems Bennett selects as representative: "Do you think Stoddard would have represented me by that 'Mercedes'—an artificial bit of make-up?" (qtd. in Matlack, "Literary Career" 176).[4]

Contrarily, Janet Gray, in her anthology *She Wields a Pen: American Women Poets of the Nineteenth Century,* offers a more extensive and varied selection of Stoddard's poetry, excluding "Mercedes." "Before the Mirror" is now accompanied by "House by the Sea," "Nameless Pain," "The Wife Speaks," "One Morn I Left Him in His Bed," and "Above the Tree." But while Gray's anthology represents her more fully (and, I believe, more adequately), Stoddard's position within an evolving canon whose key founding principle is the "cultural work" performed by the literary text remains, to say the least, an extremely marginal one. In the editor's introduction, Gray locates herself firmly in the mainstream of feminist cultural studies orthodoxy in arguing that "we need to explore not just the formal qualities of the text itself but the cultural work that such an utterance, localized in time and space, might do" (xxxv). Since women poets "wrote in the context of their participation in groups and movements whose purposes extended beyond literary production" (xxx), the poetry selected for the anthology "with few exceptions, appeared in print in the context of social purposes beyond the making of poems" (xxviii–xxix). A perusal of the anthology reveals Stoddard to be one of the anthologist's "few exceptions," an exceptional status reinforced by Gray's brief explanatory note on the Stoddard selections: "Like her fiction, [Stoddard's] poems show the influence of such Gothic authors as Emily Brontë in depicting family tensions, incest and decaying households" (97). Gray's pigeonholing of Stoddard as a Brontë-inspired gothicist makes the "cultural work" of her poetry, especially in the larger American context of sentimentalism evoked by the volume's other selections, somewhat opaque to say the least.

In these two anthologies we can see how scholars of nineteenth-century American literature, through the institution of literary study, have set about constructing a canon of women's poetry; we are also witness to how the selectivity of this institutionalized canon might effectively govern and delimit literary study and instruction. Bennett accords Stoddard's poetry marginal status on comparative aesthetic grounds: Stoddard's poetry is just not as formally distinguished (or good?) and, hence, not as significant as the poetry of, say, Elizabeth Oakes Smith. Gray complicates the question of marginality by granting the same work *exceptional* status (in both senses of the word) as a poetics on the margin; Stoddard's poetic text does not fit easily in Gray's anthology because it is, in some sense, *other* to the established category narrative, but perhaps worthy of a more substantial representation for precisely that hint of *otherness.*

If Stoddard's different representation within these contemporary anthologies begs the question of what it means to be a *marginal* poet, her own poetic text offers a sustained and detailed meditation on precisely that issue. This was a poet only too aware of her own marginal status, of her own difficult self-location in the gap between residual and emergent nineteenth-century poetic categories. Stoddard's consequent attempt to create an artistic space for herself by interdigitating mutually incompatible elements ensured that she was already, in her own lifetime, quite simply an uncategorizable poet.

Certainly, while she could not escape its stock conventions, Stoddard had little intuitive sympathy for the prevalent subject matter of the women's poetic establishment.[5] Although women's poetry of the period was not as engaged with public issues as women's fiction, Elizabeth Petrino observes that while conforming to the "dominant narratives concerning women's lives," the poetry also often promoted "a sense of social cohesion" and "a forum from which to address issues of national importance, such as slavery, alcohol abuse, animal rights, children's education, woman's suffrage, and the forcible removal and divestment of Indians from their lands" (208). That Stoddard's poetry would eschew "social cohesion" is not surprising. In her early newspaper columns, Stoddard questioned the efficacy of popular reform movements. Her temperamental opposition to moral reform in all its guises is evident in this wry *Daily Alta* column: "I have intimated a doubt whether purity can be legislated into men by the imprisonment of lewd women, so I doubt whether law can keep a man sober. . . . The tendency of all life is to excess" (19 May 1855). Excess, we might note, is also a defining feature of Stoddard's own remarks on the position of women in the nineteenth century. While in recent years scholars have argued that much of the women's poetry of this era is concerned with a subtle negotiation of the paradoxes of their "Angel in the House" status, there is precious little subtlety evident in Stoddard's addressing of the issues of paradox and subterfuge in women's subaltern status in her fiction, journalism, or poetry.

Stoddard had equally little sympathy for the poetic innovations of Whitman and Dickinson. Of *Leaves of Grass* she notes, "It was neither read nor noticed much; but it made some sensation. Everything that convention says shall not be said, is spoken in that book. It is the experience of a thoughtful, talented, licentious man. What he knew, he wrote, and he knew a great deal that may be called immensely nasty" (*Daily Alta California,* 9 Nov. 1856).[6] Her reading of Dickinson was no more sympathetic. In a letter to Julia Dorr, Stoddard observes, "I see very little in her favor—She is confused, broken, a kaleidoscope without any color. . . . There was not the slightest excuse for her eccentric ways, such as the Brontes can afford to be, for they were honest and wholesome" (qtd. in Matlack, "Literary Career" 601).[7] For Stoddard, the "nasty" and "trashy" Whitman and the "eccentric" and "broken" Dickinson both foregrounded the problem of "wholesomeness."

Curiously, a common critique of Stoddard's fiction was its own occasionally "unwholesome" nature. In a revealing exchange of correspondence with James Russell Lowell, who suggested that her fiction at times went too near "the edge," presumably the "edge" of propriety, Stoddard responds, "Your warning strikes me seriously—Am I indeed all wrong, and are you all right about the 'going near the edge' business. Must I create from whose, or what standard" (qtd. in Matlack, "Literary Career" 185). She proceeds to query "whether, in writing, one should aim at entering a circle already established—or making one." The question suggests that Stoddard was only too aware of her own problematic placement within any contemporary literary "circle." To innovate, to make one's own circle, necessitated a movement "near the edge" of the boundaries that circumscribed expression, a crossing of established "standards." This necessitated the transgression of the liminal threshold that Dickinson would memorably describe as "Going out Beyond Circumference." But the edge of poetic innovation (as Whitman would discover) limned the boundary line of conventional morality: a new innovative poetics demanded a leap into "unwholesomeness" that would, inevitably, seem "eccentric" to conventional nineteenth-century tastes. Stoddard stood on the poetic edge, on the margin, but was unable to go beyond; incapable of succeeding completely within the established circle of sentimentalism, fearful of (and tempted by) the crushing influence of a male poetic tradition, she was equally incapable of inscribing a new one.[8]

Drawing on the thematics of sentimentality but comprehensively rejecting the models of social cohesion that sentimentalism typically promulgated, Stoddard celebrated the intrinsic Romantic values of freedom from social constraints, heroic individuality, and passionate personal expression. At the same time, while her poetry intimates a brooding awareness that inherited formal constraints would stymie the expressive power of the female poet, Stoddard also proved incapable of appreciating the poet who performed a similar fusion of disparate elements within the perimeters of a complex formal experimentation: Emily Dickinson. As a result, Stoddard's poetry is neither an archaic curiosity nor an aesthetic failure: this tense, gnarled, conflicted verse, a revelatory poetics of the interim, in fact, serves effectively to complicate some of our most basic notions of poetry by nineteenth-century American women. Again, Stoddard's poetry ultimately deserves study not merely because it serves to remind us of the monolithic and exclusionary nature of our critical categories but also because her self-identity as a poet was constructed, at least in part, from her awareness of her *own* liminality, her in-between status, her own peculiar knowledge of the gap. Locating her poetry within that gap, Stoddard presents us with a uniquely different and complex meditation on the question of gender and poetic authority in nineteenth-century American women's poetry.

Without question, Stoddard's initial association with her husband's poetic circle reinforced her awareness of difference. It may be that her desire for recognition and acceptance by the male writers who surrounded her gave rise to her concern about the expressive freedom of the female poet in a male tradition. In the 1850s, Richard Stoddard and his male literary friends, with youthful poetic ambition still intact, considered themselves to be the unacknowledged founders of a new genteel American poetic tradition. At first, the energy and enthusiasm generated by this minor literary clique proved inspirational for the genteel poet's wife, whose first attempts at poetry were, by her own admission, critiqued and edited by her husband. Looking back on those initial efforts, Stoddard observes, "I cannot say whether it was from sympathy or the fervor of poesy, but I, too, attempted to be an Arcadian. I began some verses which cost me infinite strivings and labor, and I never forget the sublime patience of my fellow-poet as I produced a line and read it. He did not ridicule me, or laugh at me, but let me do it. At the proper time and occasion he was the severest critic, and his fiat of 'This won't do' was final" (qtd. in Matlack, "Literary Career" 114). Letters written by Stoddard during the 1850s, though, indicate a more difficult negotiation with the "severity" of her husband's criticism. In early 1854, she confesses to her friend Margaret Sweat, "I have old habits of reading and impressions to contend with. Of all the rules of art I am shamefully ignorant. I can't make my ideas melodious." Stoddard's interesting choice of words to describe her schooling in metrics indicates that learning these "rules of art" was for her a poetic *workshop* in every sense of the word, a form of indentured servitude. "To succeed," she admits, "I shall have to go through a terrible apprenticeship." Moreover, the master tradesman from whom she was learning her craft was not always "sublimely patient": "Stoddard is a severe master and I get so discouraged that I *cry* dreadfully" (qtd. in Matlack, "Literary Career" 114–15).[9]

This struggle to find her poetic voice in the face of an overwhelmingly influential *other* would be a defining feature of Stoddard's poetic career and the central theme of a number of her poems: the identity of the powerful other would change, and poets more influential than her husband would occupy the position, but the encroachment of the male precursor upon individual poetic autonomy and the resultant dialogism is a recurring concern. Of course, the female artist who seeks freedom from the formal restrictions of gender may, of necessity, have to break away not only from the influence of particular male precursors but also from the formal laws they legislate. At least that is the argument of the allegorical "The Wolf-Tamer," a poem that ponders the consequences of the wild outsider's succumbing to the narcotic music of influential pied pipers. The title of the poem is, in fact, decidedly double-edged: while we might assume that the poem will be a meditation on the art of the individual whose seductive music tames wolves, haunting ambiguities and formal incoherencies eventually combine to generate a rather different question for the reader—is our wolf-narrator *really* tamer?

> Through the gorge of snow we go,
> Tracking, tramping soft and slow,
> With our paws and sheathed claws,
> So we swing along the snow,
> Crowding, crouching to your pipes—
> Shining serpents! Well you know,
> When your lips shall cease to blow
> Airs that lure us through the snow,
> We shall fall upon your race
> Who do wear a different face.
> Who was spared in yonder vale?
> Not a man to tell the tale!
> Blow, blow, serpent pipes,
> Slow we follow:—all our troop—
> Every wolf of wooded France,
> Down from all the Pyrenees—

Shall they follow, follow you,
In your dreadful music-trance?
Mark it by our tramping paws,
Hidden fangs and sheathed claws?
You have seen the robber bands
Tear men's tongues and cut their hands,
For ransom—we ask none—begone,
For the tramping of our paws,
Marking all your music's laws,
Numbs the lust of ear and eye;
Or—let us go beneath the snow,
And silent die—as wolves should die!

At first glance, the poem merely provides further evidence of a poet's struggle to master the intricacies of meter and rhyme, of Stoddard's self-confessed inability to make her ideas "melodious." In this case, though, the formal incoherencies are thematically significant if we consider "The Wolf-Tamer" to be an extended allegory of female poets' subservience to male poetic standards, a study of their entrapment by "music's laws." This wolf tamer certainly has the power to enthrall the following wolves, symbols of all that is wild and untamed, but whether he himself escapes the "music-trance" that so enraptures them or is also subject to his own hypnotic self-delusion is rather ambiguous ("Shall they follow, follow you, / In your dreadful music-trance?"). The wolves may "crowd" and "crouch" to the satanic temptation of "Shining serpents!" but there is a powerful menace in their subservience, in the latent threat of "sheathed claws" and "hidden fangs" and in the blunt admission that "When your lips shall cease to blow / . . . We shall fall upon your race." Indeed, all around are evidence of retaliatory massacres that artistically silence ("Not a man to tell the tale") and mutilate ("Tear men's tongues and cut their hands") in a decidedly gendered way. The wolf-speaker confesses that "Marking all your music's laws / Numbs the lust of ear and eye," but the numbing process is clearly incomplete insofar as she does not, in fact, "mark" those laws at all consistently, or if she does, it is in the sense of "marking" as defacing. For the rhythm of the poem involves a continual breaking out of any established rhyme scheme followed by an abrupt return to temporary regularity. These movements back and forth mimic the wolf-speaker's attempts to break from the spell of the tamer, from the "music's laws" that lull and calm, shackle and bind. The almost complete disintegration of the rhyme scheme in the middle of the poem—"troop / France / Pyrenees / you / trance"—indicates the speaker's temporary escape from the narcotic suggestion of regular musical patterning. The interpolation of lines of irregular scansion— "Blow, blow, serpent pipes"; "For ransom—we ask none—begone"; "Or —let us go beneath the snow"—are further indications of chafing conflict, of an angry animal chewing at the bindings. Readers are left to ponder whether the wolves' "Tracking, tramping soft and slow" is a quiescent following or the possibility of a hunt-in-progress. Certainly, if this wolf is tamer, she is hardly tame. This swinging across the "gorge of snow" (a symbolic journey that, perhaps, suggests the necessary following of the established route of an influential other across the white abyss of the page) cannot end well for both parties involved. If the wolf/ writer is to remain nonthreatening and to be required to suppress her natural (and revolutionary) instincts, she prefers a "silent" death "*beneath* the snow,*" a subterranean and subtextual route. Better silence and death as an unknown than the passive tracking that demands a succumbing to the "serpent pipes" of influential others.

The "serpent pipes" of the likes of Richard Stoddard, George Boker, and Bayard Taylor did not prove to be terribly compelling. As this early satirical sketch of "the literary visit" indicates, Stoddard was soon able to dissect the shortcomings and pretensions of her husband's literary salon: "A finds B writing a poem. A insists on B's reading it. B reads and A says 'glorious.' Then A takes a manuscript from his pocket, which B insists will be read. A reads and B says 'glorious.' A asks if B has seen his last squib in Young America. B asks if A has seen his last review of that book by Muggins. Each man puts his feet on the sofa (no, literary people don't have sofas)—somewhere above his head—and then Tennyson, Browning, Longfellow, and their faults are discovered" (*Daily Alta California,* 20 Jan. 1856). In fact, Stoddard's initial poetic sympathies were with Alfred, Lord Tennyson and Browning, and her first efforts demonstrate that the poetic ephebe's greatest weakness was a too close imitation of those male Victorian influences.[10] Her artistic project, like that of her idols the Brontës, would involve accessing the power of the male tradition by establishing a complex dialogic relation with it.[11]

Especially striking in this context is "Before the Mirror," an obvious attempt by Stoddard to clear an autonomous imaginative space for herself as a female poet in a male tradition. In the famous precursor poem, Tennyson's hermitic "Lady of Shalott" grows weary of the shadow world of her tower and leaves her secluded existence. But upon entering the world of human passions for the first time, she is destroyed. The poem is obviously an extended Tennysonian meditation on the limitations of the poetic imagination: it is a study of the necessary insularity and enclosure of the artist, of the consequent inability to develop a potential existence into an actual life, and of the difficult, possibly fatal, process of becoming vulnerable to human passion and so fully sympathetic to the human condition. A closer acquaintance with the world of mortal passions may precipitate the death of the imagination unless, presumably, the imagination becomes capable of refiguring death itself. In Tennyson's poetic allegory, the imagination leaves the mimetic world of visionary joy and the lure of beauty and shadows for the real world and dies: it is, in other words, an imagination that fails to negotiate successfully the transition from "Lotus Eaters" to "In Memoriam." In a poem concerned with the danger of the mirror, of living in the mimetic world of art, Tennyson's decision to represent the imagination as a female figure obviously provides a problematic model for the female reader of his poetic text, perhaps especially for a reader with poetic ambitions. The Lady's recognition that the only way to break the circle of desire is to annihilate the self makes the poem that bears her name a curiously suicidal text: if imagination in ladylike form must die in order that her creator might develop as an artist, what does that indicate about the female imagination?

In "Before the Mirror," Stoddard's first-person speaker immediately identifies with the situation of the Lady ("Now, like the Lady of Shalott") and so immediately provides an interesting revision of the precursor poem—the object of the initial study is now a more developed speaking subject and the allegorical woman, the lady-as-figure-of-the-imagination, is contoured in flesh.

Now, like the Lady of Shalott,
I dwell within an empty room,
And through the day, and through the night,
I sit before an ancient loom.

And like the Lady of Shalott,
I look into a mirror wide,
Where shadows come, and shadows go,
And ply my shuttle as they glide.

Not as she wove the yellow wool,
Ulysses's wife, Penelope;

By day a queen among her maids,
But in the night a woman she,

Who, creeping from her lonely couch,
Unraveled all the slender woof:
Or with a torch she climbed the towers,
To fire the faggots on the roof!

But weaving with a steady hand,
The shadows, whether false or true,
I put aside a doubt which asks,
"Among these phantoms what are you?"

For not with altar, tomb, or urn,
Or long-haired Greek with hollow shield,
Or dark-prowed ship with banks of oars,
Or banquet in the tented field;

Or Norman knight in armor clad,
Waiting a foe where four roads meet;
Or hawk and hound in bosky dell,
Where dame and page in secret greet;

Or rose and lily, bud and flower,
My web is broidered. Nothing bright
Is woven here: the shadows grow
Still darker in the mirror's light!

And as my web grows darker too,
Accursed seems this empty room;
I know I must forever weave
These phantoms by this fateful loom.

Cursed she may be, but Stoddard's "Lady of Shalott" chooses to remain in her room. For her, the fact that the "shadows grow / Still darker" merely ensures that "my web grows darker too." This is an artist who, for her own protection, "put[s] aside" questions of identity ("Among these phantoms what are you?"), presumably in the knowledge that she, like that other weaver, Penelope, has the incendiary, destructive passions of a tower-burning woman, accepting instead that she is fated to "forever weave." It is worth recalling the extent to which the precursor poem is an extended *reflection* on the imaginative process. Tennyson's "Lady" is weaving by the reflected surface of the mirror when the entrance of a mirror-shattering male figure breaks her mimetic observation of the world. When the reflection of Lancelot in the nearby river is itself re-reflected in the surface of her mirror, the reflection of reflections, the secondary nature of the mirroring, breaks through the cocooning of mimetic protection: "From the bank and from the river / He flash'd into the crystal mirror." The formal shape of the poem duplicates this image of double-mirroring: the death of the imagination dubbed "Lady of Shalott" within a poem also titled "Lady of Shalott," whose stylistic borrowings from Percy Bysshe Shelley and John Keats Tennyson is signaling his imminent movement beyond, is an intimation of imaginative destruction in the interests of imaginative growth, a reflection upon the power of reflections that precipitates, for the poet, a voyage beyond the mirror of precursor influence.

What Stoddard's text provides is a further mirroring of Tennyson's mirror-text, a reflection to the third degree that returns the "Lady" to the safety of her room. Just as her speaker sits before her "mirror wide," so Stoddard herself confronts—and ultimately rejects—a "mirror-text" in which she can find only a deathly reflection. "Before the Mirror" indicates not merely a spatial positioning (the poet who sits before the mirror) but a temporal one (the poet who considers a return to a time before the mirror held such significance, before the precursor model became imaginatively seductive): the list of "bright" material that remains unwoven—the Greek myths and Arthurian idylls, the flowers and "bosky dells"—evokes Tennyson's primary image bank, and in this context, the precursor poet functions himself as Stoddard's Lancelot—an attractive, seductive, dangerous male influence encroaching upon the female imagination. But Tennyson-Lancelot is here rejected.[12] Recognizing the extent of his threat to the integrity of the female imagination—however dark the shadows of its unconscious depths—this Lady, if tempted, will not be lured out: she is not leaving her loom.

Tennyson's lady in the tower was a central icon of the nineteenth century to the extent that she had become a pervasive cultural image. Jennifer Gehrman argues that the poem "codified the systematic bondage and exploitation of women" (123) as an extreme representation of the Angel in the House and, further, that the "similarities between Tennyson's medieval beauty and the standards imposed on real women in the nineteenth-century are obvious" (123). Therefore, when a popular writer like Elizabeth Stuart Phelps chose "The Lady of Shalott" as the subject for a short story, her satirical and revisionary intentions were self-evident. The argument of Phelps's story is, in fact, didactic: the "Lady" must leave her seclusion. For Gehrman, Phelps's contention is that "seclusion from the world is not a viable option for the woman artist who sees herself and her art as dynamic agents of social change" (Gehrman 125). Obviously, Stoddard's is a very different reading of Tennyson's "Lady," pondering whether the female poet's "seclusion from the world" might be symptomatic of a more fundamental problem: how can the female artist hope to be a "dynamic agent" of change from within the confines of an oppressive and stifling male literary tradition? In her own intrapoetic negotiation with Tennyson as influential male precursor, and via what approximates to the corrective swerve of a Bloomian clinamen, Stoddard tries to clear imaginative space for herself as a female poet in a potentially deathly male tradition. The anxieties regarding representation that precipitates Stoddard's sounding of the intertextual depths of artistic creativity in this poem reveal her to be perhaps a more astute reader than her contemporaries of the full extent of the "Tennyson problem." Stoddard is not evading the issue of the possibly negative cultural effects of Tennyson's poetry upon female representation: she is offering a more complex analysis of the problematic situation of the nineteenth-century female artist in the male tradition.[13] In Phelps's story, for example, the solution is obvious—it is time for the lady to leave her pseudoprison in the phallic tower and set about changing the world. For Stoddard, however, there can be no real escape from the tower into a world ultimately constructed on identical phallologocentric principles.

Drawn to the male Romantic tradition and yet unsure of her own self-location as a woman within it, Stoddard was simultaneously attracted to the thematic concerns of her female peers. As Paula Bennett observes, sentimentality is the "inescapable fact in much nineteenth-century poetry" (*Anthology* xxxviii). Traumatized by the death of her first child, Stoddard too entered the poetic landscape assiduously cultivated and refined by Lydia Sigourney and her poetic progeny—the child elegy. The sentiments of "One Morn I Left Him in His Bed" are thoroughly conventional:

One morn I left him in his bed;
A moment after some one said,
"Your child is dying—he is dead."
We made him ready for his rest,

Flowers in his hair, and on his breast
His little hands together prest.

Similar sentiments—and the standard proliferation of flower imagery—
reappear in "Unreturning":

But he, who once was growing with the grass,
And blooming with the flowers, my little son,
Fell, withered—dead, nor has revived again!

These two poems, however, constitute the full extent of Stoddard's uncomfortable foray into the cult of death ubiquitous in nineteenth-century
American women's poetry. Petrino maintains that the child elegies usually console parents by urging a comparison of "their child's perhaps
eventually painful state on earth with its blissful existence in heaven,
and they look forward to a comforting reunion between parents and
child after death" (56). Typically, such poems project the spiritual and
affective values inscribed in the Christian evangelical interpretation of
women's sphere. In an era of high infant mortality, the exemplary and
pious character of the dying child was an integral part of that interpretation. In Stoddard's elegies, however, we find neither a suggested comparison with the child's blissful heavenly existence nor any indication of
reunion in the afterlife. Stoddard's extreme skepticism regarding the efficacy of institutional religion, an uneasiness displayed frequently in her
fiction, makes her, in fact, temperamentally unsuited to funerary verse.
If typically in such elegies "the dying child teaches a lesson in holy
living to its parents" (Petrino 56), the lesson of "holy living" was one
that Stoddard was unwilling to accept personally. Her poems begin
with a child's death, but they make no effort to display the logic by
which the survivors can learn to deal with their loss. Although Stoddard
adopts the standard conventions, she seems constitutionally incapable of
providing the consolation offered by Sigourney and other nineteenth-
century American female elegists. Stoddard's child elegies, with their
failed gestures of sympathetic comforting ("Mothers, who mourn with
me to-day, / Oh, understand me, when I say, / I cannot weep, I cannot
pray"), in fact, flirt with a bleak existentialism. Stoddard adapts the sentimental mode but has a lack of personal commitment to the subject:
adhering to the cultural form and yet comprehensively failing to perform the necessary cultural work of sympathetic comforting, her child
elegies are essentially stillborn.

Of course, the capacity to experience and endure pain, suffering, and loss are also intrinsic to the sentimental subject. And the pain of separation is the central theme of a number of Stoddard's poems. Lines like these—"You left me, and the anguish passed, / And passed the day, and passed the night— / A blank in which my sense failed"—conjure up that familiar Dickinsonian landscape of the aftermath where "Pain—has an element of Blank—" (650). For both Stoddard and Dickinson, not only is pain in itself indefinable and unnameable, a wordless void, but the reason for the specific anguish is necessarily unspoken and, so, fundamentally ambiguous (an ambiguity reinforced, in the lines above, by the dual sense of "passed"). The precise cause of the loss of the beloved (is it merely a broken engagement or the ultimate broken engagement of death?) is left unstated; consequently, the potential for possible reader implication in the "secret sorrow" is infinite. On other memorable occasions, however, pain is a consequence not of separation from the beloved but of his continued presence. An obvious example is the poem "Nameless Pain," whose opening stanzas are these:

> I should be happy with my lot:
> A wife and mother—is it not
> Enough for me to be content?
> What other blessing could be sent?
>
> A quiet house and homely ways,
> That make each day like other days;
> I only see Time's shadow now
> Darken the hair on baby's brow!
>
> No world's work ever comes to me,
> No beggar brings his misery;
> I have no power, no healing art
> With bruised soul or broken heart.

While the poem's disaffected speaker will conclude with the observation "I still should pine / If any other lot were mine," this is not, in context, a terribly convincing assertion. The "nameless pain" is, in fact, nameable: it is the stultifying inertia of an unfulfilled life. This is a sentiment even more strikingly conveyed in "I Love You, But a Sense of Pain," a poem of such interest that it deserves quoting in its entirety:

I love you, but a sense of pain
Is in my heart and in my brain;
Now, when your voice and eyes are kind,
May I reveal my complex mind?

Though I am yours, it is my curse
Some ideal passion to rehearse:
I dream of one that's not like you,
Never of one that's half so true.

To quell these yearnings, vague and wild,
I often kneel by our dear child,
In still, dark nights (you are asleep)
And hold his hands, and try to weep.

I cannot weep; I cannot pray—
Why grow so pale, and turn away?
Do you expect to hold me fast
By pretty legends of the past?

It is a woman's province, then,
To be content with what has been?
To wear the wreath of withered flowers,
That crowned her in the bridal hours?

Still, I am yours: this ideal strife
Stirs but the surface of my life:
And if you would but ask once more,
"How goes the heart?" or at the door

Imploring stand, and knock again,
I might forget this sense of pain,
And down oblivion's sullen stream
Would float the memory of my dream!

Again, the conclusion of the poem ("I *might* forget this sense of pain")
cannot undo the earlier detailed expression of marital unhappiness. The
depths of frustration suggested here—the need of a "complex mind" to
leave behind, if only momentarily, the "withered flowers" of marriage

in order to rehearse an "ideal passion"—clearly extend far below the "surface" of the speaker's life. What the reader will most likely remember is the "quelling" of the wife's "ideal" yearnings by the child's bedside, the "turning away" of the husband-addressee from the "revelation" of his wife's previously suppressed complexity, and the implication of adulterous possibility in "I dream of one that's not like you." In an era when the ideology of the domestic was sanctioned by sentimental religiosity, there is considerable significance in this speaker's admission that "I cannot weep; I cannot pray." The poem is saturated with a sense of unfulfilled potential, of repressed and possibly insatiable desires, and, most of all, of the crippling stasis of power-inflected gender relations.

Other Stoddard poems elaborate this critique of gender relations built on "pretty legends of the past" by focusing on the vulnerability of women in a patriarchal culture that privileges youth and reproductive functionality. In "The Queen Deposed," the monarch, who has been replaced by a younger woman capable of bearing her husband an heir, muses, "Babes make or mar our queenly fate— / My woman's life is done." The scathing social satire of "Vers De Societé," on the other hand, offers a brief sketch of the life of the new "queen" and, thereby, provides a pithy analysis of how women's economic dependency may ultimately be a form of prostitution injurious to all parties:

> Tiger of fifty! So you've bought
> This pretty girl in the Honiton lace.
> Now she's abroad, she quite forgets
> She shudders in your embrace.

The most striking feature of many of these poems is the fact that, while it has been observed that women's literature in nineteenth-century America is subversive of patriarchal values subtextually, functioning as a "literature of implication" (Dobson, *Dickinson and the Strategies of Reticence* 123), and that this implicatory power is evident in a degree of ambivalence in women's poems about marriage (Walker, *Nightingale's Burden* 50–52), Stoddard's critique of gender relations is often strikingly overt and absolutely unambiguous. Joanne Dobson has argued that women's literature of the period, "to be acceptable to conventional writer and reader, had to screen out, sublimate, or otherwise disguise insistent but culturally threatening personal energies" and, as a result, that "the personal was a problematic subject for women in a way that it was often not for men" (Dobson, *Dickinson and the Strategies of Reticence* 24). The personal was only a problematic subject for Stoddard to the extent that she, like her heroine Cassandra Morgeson, had little talent for sublimation and disguise. That her contemporaries were aware of a problematic difference grounded in distinctive individuality is evident in this 1896 review of her poetry in the *Dial* (20: 111): "[With] Mrs. Stoddard's volume, we are in the presence of poetry in a more serious sense. It would be difficult to do justice to the intensity of noble feeling that throbs beneath the stern grave simplicity of these poems. . . . In all her choir of American singers, there is *no woman's voice more distinctly individual than this, or more compulsive in its appeal*" (emphasis added). Once again, it is the "compulsive" nature of this "distinct individuality" that ensures Stoddard such a difficult placement in the evolving canon—that same distinctive individuality, in fact, is what made Stoddard somewhat unacceptable to conventional readers of nineteenth-century women's literature then *and* now.

Annie Finch has argued that the sentimental poets' difficulty in engaging nature is a consequence of their lacking the privileged central lyric self of male writers.[14] Yet much of Stoddard's poetry emanates from a central lyric self that engages nature alone—a poem like "The Willow Boughs Are Yellow Now," in fact, begins with the declaration of willed separation:

The gray-eyed twilight lingers long,
To meet the starry night;
I walk the darkening lanes alone.
And love the sombre light.

In recent years, it has not been unusual to find scholars of this period claiming that "to contend that nineteenth-century American women's writing is worth reading—is, in fact, readable—we need to acknowledge its very different criteria for judging value, which are *based on a desire to bridge the gap between alienated selves*" (Petrino 210; emphasis added); or that "while the dominant masculine tradition focused on the insularity of the individual, the women writers *portrayed characters who were enmeshed in a community of interpersonal relationships*" (Warren 11; emphasis added). Such generalizations, asserting an inherently common core of culture and positing women's nurturing and relational qualities as naturally opposed to male domination, often verge on a dangerous essentialism. Certainly, such definitions cannot accommodate a poet like Stoddard who often strategically establishes herself as an insular self and, in so doing, as a subject very much separate from community. Stoddard is a poet who, in many ways, does not envision "the loss of human connections as the greatest tragedy" (Bennett, *Anthology* xxxiv). In fact, she begins "Music in a Crowd":

> When I hear music, whether waltz or psalm,
> Among a crowd, I find myself alone; . . .

She concludes the poem with a sentiment of complete separation from communities of "men and women" alike:

> They were a Vision, though. And are these real,
> These men and women, moving as in sleep,
> Who, smiling, gesture to the same Ideal,
> For which the music makes me weep?

The images of separation and isolation proliferating in Stoddard's poetry reach their fruition (in every sense of the word) in one of her best poems, "Above the Tree." Apparently commencing in dialogue with Tennyson's "Ulysses," this poem becomes a deeply personal meditation on reputation and literary legacy. The frustrated aspiration for literary achievement and recognition expressed in this poem is, I believe, quite unusual for women's poetry in this era:

> Why should I tarry here, to be but one
> To eke out doubt, and suffer with the rest?
> Why should I labor to become a name,
> And vaunt, as did Ulysses to his mates,
> "I am a part of all that I have met."
> A wily seeker to suffice myself!
> As when the oak's young leaves push off the old,
> So from this tree of life man drops away,
> And all the boughs are peopled quick by spring
> Above the furrows of forgotten graves.
> The one we thought had made the nation's creed,
> Whose death would rive us like a thunderbolt,
> Dropped down—a sudden rustling in the leaves,
> A knowledge of the gap, and that was all!
> The robin flitting on his frozen mound
> Is more than he. Whoever dies, gives up

Unfinished work, which others, tempted, claim
And carry on. I would go free, and change
Into a star above the multitude,
To shine afar, and penetrate where those
Who in the darkling boughs are prisoned close,
But when they catch my rays, will borrow light,
Believing it their own, and it will serve.

This is not merely the tree of life but also that of literary reputation: the tree-as-canon, if you will. In fact, it would seem that to an uncanny degree, Stoddard herself anticipated the concerns with canonicity detailed in this collection of essays. The "sentiment" to which this poem directly corresponds can be found in this 1876 admission to Elizabeth Akers Allen: "No one knows what a literary ambition I had, nor how my failure has broken me" (qtd. in Matlack, "Literary Career" 524). Recognizing that the "labor to become a name" has been in vain and the scant compensation in being "a seeker to suffice myself," Stoddard anticipates her own erasure from the historical record, recognizing that her own literary legacy is merely to be a "knowledge of the gap." This is a dispassionate vision of literary history as a perpetual intertextual weaving in which "tempted" others have "claimed" "unfinished work," appropriating "borrowed light" as their own. "Above the Tree" is the dark sister poem of Dickinson's "The Poets light but Lamps." For Dickinson, the hope is that the poetic lamps "inhere" like stars, with a "vital light" sufficient to draw the attention of reader/astronomers ages hence. In Stoddard's bleaker vision of literary history, "freedom" also is imagining the poet a distant star, here a sun casting its rays across interstellar spaces—an unknown, unacknowledged origin—whose light, "caught" by impervious others, survives the demise of its source but is scarcely "vital." The conclusion that this light will not merely "serve" others (by providing them with light) but that the gesture will also "serve" the speaker-poet (as a sad but sufficient legacy) is scarcely convincing. This is not merely one of Stoddard's most personal poems, it is one of the saddest poems in nineteenth-century literature. It also conclusively demonstrates that if, in Bennett's words, this was an era when poetic talent was "scattered diffusely through a population of unknowns" (*Anthology* xl), this was a poet who did not want to be unknown, although she may have come to accept the inevitability of the scattering diffuseness of her own poetic light. If, to quote Joanne Dobson, the "sentimental crisis of consciousness is not so much an anxiety regarding the ultimate nonbeing of the self as it is the certain knowledge of inevitable separation—whether temporal or eternal—from the others who constitute the meaning of one's life" ("Reclaiming" 267), then the crisis of consciousness for Stoddard, contrarily, was the fear (and, increasingly, the certain knowledge) of inevitable separation from the later audience she anticipated, a separation whose consequence constituted in many ways a fundamental form of artistic nonbeing.

In *Contingencies of Value,* Barbara Herrnstein Smith notes that texts cannot become canonical unless they are seen to endorse the hegemonic or ideological values of dominant social groups: it would be naive to believe that the establishment of a canon of nineteenth-century women's poetry by feminist critics, newly ascendant in the academy, will not also be a significant hegemonic and ideological enterprise.[15] In a gesture now foundational in the formation of the poetic canon, scholars of nineteenth-century women's literature often dissolve the aesthetic in a general attack on the "poetics of presence." Tim Morris, maintaining that the American poetic tradition developed around the suspect "values of originality, organicism, and monologic language" (*Becoming Canonical* xi), argues that the "poetics of presence should be abandoned as an assumption of reading" since "feminist countermoves cannot be successful if they rely just as uncritically on the values of presence" (10). Claiming that since "the egocentric model of poetry is based on the male-defined poetic tradition of romanticism," Annie Finch argues that those who "did not struggle with that tradition . . . offer a gynocentric alternative model for critics of women's poetry" (4). One problem with a gynocentric alternative model distinguished by, in Finch's words, the "lack of a privileged central self, in conjunction with the elevation of public, communally shared values such as religion and family love" (5) is that there is no place within it for a poet like Elizabeth Stoddard.[16] Processes of selection and exclusion, the requirements of an explanatory master narrative, always distinguish canon formation: the example of Stoddard provides us with a useful and revelatory view of a significant fault line in the narrative of the developing canon of nineteenth-century women's poetry. If literary value is, indeed, an artifact of the cultural and material elements that surround a work's production and reception, then the status of Stoddard's poetry in contexts (past and present) that foreground and privilege the cultural work of the sentimental text will inevitably seem slight. But that assessment speaks more to the confines and limitations of the established paradigm than to the intrinsic worth of the particular poet. On 6 March 1859, Bayard Taylor wrote on the outside of an envelope containing a letter to the Stoddards, "To the Stod-dardess, (a wild female specimen of the poetic animal)." Finding a place for the "wild female specimen" in a canon that has, to date, been pri-marily focused on the significance of the domestic species may well, in time, prove to be a revelatory project for contemporary scholars of nine-teenth-century women's literature.

NOTES

I thank Ellen Weinauer for her careful and thorough reading of previous versions of this essay.

1. Recent critical literature that attempts to complicate our understanding of sentimentalism in nineteenth-century American women's literature would include Dobson's "Reclaiming Sentimental Literature"; Bennett's "Not Just Filler and Not Just Sentimental: Women's Poetry in American Victorian Peri-odicals, 1860–1900"; and Susan K. Harris's *Nineteenth-Century American Women's Novels.*

2. In her own effort to identify and unravel the complex strands of nine-teenth-century women's literature in America, Joyce Warren resorts to placing Stoddard in the problematic category of "questioner" (72).

3. Douglass's suspicion of sentimental literature centers on what she viewed as its straightforward reveling in a hypocritical masochism. In response, Tomp-kins, Baym (*Woman's Fiction*), and Dobson ("Reclaiming") have argued that scenes of submission are a subversive strategy and that representations of pain and suffering permit readers to imagine themselves in the victim's place and thus, eventually, to recognize and contest the patriarchal forces that create and sustain the painful experience. In recent years, more nuanced readings of senti-mental power by Karen Sanchez-Eppler and Marianne Noble, among others, have recognized the power of sentimentalism in the development of a social-protest fiction while simultaneously querying the moral and aesthetic value of a literature that derives its subversive power from the representation of suffering.

4. In his 1874 revision of Griswold's anthology, Richard Stoddard noted that "a new race of female poets . . . with a wider range of thought in their verse, and infinitely more art" (7) had emerged since the first publication of the volume in 1848 and, in discussing the "force" and "originality" of the poets he had added, pointedly observes that the readers of an earlier generation would not have appreciated it.

5. Cheryl Walker argues that by midcentury "the dominant members in this women's tradition must have seemed to younger women poets like an es-tablishment" (87). Stoddard's predilection for composing in blank verse also sug-

gests a willful resistance to the typical formal structures of American women's verse in this period and may constitute an anti-establishment gesture.

6. Stoddard reiterates her distaste in an 1860 letter to Stedman: "I have been looking over Leaves of Grass. The author leaves himself no privacy, and I think he is very trashy and laughable" (qtd. in Matlack, "Literary Career" 163).

7. In a letter of 1892 to Lilian Whiting, Stoddard observes sharply, "An eccentric arrangement of words—or ebullition of feeling do not constitute poetry" (qtd. in Matlack, "Literary Career" 470). This reaction is surprising since the two Massachusetts writers had a great deal in common. Describing the Dickinson family's Amherst homestead, T. W. Higginson informs his wife: "If you had read Mrs Stoddard's novels you could understand a house where each member runs his or her own selves" (16 Aug. 1870, qtd. in Leyda, 2: 151). Besides some striking biographical similarities, Dickinson and Stoddard also moved, albeit obliquely, in similar literary venues. In March 1864, for example, the magazine *Round Table* published Dickinson's poem "My Sabbath" (no. 324). Charles Sweetser, the editor of the magazine, had been a neighbor of the poet and remained a frequent visitor to Amherst. In the early 1860s, Richard Stoddard was one of the subeditors of *Round Table* and a frequent contributor to the magazine. Possibly as a favor to Richard, Sweetser would write a review of *Two Men* in 1865.

8. Bayard Taylor's comparison of Stoddard to Elizabeth Barrett Browning suggests another interesting poetic relation. Taylor, who knew both women and who would, later, have considerable issues with Stoddard's pungent forthrightness, observed in a letter of 4 August 1856: "E.B.B. reminded me of E.D.B—only she is less profane and pugnacious" (134).

9. In his reminiscences, Stoddard's own recollection is that "the habit of writing is sometimes catching, and my wife finally discovered when she caught herself penning little essays, and poems, and stories, which she brought to me in fear and trembling. She had a fine intellect, but it was untrained, and all that I could do for her was to show her how to train it. She was not cursed with mediocrity, but had the misfortune to be original" (114).

10. In "Mercedes," a weak and hackneyed attempt to replicate the Browning dramatic monologue of the obsessed lover, this is especially evident.

11. The writer who once lauded *Jane Eyre* as a "daring and masculine work" (qtd. in Matlack, "Literary Career" 168) craved respect as a writer who wrote with the freedom of a man, albeit on her own revisionary terms.

12. Stoddard once noted wryly, "Tennyson is a monstrous fine poet. We all try to imitate his sweet, laborious art; but we fail" (*Daily Alta California,* 20 July 1856).

13. The danger of imitation, of course, is that it ultimately leads to stul-

tification and the stifling of the poet's own voice. Like many of her contemporaries, Stoddard was tempted to traffic in clichéd Romantic tropes and over-
wrought, archaic diction. The openings of the poems "Achilles in Orcus" ("From
thy translucent waves, great Thetis, rise!") and "Closed" ("The crimson dawn
breaks through the clouded east / And waking breezes round the casement
pipe") display this tendency only too well. On occasion, Stoddard also displays
a predilection for the excesses of gothic poetic architecture. This is evident
not only in the adjectival imprecision of her gothic vocabulary in the allegorical "The House of Youth" ("The *mottled* sand-bird runneth up and down /
Amongst the *creaking* sedge, / Along the *crusted* beach" [emphasis added]) but
also in the more elaborately rhetorical sub-Poeisms of "March":

> Roar from the surf of boreal isles,
> Roar from the hidden, jagged steeps,
> Where the destroyer never sleeps;
> Ring through the iceberg's Gothic piles!

The young writer who claimed, "I long to probe with sensation the abyss of
life" (qtd. in Matlack, "Literary Career" 74) was drawn to the abysmal excesses
of Poe's "boreal isles" and "Gothic piles," and as these lines suggest—"I heard
in dreams the sweet joy-bells: / I woke to see a woman pale / Tear apart my
bridal veil, / With flaming eyes and hideous yells!" (qtd. in Matlack, "Literary
Career" 116)—often borrowed more from the "sensational" qualities of the
Brontë novels than from the stylistic restraint and precision of Emily Brontë's
poetry.

14. Stoddard's poetry is often most effective when brought, literally and
figuratively, closer to home—that is, when it returns both to the natural landscape surrounding Mattapoisett that inspired the setting of *The Morgesons* and
much of her short fiction and, simultaneously, to the domain of the Wordswor-
thian lyric self. In the conclusion of "From the Headland," for example, we
discover a superb poet of the seascape:

> Here, but the wiry grass and sorrel beds,
> The gaping edges of the sand ravines,
> Whose shifting sides are tufted with dull herbs,
> Drooping above a brook, that sluggish creeps
> Down to the whispering rushes in the marsh.
> And this is all, until I reach the cliff,
> And on the headland's verge I stand, enthralled
> Before the gulf of the unquenchable sea—

The sea, inexorable in its might,
Circling the pebbly beach with limpid tides,
Storming in bays whose margins fade in mist;
Now blue and silent as a noonday sky.

Stoddard often found in the waters of Buzzard's Bay the reflection of her own psychological processes—a convenient reconciliation of the Romantic contraries of measured blue calm and the ever-present threat of tempestuous explosion. The rocks of Ned's Point, Mattapoisett, were Stoddard's "Tintern Abbey." In this poem, a suitable companion piece for *The Morgesons,* the journey from the "sluggish" brook and "whispering rushes" to the "verge" of the headland (Stoddard's "edge of things") and the vision of "inexorable" and "unquenchable" strength the "gulf" provides is the most thoroughly imaginative of voyages. As always, the rock-cleft promontories of the southeast coast of Massachusetts offer the poet a convenient map of (and to) her imaginative process: a Romantic vision from the *headland* indeed.

15. Among the most significant discussions of canon formation in American literature are the critical texts by Tompkins, Lauter, and Kolb. For a pithy critique of the New Americanist attempt at canon reshaping, see Crews, "Whose American Renaissance?"

16. John Guillory has noted that an author's inevitable reemergence often compromises the "pluralist critique of the canon" whose founding strategy is the dissolution of that author's "privileged central self": "The primacy of the social identity of the author in the pluralist critique of the canon means that the revaluation of works on this basis will inevitably seek its ground in the author's experience, conceived as the experience of a marginalized race, class or gender identity. The author returns in the critique of the canon, not as the genius, but as the representative of social identity" (10).

Elizabeth Stoddard as Returned Californian

A Reading of the *Daily Alta California* Columns

Margaret A. Amstutz

Before Elizabeth Stoddard attempted either short or long fiction, she enjoyed popularity through more pedestrian labor as a newspaper columnist. As the "Lady Correspondent" from New York City to San Francisco from 1854 to 1858, Stoddard submitted biweekly columns to her San Francisco readership that offer a cynical, biting, sardonic, and occasionally dreamlike look at her urban surroundings and the rural New England of her childhood. In a thorough overview of Stoddard's writing life, James Matlack describes Stoddard's journalistic venture as a "campaign . . . that displayed her skills as an author in an entirely convincing manner" ("Literary Career" 122). "Campaign" is an appropriate term here, for although uneven in tone and content, these columns collectively demonstrate a self-conscious young female author's ongoing, directed attempts to challenge convention and to indulge in experiment with journalistic form. The first daily newspaper in the West, the *Daily Alta California* offered Stoddard a unique venue that, she later confessed, taught her "to write prose and the earning of money. Every month I received a check for twenty-four dollars, which possessed many imaginative possibilities that were never realized. At any rate, I was the first female wage-earner that I had known, and it gave me a curious sense of independence" (qtd. in Matlack, "Literary Career" 126). The rhythm of these checks and the steady schedule of biweekly submissions could have fostered a conventional writing style in this early period of a young writer's life. However, for Stoddard, this was hardly the case. Indeed, while the economic possibilities of twenty-four dollars per month may have gone unrealized, the literary rewards were precisely the "imaginative possibilities" inherent in the medium in which Stoddard was maturing as a writer.

In their exploration of her writing career, Lawrence Buell and Sandra Zagarell identify Stoddard's "literary debut" as a correspondent to the

Daily Alta as the foundation for her narrative vision, "rooted in the contemplation of the kind of small, ancient, ingrown New England seaport
town in which she grew up" (*The Morgesons* xv).[1] Undoubtedly, Stoddard's fictional treatment of New England is indebted to her early journalism and the thematic exploration that these biweekly columns afforded her.[2] Yet to be taken on by scholars, however, is a more specific
examination of the role that the young writer's bicoastal correspondence
played in her exploration of authorship, in particular her self-conscious
investigation of the discursive spaces within which she might locate her
own evolving authorial voice. In the *Alta* columns, Stoddard identifies
herself as a woman looking westward: the possibilities of an envisioned,
distant California significantly inform her nascent literary imagination.
Her accounts of local New York and her pilgrimages to her native Massachusetts convey an unsettling sense of "otherness" in the midst of
the familiar—land, family, and body—that would come to mark Stoddard's best fiction in later years. The medium of bicoastal journalism provided a critical contribution to the development of Stoddard's literary
imagination, as she came to situate herself in relation to three distinct
locales: New York City (where she lived); Mattapoisett, Massachusetts
(her birthplace and frequent summer home); and San Francisco (where
she imagined her readers to be). As a result, in the *Alta* columns we find
Stoddard, through the deliberate triangulation of alternate geographies
for self-identification, able to test both her largely rural New England
homeland and the problematics of urban culture, in cities both near and
far. Simultaneously, in seeking to define herself as an author, Stoddard
boldly engaged contemporaries from Fanny Fern to Nathaniel Hawthorne in her description and commentary, placing herself implicitly in
dialogue with her literary peers. In this way, Stoddard crafted her own
distinctive narrative voice, locating her idiosyncratic authorial vision
against the backdrop of an expanding American literary consciousness.
Stoddard's columns thus afforded her an apprenticeship simultaneously
intertextual and interstitial; not only did she locate her own voice as a
writer in relation to the texts of her significant contemporaries, but she
also found the means—through the situated triangulation of landscape
for her immediate audience—to begin the process of charting an alternate cartography of the self.

Stoddard establishes her desire for literary distinction early in the columns' run, both in her repeated calls for American literary achievement
and in her attempts to distinguish herself from her female contemporaries. Indeed, even in jest, Stoddard expresses her desire for American ac-

complishment. Complaining of the bothersome mosquitoes on a late-August night in New York, she writes in an early column, "Who has written the song of the skeeter characteristically? No one. Like the American Epic, in spite of Buchanan Read, it remains to be done. Abstractly, I respect the mosquito; he is apparently an insignificance, but he sings and stings satanically. I am but a small bit myself; so I admire power in smallness" (20 Aug. 1855).

Already, in her first year as a columnist, her powerful self-confidence is apparent and inextricably connected to the belief that the individual, creative American voice would have a "stinging" component. Stoddard relishes that "satanic" sting, asserting in her initial column that her success will not be secured through the safe route of conventional—that is, pious or sentimental—rhetoric. In her introductory letter she scorns the "pugilism of Fanny Fern, the pathetics of Minnie Myrtle, or the abandon of Cassie Cauliflower," writing instead—she claimed—"letters containing facts and opinions" (8 Oct. 1854). While her future columns do make frequent reference to the domestic world, Stoddard regularly eschews the narrative styles of her female contemporaries, preferring instead to take a dry, witty, and often reflective approach to her material. But Stoddard's criticism, at least in the case of one of her fellow journalists, belies in part her claims for distinction. For all of Stoddard's criticism of Fanny Fern's "pugilism," her own work is often stylistically akin to Fern's in her saucier journalistic moments; contemporary reviewers who labeled Fern's work as "unfeminine" and "vulgar" echo observations made of Stoddard's own writings (cited in Warren 109). Inevitably, for Stoddard, Fern modeled confidence in the first-person journalistic narrative while succinctly demonstrating the possibilities (and limitations) of satirical commentary. As America's first woman newspaper columnist, Fern made a highly successful living from her journalism. With the 1853 publication of *Fern Leaves from Fanny's Portfolio* garnering sales close to one hundred thousand in the United States and abroad in its first year of publication, a bar had been set for female authorship in terms of audience, financial success, and journalistic enterprise (Fern xvi).

Distinguishing Fern and Stoddard conclusively, however, is the question of audience. Fern's columns prior to their collection in *Fern Leaves* ran in the *Olive Branch,* the *True Flag,* and the *New York Musical World and Times* for a primarily northeastern readership.[3] Stoddard, in contrast, was offering biweekly accounts of her local environment for a distant California audience, whose relationship to the content of her columns was one of recollection, association, or imagination. The miles between writer and reader granted Stoddard a measure of imaginative (and rhetorical) license that she continually incorporates in her journalistic descriptions. Indeed, rather than offering the promised direct description of her surroundings, Stoddard is liable to claim, "The world is in a haze this morning; the world is where we may happen to be. Possibly our morning is tropical; the jolly sun may be shining on the bald heads of the just, and patent leathers of the unjust; and life may seem bustling and well-to-do, but I do not realize it." Her surroundings assume "the muffled, misty hue of the atmosphere. The figures in the landscape look like gliding spectres, and their voices are faint and far away" (19 Feb. 1855). Here and elsewhere in the columns, Stoddard flecks her world with shades of gray, shards of memory and emotion tincturing the narrative account, refining concrete details away. Throughout her tenure with the *Daily Alta,* Stoddard's columns freely stray in this manner from the "facts and opinions" that she has previously claimed would be her focus. With her audience merely a distant image, a western mirage, Stoddard has a much different task than a journalist writing for a familiar local readership. The remoteness of that distant audience provides an opportunity to offer on occasion a more imaginative, romanticized presentation of the contemporary scene.

Stoddard's columns thus serve her both as an entrance into the literary arena and as a venue for narrative license, suggesting that she, much like the women whose work she critiques, takes advantage of the freedom (and the public forum) afforded the nineteenth-century (male or female) journalist. As Nancy Walker notes in her biography of Fanny Fern, the authority of the columnist emerged in the mid–nineteenth century from a blend of political impulse and individual expression, with columnists viewed as "educated, alert citizens possessed of the right to express their opinions in print" (23–24). Stoddard clearly takes advantage of the "right to express" her opinion (a tendency for which she became widely known both in her work and in her personal relations in later years). At several points in her correspondence, for example, Stoddard-as-Lady-Correspondent is critical of perennially popular women writers for their feebleness in wrestling with the landscape of the self, particularly the emotional depths and heights of passionate sensibility. Noting the prolific publication of works by women, she argues that "no one book has been written by a woman of erudition; no metaphysical tale, novel or poem; no story that holds in analysis the passions of the human heart. . . . The eight books in ten are written without genius; all show industry, and a few talent" (22 Oct. 1855). In chastising Harriet Beecher Stowe, Stoddard recounts the story of "an old lady whose son took a prize at the Olympic games" who "advised her son to die while he was a victor, lest he should try to win some future prize and fail. So with Mrs. Stowe. I wouldn't really advise her to die, (for she mightn't be quite prepared, notwithstanding her husband is a minister,) but I would advise her to rest on the laurels of 'Uncle Tom'" (19 June 1855). Such comments exhibit the brash confidence of a young writer, but when viewed in conjunction with the four-year stream of columns from New York to California, they also reveal Stoddard's alternate vision of female authorship, suggesting that the female writer's active and ongoing literary experimentation in a public setting should directly challenge or even upset the boundaries for expression of the individual consciousness.

Stoddard's willingness to experiment as a writer is, of course, evident in her short and long fiction—and evidenced as well by her struggles to find an audience for that fiction. Stoddard's *Alta* columns anticipate her later fictional tendencies in this regard: in them we witness Stoddard's early efforts to put her ideas about literary experimentation into practice. (Indeed, her popularity as a columnist, particularly when compared with her lack of popularity as a writer of fiction, reminds us of the comparative license granted the [female] journalist.) We are also able to see how the destabilizing medium in which she first worked as a writer facilitated such experimentation. Any discussion of the *Alta* letters' collective importance in Stoddard's emerging literary imagination must acknowledge the adventuresome, risk-filled course of their journey: columns written in summer on the rocky Mattapoisett shoreline journeyed from New York to San Francisco via two steamers—one in the Atlantic, one in the Pacific—and onto the railway that carried the letters between these oceans across the fields of Nicaragua (Matlack, "Literary Career" 127). On occasion, Stoddard actually meditates on this journey and its ability to destabilize her work with an appealingly self-deprecating humor: "I have received and read my first printed letter in the *Alta California,* and am confounded at its length," she notes in a very early column:

> I knew that a woman's tongue was garrulous, but never till now knew that her pen might have the same complaint. The experiences of this letter, as a traveller, must have been remarkable. I detect foreign airs about it.
> "Setters from Idlewild!" Oh Proof Reader, is thy servant a dog,

that she should do this thing? Is Willis to be accused of breeding puppies? I wrote "Letters from Idlewild." (17 Dec. 1854)[4]

The humor loosely cloaks the sentiment that the letter has assumed a life of its own during the journey, that the chosen genre of the Lady Correspondent dictates a problematic textual transmission, an inevitable diffusion of the authorial intent of the original. The sheer distance traveled by these papers thus elevates them in the imaginative realm: Stoddard's texts become as metaphorically fluid and unstable as the literal vehicle that joins their communicative circuit. Those "singing" waters are, of course, frequently personified in Stoddard's own Romantic inscription —reminding us once again of her fusion of "facts" with emotion, the "real" with the imaginative: "But to come to the truth and beauty of my surroundings. Here rolls the everlasting sea. On the day of my birth its voice was uplifted; on the day of my death, its song will be the same." She is both fascinated and troubled by the New England sea, viewing it as "deaf and sightless . . . unpitying. . . . Ever in motion, yet within impassible [sic] barriers, it seems a type of the soul on earth, fretted by and chained to the body" (24 Oct. 1855). It may be that the long ocean voyage of her columns cemented Stoddard's fascination with the waters of Buzzard's Bay to such a degree that in her later fiction she naturally ascribed to the sea decidedly empathic and communicative powers. In one memorable passage from *The Morgesons* the sea actually echoes the imprisoned, passionate nature of the narrator's mother, "murmuring softly, creeping along the shore, licking the rocks and sand as if recognizing a master" (63). Contemplating this vastness weekly as a young writer, Stoddard, perhaps not surprisingly, would later claim this space in her fiction as an avenue for the expression of natural desire or, in this particular case, animal-like masochistic subservience. In Stoddard's work, the sea typically represents intense longing, seething animal passion barely contained by the seawalls of social structure, a boundary usurping elemental force, even as it exists as a concrete entity that drives, in a very real sense, the economic life of coastal New England.

If the medium through which the *Alta* columns were largely transmitted is fluid, so, too—perhaps in a mirroring response—is the identity of the Lady Correspondent herself. Inspired perhaps by the distance afforded her by her imagined identification with her California readership, Stoddard, as she details her visits to the New England of her childhood, assumes the dual roles of traveler and observer. Having wandered both the physical streets of New York and the imagined byways of a distant California, Stoddard positions the Lady Correspondent as "a pilgrim and a sojourner, but not a fashionable one." Recounting a return to the New England seashore in this early column (24 Oct. 1855), Stoddard assumes the role, at least initially, of an expatriate returning to the land of her birth. There, however, she finds the myth of Yankee resourcefulness undercut by the economic fluctuations of the shipbuilding industry. The sea that carried Stoddard's letters across the miles to the West Coast captures her imagination not by affirming the constancy of a mythologized New England but, rather, by the way in which it serves as a mere witness to the illusion of constancy: "The sandy soil of the village grave yard hides generations of my race. The old slate stones level with their mounds, and covered with moss, the upright marble slabs with their names freshly cut have neither age nor date to the deaf and sightless sea" (24 Oct. 1855). In the eyes of the returning pilgrim, the broken promise of the New England cemetery is its doomed attempt to record the generations for posterity. Stoddard makes the same observation in *The Morgesons* (1862), emphasizing the "strength in the narrowest affinities" one finds in the present, in contrast to the "still more profound darkness" to be found in the "antiheraldic memory" of the Morgeson lineage (8). As in the journalistic work of the apprentice author, in this later text the physical surroundings hardly prescribe the landscape of the self. The New England cemetery soil holds little familial security for Stoddard's narrator Cassandra in *The Morgesons;* rather, she remains a transient being, engaged in possessive individual encounters with the present. This, too, we might remark, was precisely the self-location of the Lady Correspondent of the *Daily Alta* columns.

In general, the Lady Correspondent's imaginative travels in the columns—indeed, the transient nature of the journalistic medium itself—provide both perspective and content. Most often, the instability of her own identity invariably emerges from her attempts to conceptualize the distant western city. However, as the Lady Correspondent illustrates in her first column to the *Daily Alta,* her later self-identification with California was not immediately apparent: "All of the world, that is, our half of it, has been for weeks drying up. The country is crisp, brown, and fiery. In the city we are dust-bound. . . . The reporters are writing their last letters from Saratoga and Newport. . . . I am willing to confess to you Californians, who believe in the Pacific and Sandwich Islands, that the mineral waters of Saratoga are unknown to my palate, and that I have only seen Newport afar off" (8 Oct. 1854). Stoddard's impulse in this initial letter is, clearly, to underscore the dichotomy of near and far, to locate herself firmly in a New York distanced from her readership. However, as her correspondence continues, the identification with any one particular place becomes less certain, and Stoddard's identity as a New Yorker is increasingly destabilized; by 1856, she alternates between confessions of attachment to the city ("I love New York, stiff, ugly and incongruous as it is," she states on 9 November) and a more familiar association with the New England region, with its "Congregational fast days. . . . Instead of the ordinary noon–day meal, the folks had only pies and cakes, and cold coffee in mugs. . . . But at sundown the pious but rejoicing village sat down to a Yankee tea, the like of which can never be had out of New England" (9 Mar. 1856). Increasingly, it would seem, Stoddard's imaginative journey to California places her Lady Correspondent in the tradition of pilgrim/sojourner, a role that she adopts with no little self-awareness. Emily Budick identifies in nineteenth-century American authorship a "questioning of the authority attached to language and literature and the social institutions they promote" (78). Stoddard's own questioning begins in the Lady Correspondent's repeated pattern of exploration and account; having envisioned her native New England from a traveled perspective, her loyalties to place are refreshingly subverted as she contemplates the triangulation of three locations that come to figure mutually encroaching temporal dimensions —past (Mattapoisett), present (New York), and future (San Francisco).

Of course, the *Daily Alta* columns also allow Stoddard "to experiment with tone," as Buell and Zagarell note (Stoddard, *The Morgesons and Other Writings* 312), particularly in her sketches of New England. The New England landscape, with its evocation of tastes and smells, would have been familiar to many of her San Francisco readers. As the Lady Correspondent reminisces, "A Yankee sea-coast tea differs from an inland or mountainous tea. With mournful smacks of the mouth, I recall the former: small quahogs with melted butter poured over them; creek oysters in the shell; broiled split eels; hot biscuits" (9 Mar. 1856). Yet the *Daily Alta* columns rarely settle for nostalgia for the rural environment, in part because that environment is the product of a decaying past. In contrast, the imaginative prospect of San Francisco, the developing urban city of the future, is perpetually reshaping and energizing Stoddard's vision; as she queries, "By the way, what do the rich San Franciscans do to keep out of boredom?" (22 Oct. 1855). Upon her return to Mattapoisett in September, Stoddard debunks the Romantic aspects of the township, labeling its people as "a scaly set" and identifying " 'an ancient and fish-like smell' . . . apt to pervade its premises" (24 Oct. 1855). Her pointed prose exposes as fraudulent those New England characteristics elevated to the realm of American myth by Washington Irving and James Fenimore Cooper, the surmised Yankee stoicism and the quaint charm of the New England township: "The ploughman wonders why the 'granite soil of New England' should be a favorite phrase with orators: he and his oxen think it a deuced bore." The patterns of "puritanic" New England are thus infused with "the saline qualities of the atmosphere" (24 Oct. 1855). In these and other accounts of Stoddard's pilgrimage to her native Massachusetts, she increasingly assumes the position of marginalized and critical observer. Rather than brooding self-examination, her rhetorical response to "otherness" in the midst of the familiar New England setting is a rapidly paced blend of dry observation, critical wit, and brief introspection. Envisioning herself as a visitor in her native New England, Stoddard assumes increased narrative license and, in a direct reassessment of Massachusetts facilitated by an assumed outsider's perspective, her chronicle continually and pointedly demystifies the rural setting.

Interestingly, a private link between Stoddard and a specific other may have been inscribed within the public forum of these columns. Matlack argues for the importance of one particular California reader, noting that Stoddard's younger brother Wilson Barstow was a resident of San Francisco for four and a half years during the period of Stoddard's columns. Matlack calls the letters a private dialogue with Wilson in the guise of a public conversation, "letters to her brother" that gave her "a powerful private motive in her wish to have a regular if unconventional means of communicating with [him]" ("Literary Career" 128). While the columns depict Stoddard's relationship with her brother as one of sincere affection and illustrate the pangs of separation, the presence of her brother in the *Alta* readership perhaps indicates something other than private correspondence between the two. Even as she conceives of her brother as a primary audience, Stoddard also indicates that she views her role as a writer to be one of public performance. Comparing herself to a ballet dancer who continues to dance in the midst of sadness, she states, "I have a grief to struggle with, a malady that has its origin in California—the separation of my family. But I must keep up my dancing for all that" (21 Sept. 1856). Indeed, rather than merely holding a private dialogue with Wilson, Stoddard uses the forum of the columns to identify more generally with her Californian audience and to insert herself, in a thoroughly performative way, as a chronicler of the widening canvas of individuals who exist in relationship to others in a transcontinental frame.

Stoddard, in fact, presents her Lady Correspondent as a part of that broader American phenomenon, associating herself with stereotypical figures accompanying westward expansion. The mystique of California includes both the figure of "the Returned Californian"—a stereotype markedly noticeable in New York and a personage to whom Stoddard repeatedly refers in later columns—and those of the "California widows," those women left behind as their husbands traveled westward. By identifying herself as a "California brotheress," Stoddard aligns herself with those women in her local surroundings whose husbands are absent. More interestingly, her repeated references to the "Returned Californian" walking the streets of New York in brazen dress, recklessly spendthrift, evidences her early refining of the type of character development that would manifest itself in her later fiction. With these figures, Stoddard's biweekly columns become a testing ground for her construction of abbreviated, memorably detailed portraits of minor characters. Take, for example, the portrait she paints of Cassandra's Grandfather Warren in her first novel *The Morgesons*, "a little, lean, leather-colored man" whose characteristics serve as an index to his native New England: "He chafed his small, well-shaped hands continually; his long polished nails clicked together with a shelly noise, like that which beetles make flying against the ceiling" (*The Morgesons and Other Writings* 28). This brief sketch illustrates the development of Stoddard's "shrewd eye for the significant or absurd detail" and represents, presumably, one of the rewards of her journalistic apprenticeship to which Buell and Zagarell point in their discussion of her *Daily Alta* years.

However, the character sketches practiced by Stoddard in the columns also hint at Stoddard's deeper intentions for authorship. She deems the Returned Californian "an index to the progress of California" with "as marked an individuality as a Vermonter or a Kentuckian" (17 Dec. 1854). Initially an uncouth, bearded figure dropping gifts of gold nuggets on his friends, the Returned Californian evolves in Stoddard's eyes into a dramatic personage who makes "mysterious" entrances; travels by carriage rather than omnibus, visiting tailors and Tiffany & Young; then emerges as "the perfect butterfly . . . inwardly delighted with his appearance," sporting "the biggest diamonds, the most enamelled of all watches," and appearing to be "much astonished at the cheapness of things" (17 Dec. 1854). Inherent in her description are two themes: the suggestion of a city of possibilities in the distant West whose community lends itself to the development of such flamboyant figures; and the psychological impact of accumulated material possessions, as the individual, weighted by a collection of goods, becomes an urban spectacle. These stories are only suggested, not detailed, but it is the perspective of the imaginative journey to California that enables the generation of such character sketches. The minor characters she depicts were her creative entrée as social commentator, and in approaching the New England setting and character with the visionary perspective of her *Daily Alta* journalism, Stoddard would in her later fiction use similar figures to criticize the social conventions of the New England community with vigor and force.[5] Thus, the transient vision of the Lady Correspondent renders Stoddard, too, a Returned Californian of sorts, providing her with the dual perspectives of both participant and observer and ultimately facilitating the creation of a unique (and very different) authorial persona.

Entering the public arena to offer an imaginative, romanticized presentation of the contemporary scene, the female writer also had to cope, inevitably, with the influence of significant male precursors who claimed it as their own domain. If California was still largely to be discovered in literature, New England was a literary landscape densely populated and well traveled. For Stoddard, the "return" to New England of the "Lady Correspondent" was also simultaneously a return to that densely populated textual landscape, to the landscape of the region's literature, and thus an intertextual (as well as interstitial) return. As a writer, Stoddard had to clear imaginative space for herself in a patriarchal tradition; to a degree, her journalism gave her a chance to establish her own authorial legitimacy through the conduit of that tradition and, at the same time, to contest the ground of the tradition itself. The *Alta* columns provided Stoddard with an opportune *revisionary* platform, in Adrienne Rich's sense of the word—in them, Stoddard could engage in the "act of looking back, of seeing with fresh eyes, of entering an old text from a new critical direction . . . to know the writing of the past, and know it differently than we have ever known it; not to pass on a tradition but to break its hold over us" (35). Indeed, Stoddard's most ambitious, if significantly more covert, attempt to position herself in the literary arena of her day can be found in an early column that provides a curious engagement with the work of Nathaniel Hawthorne—in particular, with two of Hawthorne's sketches, "Night Sketches" (1838) and "Hall of Fantasy" (1843).

As Matlack and others have indicated, Hawthorne's influence in Stoddard's life cannot be understated: aside from being the prominent American novelist of the period and a distant relative, Hawthorne is recognized by Stoddard herself as one of "three names I owe much to: Hawthorne, Lowell, Stedman" (qtd. in Matlack, "Literary Career" 556). The exploration of the individual psyche in Stoddard's fiction is a clear acknowledgment of Hawthorne's patterns, of his influence in American literary development. Buell and Zagarell note that Stoddard's later fiction "accentuates" the "psychological intensity which Hawthorne often neutralized through coyness or urbanity" (xv). In a column from 1854 in which Stoddard recounts her visit to the New York Crystal Palace, we see the public debut of Stoddard's fascination with Hawthorne and her conscious experimentation with his narrative style. We might also recognize the spirit of complex contention with which she approaches her formidable male precursor. For if Stoddard makes use of Hawthornian patterns of investigation, her mission *to* the Crystal Palace evidently constitutes, at the same time, a deliberate textual infringement of the Hawthornian imaginative patent. Nancy K. Miller, while adapting many aspects of French poststructuralist theory for her own purposes, rejects its definition of intertextuality in order to posit an alternative "theory of text production" she dubs "Arachnology."[6] Arachnology is an exploration of the forms that a "female signature" takes in the traditions of women's writing, an examination of the interweaving of texts as an activity centered in an embodied and gendered agent. Miller's woman writer is conceived as a subject in history with the capacity to participate in a limited "political intertextuality." As she contends with the writings of Hawthorne, Stoddard's "weaving" of what she calls her own "baseless dream" in this *Alta* column is an early attempt at precisely such arachnid revisionism.

Stoddard's provocative account of the fading days of the New York Crystal Palace exhibition appeared in early November 1854.[7] Organized in 1852 in the wake of the successful 1851 Crystal Palace exhibition in London, the New York Crystal Palace was to be an "exhibition of the industry of all nations," showcasing military weapons, consumer goods, inventions, art, and a plethora of tastes and smells of places near and far. Like its London counterpart, the New York Crystal Palace aspired to collect the most sophisticated of human achievements under a single roof. In actuality, the exhibition proved to be a great disappointment, and Stoddard's narrative offers a pensive depiction of its shortcomings, noting its "half deserted arcade" and the "lonely few" who continued to make their visits (5 Nov. 1854).[8] Notably, however, the Lady Correspondent's analysis of the Crystal Palace exhibit is interspersed with a description of her husband Richard Stoddard's literary circle, reviews of recent book publications, and a report on the Metropolitan Theatre. The writer thus presents her commentary as that of an individual enmeshed in the literary and cultural issues of the day. Choosing to engage the work of Hawthorne, by that time a long-established literary figure, Stoddard uses her narrative to stake her own definitive claim in the profession of authorship. She does so by intentionally shaping her column as a countertext that adapts, assimilates, and transforms the precursor's text.

The dream narrative form of this particular column mirrors closely the circumstances suggested in Hawthorne's "Night Sketches," in which the narrator's leisurely confinement within a room on a rainy day permits him free rein to "summon up a thousand varied pictures" in the imagination (225). As in "Night Sketches," Stoddard's narrator also wanders allegorical halls, contemplating the figures found in the recesses of the creative imagination. Indeed, Hawthorne's "Hall of Fantasy" was a natural model for the re-visionary writer in this regard: his descriptions of "cities to be built, as if by magic . . . of mighty rivers to be staid in their courses, in order to turn the machinery of a cotton-mill" are peopled by "the inventors of fantastic machines" and so not unlike those exotic international exhibitors Stoddard observes in the Crystal Palace ("Hall of Fantasy" 247). Commencing with a description of the Lady Correspondent wandering the abandoned halls of the exhibit, Stoddard identifies the lingering patrons as "exiles, condemned to do the exhibition"; one couple, she notes wryly, is "evidently tired of life, and might have been looking for a suicide apparatus" (5 Nov. 1854). Having missed the height of its glory, the transient viewer of the Crystal Palace can observe only a barren space, a physical and psychic emptiness. The detritus of the echoing hall is a wearisome collection of leftover merchandise from an "experiment of an exposition of Art and Industry [that] has so far failed" (5 Nov. 1854). The Lady Correspondent's interest in the public exhibition, however, shifts quickly from its material contents to the vacant spaces now affording an opportunity for the industry of private imagination. That imaginative voyage, by virtue of its journalistic transmission, is rendered public, in its turn, for her distantly imagined Californian audience.

Lingering for a few paragraphs on the confirmed financial disaster of the exhibition itself, Stoddard observes, "In a remote corner of the

Crystal Palace I wove a new fabric, the baseless one of a dream. It is the only one there, and I shall prosecute any infringement of my patent. I imagined myself there at night, when our common life is barred in the folds of sleep. The grotesque became visible, and the will was able to realize all it desired" (5 Nov. 1854). The fabric of this dreamscape includes a suit of armor that "clanked down the stairs, to chat with a silk undershirt" and surreal social engagements between the international goods: "A Merrimac print made overtures to the goat-hair shawl of India, while the Gobeliu tapestries looked on, silent and disdainful." From an imagined conversation of Eve and Venus on "the nature of the apple" to Washington's getting "off his high horse to look for Martin Luther" to biblical figures' parading by in tandem, the halls of the Crystal Palace are filled now with the tumult of the Correspondent's raveling fantasy: "The shout of joy, the wail of despair, the infant's babble and the sigh of death began and ended the riddle of life, and so was fulfilled to me the mission of the Crystal Palace" (5 Nov. 1854). Even as she engages in this dreamlike fugue, in the Crystal Palace/Hall of Fantasy column, we find Stoddard exploring the notion that such aggregate fantasies, the sort of fantasy that in Hawthorne's fiction so often turns to darkness, are inherently dangerous, Romantic detours from the concrete and tangible. Perhaps for that reason the narrator concludes her sketch with a jolt of horse-drawn reality: "When I jolted home in a matter-of-fact omnibus, I tried to decide between the difference of life as a dream and a reality, and whether the world is not one vast lunatic asylum, whose patients are only to be cured by death. I was not shaken from this strange mood, till I found the omnibus man had given me a bad shilling!" (5 Nov. 1854).

Why, we might ask, would Stoddard select this particular narrative form for her California readership? For one thing, haunting the "Crystal Palace" column is the specter of economic disaster. This is a report of simultaneous cultural and economic exhaustion—and is, moreover, in sharp contrast with the successes of London's Crystal Palace, a particularly *American* failure. Frequently, Stoddard's columns evidence a harsh critique of the inequities of wealth distribution in New York: "We are not a well people commercially," she writes in 1854: "Wall street has a constriction. The bulls snuff and paw. The bears growl and dread being stirred up. The cholera here, and the yellow fever South, have delayed the buyers, and there is therefore an overstock of goods in our market. Failures, crashes and crises are anticipated. But how few will be affected?" (22 Oct. 1854). As troublesome as individual poverty is, the result of such economic instability is an erasure of individuality for those who lose their fortunes, an absence of self in the midst of the teeming city where "somebody will move from the Fifth Avenue to the Second, and then be seen no more forever at opera, ball, and Grace church" (22 Oct. 1854). Economic instability leads to a form of living death; Stoddard characterizes these hopeless individuals as "rent vampires," who move from apartment to apartment in New York, seeking hope in the next "disagreeable place" of residence but seemingly losing their souls in the process (19 Mar. 1855). For Stoddard's California readership, the message is one of caution at the well of opportunity, a warning for the growing cosmopolitan cities of the West. The Crystal Palace exhibition in New York is a failed experiment in urban planning: that Stoddard should choose to present it to a California readership engaged in their own ongoing experiment in urban design, the emerging architecture of San Francisco, is perhaps not at all surprising in context.

At the same time, the pervasive fear of erased individuality and self-dissolution is also the key concern in Stoddard's intertextual engagement with Hawthorne's sketches. Stoddard's bold adoption of Hawthorne's sketch for a public audience illustrates the extent to which his images permeated her own imagination. In these early years, Stoddard *was* reading Hawthorne, attentively. As a model for both style and intellectual questioning, Hawthorne colors Stoddard's journalism and later fictional works most distinctively in those passages that imbue reality with the dreamlike state of fantasy (passages that—in Stoddard's re-visionary perspective—often come, contrarily, to tincture the fantastic with concrete detail). As Buell has argued, both writers specialized in a New England "provincial gothic" fiction that was "most powerful when operating somewhere in between the imaginary poles of romance and realism, interfusing both approaches." However, while Hawthorne identified himself as a romancer, Stoddard did so more ambivalently and "was quick to defend the mimetic accuracy of her portrayals" (*New England Literary Culture* 367). Moreover, Hawthorne was a *real* presence in Stoddard's life, as well; both Elizabeth and her husband were indebted to him for his assistance in placing Richard in a position in the New York Custom House (Moore 122). The revision of Hawthorne's "Hall of Fantasy" is, therefore, an opportunity for Stoddard to assert her own artistic ambitions and to commence a search for the autonomy of her own narrative voice in what was a context of *personal* economic anxiety. Such a revision is also the exploration of a parallel literary dependence potentially as crippling to self-autonomy as any economic relation. In Hawthorne's sketch, the American man of letters has a tenuous place in the display of literary achievement. In Hawthorne's allegorical Hall, the bust of Charles Brockden Brown occupies "an obscure and shadowy niche" in comparison with the light-flooded pedestals bearing figures of European literary dominance. Brown is "reposited" in the shadows less by Hawthorne himself—the curator of this fantasy—than by the "realms and imaginations" of those who contribute to this collective fantasy ("Hall of Fantasy" 247). In her revision of Hawthorne's fantasy, Stoddard questions the notion that the placement of Brown in a "shadowy niche" is detrimental when she claims for herself a similar spot in her own dream-vision and celebrates the solitude of "a remote corner of the Crystal Palace" in which to weave "a new fabric." In this place, she celebrates the individualism of the literary imagination, recognizing and accepting that its prospect is possible erasure from the literary record, while giving a wry nod to the form she appropriates: "It [her dream-fabric] is the only one there, and I shall prosecute any infringement of my patent" (5 Nov. 1854).

In the fantasy of the Crystal Palace, Stoddard questions the role (and survival) of the Romantic author in an increasingly complex (and industrial) nineteenth-century culture. Her effort to do so is also, like Hawthorne's own, situated at least in part in relation to canonical British predecessors: in Stoddard's case, the singularly important female antecedent is Charlotte Brontë. Like Stoddard, Brontë recorded her impressions of a Crystal Palace exhibition—this one in London—in two letters written 30 May and 7 June 1851 to her father, the Reverend Patrick Brontë. She found it on her first visit to be "like a mighty Vanity Fair—the brightest colours blaze on all sides—and ware of all kinds—from diamonds to spinning jennies and Printing Presses, are there to be seen—It was very fine—gorgeous—animated—bewildering." Brontë returned a week later, and after a second viewing she was much impressed by the vastness of the place: "Its grandeur does not consist in *one* thing but in the unique assemblage of *all* things . . . it is such a Bazaar or Fair as eastern Genii might have created. . . . The multitude filling the great aisles seems ruled and subdued by some invisible influence—Amongst the thirty thousand souls that peopled it the day I was there, not one loud noise was to be heard—not one irregular movement seen—the living tide rolls on quietly—with a deep hum like the sea heard from a distance" (qtd. in Barker 324). The "unique assemblage" of which Brontë writes is, of course, the central concept of the Crystal Palace itself—impression by collection, not by connection, nor pattern, nor even central, climactic exhibit. It is this same amalgamation that Stoddard adopts in her own refracted descriptions of silk shirts, armor, and goat-hair shawls. In pointing to the "elliptical dialogue, abrupt juxtaposition of scenes, [and] lack of narrative explanation" of Stoddard's first novel (xix), Buell and Zagarell accurately identify a Stoddardian predilection for an amalgamation of sensory impression, a "Crystal Palace" effect that we find Stoddard first experimenting with in this early column. In this way, not only did the *Alta* columns permit Stoddard the creation of a discursive space in which to imagine herself intertextually, a "shadowy niche" of her own, but her journalistic venture is also instrumental in facilitating the carving out of her own imagined space as an author, an exercise in voice acquisition. In Stoddard's Crystal Palace column, and more generally throughout her four-year tenure as a journalist, we discover the columnist's willingness to loiter in abandoned spaces and to explore the dark fantasy of the soul at uncommon moments—not in the long past, as Hawthorne might have done, but within the immediate flux of contemporary life. That a column such as this one should introduce several themes that later proliferate in Stoddard's novels—the notion of "exiles" displaced in a cultural setting; the necessity of living the experiential life, as the Lady Correspondent "touched and poked exposed goods"; even the humor-cloaked fear of the "lack-lustre" life of the walking dead and the call to wake to a more thoroughly Emersonian vibrant existence—is not at all surprising: Stoddard has found her own literary voice via a significant dialogic journey through the voice of the other.

As previous scholars have observed, the influence of Stoddard's early journalism on her later fiction is unquestionable. The cartography of the Stoddardian imagination was detailed on a transcontinental map, and it was a westering vision that Stoddard would later bring to focus on the details of her fiction. If Stoddard's literary imagination was "rooted in the contemplation of the kind of small, ancient, ingrown New England seaport town in which she grew up," it was also, perhaps more significantly, contoured by her distanced contemplation of a faraway San Francisco. In her *Daily Alta* columns we can find an ample demonstration of the effect this perspective had upon Stoddard-as-author in her developmental years. The imaginative journey to California by way of the *Alta* columns ultimately offered her a vision of authorship trained to question in sharp vignettes the complexities of contemporary American society while providing her with an outsider's perspective on the pressingly familiar. The young writer who once argued that "the true way to write a book of travels is to make a champagne affair of it; let us have in its pages foaming draughts of life; stinging, clear and pleasant bubbles"

(5 May 1855) would in later years specialize in precisely that—an intoxicatingly Romantic realism of kaleidoscopic details that, sharply noted and pungently observed, return *in their turn,* a century later, to sting still.

NOTES

1. See Buell and Zagarell, "Biographical and Critical Introduction" for a complete treatment of Stoddard's New England heritage.

2. On the influence of Stoddard's journalism on her fiction, see also Weir, "Our Lady Correspondent"; Buell, "Provincial Gothic: Hawthorne, Stoddard, and Others" in *New England Literary Culture;* Zagarell, "The Repossession of a Heritage"; Reynolds, *Beneath the American Renaissance;* and Susan K. Harris, "Stoddard's *The Morgesons:* A Contextual Evaluation."

3. Buell and Zagarell have made a parallel distinction between Stoddard and Fuller, since Fuller was writing to an established community in a cultural center and was featured in more respected publications (Stoddard, *The Morgesons and Other Writings* 312).

4. "Willis" refers to N. P. Willis, one of many contemporary writers whom Stoddard alternately criticizes and praises in her columns; even as she scorns his choice of titles, "Fun-Jottings, or Laughs I have taken a pen to," she acknowledges that "he often lends a hand to fledglings in literature, and praises them generously. Moreover, he glorifies and believes in women. God bless him!" (8 Oct. 1854).

5. Buell and Zagarell note Stoddard's development as a social commentator as well, focusing on the eastern market and her sketches of New England life; see xv.

6. See Miller, "Arachnologies."

7. For a discussion of the Crystal Palace and Victorianism, see Briggs, *Victorian Things.*

8. See Richards, *A Day in the New York Crystal Palace* (1853) in the Hargrave Collection of the University of Georgia. This abbreviated travel guide to the Palace reveals that the exhibition fell short of expectations, for the scale of the project was not equaled by its level of quality. Unable to explain the lack of participation by American artists, the author of the guidebook is left with the vague "regret that they have left the field almost entirely to foreign exhibitors" (164). Like the narrator of this Crystal Palace guidebook, Elizabeth Stoddard was concerned with the lack of an American presence in the expanse of European artistic endeavor, a concern marking many mid-nineteenth-century American fictional and journalistic texts.

3

Haunting the House of Print

The Circulation of Disembodied Texts in "Collected by a Valetudinarian" and "Miss Grief"

Paul Crumbley

In "Collected by a Valetudinarian" and "Miss Grief," Elizabeth Stoddard and Constance Fenimore Woolson build short stories around texts that never appear.[1] The female narrator of Stoddard's 1870 "Collected" reads a dead woman's diary chronicling the deceased author's creation of a novel that the narrator deems unpublishable but that nonetheless powerfully relates "the truth about us women" (306). Similarly, the male narrator of Woolson's 1880 "Miss Grief" is deeply moved by a female writer's unruly manuscripts that he nevertheless ultimately rejects because "her perversities were as essential a part of her work as her inspirations" (265). These disembodied texts haunt the stories in which they figure primarily through the effect they have on those who read, write, and hear them. By pointing to manuscript compositions that have great power but are incapable of print publication, these stories achieve two objectives of particular importance to nineteenth-century American women writers: they illuminate the extent to which print conventions constrain literary representation, and they draw attention to human experience—in these instances, female—that lies outside the protocols of print culture. By presenting female authors who are from the beginning sickly and who eventually die unpublished, Stoddard and Woolson connect failed female health to the inadequate circulation of a print record that embodies the experiences of real women.

For both writers, then, literary circulation emerges as a central underlying trope in which the health of the nonconforming female writer is linked to the reading public she relies on for the absorption and dissemination of her work. Simply stated, the healthy circulation of literature requires that all persons who acknowledge its value act as transmitters within a circuit connecting private creation to public benefit. Cast in this light, one of the most intriguing dimensions of both stories is their investigation of gift-based distribution as an alternative to consumer-based print publication. In *The World of the Gift,* Jacques T. Godbout explains that gift networks can indeed "transform the producer-user relationship" from a "binary utilitarian" system to one that operates "according to rules that are not those of the public institution and differ from it essentially in not making a distinction between . . . producer and consumer" (166). Such an alternative system offers writers a means to distribute uncensored writing through readers who actively collaborate in the circulation of texts. Consequently, gift distribution provides a means of assessing the practical viability of even the most severely limited circulation as a means of preserving unruly female texts. What these stories show, however, is that the ultimate benefit to the individual writer and the culture she inhabits must be assessed according to the potential collaborator's effectiveness in expanding circulation.

Stoddard and Woolson stress the importance of audience by presenting female writers who conduct their artistic lives outside conventional print culture, a position which means that neither writer enjoys the luxury of public support nor the pain of public rejection; instead, they fear not the loss of a public readership but, rather, the possibility of no readership whatsoever. While male authors like Herman Melville and Nathaniel Hawthorne also struggled with questions of artistic integrity—in their personal lives as well as in their fiction—their positions differed significantly since they both achieved public recognition by successfully utilizing existing systems for print circulation. This meant that for them, the problem lay in making those systems responsive to artistic innovation, not in gaining access in the first place.[2] In her discussion of Stoddard's public and critical reception, Lisa Radinovsky points out that Stoddard herself knew only too well how difficult it was for a nonconforming female writer to win a public readership. While critics received her novels positively, Stoddard's bold rejection of "the pious, pure, submissive and domestic" ideal conveyed by the Cult of True Womanhood cost her dearly in terms of public support: "eccentric women like Stoddard were often stigmatized as unnatural, unwomanly threats to middle-class ideals . . . especially when their unorthodox views entered the public sphere" (Radinovsky, "Against All Odds" 266). When Stoddard's narrator learns that the female artist, Alicia Raymond, is "a woman of genius" (289) and Woolson's narrator identifies the protagonist in that story as a woman who "possessed the divine spark of genius" (257), both characters are immediately set apart as eccentrics and, therefore, suspect. As Radinovsky notes in her discussion of Stoddard, "The very few women who were described as geniuses were apt to be called diseased, vulgar, coarse, and unwomanly, as if they could not be both geniuses and real women" ("Against All Odds" 267). Radinovsky demonstrates the currency of this view by citing the following statement from Cesare Lombroso's 1863 book *The Man of Genius:* "there are no women of genius; the women of genius are men."

In keeping with this theory, the female narrator in "Collected" describes the setting where the deceased writer composed her novel as an isolated haven where "neither laws nor men could trouble a solitary stranger," at the same time concluding that the author could never "have been induced to publish anything" even though "we should have a better literature" if she did (307). Likewise, in "Miss Grief," the male author who narrates the story acknowledges that the dying Miss Moncrief "had the greater power" (268)—despite her rejection of all his editorial advice—but nonetheless arranges to have her unpublished drama "destroyed unread" upon his death (269). Sharon L. Dean illustrates Woolson's sensitivity to the inhibiting presence of editorial demands by referring to a letter Woolson wrote to Henry James in which she objects that even at the turn of the century it was impossible for a woman to be "a complete artist" (186). In a manner entirely consistent with this statement, "Collected" and "Miss Grief" show that print culture in nineteenth-century America was so resistant to the original contributions of female writers that even the most talented among them could be deprived of cultural support.[3]

Lawrence Buell and Sandra Zagarell have observed the strong parallels "in attitude, upbringing and milieu" that link Stoddard's life to that of Emily Dickinson, who is arguably the best-known nineteenth-century writer to have declined print publication (Buell and Zagarell xii).[4] Striking as the biographical similarities are, the links uniting Dickinson to the fictional authors of Stoddard's and Woolson's stories may be even more impressive. Through her correspondence, for instance, Dickinson clearly engaged in the sort of gift-based circulation that Alicia Raymond and Aarona Moncrief attempted. Especially in her letters to Helen Hunt Jackson and Thomas Wentworth Higginson, the differences between gift and commercial economies emerge with stunning clarity. The Jackson correspondence shows the successfully published Jackson attempting to secure print publication for a clearly resistant Dickinson. Having explained to Jackson that she is "unwilling" and "incapable" (*The Letters of Emily Dickinson* 563), Dickinson repeatedly asks Higginson's assistance in eluding Jackson's efforts (562–63, 566). Similarly, in her earlier letters to Higginson, Dickinson famously declared that "to publish" was "foreign to my thought, as Firmament to Fin" (408). Though she clearly desired communication with both Jackson and Higginson, Dickinson appears to have been much more interested in gift circulation than print publication.[5] Ironically, Dickinson's sustained correspondence with Higginson—who consistently doubted her readiness to enter print—was a primary reason her work has endured, as his editorial collaboration with Mabel Loomis Todd ultimately secured a broad public readership. In this sense, then, Dickinson exemplifies the circulation potential that remains unrealized in "Collected" and "Miss Grief."

The degree to which Stoddard and Woolson are concerned with the exclusion of female authors from positions of cultural authority may be seen through the way both stories present vague and disturbingly disembodied roles for central female characters. This approach draws attention to the near invisibility of women not fully engaged in authorized forms of female conduct, while also magnifying the double bind whereby women writers who seek print visibility must conform to the social expectations that prevent female originality from becoming part of the official literary record. In Stoddard's case, the "valetudinarian" protagonist is an ailing widow who discovers comfort in the presence of another widow, both of whom appear to confirm one well-known female stereotype, that of the helpless widow. Miss Grief, Woolson's semi-eponymous woman writer (whose real name is Moncrief), is an aging spinster whose actual life is so clouded by culturally imposed stereotypes about spinster authors that the conventional male narrator appears incapable of viewing her as a distinct individual. These framing procedures establish a pervasive cultural inclination to erase the presence of nonconforming women, an inclination that women writers must overcome if their writing is to succeed in conveying a more accurate picture of the lives American women actually lived. This is precisely the point Helen Hunt Jackson makes in her poem "Found Frozen," in which her speaker describes the way "they who loved her with all the love / Their wintry natures had to give" erase the suffering of a deceased woman's actual life by writing "across her grave / Some common record which they thought was true" (20). Perhaps it was her desire to displace the false but all too common public record of women's lives that prompted Jackson to seek publication for Dickinson.

From the opening pages of "Collected," Stoddard draws attention to the way conventions that inform the "common record" collectively obscure female identity. After not having revealed the narrator's name for the first fifth of the story, Stoddard finally does so after giving her married name first, revealing her first name in the following paragraph. And in the paragraph after that we learn that Alicia Raymond, the female writer of genius, has lost what limited fame had been hers when her father died and all efforts to promote her work ceased (288–89). To show that the concealment of a distinctive female identity revealed in these instances is a pervasive feature of society, Stoddard includes within her narrator's gaze both the "occasional" village woman who "now and then appeared" wrapped in shawls (285) and her future friend, Helen Hobson, whom the narrator describes as bearing "a shadowy resemblance to myself, in as much as she was dressed in mourning and looked delicate and feeble" (288). By linking the anonymous village woman to the narrator and her friend, who are also village women—at least temporarily—Stoddard's opening pages convey the general impression of a society in which women fail to achieve full embodiment.

This impression of cultural disembodiment is further reinforced when the ever-present hotel manager, Mr. Binks, introduces the narrator and Mrs. Hobson with the twin observations "Birds of a feather flock together" and "By your looks I conclude you have them 'ere mysterious complaints which make women so unaccountable. My wife was the same; first and last, she cost me a couple of hundred in patent medicines" (288). Not only does Binks automatically categorize all ill women as of a single type, but he appears to have no clear recollection of distinguishing personal features that would set his own wife apart from other similarly constituted women. Instead, he points to the inconvenient expense of patent medicines that he clearly views as the natural resort of all similarly indisposed women. Throughout his conversation he conveys a good-natured patronage of female quirkiness even as his words inadvertently reveal how commercial enterprise accommodates precisely the eccentricities he so derisively dismisses. Apparently without conscious forethought, his words show that these very eccentricities of the female constitution define the type of woman who purchases patent medicines and frequents the establishment upon which his livelihood depends, thus providing an economic foundation for the perpetuation of female enfeeblement.

Despite the humorous presence of Mr. Binks (he provokes Helen and Eliza's first laughter [288]), his comic relief underscores the easy dismissal of fictional females that all too clearly illustrates a widespread social denial of female seriousness, a denial often debilitating for female authors in the real world. Woolson provocatively identified Stoddard as an example of the negative effect writing can have on female health when, upon hearing that Stoddard was ill in 1876, she asked Edmund Clarence Stedman, "Why do literary women break down so?" (qtd. in Weimer xviii). Joan Myers Weimer further demonstrates Woolson's awareness that she formed one of a community of women writers who suffered debilitating somatic responses to writing by quoting a letter Woolson wrote to Samuel Mather. In that letter, Woolson states that while she suffered the "(comparatively) small trouble of lameness," her suffering "sinks to nothingness beside the terrible nervous prostration her friend Frances Hodgson Burnett suffered every time she finished writing a book" (xix). Cheryl B. Torsney gives special emphasis to the extent that Woolson saw discomfort as an accompaniment of writing: "The happiest women I have known belonged to two classes; the devoted wives and mothers, and the successful flirts, whether married or single; such women never write" (19).

The awareness registered in these passages informs the approach Stoddard and Woolson develop in "Collected" and "Miss Grief," showing that for each woman the relation of writing to health raised important questions; but as we shall see, the stories' explorations of health and writing tend to view the questions themselves as more productive than attempts to resolve them. Lying as they do behind the events of each story, these questions enable both writers to oppose mind-body and text-body binaries as a way of evoking heteroglossia unique to the female writer's contemplation of public utterance. Mikhail M. Bakhtin's definition of "heteroglossia" as the closest "conceptualization as is possible of that locus where centripetal and centrifugal forces collide" (428) here applies to the multiple conflicting discourses that Stoddard and Woolson use to frame the experience of dissenting woman writers. Among these, the pressure to present a fictional self consistent with society's expectation of a privatized domestic woman runs up against the woman writer's desire to reach an audience responsive to writing that seriously challenges conventional knowledge through innovations in style and content. Most pointedly, both stories also show that, far from promoting female health, privatization can, in fact, have a negative effect by foreclosing communication and thus thwarting expressive impulses the exercise of which is essential to overall health.

As Cynthia Davis has advised in her analysis of medical science and literary form, the serious effort to "examine bodily and narrative forms as analogous entities" (3) must proceed with the understanding "that medical definitions of embodied identity were—contrary to received

knowledge—both complicated and unstable" (2). Nowhere is the instability of medical definitions more evident than in Edward H. Dixon's
popular medical advice book, *Woman and Her Diseases.* "From her position in the social scale," he writes in his introduction, "she is subjected
to so many causes of physical degeneration from the evident design of
nature . . . that it seems but an act of humanity to make an effort for
her instruction in some of the evils that so constantly beset her" (5). In
her assessment of Dixon, Diane Price Herndl states, "Like other books
in the genre, Dixon's reveals the conflicting messages of medical thought"
whereby "woman is both innately sick and responsible for her poor
health" (35).[6] Pronouncements like Dixon's, which Herndl sees as typi-
fying nineteenth-century medical science, have led her to agree with
numerous other critics who also view "patriarchal culture as potentially
sickening for women and as defining women as inherently sick, especially
when they resist its norms" (7).[7] Notable contemporaries of Stoddard
and Woolson, who also understood writing as linked to the debilitating
influence of patriarchal culture, include Charlotte Perkins Gilman and
Edith Wharton, both of whom Herndl describes as having written "illness into their texts, leaving themselves apart from it, not invalid women"
(128). The most famous and perhaps the most public declaration of a
woman writer's rejection of the patriarchal medical establishment is
Gilman's explanation in "Why I Wrote the Yellow Wallpaper?" that she
wrote that work with the express purpose of rejecting S. Weir Mitchell's
rest cure, founded "on the solemn advice to 'live as domestic a life as far
as possible,' to 'have but two hours' intellectual life a day,' and 'never to
touch pen, brush or pencil again as long as I lived'" (348). Davis presents
Louisa May Alcott, Dr. Harriot K. Hunt, and Margaret Fuller as similarly
taking up the pen "in hopes of not simply minimizing or escaping suffering but alleviating it" (55). As these observations suggest, Stoddard
and Woolson reflect a sensitivity to the connection of writing with
health that found broad support in advice literature, as well as in the
work of other women writers.

Stoddard gives special attention to the internal psychological and
emotional forces that further complicate the management of female
bodies by not limiting her analysis to external social and cultural forces
that seek to dictate women's behavior. More disturbing even than the
near invisibility of women is the experience of interior turmoil that
Stoddard urges her readers to associate with a disruption of mental fac-
ulties. The first sentence of "Collected" quickly injects evidence of the
narrator's troubled search for a vanished self that directly links health to

emotional state and sets up the narrator's contradictory thought process. She describes herself as revisiting "an old village on our sea-board" where she actively seeks "something lost, *i.e.,* health and to appease a heart disquieted by grief," in pursuit of which she will "remain as long as the perturbed ghosts, my present rulers, [will] permit" (285). Here we see that the narrator, Eliza Sinclair, perceives herself as simultaneously having "lost" health while also passively submitting to "ghosts" that dictate her actions. We soon learn that though Eliza ostensibly wishes to recover the health and equanimity of her past, she is guided by the words of "the medieval Balzac" whose advice to *"Hide your life"* she takes to heart, stating her intent to "lose myself" in the woods and sand barrens where she knows she will find "arrow-heads, and the Indian skulls" of a once-flourishing culture (286). Stoddard's determination to establish a parallel between the artifacts of Native American culture and the fate that Eliza faces compels consideration of the crucial role self-awareness plays in making possible the circulation of texts that then become critical to the historical survival of cultures. The near erasure of Native American culture from the cultural landscape of the United States portends a similar future for women's culture if steps are not taken to secure the stories capable of perpetuating an accurate account of life within that culture.

Throughout "Collected," Stoddard interweaves passages establishing the pernicious influence of widely held beliefs about the sanctity of women's private lives that are not only incommensurate with female experience but that can have the effect of preventing women from acknowledging the authority of their own histories. The first of these takes the form of an exchange between Eliza Sinclair and Helen Hobson in which both appear to understand that female history is a private matter: "Mrs. Hobson never told me her history; I never asked it. Having no wish to reveal mine, why should I demand hers?" (288). Mr. Binks's words succeed this exchange with a disclosure that once again associates female sickness with monetary value while effectively defining the cultural vacuum that surrounds the experiences of women who deviate from the mainstream. "I am an inquisitive man," he avers, "but I never asked Mrs. Hobson a question, and I am never going to. She is as good as gold, and as sick as Lazarus" (289). Mrs. Hobson herself then observes the cultural outcome of such punctilious determination not to violate female privacy when she reports Binks's often-repeated pronouncement that "one half of the world does not know how the other half lives"

(289). Once again, the story asks readers to think about the internal contradictions that prevent a woman like Helen Hobson from realizing that her own refusal to communicate details of her personal history makes her complicit in the social denial of female embodiment that she so deplores.

Like "Collected," "Miss Grief" quickly conveys the impression that culturally based assumptions that bear directly on female embodiment and literary circulation obscure the actual composition of women's lives, only Woolson makes an even more pronounced effort to show that male assumptions about women diminish the visibility of all women, not merely the "eccentric" or the marginal. To achieve this end, Woolson sets her work in cosmopolitan Rome, uniting two divergent poles of the female social spectrum by introducing the drab Miss Moncrief and the sparkling Isabel Abercrombie in the same paragraph. Doing so juxtaposes the "eccentric and unconventional," "shabby, unattractive, and more than middle-aged" Moncrief with the socially brilliant, youthful, and much-sought-after future wife of the narrator (249, 251). Upon first mention, Miss Moncrief is identified not by the visiting card conventionally left by members of polite society but by an orally transmitted name that is garbled as it circulates from the manservant to the narrator. That the female writer's name is altered from Moncrief to "Grief" conveys the grief encountered by female writers who seek a clear viewing of their work. However, the narrator applies the mispronounced name to himself only, waggishly punning that he shall continue to "not be at home" to grief "if she continues to call" (249). Such quick translation into the interior domain of male thought is consistent with the story's opening line, in which the narrator readily admits "that I am conceited" and shortly thereafter acknowledges that he is "amiably obedient to all the rules and requirements of 'society'" (248).

Woolson makes her point that male authors like her narrator introduce into their writing false assumptions about female behavior by showing that this particular author is unable to continue composing once he actually encounters a woman whose behavior is inconsistent with the pattern that guides his thoughts. This violation of supposed norms takes place when Isabel Abercrombie, the woman he is courting, does not act as he thinks she should. "I had constructed a careful theory of the young woman's characteristics in my own mind, and she had lived up to it delightfully until the previous evening, when with one word she had blown it to atoms and taken flight, leaving me standing, as it were, on a desolate shore, with nothing but a handful of mistaken inductions wherewith to console myself. I could not write, and so I took up a French novel (I modeled myself a little after Balzac)" (250).

In a manner consistent with both the Stoddard and the Woolson stories, the offending conduct is not described. Similarly, the ultimate concealment of Miss Moncrief's writing and Alicia Raymond's novel will further demonstrate that only socially acceptable forms of female embodiment make their way onto the printed page. In this context, the narrator's recourse to Balzac functions to expose both the narrowness of his own conception of female behavior and the precarious foundations of any exclusively male effort to depict female experience realistically. Given the narrator's deliberate modeling of himself on Balzac, we can also see embedded in this passage Woolson's implied assertion that the circulation of male-authored texts reinforces notions of female embodiment badly in need of the corrective balance offered by a female point of view. We may also detect here a parallel with Stoddard's allusion to Balzac, wherein she also uses the influential male writer to illuminate the way literary representation can negatively inform social expectation.

What is required to balance the influence of Balzac, however, is not merely the presence of female writers; rather, Woolson and Stoddard appear to share a desire for women writers who enjoy the consultative power of a Balzac. For this reason, the problem at the heart of both stories turns on the ability of a female writer who possesses original literary power to achieve the circulation essential to becoming as influential as a major male writer. For Miss Moncrief, the path to circulation begins with an established male writer whose work she respects. "I have read every word you have written," she eventually declares to the narrator upon meeting him after seven failed attempts (252). She then describes a particular passage within the narrator's work that "was secretly [his] favorite," despite the fact that an otherwise adoring public "had never noticed the higher purpose of this little shaft, aimed not at the balconies and lighted windows of society, but straight up toward the distant stars." In response, the narrator admits that "she had understood me—understood me almost better than I had understood myself." Following this exchange, the narrator grudgingly acknowledges, "You have bestowed so much of your kind attention upon me that I feel your debtor" (253). He then acts to remove the debt by offering his services, indicating an effort at reciprocity through his willingness to assist with the contents of a box he knows contains a manuscript: "It may be there is something

I can do for you—connected possibly with that little box." At this point, Miss Moncrief responds with words that undermine the narrator's proposal of a materially based reciprocal exchange by introducing the possibility of an alternative, non-material economy. Instead of graciously accepting whatever limited assistance he can provide, she acknowledges that while his opinion may be of little value "in a business way," it might nonetheless "be—an assistance personally."[8] These words bring into Woolson's text a set of values that oppose the leveling force of marketplace reciprocity with the singularity of a personal gesture.

By posing the possibility that personal response may provide a preferred alternative to commercial publication, Woolson introduces the discourse of gift exchange that brings with it an alternative form of circulation. According to the definition of gift Lewis Hyde has provided in *The Gift,* an essential feature of gift exchange is the opening of a special relation with the world and others achieved fully through circulation, so that the gift is "consumed" through an exchange process not dependent on abstract value (9).[9] To track this kind of circulation, it is important to shift attention from publication and print distribution to affective response and the establishment of community identity. Godbout's definition of the gift as "any circulation of goods or services with no guarantee of recompense in order to create, nourish, recreate social bonds between people" (20) might usefully be applied to the above circumstance involving Miss Moncrief and the narrator. Woolson's displacement of the impersonal "business" dimension of commercial exchange with Miss Moncrief's desire for something more like understanding, sympathy, or even friendship reflects the extent that the story deliberately examines the power gifts have to create significant social bonds.

However, as Stoddard's and Woolson's stories have raised the issue of authorial influence, we ought to examine the ways in which the circulation of gifts contributes to the establishment of hierarchical relationships. Annette B. Weiner provides just such an analysis by distinguishing between "alienable properties" that may be "exchanged against each other" and "inalienable possessions" that function as "repositories of genealogies and historical events, their unique, subjective identity [giving] them absolute value placing them above the exchangeability of one thing for another" (33). As Weiner makes clear, the category of inalienable possessions is broad, containing language in the form of "myths . . . songs, and the knowledge of dances," as well as material objects like "human bones, sacred stones" and "woven fabrics" (37). Ownership of these inalienable possessions introduces difference into the otherwise reciprocal exchange of gifts by investing certain gifts with a power that radiates from the inalienable possession. In Weiner's words, "the motivation for reciprocity is centered not in the gift per se, but in the authority invested in keeping inalienable possessions" (40). The outcome is a social system within which the ownership of inalienable possessions "makes the authentication of difference rather than the balance of equivalence the fundamental feature of exchange." Within such a system, the distribution of gifts may serve to affirm the superior authority of one giver despite the superficial appearance of equivalence. If, as Hyde has argued, talent and inspiration are gifts just as the ability fully to appreciate a work of art is (xi–xii), then Miss Moncrief's perception of the narrator's instance of isolated brilliance initiates an exchange of gifts that may coincidentally reveal a fundamental difference based on authorial power that here acts as an inalienable possession. As Mary Louise Kete has argued in *Sentimental Collaborations*, for nineteenth-century Americans "the inalienable possession of a self fundamental to liberalism is produced through a free circulation of gifts of the self" (53). In the case of Stoddard and Woolson, the inalienable possession is the self's power to produce literature that sets the gifts of certain writers apart from the products of lesser talents.

To assess fully the presence or absence of such a distinction and its bearing on Miss Moncrief's status as a writer capable of literary influence, we need to examine the narrator's response to the manuscripts she gives him. Much to his surprise, the narrator finds that he is unable to put down the drama Miss Moncrief hands him at the conclusion of their first meeting. He stays up half the night reading it, and Woolson's words clearly convey his astonishment: "No one could have been more surprised than I was to find myself thus enthusiastic" (256). When Miss Moncrief returns to his rooms to hear his judgment, he provides additional language that not only expresses his appreciation for her gift but also acknowledges that she possesses ability beyond his own. "It seemed so pitiful that she should be trembling there before me—a woman who possessed the divine spark of genius, which I was by no means sure (in spite of my success) had been granted to me—that I felt as if I ought to go down on my knees before her, and entreat her to take her proper place of supremacy at once" (257).

Up to this point, the narrator has merely reciprocated by reading her work after having learned that she has read his. The unexpected discovery that hers is the greater talent, however, upsets the system of reciprocity, creating a dilemma for the narrator, who now sees both that Miss Moncrief has the inalienable possession of literary power and that commercial success has not proven his ownership of a similar ability. Despite this discovery, he resists the impulse to acknowledge her superiority openly and, instead, denies the difference by attempting the impossible task of employing his inferior talent to make her work commercially palatable. This effort is, of course, doomed from the beginning, leaving the frustrated narrator to admit, "I began; and utterly failed" (264).

Woolson's decision to focus on the narrator's recognition of Miss Moncrief's talent, in combination with his inability to give the work a form suitable for publication, establishes one of the central economic conflicts that ultimately impede the public circulation of works by nonconforming women. To understand this conflict, it is important to look at the way Miss Moncrief ceases to have an interest in the publication of her work and seems content to die happy in the knowledge that her gift has been received by at least one writer whose ability she respects. This difference in point of view becomes evident after the narrator falsely informs the dying Miss Moncrief that he has found a publisher for her drama (266). He assumes that lying to her about publication will make her happy, but the text does not support such a conclusion. Miss Moncrief does admit that she had "never known what it was . . . to be fully happy until now," but she makes this admission *after* the narrator has told her a story (267). At the moment she first hears his lie that her drama has been accepted, her response to the narrator is, "Tell me." He then fulfills her wish with "a romance invented for the occasion," one with which he readily admits "none of [his] published sketches could compare." In his own mind, he acknowledges that the telling of this lie "will stand among my few good deeds . . . at the judgment seat." What Woolson seems to be showing here is that Miss Moncrief is grateful for the story the narrator has spun, for the return of the gift of story, rather than for the news of publication. Had publication been her aim, she would surely have urged the publication of her other manuscripts, but this she does not do. Instead, she designates the narrator as executor for one work only, her drama; her other manuscripts, which she describes as her "poor dead children," are, in her words, to be buried with her, "unread, as I have been" (268). This final statement conveys Miss Moncrief's understanding that the real story of her life has never been read and that the revisions she knows to have been undertaken by the narrator have at least partially erased the distinctive features of her life. She knows, in other words, that beyond helping the narrator tell a better story than anything he has previously published, her life has failed to enter circulation and become part of the official record of her culture. Equally important, her description of her manuscripts as "dead children" indicates her awareness that her flesh-and-blood existence is intimately linked to the successful circulation of her art.

In "Collected," the positive health benefits that potentially follow from circulation do not register in the author, Alicia Raymond, who has died before the story begins, but rather in Eliza, the person who receives from Helen the gift of Alicia's diary. Following her initial reading of Alicia's diary, Eliza ponders the possibility that reading the work has placed her in contact with forces capable of improving her health: "Maybe I am sent here to be aided by her," she wonders out loud to Helen (296). Helen's response seems to confirm the power Eliza has detected: "'Be then,' she exclaimed, 'my atonement,'" as if Eliza's reception of the gift has provided the proper channel for a force that Helen has been unable to accommodate. If this is the case, both women are shown to benefit either physically or spiritually from the continued circulation of the diary. One question, then, that the Stoddard and Woolson texts both pose is whether the immediate gratification experienced by the writer, or the long-term benefits to readers that come through circulation within a restricted community of able readers, actually provides an affirmation of authorial power sufficient to justify a lifetime of public obscurity. The physical and emotional suffering so apparent in the female authors at the centers of these stories necessarily vexes any answering of this question.

Stoddard's presentation of a gift-based distribution system does, however, provide evidence of some immediate benefit to readers, though any ultimate assessment of the system must be based on the degree to which the distinctive force of the author begins to influence public culture. As Ellen Weinauer astutely observes in her analysis of "Collected by a Valetudinarian," Stoddard situates literary circulation within a gift economy constituted by "an extended, affectively-connected, mixed gender family" made up of Helen, Eliza, Alicia's brother, and his bride-to-be, Julia (168). What is more, Stoddard appears interested in providing a set of gifts uniquely suited to cultural circulation. The first and most prominent gift is the house where Alicia Raymond and her brother lived for six years. Significantly, the house is located on "Bront's Point" (293), suggesting a link to the Brontë family. When we learn that the house was given to Helen (290), that it is the house where Alicia's mother was born (292, 293), and that Helen would like Eliza to assess the value of the manuscripts the house contains (295), we recognize the basic features of a gift economy with potential public appeal. We also see that the house metonymically and materially links Alicia's manuscripts at the same time that it provides a matrilineal line of descent that might prove valuable in defining a literary history patterned on the Brontë family. Accordingly, the house acquires significance as the locus within which Alicia's talent serves as the inalienable possession that infuses her multiple manuscripts with a potency like that which Helen has earlier attached to "a scrap of [Charlotte Brontë's] handwriting" (290).

The significance of Charlotte Brontë, both as a female writer and as the emblem of female literary history, has already been established by the time the circuit of gift exchange that involves the house and manuscripts enters the story. At the time Alicia Raymond is first mentioned, Helen immediately compares her artistic struggle with that of Charlotte Brontë, giving special emphasis to the way the entire family, including both parents, shared hardships prior to any public recognition of literary greatness (289–90). In making these associations, Helen appears to be reflecting on her own blood relation to Alicia, who was her cousin. It is also at this moment in the text that Helen announces her possession of "a scrap of [Charlotte Brontë's] handwriting," thereby introducing into the text the circulation of gifts within an economy founded on the inalienable possession of literary ability. Helen's observation that "Alicia discerned a world of beauty and truth that made an everlasting happiness for her great soul, as did Charlotte Brontë" (290) shows that in her mind the two families possess a common history and that perhaps her own life might be touched by a like greatness. With clear signs of eagerness, then, both Helen and Eliza seek to emulate this sterling example of female artistic achievement. "'Dear Helen,' Eliza queries, 'how shall we idlers be taught this ideal happiness?'" (290). This is the question that immediately precedes the introduction of the primary gifts in Stoddard's story, both of which acquire meaning as part of Helen and Eliza's efforts to embody the truth that guided Alicia Raymond, thus bringing into the story an authoritative precedent for literary embodiment descending not from Balzac but from Brontë.

The movement of the house and the manuscripts from Alicia to Helen to Eliza potentially affirms each woman's inclusion within an expanding female group whose identity springs from recognition of the power dispensed by the house and the gifted writer. In this way, material and non-material, house and inspired art, body and mind are fused, the value of the one entering into and informing the other. Such a pairing of binaries indicates the way group identity and the proper management of the gift economy can transform discarded manuscripts into a potent literary corpus capable of bringing hope and health to Eliza and Helen, thus unifying producer and consumer in the manner pointed to by Godbout. Viewed from this perspective, Stoddard's story demonstrates that the proper circulation of texts within a gift economy corresponds significantly with the health of those whose role it is to oversee expanded distribution. In this particular case, the management of Alicia's house—descending at it does from mother to daughter and located on Bront's Point—and the treatment given the manuscripts become important symbolic indexes that register the reverence or lack thereof shown for the female body.

Stoddard presents the challenge circulation poses to Eliza and Helen through the answers Helen provides to Eliza's questions about how the two of them might acquire the "ideal happiness" Alicia discovered (290). Helen's response is both direct and revealing: "As soon as we can be made to believe that what is called material or positive happiness is no more truthful or exact than that named visionary or romantic happiness." Through these words, Helen admits that "we" have more confidence in the happiness rooted in materiality than in that arising from the spirit. This crucial and potentially destructive self-awareness reveals a fundamental dualism at odds with the collapse of binaries so essential to embodiment within a gift economy. It comes as no surprise, then, that immediately following Helen's observation, Eliza steps out of the female circle of perception and describes the picture she imagines the two women present within the gaze of Mr. Binks. "We were a couple of faded, middle-aged women, clad in black garments," she resignedly acknowledges. "Why should such indulge in aspirations for happiness, or the expectation of doing any farther [sic] work in this gay world?" In like fashion, Helen describes the house and its surroundings as void of spiritual promise: "[Alicia] gave it to me; the spot, worthless as it is, has chained me; the ground about it is barren; nobody would think of bringing it under cultivation." In what appears to be a last fleeting effort to locate spiritual potential within the house and dispel an entrenched mind-body dualism, Helen proposes that she and Eliza inhabit the home together: " 'Suppose, Eliza,'—and Helen brightened at the thought— 'that you and I should occupy the house?' " Eliza dismisses this proposal in language that effectively communicates her view that the house has become an empty shell: "But we should have to leave out the genius which has made such an impression upon you, and, I confess, upon me also." These quick exchanges illustrate the extent to which Eliza and

Helen—despite their hopes—see the house as utterly vacated by the vitality that once dwelt within. This failure to perceive within the structure any seeds for future growth reflects the extent to which each woman has lost confidence in the generative power of Alicia's art and of her own body, adopting, instead, the male construction that casts them as "faded, middle-aged women" who entertain no "aspirations for happiness." Finally, Eliza's rejection of Helen's offer of joint habitation suggests that for her the weight of individual resignation exceeds her ability to imagine the generative power of collective effort. In this way, the two women fail to meet Helen's challenge to accept the reality of visionary truth that they must embody if they are to promote the further circulation of Alicia's manuscripts.

In the light of this shared resignation, Helen's decision to sell the house comes as no surprise. As she explains to Eliza, "Since you came I have decided to settle my affairs so far as that old place is concerned. When Alicia's papers are looked over and every thing removed I will sell the house. When you leave the town I will go also, for I can no longer endure it" (295). The logic behind Helen's actions suggests that for her, a future in the old house may have been possible if someone capable of comprehending Alicia's writing had been willing to take up residence with her; she needs to know that the house is the locus for significant artistic accomplishment that she has sensed but cannot fully confirm. Following Eliza's refusal, Helen is left with the haunting sense of having had a passing acquaintance with greatness, a sense that she is incapable of translating into the basis for meaningful future action. In terms of the circulation of gifts, the sale of the house in combination with the imperfect union of the two women suggests a failure to discover the potential for cultural reproduction so central to the circulation of gifts. As Weiner has succinctly stated, "The processes of cultural reproduction involve the heroic ability to reproduce more of one's self or one's group through time by asserting difference while defining an historical past that looks unchanging" (48). By selling the house and failing to embody visionary truth, Eliza and Helen relinquish the difference offered by Alicia's talent and accept, rather, the sameness society imposes on "faded, middle-aged women, clad in black garments" (290). They also fail in their effort to follow the path that Alicia took, the path that Stoddard presents as descending from Brontë rather than Balzac.

In the closing pages, the story provides what might be the purest example of a gift exchange directly affecting Alicia Raymond. Significantly, the event takes place in the pages of Alicia's diary, a work that

Buell and Zagarell have described as growing out of Stoddard's own "manuscript journal" (Stoddard, *The Morgesons and Other Writings* 308 n. 8), thus positioning this particular gift exchange in that portion of the story that most nearly approximates the actual author's own life. For this reason, the details of the scene bear close scrutiny as a source of information about Stoddard's personal understanding of the circulation potential inherent in gift exchange. On the second-to-last page of the story, Alicia reads to Julia, her brother Alton's fiancée: "[Julia] clapped her hands at first, then grew silent; as I read on her delicate cheek crimsoned, her eyes blazed, she moved near me, took my hand, and kissed it" (306). After the reading, Julia expresses her astonishment at Alicia's courage in daring to "tell the truth about us women." Along with her surprise at Alicia's courage, however, Julia also expresses her amazement that a woman as reclusive as Alicia could write with such discernment about shared female experience. "I did not know that one could create without experience," she remarks. To which Alicia enigmatically replies, "Nor can one; like Ulysses, I am part of all that I have seen; and much good it has done me, hasn't it?" This reference to Tennyson's Ulysses is followed shortly, in the last diary entry, with words that allude to yet another literary traveler, this time Melville's Queequeg,[10] after whom she patterns her own signature: "Alicia Raymond—her mark."[11] Through this gesture, Stoddard would appear to be conflating the fame of the classic hero with the obscurity of Ishmael's native companion whose language escapes the interpretive powers of the Americans who surround him. Alicia herself appears entirely aware of the fact that while her work possesses power comparable to that of classic literature, it may ultimately fail to enter circulation and to contribute to the life of the culture embodied in its pages. Nevertheless, she does remark in her diary that she is "glad" that Julia now "knows a thought of mine," expressing in these words the momentary happiness that the imparting of her gift has afforded her. In consideration of the fact that Alicia's words take the form of diary entries that expand on Stoddard's own journal, we may conclude that Stoddard has not only established a personal link with Alicia Raymond but also presented through Alicia the difficult authorial challenge of weighing the immediate gratification of limited circulation against the delayed gratification of extended circulation that might follow publication. Helen may well sum up the high stakes at play in such a quandary when she comments on the sort of fame Alicia had so far been denied: "Talk about Chatterton and Keats—if they did not live in their lifetime, they do now, while Alicia's memory only exists in mine and that of her brother" (289).

For both Stoddard and Woolson, the central struggle of the nonconforming female artist lies in balancing contrary requirements: that writing take place outside the demands of social convention while retaining contact with a public readership sufficient to ensure cultural consumption. Weinauer effectively poses Stoddard's authorial predicament, writing that "it is, finally, as much the lack of consumption as consumption itself that threatens the author" (174). However, Weinauer's conclusion that through "Collected" Stoddard's "reworking her own journal and representing it as Alicia's" enables her to circulate "a most 'private' text in a most public forum: *Harper's New Monthly Magazine*" (176), overlooks not only the fate of Alicia's novel but her health as well. Even so, Weinauer's analysis does usefully flesh out authorial alternatives that appear in Stoddard as well as in Woolson. According to Weinauer, "Eliza does not merely 'collect' and preserve the diary: she publishes it, including it in her story" (176). Weinauer further argues that Stoddard's inclusion of her own journal in Alicia's diary blurs "the lines between private and public property" so that when "Alica Raymond makes a gift of her [diary] . . . so too does Stoddard make a gift of herself" (177). What is, perhaps, most interesting is that Weinauer's logic might also be applied to Woolson's story, yielding the conclusion that her narrator acts as Eliza does by incorporating the private writing of Miss Moncrief in his public story. The implication, then, is that like Stoddard, Woolson, too, discovers the means to circulate a private truth within a public medium. Due, however, to the fact that both stories contain literary works that never appear, the circulation Weinauer outlines is incomplete: that is, it fails to embody the female work Stoddard and Woolson describe in their stories.

Trapped by the desire to produce honest accounts of female experience in an era that demanded standardized narratives of women's lives, writers like Stoddard and Woolson chose to write about the inability to embody texts that delivered more of the truth about nonconforming women than print culture would allow. In this regard, "Collected by a Valetudinarian" and "Miss Grief" emerge as narratives that not only detail the multiple vexations faced by female writers but also provide accounts of a cultural illness that affected many women. As illness narratives, the texts proceed as if their authors were patients describing the conditions of their enfeeblement, hoping that among their readers will be doctors capable of diagnosing and correcting the problem. Gay Wilentz has written in *Healing Narratives* that through such narratives "it is hoped that something lost, in this case one's health, can be regained through the doctor's interpretation" (16). Indeed, Stoddard's opening lines in "Collected" so closely resemble Wilentz's contemporary phrasing that it is difficult not to read them as an appeal for diagnostic assistance: "Traveling this year in search of something lost, *i.e.,* health . . . I revisited an old village on our sea-board for the first time in many years" (285). Perhaps the primary achievement of these short stories is that through them Stoddard and Woolson provide modern readers with the description of an ailment for which nineteenth-century culture could offer no effectual cure.

NOTES

1. "Collected by a Valetudinarian" first appeared in *Harper's New Monthly Magazine* in 1870. All quotations are from Stoddard, "Collected by a Valetudinarian," in *The Morgesons and Other Writings.* "Miss Grief" appeared in 1880 in the short-story collection titled *Rodman the Keeper* (Torsney 70–72). All quotations are from Woolson, *Women Artists, Women Exiles: "Miss Grief" and Other Stories.*

2. Much has been written about Melville's and Hawthorne's struggles to sustain the popular and critical acclaim they received for their early publications. For more on Melville's struggle, see especially "Melville's Misanthropy" in Brown, *Domestic Individualism.* For more on Hawthorne, see Brodhead, *The School of Hawthorne,* particularly "Late Hawthorne, or the Woes of the Immortals."

3. In an 1876 letter to Elizabeth Allen, Stoddard describes the devastating effect poor sales had on her confidence: "No one knows what a literary ambition I had, nor how my failure has broken me" (*The Morgesons and Other Writings* 344). This sentiment is echoed in an 1891 letter to Stedman in which she makes it clear that critical praise is no substitute for the failure to achieve broad public circulation: "The failure of my novels is the 'black drop,' when they are praised, and it chokes me into silence" (*The Morgesons and Other Writings* 337).

4. See also Weinauer 172.

5. For a more detailed discussion of the gift economy and the Dickinson-Jackson correspondence, see my essay "'As if for you to choose ——': Conflicting Textual Economies in Dickinson's Correspondence with Helen Hunt Jackson." For a more in-depth discussion of parallels linking Dickinson's correspondence

with Higginson to Woolson's "Miss Grief," see the conclusion to my book *Inflections of the Pen: Dash and Voice in Emily Dickinson.*

6. Of the numerous examples from advice literature that blame women for their physical enfeeblement, I will cite two here: William A. Alcott's 1838 book *The Young Wife, or Duties of Woman in the Marriage Relation,* especially his chapter "Domestic Economy" (152–77); Reverend Daniel Wise's 1869 *The Young Lady's Counsellor: Or, Outlines and Illustrations of the Sphere, the Duties, and the Dangers of Young Women,* especially 152–99.

7. Other critics who have pointed out the debilitating influence patriarchal culture has had on female health include Gilbert and Gubar in *Madwoman in the Attic,* Smith-Rosenberg in *Disorderly Conduct,* Ehrenreich and English in *Complaints and Disorders,* and Showalter in *The Female Malady.*

8. Other instances of Miss Moncrief's ambivalent relationship to publication appear on 254, 259, and 263. In each of these passages, an argument can be made that Moncrief actually seeks the publication of her work. My position is that the logic of gift exchange in combination with the undeniable ambiguity of these passages supports the conclusion that she only appears to desire publication in an effort to pacify the narrator.

9. What Hyde means by "consumed" is that the gift "moves from one hand to another with no assurance of anything in return" (9); in this way, the relationship between giver and receiver differs from that of the marketplace, where the giver expects an equivalent return. In the gift economy, the giver surrenders all expectations of a specific return; the transmission of the gift is the consummation beyond which the giver expects nothing. However, as Marcel Mauss has pointed out in his study of the gift, the circulation of gifts within a social system proceeds according to general principles: "In the distinctive sphere of our social life we can never remain at rest. We must always return more than we receive; the return is always bigger and more costly" (63). Given this dynamic of gift exchange, we can observe the movement of the gift that Miss Moncrief has bestowed on the narrator to see if he, indeed, meets and, thus, confirms the demands of the gift-based economy.

10. There is ample evidence to support the likelihood that Stoddard read *Moby-Dick.* As Zagarell points out, Stoddard published "a brief sketch in the Duyckinck brothers' *Literary World* in 1852" ("Profile" 42) within months of the *Literary World*'s "two-part review" of *Moby-Dick,* written by Evert Duyckinck, that caused Melville such distress (Robertson-Lorant 290). That Stoddard was a "distant cousin" of Nathaniel Hawthorne, to whom she sent a complimentary copy of *The Morgesons* ten years later (Zagarell, "Profile" 43), suggests that she was aware of his literary tastes and knew of his friendship with Melville, as

well as his support for *Moby-Dick* during the period she wrote for *Literary World*. As an experimenter in stylistics and form herself, Stoddard would almost certainly have read the work that attracted so much attention. The fact that Stoddard's husband, Richard Stoddard, worked for the New York Custom House at the same time Melville did and that he wrote a review of *John Marr and Other Sailors* in 1888 lends further support to the idea that Elizabeth Stoddard was familiar with Melville's published work (Robertson-Lorant 501, 587).

    11. The obvious allusion is to the chapter in *Moby-Dick* titled "His Mark." In this chapter, Queequeg signs the ship's articles by making a mark that duplicates a tattoo on his arm. To show Queequeg's mark, Melville included a hand-drawn representation of the tattoo surrounded by Captain Peleg's words, also written by hand: "His Quohog mark" (85). Melville's surrounding of the exotic Queequeg's mark by the hand of an enterprising capitalistic male may have had special resonance for Stoddard's Alicia, who was about to release her manuscripts on a journey of unknown destination while she herself, like Queequeg, was about to set sail on a journey from which she would never return (Stoddard, *The Morgesons and Other Writings* 307). Equally intriguing is the fact that the tattoo forms part of a language imprinted on Queequeg's body which Melville later describes as "a complete theory of the heavens and the earth, and a mystical treatise on the art of attaining truth" (366). This, in combination with the fact that Queequeg remains "a riddle . . . unsolved to the last" (366–67), may have recommended to Stoddard that she use Melville to show that like Queequeg's "treatise on the art of attaining truth," Alicia's "world of beauty and truth" (Stoddard, *The Morgesons and Other Writings* 290) would also fade from the world unread by her contemporaries.

2
GENDER, SELFHOOD, AND THE DISCOURSE OF DOMESTICITY

4

"I Am Cruel Hungry"

Dramas of Twisted Appetite and Rejected Identification in
Elizabeth Stoddard's *The Morgesons*

Julia Stern

> Both would have annihilated my personality, if possible, for the sake
> of comprehending me, for both loved me in their way.
> Cassandra Morgeson, reflecting on her relations with sister Veronica
> and brother-in-law to-be, Ben Somers

> How incapable they are of appreciating what they cannot appropriate
> to the use of their own idiosyncrasies.
> Cassandra Morgeson, remarking on the inability of the Pickersgill
> Somers women to appreciate her in all her alterity

In 1862, during the final decade in which American women avidly
wrote and consumed works of sentimental literature,[1] Elizabeth Stoddard composed and published *The Morgesons,* a novel that might have
been mistaken for that of Emily Dickinson had she been known as a
writer of fiction.[2] Gnomic and elliptical in style, gothic in characterization and plot, and presciently modernist in form, Stoddard's book
was critically lauded and promptly ignored in its own day; indeed, into
the early twenty-first century, *The Morgesons* remains the generic "odd
man out" in reevaluations of American women's writing, patently rejecting the literary conventions, affective atmosphere, and moralistic
manifest narratives of many works produced between 1850 and 1870 by
American women.[3] Notoriously "difficult," this text has continued to
resist the sort of exegetical attention that would not only account for
Stoddard's representation of female sadism and masochism but also assert an informing relation between her aphoristic, fragmented style and
the decidedly antisentimental valence of her story. Taking up that challenge, I will argue that in language, characterization, and theme, *The
Morgesons* proceeds by a narrative physics of nonidentification, nonin-

trojection, and tragic incorporation. Featuring variations on the motif of perverse consumption, Stoddard's book offers a dialectical rebuttal to the women's tradition inaugurated by Warner, Stowe, Cummins, et al. whose works constitute its literary milieu. With *The Morgesons*, Stoddard allows us to reimagine a postsentimental genealogy for American women's fiction of the Civil War and post–Civil War eras.

Unlike the "pie[ous] and pie-making" women in the novels of the domestic sentimentalists,[4] nearly every major character in *The Morgesons* maintains a troubled relation to desire.[5] The narrator's sister Veronica subsists on a regressive diet of milk and buttered toast, the automaternal dimensions of which are suggestive indeed; Locke Morgeson, the novel's patriarch, is known for what the American Psychiatric Association's *Diagnostic and Statistical Manual* (the DSM IV) might call compulsive shopping and speculating disorders; distant cousin by marriage Alice Morgeson is occupied monomaniacally by child-rearing; and Alice's husband, Charles, expresses an exclusionary passion for hothouse gardening and horse-breaking. Across multiple generations, the Pickersgill–Somers family is notorious for alcoholic self-immolation (Ben and Desmond); in lieu of drink, they control their kindred by means of inappropriate sexuality and economic tyranny (Mrs. Somers). All are figures of twisted appetite, the subject of this chapter, which draws upon Nicolas Abraham and Maria Torok's psychoanalytic work on identificatory disturbances, those failures to "introject" or take inside the self-representations of objects lost outside in the world or within the mind.[6]

In the psychoanalytic literature, a crucial distinction exists between "introjection" and "incorporation." Introjection involves the careful sorting of complex representations of the lost object so as to allow the ego to take in, digest, and internalize the loss—what Freud calls *mourning;* in contrast, "incorporation" entails the swallowing whole, the non-digestion, the incomplete assimilation of the lost object, its encryptment or live burial in the ego—what Freud calls *melancholia.* Torok writes, "Incorporation is invariably distinct from introjection (a gradual process) because it is instantaneous and magical" (113). Understanding the ways in which Stoddard's characters do not identify with—or fail to internalize—the people and things populating their emotional landscapes, the perverse ways in which they relate to their own desires, illuminates the antisentimental project in which their creator is engaged.

The uniqueness of Stoddard's position in mid-nineteenth-century American literary history becomes most clear by reading *The Morgesons* against the genres that dominated its author's culture, particularly the women's sentimental novel. This fictive form is predicated on the capacity to evoke in the reader a sense of fellow feeling for characters undergoing duress: as Adam Smith hypothesizes in his *Theory of Moral Sentiments* (1759), sympathy itself requires the spectator's affective identification with the plight of the person viewed, following which occurs an emotional migration or translation of feeling as the viewer comes to imagine taking the afflicted figure's place. To sympathize adequately with a friend whose son has died, for example, it is not enough, Smith argues, to conceive of forfeiting one's own male offspring; instead, one must imagine, through a process of emotional extension and transference, becoming the very friend, suffering the loss of that specific child in all his particularity.

Literary theorists of sympathy like David Marshall and Julie Ellison, writing on the British tradition, and Elizabeth Barnes and Julia Stern, studying its American counterpart, as well as scholars of sentiment such as Ann Jesse Van Sant, Janet Todd, John Mullen, J. G. Barker-Benfield, Ann Douglas, Jane Tompkins, Gillian Brown, Cathy N. Davidson, Philip Fisher, Shirley Samuels et al., Eva Cherniavsky, Bruce Burgett, Mary Chapman, and Glenn Hendler, have spent the last twenty-plus years exploring the connection between fictive forms predicated on affective identification and their political and cultural implications. This massive scholarly effort has enabled the recovery of entire canons of late-eighteenth- and mid-nineteenth-century Anglo and American women's writing, which include Buell and Zagarell's fortuitous reintroduction to American readers of Elizabeth Stoddard and *The Morgesons*. In the course of doing this vital work, however, critics—including myself—have failed to be mindful of the ways in which novels working in the absence of sentimental formulae, far from proving out of sync with, if not actually unassimilable to, the dominant terms of this mid-nineteenth-century discourse, may, in fact, engage in trenchant philosophical and political critiques of sentimentalism's very premises.

That is, it is no longer enough to diagnose, along with many late-twentieth- and early-twenty-first-century readers of *The Morgesons*,[7] Stoddard's epigrammatic style and disassociative form as interpretive obstacles for her audience, which finds difficulty recognizing the legibility of the characters or comprehending the nonlinear nature of the plot. Instead, taking epigram and disassociation as heuristics, and extending our grasp of the novel's pervasive disruption of readerly identification to the dynamics inside Stoddard's story itself, including the vexed logical relation of sentence to sentence or paragraph to paragraph, may open a context for resituating *The Morgesons* squarely within a literary history any relation to which, until now, it seemed to disavow.

Written at the beginning of the American Civil War, an event that remains unmentioned in the novel,[8] *The Morgesons* is the story of a house divided. Accordingly, the novel parses its characters, delineating those who live through the body—eating with zeal or drinking to excess (the Surrey matrons who come for tea, Cassandra, and the innkeeper Mrs. Tabor; and Ben, Desmond, and the Pickersgill-Somers ancestors, respectively)—and those who dwell in the spirit (Veronica, Mrs. Morgeson). Stoddard associates embodiment with the literal and the material in the representational economy of her novel, while she links otherworldly orientation to the figurative and the ethereal. The following remark, then, offers both a revelation and a tautology: "It is the literal you will hunger for, dear Ben."[9]

Cassandra's doubt-evoking observation about the impending, potentially ill-fated marriage between her friend Ben Somers and her anorexic sister Veronica, to whose masochistic regime we return in what follows, belatedly telegraphs the book's abiding interest in struggles between ideality and materiality, spirit and body. Very early on, Stoddard's narrator-protagonist explains that she "became a devourer of books which I could not digest, and their influence located in my mind curious and inconsistent relations between facts and ideas" (56).[10] Orally aggressive—voracious when hungry and notably sharp tongued—Cassandra possesses none of the powers of assimilation that would enable her to absorb the very objects with which she passionately engages, the ideas of Milton, for example, or the affective otherness of her own sister and mother. Instead, the narrator is beset by inchoate longings, the satisfaction of which she cannot achieve, lacking as she does the "digestive" resources of her inward-turning sister and mother.

Often ravenous and rarely self-denying, yet haunted by an inexplicable emptiness, Cassandra Morgeson, not Ben Somers, "hungers for the literal"—that which supports her flourishing body but bypasses the nourishment of a mind and heart craving physiological stimulation rather than mental expansion. Put another way, the narrator "hungers for the literal" because things of the spirit do not satisfy her peculiarly embodied longings. In that regard, Cassy is utterly unlike her bookish sister Verry, whose nickname itself suggests the Latin noun *veritas*—truth—which with justice and goodness constitute the central topoi of the idealist philosophy Stoddard identifies with Veronica.[11] Impishly bizarre and uncommunicative as a child, rarely engaging in games with Cassandra and then only to play tricks on her, to which her sister responds with sadistic violence, Veronica becomes attached to Cassy only following the death of their mother, when both women are in their mid-twenties.

As an adolescent, however, unable to identify with the gregarious members of the Morgeson household—father Locke and sister Cassandra—Veronica ultimately develops sympathy and concern for the family's servants as well as for the poor, outcast, or otherwise abject figures dwelling in her Surrey community. Object attachment within the natal family may be perversely disrupted, but the romantic Veronica feels kinship with fellow sufferers in the larger social arena. This dimension of what primarily is a nonrealist plot ironically links the novel to the very issues that concerned socially committed writers like Rebecca Harding Davis, who put at the center of their fiction the world of labor and the fate of the working poor in the 1860s, the decade in which Irish immigration to America was swelling, as Hepsey's reference to the ubiquity of "Paddy Margaret" suggests (215).[12]

Nor does Cassandra resemble her intellectually precocious counterparts in the women's fiction of the decades surrounding the publication of *The Morgesons;* in this regard particularly, the character throws a convention-shattering curveball to those twenty-first-century readers expecting another Ellen of Susan Warner's *The Wide, Wide World* (1850), Gerty of Maria Cummin's *The Lamplighter* (1854), Edna of Augusta Evans's *St. Elmo* (1866), or Jo of Louisa May Alcott's *Little Women* (1868). A common source of readerly identification between both nineteenth-century and later audience members and the "girls in the books" (*Little Women* 208) is the fact that fictive heroines are bookworms par excellence, thus mirroring the very figures examining them. That Cassandra Morgeson gets little out of her reading marks Stoddard's anti-interpellative gesture toward her audience, a kind of "in your face" affront to the reader seeking to identify with the female protagonist.[13]

Contra the fictive, sentimental, book-loving contemporaries who anticipated and succeeded her, Cassandra hates school, retains nothing from early educational forays in Surrey and Barmouth, and later shows interest only in Byron's poetry, itself nineteenth-century shorthand for literature *dangereuse.* Beyond the volumes of *Childe Harold* and the like that they keep in their guest bedroom, Alice and Charles Morgeson read newspapers exclusively, suggesting that their narrowly pragmatic focus is delicately seasoned with the hint of the sexually outré, an appetite for action and violence (daily journalism) and the genteelly erotic (*Don Juan* and so forth). Of the characters noted above, one can imagine only Jo

March reading Byron, and then exclusively under the strict tutelage of her middle-aged husband, Professor Bhaer, a scholar of Romantic literature by way of Goethe the philosopher rather than the German novelist notorious for introducing fatal lovesickness to eighteenth-century fiction.[14]

It is in this literary-historical context that we might interpret the all-night reading session Cassandra undertakes within hours of arriving at Charles Morgeson's Roseville home. Devouring in one sitting her cousin's complete works of Byron (who himself famously was accused of engaging in incestuous relations with his half sister), the narrator virtually trumpets her illicit longings for Charles. Sensual excitation here clearly displaces any veneer of literary appreciation, as the poetic language arousing the narrator's nervous system bypasses her intellect entirely. In an earlier passage, in which she notes that "no thought remained with me long" (10), Cassy recognizes what we might call her abiding "digestive disturbance"—a phrase that usefully underscores the figurative connection between the consumption of food and the taking in of the external world of persons and things as described by object relations psychoanalysts such as Ferenczi, Abraham, and Torok.

Figuration itself, the process by which things are represented through comparison, in which words substitute for one another, involves the very workings of identification, exchange, and taking-in. Diana Fuss writes: "Freud's scientific theory of identification is entirely predicated on a logic of metaphoric exchange and displacement. Metaphor, *the substitution of one for the other,* is internal to the work of identification" (5). In a similar vein, writing not about identification but about its failure, incorporation, Torok notes, "But the fantasy of incorporation merely simulates profound psychic transformation through magic; it does so by implementing literally something that has only figurative meaning . . . [one important procedure constituting] the magic of incorporation: *demetaphorization* (taking figuratively what is meant literally)" (126).

In her protagonist, Stoddard represents a character with few connections to the affective domains of others. Indeed, an even more psychoanalytically oriented critic than myself might trace the attachment disorder plaguing the fictional Cassandra to the eccentric family of origin Stoddard limns in great detail, focusing as she does on a mother whose dreamy indifference to both reality writ large and its local unfoldings in the inner lives of her children fosters disassociation rather than nurture. Emblematizing Mary Morgeson's rejected engagement with the physical world are her gaping-eyed shoes, from which she has removed the laces so that she can manage her footwear without being annoyed by the flapping strings she cannot be bothered to tie.[15]

Stripping shoes of their laces would seem a relatively innocuous response to the pull of reality's imposing demands, but in the quietness of the gesture lies a violent retort to the outer world. If thy shoelace offends thee, pluck it out, the motion asserts; and it is just this penchant for delicate but brutal discipline that prompts Mary Morgeson to accede to her sister's plan to improve Cassandra's education at Barmouth, the puritanical town in which the Warren girls were raised by an unforgiving father. Mrs. Morgeson's decision to send Cassy away, coupled with her refusal to visit her beloved daughter during the Barmouth year because it would require a return to her childhood home, has mystified readers and critics alike: how can we understand the apparent sadism underlying the behavior of this otherworldly, if mechanistically pious, evangelical Christian mother?[16]

To be sure, a malicious strain clearly underlies almost every encounter that takes place between members of the extended Morgeson-Warren family: witness Grandfather Warren's shotgun massacre of the pigeons roosting in the pigpen; this sadistic deed comes in direct response to Cassy's expression of concern about the "beautiful pigeons who live on the roof" (44), which have arrogated food intended for the pig and thus, according to Grandfather Warren, must be driven away from the property. (Aunt Mercy later explains to Cassandra that had she not declared her attachment to the birds, Grandfather Warren would have spared them.) Without discounting the importance of intrafamilial sadism in *The Morgesons,* I consider Mary Morgeson's unsympathetic treatment of Cassy during the Barmouth section of the novel in the light of an equally important theme, pertaining to what the narrator herself has called a hunger for the literal or, more precisely, the impossibility of the figurative, a variation on the motif of disrupted identification.

Rather than attempting to explain to her daughter the restrictive rigors of a stultifying girlhood, Mrs. Morgeson sends Cassy to Barmouth to *repeat* that experience exactly. Megan Glick notes that in sending Cassandra to Barmouth to reenact her early life, Mrs. Morgeson attempts to script a scenario of Smithian sympathy in which, emotionally, Cassy would come to take her mother's place.[17] I would qualify Glick's insight by adding that because Mary Morgeson's scheme for Cassy's experiential "transport" unfolds literally rather than imaginatively, it is destined to fail. When the literal usurps the figurative, sympathy is impossible. Understood in another register, one could argue that through an act of violent substitution, thrusting her daughter into what has been her place, Mrs. Morgeson deputizes Cassandra to perform the work of emotional self-translation that she herself has disavowed. But rather than becoming illuminated by living out her mother's perverse behest, Cassy is damaged by its brutality, with sadism and masochism having displaced the possibility of fellow feeling.

It is as if Cassy can come to understand her mother's tortured history only through a literal recapitulation at the level of bodily encounter. Mary Morgeson writes to Cassandra during the period of her trial in Barmouth: "One of these days you will feel a tender pity, when you think of your mother's girlhood. You are learning how she lived at your age . . . I thought you would, by and by, understand me better than I do myself, for you are not like me, Cassy" (46). Thus the heroine's sojourn at her grandfather's might be thought of as the first iteration of Stoddard's scarring and tattooing motif,[18] though the traces of these early impressions are written on her spirit, rather than on her face as they will be in the case of her later wounds from the carriage wreck that kills Charles Morgeson, or on her limbs as in the instance of the love tattoo imprinted on the arm of her friend Helen.[19]

If Mary Morgeson is incapable of imagining nonviolent methods for routing feelings of attachment to a favorite daughter, Cassandra herself reveals a startling level of insensibility to her mother's actual physical condition. In a relatively faithful depiction of a nineteenth-century upper-middle-class New England household,[20] where birth, sickness, death, and postmortem preparations take place at home, is it plausible that a thirteen-year-old girl would fail to notice her mother's pregnant body changing over the course of the nine and a half months in which they have lived together under the same roof? As Diana Fuss notes in *Identification Papers,* citing Judith Butler's own work on the subject of identification in *Gender Trouble* and *Bodies That Matter,* "what at first may appear to be a refused identification . . . might in some cases more accurately be termed a disavowed one—an identification that has already been made and denied in the unconscious. A disidentification, in other words, may actually represent an 'identification that one fears to make only because one has already made it.'"[21]

While neither Cassandra nor Veronica seems remotely aware of her mother's physiological condition, each is acutely sensitive to the larger issue of disturbed maternal-filial relations.[22] Near the beginning of her narrative, Cassy breezily remarks that Mrs. Morgeson "did not love [Veronica] as she loved me; but strove the harder to fulfill her duty" (13).

Though we can dismiss this self-serving analysis on the grounds that fierce sibling rivalry distorts the reliability of Cassandra's perception, it is true that Veronica herself everywhere seems motivated by a longing for her mother's love. In a virtual textbook working out of Freud's theory of compensation, Veronica fails to receive maternal affection and so comes to serve as a mother-surrogate to those parentless figures surrounding her.[23] Transforming her own unsatisfied appetite, she offers care to creatures of the natural world as well as to underprivileged members of the social order.[24]

Veronica is the sole member of the Morgeson family to appreciate the orphaned, stunted serving girl, Fanny, for her odd beauty and keen intelligence. Ostensibly taken in by Mrs. Morgeson when her mother dies, Fanny is neglected entirely by Cassy and Verry's mother; and so, witnessing the suffering of a difficult, fitful young girl, one to whom her mother remains indifferent—that is, coming to identify with Fanny as a fellow outcast within—Veronica takes up her cause and succeeds in humanizing her. Though Fanny is based on the real-life servant who married Stoddard's father after the death of her mother (though in the wish-fulfillment-driven universe of autobiographically based fiction, Fanny is rejected by Locke Morgeson in favor of the rich and glamorous Alice Morgeson; and thus the girl reverts to the emotional custody of Cassandra),[25] we might also think of her as *The Morgesons*'s white, working-poor version of Harriet Beecher Stowe's Topsy, a parallel to which I will return. Though Cassy will tangle with Fanny in a scene I will examine later, the fiery servant girl will become, ultimately, an indispensable member of the intentional family Cassandra constitutes from the ashes of Morgeson domesticity at the novel's conclusion.

Constitutionally, Stoddard's only champion of the disenfranchised is incapable of attending to her own physiological needs: from her earliest days, Mary Morgeson's younger daughter has refused to consume any foods other than milk, buttered toast, and simple crackers;[26] and she has been subject, as well, to frequent bouts of violent illness. What is "wrong" with Veronica? Is her restricted eating a response to hysteria, agoraphobia, or even Asperger's Syndrome, a form of autism in which sufferers often exhibit remarkable talents, such as the sort of savant-like musicality Stoddard bequeaths to Veronica?

It makes great sense, historically, to attribute Veronica's "mysterious illnesses" to hysteria; the third quarter of the nineteenth century marked the heyday of diagnosing this condition in the cases of the very sort of young, white, upper-middle-class, and relatively educated women Stoddard portrays in *The Morgesons*. Certainly, Veronica's swooning condition—the "fits" Cassy describes taking hold of her sister for hours at a time—is congruent with the symptoms that Freud and Breuer describe in *Studies on Hysteria* (1895) and that Freud notes in his famous case history of "Dora," titled "Fragment of an Analysis of a Case of Hysteria" (1901), though Verry does not speak in unknown foreign languages, nor does she exhibit muteness or paralysis. The agoraphobia to which I refer is part of a wider hysterical symptomatology described by Charlotte Perkins Gilman in her virtuoso feminist novella "The Yellow Wallpaper" (1896), a fictional account of what today would be diagnosed as postpartum psychosis, which she based on her own psychiatric break and "cure" at the hands of the famous American doctor S. Weir Mitchell, celebrity neurologist of the late nineteenth century. The notion that Veronica is afflicted with Asperger's Syndrome, a condition on the autistic continuum marked by oversensitivity to stimulation of all kinds, the failure to make emotional attachments of meaningful depth (also described as an inability to feel empathy), and, occasionally, intellectual or artistic powers usually identified with so-called savants, is Dana Bilsky's.[27] Bilsky's compelling claim, however, does not account for how Veronica is able to relate empathically to Ben Somers and Fanny at the end of the novel.

While any one of these diagnoses is persuasive, I suggest a more simple reading: emotionally famished in the face of her mother's withheld love (itself a product of Mary Morgeson's disavowed identification with an eccentric child?), Veronica dramatizes in vivid terms the family's conflict over the issue of nurture per se.[28] Scripting not only her own physical and emotional disability, Verry also dictates the household's solicitous responses to her mysterious maladies.

Tellingly, it is the female servants, Temperance, Hepsey, and Fanny, who fly to Veronica's aid during her "spells." Mrs. Morgeson at best serves as a second-string nurse's aid to Temperance and Fanny, who wage battle on the front lines of Veronica's care; and Fanny quickly comes to learn the precursor symptoms of Veronica's affliction, accurately predicting in advance when an episode will occur. Neither Locke nor Arthur nor any of the "boys" who come to work for the family has anything to do with tending to Verry, underscoring Stoddard's point that what Veronica craves is the motherly touch afforded by the warm-hearted, working-class, hired female help. Regulating what she ingests—the primary components of the nineteenth-century Anglo-American nursery regimen as well as obvious symbols of basic, biological, maternal provision—Veronica orchestrates what her family takes into its hearts and minds: the ongoing fear of her death in the face of self-starvation or as a result of a bafflingly incurable disease.

In a detail that offers a fascinating and beautifully observed counterpoint to Verry's self-denial,[29] the Morgeson servants frequently apprise the decidedly nonphilanthropic Cassandra that her emaciated sister is off feeding others: whether they are the poor of Surrey, whom she succors with baskets of provisions, or the "cadaverous" and significantly "motherless" missionary children, to whom she sends sugarplums and picture books after discovering them in a Boston hotel dining room on the eve of their voyage to India, eating only bread and water (65). That the wasted children snarl with rudeness in the face of Veronica's generosity only underscores the uncanniness of her identifications.

Given Veronica's decidedly antisocial impulses, the fact of her responsiveness to the abject children whom she nurtures at the Boston hotel by bequeathing luscious sweetmeats and storybooks would appear to expose a contradiction in her ordinarily reclusive character. In fact, Verry's relative sensitivity to the needs of less-privileged others is not incongruent with a widely known practice of her father's, one that some readers find confusing: Locke Morgeson's ongoing willingness, expressed in instructions to both his wife and his domestic help, to host and even to house flocks of distant hungry relatives and, at times, virtual strangers asserting vague and unverifiable claims of kinship.

One can speculate on the motivations for such largesse: Locke Morgeson may wish to flaunt his wealth in a display of the sort of nineteenth-century beneficence that translates directly into social power,[30] while Mrs. Morgeson's willingness to open the family home may be rooted in altogether different notions involving Christian charity. Whatever the reasons driving this couple, one irony abides: while the nuclear Morgeson family members share virtually no interests, desires, or concerns in common and spend as little time together as possible, the fragile confines of their awkward domesticity are permeated continually by the freeloading outsiders to whom Veronica attends and from whom in disgust Cassandra flees (22–23).

Cassandra Morgeson disdains identification *tout court,* living in and for the literal alone; Veronica Morgeson takes into herself only what we might call "Romantic" objects—things naturally beautiful or socially outcast.[31] So exclusively does she dwell on the plane of the spirit that when their mother dies, Verry begs Cassy, "Let us keep her away from the grave" (206). Ben and Desmond Somers, along with their mother,

engage in a third tragic version of perverse consumption, the identificatory disturbance that, working as if by magic, is incorporation. Alcoholism is the Bellevue Pickersgill family "curse" (the term is Charles Morgeson's), though the disease,[32] while carried along the distaff line, most
vividly expresses itself in Mrs. Somers's male children. Vacillating between sobriety and drunkenness in Roseville, Ben marries Veronica in
Surrey, and soon after he dies there, presumably of the ill effects of perpetual intemperance, euphemistically termed "the groundplan of the
Bellevue Pickersgill character" that "cannot be altered" (252).

Emplotting Ben's self-extinction through alcohol over against his
brother's heroic battle for sobriety, which Desmond ultimately wins,
Stoddard most vividly—and fatally—depicts the aftereffects of appetite
gone awry. But Ben's seemingly inevitable plunge into obliteration
marks only the final stage in an ongoing, futile attempt at self-medica-
tion: unlucky enough to have been born into a family in which ineffective and drunken men (his father is a gout-stricken, bedridden non-
entity) have forfeited moral authority to a power-hungry woman, he
has taken in the mother's milk of Bellevue Somers's poisonous ambition.

Contra the ethos of maternal sacrifice that saturates the sentimental
novel against which Stoddard is writing, Mrs. Somers's fecundity becomes the improbable medium for total domination of her children. In
that regard, it is fascinating to juxtapose two episodes in *The Morgesons*
that ostensibly seem unrelated but that both focus on maternal nurture
gone awry. The first involves Mrs. Somers's recent and belated maternity,
about which characters in the novel repeatedly comment, underscoring
the medical and cultural aberration at work when a nearly fifty-year-old
matron living in the mid–nineteenth century has a child following a
fifteen-year hiatus and in the company of an invalid husband.

We can usefully contrast Mrs. Somers's unexpected fertility with an
earlier moment in which Cassandra wages a three-week battle between
life and death following the crash that has killed Charles and scarred and
traumatized her. When Cassy regains consciousness, the newly widowed
Alice Morgeson supervises her nourishment, feeding her a chicken
broth that has been prepared using only tiny pieces of meat. In rationing
how much soup Cassandra can consume per hour, Alice will not allow
the young woman to ingest any of the poultry the potage had contained.
Alice begins: "'The hour is up; I will get your broth.'" Cassy replies,
"'Bring me a great deal.' She came back with a thin, impoverished liq-
uid. 'There is no chicken in it,' I said fearfully. 'I took it out.' 'How could

you?' And [Cassandra] wept. She smiled. 'You are very weak, but shall have a bit.' She went for it, returning with an infinitesimal portion of chicken. 'What a young creature it must have been, Alice!' She laughed, promising me more, by and by" (124).

In this scene, Alice Morgeson governs what erstwhile sexual rival Cassandra may "take in" to her body. While Cassy remains utterly dependent on Alice's care, the widow Morgeson sadistically reworks the relations of desire, agency, and sensual satisfaction from which she was excluded during the (unconsummated) love affair between her husband and this younger distant cousin. The "fetal" chicken, as I like to think of it, stands in for many blasted hopes, including that of a sexual future for Charles and Cassandra; and Alice's withholding of its flesh suggests what we might consider a concretizing wish to regulate Cassy's mourning for Charles by controlling what she "ingests." Here, the literal stands in for the figurative—or, inversely, the figurative stands in for the literal. Mrs. Somers's baby, who will die shortly after the dinner party episode I am about to discuss, serves a symbolic function similar to that of the withheld fetal chicken: both become the object of a maternal figure's management, withheld and displayed at the will of an angry woman attempting to commandeer the desire of her adversaries.

In her late forties, when the major health issue worrying most nineteenth-century women is impending death, not childbed fever, Bellevue Pickersgill Somers has produced a baby boy, whose unanticipated arrival impedes the distribution of Pickersgill capital held in trust until the youngest Somers male reaches twenty-one years of age. Is it fancifully Freudian to remark in this case that a mother's unnatural sexuality has paralyzed her sons? In fact, Mrs. Somers's reproductive powers quite literally blight the psychological independence and economic autonomy of Ben and Desmond, neither of whom has been educated for professions; Ben, in fact, has failed to take his degree from Harvard, having been sent down for drinking and fighting.

Bellevue Somers would seem to luxuriate in the economic vengeance she has wreaked on her male offspring, whose only offense, beyond their embarrassing addiction to alcohol and the attendant discomfiture their drunkenness causes, involves the desire to disentangle themselves from an emasculating dependence on the (matrilineal) family of origin. During Cassandra's visit to Belem, to remind the assorted company of who in the household wields ultimate power, Mrs. Somers orchestrates a dinner party the concluding scene of which may be unmatched in nineteenth-century American fiction for its cannibalistic emotional subtext:

A few days after my arrival [in Belem], some friends dined with Mrs. Somers. The daughters of a senator, as Ann informed me, and an ex-governor, or I should not have known this fact, for I was not introduced. The dinner was elaborate, and Desmond did the honors. *With the walnuts, one of the ladies asked for the baby.*

Mrs. Somers made a sign to Desmond, who pulled the bell-rope —mildly this time. An elderly woman instantly appeared with a child a few months old, puny and anxious-looking. Mrs. Somers took *it* from her and *placed it on the table; it* tottered and nodded to the chirrups of the guests. Ben, from the opposite side of the table, addressed me by a look, which enlightened me. His voyage to India was useless, as the property would stand for twenty-one years more, lacking some months, unless Providence interposed. Adelaide was oblivious of the child, but Desmond thumped his glass on the mahogany to attract *it,* for its energies were absorbed in swallowing its fists and fretfully crying. When Murphy announced coffee in the parlor, the nurse took *it* away. (169, emphases mine)

Might this passage detail an unconsummated black mass of sorts, given the decidedly Protestant if not actually transcendentalist theological context within which Stoddard is working? As farfetched as such a reading would seem, I want to suggest that Mrs. Somers's late and destructive maternity—undertaken with the keen knowledge that its fruits will obstruct the independence of her grown children—is demonic, indeed. "*With the walnuts,*" notes Cassandra, "*one of the ladies asked for the baby.*" This peculiar grammatical formulation raises bizarre and noteworthy questions: is the narrator implying that the child and the nuts are to be understood as a sequence of "items" on an unusual "menu" meant to be offered *seriatim*? That is, after the butler passes the nuts, the baby will be handed round? Or, even more frightening, are the walnuts and the infant intended to be seen as interchangeable comestibles purveyed to the assorted guests for their delectation in the penultimate course of the dinner (coffee and sponge cake remain to be served in the parlor)?

What are we to make of the fact that rather than holding her baby, or handing him from guest to guest in order that he might be admired, Mrs. Somers "puts *it* on the table" (notably not "him"), as if the baby were an inanimate object? Usually, an infant must be nearly six months old in order to sit up independently; thus, we only can imagine how his mother has positioned the two-month-old child amongst hot serving platters, dirty dishes, sharp carving knives and pointed serving forks, potentially breakable goblets, and blazing candles. (In the light of the "with the walnuts" phrase, we may assume that the servants have cleared the table of such treacherous fare, though Cassandra provides no evidence of their having done so.)

It is no accident that Desmond employs a wineglass to get the child's attention, as a goblet is the perfect symbol of his own perverse consumption. That the baby is attempting to pacify his "anxiety" (or feed his "puniness"?) may be the most heartbreaking dimension of the entire episode: he is the novel's youngest victim of motherly feeling gone to hell. Desmond actually exclaims to Cassandra, "You know what a devil's household ours is" (191). Perhaps the most nonmaternal act in the entire mammalian repertoire would be a mother's devouring of her young. Bellevue Pickersgill-Somers's symbolic articulation of her baby on the dinner table could be explicated fruitfully along such lines.

Only pages later, we see the writing on the wall for this neglected infant, as if his earlier "anxiety" and "puniness" had not telegraphed his impending doom: "'Where do you think I have been,'" Ben accuses Desmond upon the latter's return home from a walk with Cassandra. "'Where?' 'For the doctor. The *baby* is sick'; and he looked hard at Desmond. 'I hope it will live for years and years,' I said. 'I know what you are at, Ben,' said Desmond. 'I have wished the brat dead; but upon my soul, I have a stronger wish than that—I have *forgotten* it'"(191–92). Well before the end of Cassy's story, "the child is dead," indeed (244).

Though it engages comparable themes only to re-inflect them away from the sentimental heritage Stoddard rejects and toward the modernism she so uncannily prefigures, a final scene featuring perverse consumption and twisted appetite constitutes a fitting complement to the passage just discussed. On the afternoon of her would-be suicidal near dive into the sea upon hearing the mysterious refrain "Hail, Cassandra!" the shaken narrator, determined to live, returns home. Having missed the midday meal prepared by Fanny and the "Irish" Margaret, Cassy observes to her dismay the "dishes used in the kitchen" in place of the elegant china ordinarily employed in the dining room. She writes: "I pulled off the cloth and all the dishes crashed, of course—and sat down on the floor, picking up the remains for my repast . . . I continued my meal. Fanny brought a chair for me, which I did not take . . . I scarcely tasted what I ate. A wall had risen up suddenly before me, which divided me from my dreams; I was inside it, on a prosaic domain I must henceforth be confined to" (215–16).

In a novel in which an adult character starves herself when not subsisting on the food of babies, and in which an infant is served up on a dining table as if *he* were edible himself, Cassandra's abject meal of rice and chopped ham, peppered with shards of second-rate porcelain and eaten off the planking, would seem to mark another instance of communion gone awry. Or does it? What Cassandra consumes from the floor is a literalization of the figure of shattered domesticity. The symbolic wall that seems to obstruct her dreams suggests that the limits of the narrator's desire must involve a re-imagination of what can be *taken in,* for in this phantasmic scenario, she herself is located *inside* the wall's perimeter.

The novel closes with a bleak account of new walls erected: Cassy has terminated all relations with Locke and his new bride, Alice, widow of Charles Morgeson; in lieu of a concluding tableau of the circling of the sentimental family as in scenes offered by Warner, Stowe, Cummins, and Alcott, Cassy portrays an odd ménage: the young and widowed Veronica; her mute and impassive child (*itself*—the baby remains notably ungendered by the narrator, as if he or she truly is an "*it,*" the tragic victim of some sort of developmental disability passed on, perhaps, by a physically ravaged father); and Fanny, who, like the enchanted frog-prince in a nineteenth-century fairy tale, has regained human form in the face of Veronica's attention and Cassandra's new vision, the epiphany ingested in the course of an abject meal. These fragments Stoddard has shored against the Morgeson family ruins; it is as if in the characters on whom she closes her gaze, the author has imagined the Compson family seventy-five years before Faulkner's time.[33] In that regard, the Morgeson house divided has become a reconstructed dwelling, with capitalist patriarchs and their acquisitive wives forever expelled, and servants not only freed but also absorbed into the family, contra the motif of nondigestion.

At an earlier point, I drew parallels between Fanny's final transformation and the penultimate fate of Stowe's Topsy, the slave who, having known no mother, is "redeemed" and "civilized" by the love of Evangeline St. Clare. Fanny, whose heart had been as hardened by parental abandonment as Topsy's had been disavowed by the speculator who bred her, becomes domesticated via Cassandra Morgeson's respectful regard; consequently, by the end of the novel she is able to weave herself into the fabric of Cassy's remade household.

But Topsy enjoys no such luxury, for despite her creator's abolitionism, the Romantic racialist Stowe simply cannot imagine an American place for the once demonic slave, from whom she erases all rebelliousness in converting her to Christianity. Despite the depth and sincerity of Topsy's newfound piety, at the level of plot the young black woman remains too threatening a figure to remain in a nation where the law continues to sanction slavery: thus, Stowe hygienically dispatches her to a Liberian mission, where Topsy can proselytize to the "heathen"—African doppelgängers of her former self.

Between these novels, within only ten years, two women writers have come to represent the difficulty of human relatedness and connection in profoundly different ways. Stowe sketches a picture of the powers of Christianizing "love" as it breaches the color line; but she reveals, paradoxically, that the "effects" of such caritas may also entail exile or expulsion. Stoddard, in contrast, provides a moment of "recognition" bridging the divide of class that, while significantly less charged (Cassy never claims to "love" Fanny; the most that can be said is that the servant is a "different girl" ever after [247]), involves acceptance and integration. The comparative fates of Topsy and Fanny are emblematic of what I see as the beginning of a literary-historical shift, a critical re-visioning and deconstruction of the sentimental genre, and a movement toward a post-sentimental narrative imagination marked by equal parts of lyricism and fracture.

In its rejection of the formulae of its sentimental literary milieu, *The Morgesons* is a crucial, transitional book. The novel uses its radical form to interrogate the very processes of identification and sympathy on which Warner et al.'s fiction is premised. For that reason alone—if ironically, given its themes—along with "Life in the Iron Mills" and *Mary Chesnut's Civil War* diaries, among other overlooked nineteenth-century American women's texts, *The Morgesons* constitutes the vital missing link as well as a keystone in the foundation of a yet-to-be-written, post-sentimental account of literary history in the nineteenth-century United States.

NOTES

This essay is dedicated to Professor Sandra Gilbert, with abiding thanks for introducing me to Stoddard and *The Morgesons,* and to Professor Elizabeth Renker, who generously invited me to talk about *The Morgesons* to faculty and graduate students in the English Department at Ohio State University in the fall of 2000. Along with Renker's insights into Stoddard's lyricism, I am indebted to those of her colleagues, Professors Thomas Cooley for the link to phrenology, Steven Fink for meditations on romanticism, Leigh Gilmore on the workings of autobiography, Jared Gardner on the significance of incest, race, and disunion, Elizabeth Hewitt on Dickinsonian echoes and on the interplay of simile and metaphor, and Susan Williams on tableaux; additionally, I am grateful to my students and former students at Northwestern University, 1991–2002, particularly Barbara Baumgartner, Christopher Hager, Dana Bilsky, and Megan Glick, whose own work on Stoddard has enriched my understanding of *The Morgesons* and is everywhere apparent in what follows. Heartfelt thanks as well to Lawrence Buell, Rob Smith, and Ellen Weinauer.

1. Underlying this imprecise claim is my sense that Louisa May Alcott's *Little Women* (1868) marks the last major and best-selling novel of the women's sentimental tradition in nineteenth-century America.

2. In the introduction to their modern edition of Stoddard's novel, Lawrence Buell and Sandra Zagarell note that "after meeting Emily Dickinson in Amherst, Thomas Wentworth Higginson wrote his wife that she could understand the [Dickinson] household if she had read Mrs. Stoddard's novels" (Buell and Zagarell x, quoting Higginson from *The Letters of Emily Dickinson* 2: 473).

3. The following essays on *The Morgesons* form the scholarly background to what follows. See Alaimo; Buell and Zagarell, "Biographical and Critical Introduction"; Susan K. Harris, "Stoddard's *The Morgesons*"; Henwood, "First-Person Storytelling"; Matter-Siebel, "Subverting the Sentimental"; Penner; Smith, "A Peculiar Case"; Weir, "*The Morgesons*"; Zagarell, "The Repossession of a Heritage" and "Profile."

4. Mary Chesnut offered this biting characterization upon reading Susan Warner's *Say and Seal* in 1861. See *Mary Chesnut's Civil War* 65.

5. Feminist scholars studying representations of anorexia in literature have been quick to note this fact. See Nettels; and also Susanna Ryan's essay in this volume.

6. Sandor Ferenczi introduced the concept of "introjection" in 1909. Ferenczi, a Hungarian Jew and an early disciple of Freud, elaborated the psychic conditions that give rise to his crucial term: "I described introjection as an *extension to the external world of the original autoerotic interests, by including its objects in the ego* [emphasis Ferenczi's]. I put the emphasis on this 'including' and wanted to show thereby that I considered every sort of object love (or transference) both in normal and in neurotic people (and of course also in paranoiacs as far as they are capable of loving) as an extension of the ego, that is as introjection. In principle, man can love only himself: if he loves an object, he takes it into his ego. . . . I used the term 'introjection' for all such growing onto, all such including of the love object in, the ego. As already stated, I conceive the mechanism

of all transference onto an object, that is to say all kinds of object love, an extension of the ego." See S. Ferenczi, qtd. in Abraham and Torok 112.

7. I base these conclusions on the anecdotal but nevertheless compelling responses of undergraduate and graduate students to whom I have taught Stoddard's novel over the last ten years.

8. Here again we might note the apt comparison of Stoddard with Dickinson, who composes the vast majority of her poems during the years 1860–65 but who never speaks directly in her verse of the Civil War itself, though she terms publication the "auction" of the soul, a potential reference to slavery, and makes countless allusions to decidedly undemocratic political systems, which suggest a form of social critique. Scholars have discussed the fact that the Dickinson "homestead" was situated very near a local Amherst cemetery and have noted that Emily Dickinson witnessed the passing of countless funeral corteges during the Civil War years. See Sewall; see also Susanna Ryan's essay in this volume.

9. Stoddard, *The Morgesons and Other Writings,* 226. All further citations of *The Morgesons* will refer to this edition of the text and will appear parenthetically. Inspired by this quotation, Christopher Hager devotes an entire chapter of his dissertation-in-progress to exploring the relations of the literal and the figurative in *The Morgesons.* I am grateful to him for alerting me to the importance of this passage, as well as to Jared Gardner and Beth Hewitt for their provocative speculation about the role of metaphor and simile in the novel.

10. Susanna Ryan notes the passage as well.

11. Susanna Ryan reads Verry's name differently—as an index of her extremism.

12. See Ignatiev.

13. My students over the last ten years confirm this alienating experience when they contemplate why it might be that Stoddard doesn't craft an extra-intelligent protagonist or one who lives to read.

14. Though Stoddard's book obviously predates Evans's by four years and Alcott's by six, it is, nevertheless, important to consider it in the context of a generic movement that had not run its final course—the sentimental tradition in mid-nineteenth-century American women's fiction.

15. Baumgartner makes a similar point in her forthcoming *ESQ* essay on the novel.

16. Susanna Ryan reads this dynamic as a vital feature of the narrative's anti-*Bildung* teleology.

17. See Glick.

18. See Baumgartner's fine treatment of the topic. See also Putzi's essay in this volume.

19. In making this connection, I am deliberately troping on the theme of the literal by claiming that the Barmouth experience makes a figurative "impression" on Cassy.

20. Though I have just argued that Stoddard's plot does not follow conventional realist schema (consider the passages involving Cassy's dialogue with her "Spectre" or the later "Hail Cassandra" material), her delineation of character and setting remains firmly moored to a mimetic representational tradition.

21. Fuss 6–7, quoting Butler, *Gender Trouble* 112.

22. Mary Morgeson's blatantly idolatrous love for her only son, Arthur, offers support for my argument about this character's being wracked by a terror of identification with her daughters; the obvious unlikeness of a boy child to his female parent immediately enables a psychic distancing mechanism in the mother, affording a barrier against the temptation of identificatory merger that must be defended against ferociously in the case of a girl child. Fuss meditates on the violence inherent in identification: "Of course, read psychoanalytically, every identification involves a degree of symbolic violence, a measure of temporary mastery and possession . . . identification operates on one level as an endless process of violent negation, a process of killing off the other in fantasy in order to usurp the other's place, the place where the subject desires to be" (9).

23. Lacan elaborates this dynamic in the formulation about woman "not having" the phallus and so coming to "be" the phallus herself. See Cherniavsky's reading of Lacan's "to have" versus "to be" motif regarding the phallus, 68–70.

24. That poets and philosophers locate divinity in the physical world is a basic premise of romanticism from Blake and Wordsworth in England to Emerson, Thoreau, and Whitman in the United States. Thus, when Cassandra removes several baby mice from the outdoors, she has the following exchange with Verry, who asks: "'Where is the mother?' 'In the hayrick, I suppose, I left it there,' replies her sister. 'I hate you,' [Veronica] said, in an enraged voice. 'I would strike you if it weren't for this holy butterfly'" (18). In identifying the beautiful insect with the realm of the Divine, Veronica telegraphs her Romantic sensibility to a readership well acquainted with the premises of New England transcendentalism. Susanna Ryan makes a similar point in discussing the ways in which Veronica's piano playing taps into the emotional states of others (176).

25. On the parallels between Stoddard's life and her art, see Zagarell, "Profile."

26. One can only speculate on the detrimental effects of a diet composed exclusively of dairy products and carbohydrates; perhaps Veronica suffers from anemia, scurvy, nontropical sprew (an absorption disorder marked by an inability to digest wheat), and malnutrition writ large?

27. Bilsky develops these notions in her dissertation-in-progress. For current

thinking on Asperger's Syndrome, see Scott et al. and Safran. I am grateful to Bilsky for sharing these articles with me.

28. In that regard, the novel poses a fascinating counterpoint to Melville's story "Bartleby, The Scrivener, A Tale of Wall Street" (1853), which I read, among other ways, as a parable of Emersonian or Thoreauvian self-reliance run amuck. Might we see in the distinctly non-nurturing Morgeson family a similar working out of radical Romantic individualism and, implicitly, its critique?

29. Hilda Bruche, the psychiatrist who inaugurated contemporary research on anorexia nervosa, bulimia, and other eating disorders, notes that anorexics characteristically are obsessed with cookery books and culinary magazines, as well as with the preparation and sharing of food—food they themselves will not eat. Thus, Bruche notes the cases of starving women who go on cooking binges and demand that their families ingest what they have prepared. If we unpack these behaviors symptomatically, such forced feeding suggests the desire to make family members swallow what the patient herself has concocted—to mandate the "taking in"—or internalization—of what the sick member has to offer, be it a delicious dinner for or a set of bad feelings about the other figures in the family. This symptomatic detail illuminates the commonplace that anorexia is a "family" disease, an illness emanating from one member that expresses the affliction of the entire group.

30. Here again, I think of the self-described "philanthropy" practiced by the narrator of Melville's "Bartleby," whose ad hoc attempts to offer material charity to his inscrutable scrivener are laughable in the face of the exploitation he practices against his employees as a matter of office policy.

31. Indeed, Veronica "takes in" not only strangers but also those aspects of the natural world itself by which she feels compelled. Thus, her bedroom serves as a staging area for a performance of the seasons, via leaves, flowers, sticks, sky-colored paint, and grass-tinted carpet; Veronica's "nature," contra Emerson's, exists exclusively inside, as a function of her imaginative, artistic, Romantic ingestion of objects of desire.

32. Scholarship on alcoholism and temperance in the mid–nineteenth century constitutes a vast cross-disciplinary literature; for recent discussions, see Lender and Martin; Mattingly; Reynolds and Rosenthal; Rorabaugh; Sournia, Tyrell; Valverde; Vice; and Nicholas Warner.

33. Thanks to Jared Gardner for sharing this stunning political and literary insight with me.

5

"Perversions of Volition"

Self-Starvation and Self-Possession in Dickinson and Stoddard

Susanna Ryan

In 1856, in a critique of the domestic novel published in her newspaper column for the *Daily Alta California,* Elizabeth Stoddard wrote, "Why will writers, especially female writers, make their heroines so indifferent to good eating, so careless about taking cold, and so impervious to all the creature comforts? The absence of these treats compose their women, with an eternal preachment about self-denial, moral self-denial. Is goodness, then, incompatible with the enjoyment of the senses? In reading such books, I am reminded of what I have thought my mission was: a crusade against Duty" (qtd. in Stoddard, *The Morgesons and Other Writings* 325–26).[1] Stoddard's first novel, *The Morgesons,* published six years later, is a complex portrayal of the themes of self-denial and the enjoyment of the senses articulated above, and it centers on her female characters' difficult negotiations between interior and exterior experience, and between maintaining independence and expressing passion. A novel in which everyone seems to be described in relation to his or her appetite, *The Morgesons* depicts the lives of two sisters who struggle with the limitations of gendered existence; using hunger as a central metaphor, Stoddard portrays the relation between women and their appetites as a way of exploring the possibilities for female self-development and the exertion of individual will. But what the novel reveals is that appetitiveness and its satiation are inevitably bound up with the economic demands of commodity culture and the conventional narratives of heterosexual domesticity. By framing *The Morgesons* with Emily Dickinson's much-analyzed lyrics of hunger and with nineteenth-century medical texts that worry over the "problem" of female appetite, I argue for an understanding of how tropes of starvation and ingestion functioned in nineteenth-century America that moves beyond the critical focus on Dickinsonian renunciation. More specifically, I contend that Stoddard's portrayal of two young women's experiments with the boundaries of their physical bodies illuminates the compromises necessary in the resolution of women's pleasure, duty, and volition.

Stoddard's interest in female appetites is not anomalous, given its historical context: both contemporary physicians' reports on the then-famous "fasting girls" and tracts on women's sexuality display an anxious fascination with women's ingestion of food. On 18 September 1869, for example, reacting to the death from self-starvation of Sarah Jacob (otherwise known as "the Welsh Fasting Girl"), the editors of *The Lancet* issued a statement asserting that Jacob had succumbed to what they called "perversions of volition" that prolonged her fasting to excess (416). Such a diagnosis identifies two fundamental issues implicit in Jacob's rejection of food: the deviance of the act and the outrageous willfulness of it. Like a number of young women who starved themselves in Britain and America in the nineteenth century, Jacob became a public spectacle, her case arousing concern over the intersection of female desire and its enactment.[2] Around the same time, medical ideologues like the American physician Orson Fowler were cautioning young women against another "perversion of volition": masturbation. Positing abstinence from any sort of stimulation (dietary, sexual, or mental) as the cure for masturbatory impulses, Fowler admonished young women to refrain from taking almost any food whatsoever. "As to suppers," he wrote in 1851, "I recommend *none at all*. A full stomach induces dreams, or the exercise, in sleep, of those organs most liable to spontaneous action, which in this case is Amativeness[.] . . . Never fear starvation" (61–62).

The mixed messages implied in the above quotations reveal competing ideologies of appropriate behavior that complicate any form of autonomous female volition: according to the physicians attending the Jacob case, on the one hand, extreme abstinence is a perverse form of willfulness; according to physicians committed to eradicating excessive sexual desire, on the other, starvation can work as a self-regulating *cure* for deviance (as Fowler insists, "TOTAL ABSTINENCE IS LIFE . . . ABSTINENCE OR DEATH is your only alternative [56]). I do not pair these discourses arbitrarily; on the contrary, these two acts—self-starvation and self-pleasuring—are shot through with similar ideas: the exertion of control over the individual body; the consumption of the self; the management and exacerbation of excess; the enclosure of self into an impenetrable realm of self-sufficiency. Both self-starvation and autoeroticism likewise share a similar model of desire that exists through the renunciation of an object outside the self. In literary terms, these issues of nineteenth-

century women's self-denial and self-enclosure have been widely identified with the lyric poetry of Emily Dickinson: as Dickinson herself
wrote, "Great hungers feed themselves," and a number of critics have
described Dickinson as either an anorexic or an autoerotic figure.[3] But
to focus solely on Dickinson's resistant formulations of pleasure and denial is, I argue, to gloss over the complexities to be found in nineteenth-
century debates over female appetite. Dickinson revises Orson Fowler's
sexuality/abstinence schism, representing instead a secession from sexual
and economic systems of exchange—a model in which the refusal of
external stimulation *begets* pleasure, as I will discuss. But Elizabeth Stoddard's *The Morgesons,* written between the 1850s works of Orson Fowler
and the 1869 Sarah Jacob case and interacting thematically with both,
points up the impossibility of extrication from those social systems and
suggests that female appetite can be expressed only as a negotiation
within their boundaries.

Comparisons between Dickinson and Stoddard seem inevitable: both
were raised in Massachusetts, both were devout readers of the Brontë
sisters' novels, both were brought up with a conflicted relation to institutional Protestantism. (Indeed, appetite and religion often go hand in
hand in both writers' works: Dickinson's lyrics of hunger make frequent
references to God and the Divine, thereby often implying the power of
her abstinence; Stoddard's Morgeson sisters negotiate their relation to
their own desire and satiation in a New England still redefining its relation to Puritanism.)[4] Writing in a period just subsequent to the proliferation of ideological individualism and the concurrent "self-culture"
movement, Dickinson and Stoddard also share the inheritance of an
Emersonian focus on "self-reliance" and Goethe's notion of *Bildung,* or
self-education. In his influential essay "Self-Culture" (1838), William
Ellery Channing declares that self-development cannot come about
"unless we engage in the work of self-improvement, unless we purpose
strenuously to form and elevate our own minds, unless what we hear is
made part of ourselves by conscientious reflection"; such ideas mirror
Goethian, bildungsromanesque notions of self-cultivation involving influence from without to inform the developing interior (354–55). For
Goethe, as Benjamin Sax has put it, "*Bildung* included a process of self-
formation within and through interaction with the world" (250). But
this dialectic between self-development and interchange with the outside world has particular ramifications for women writing about female
processes of self-growth: bildungsromanesque opportunities for exterior
experience are entangled, for nineteenth-century women, with tradi-

tional narratives of heterosexual romance and marriage. In both Dickinson and Stoddard, these issues of socialization and exchange are literalized in the female body. Making the very physical distinction between self and other in the act of alimentary rejection or consumption, both authors present the conflict between volition and appetite; by inverting the conventions of narrative and *Bildung,* they grapple with possible models for the reconciliation of the two terms.

The figure of the self-starving woman in the texts of both Dickinson and Stoddard thus points to a larger, culturally and historically specific set of discourses in which the ingestion and/or refusal of food signifies a particular—and a particularly gendered—relation to the self and its place in the world. As Joan Jacobs Brumberg has chronicled in *Fasting Girls: The History of Anorexia Nervosa,* the phenomenon of female self-starvation dates from the thirteenth century, as a complex (and, again, a gendered) rite of religious purification. By the nineteenth century, however, "fasting girls" were less and less associated with religious martyrdom, and anorexia emerged as a diagnosable disease, one most often linked to hysteria, disordered sexuality, and troubled family dynamics— an expression of difficult interactions between young women and systems of social and sexual exchange.[5] Emily Dickinson's representation of gratifications both spiritual and personal through the hungry poetic "I" appears to hark back to an earlier, self-martyring form of fasting; but the Dickinsonian model of renunciation-as-satisfaction is only one facet of a much more complex set of cultural negotiations and redefinitions taking place around female appetite in 1860s America. If, for Dickinson, the refusal to ingest creates an impenetrable boundary within which the pleasures of self-growth can be enjoyed, for Stoddard's Morgeson sisters, self-possession is desired but elusive because there seems to be no middle ground between the enclosure of starvation and the dissipating exposure of ingestion.

In moving from Dickinson's poetry of hunger, which posits an auto-erotics of growth through emaciation, to Stoddard's *The Morgesons,* a text in which the material world intrudes upon and even shapes the individual, this essay thus moves from the paradoxical freedom of lyric form to the more realistic mode of the novel—and, too, from a spiritual model of ecstatic self-starvation to a more medicalized, even precociously psychoanalytic paradigm of identity production. Both authors employ the imagery of appetite, and both use inversion and reversal to describe an anti-teleological resistance to conventional narrative, to self-comprehension, and to object-driven models of desire. But Dickinson's sublimely unified, autoerotic self cannot translate, ultimately, to the social and relational sphere Veronica and Cassandra Morgeson inhabit. I begin, then, with a brief reading of several of Emily Dickinson's key poems on alimentary renunciation and move to an extended analysis of *The Morgesons,* in which the enclosed satisfactions of the lyric self are complicated by an appetitive imbrication with things external.

Upon Emily Dickinson's death in 1886, her sister-in-law, Susan Dickinson, wrote an obituary emphasizing Dickinson's reclusiveness, portraying her as "sitting . . . 'in the light of her own fire.' . . . [T]he 'mesh of her soul,' as Browning called the body, was too rare, and the sacred quiet of her own home proved the fit atmosphere for her worth and work. All that must be inviolate" (qtd. in Farr 9–10).[6] This allusion to the poet's self-generated heat, coupled with the reference to her imperative inviolability, aptly serves to highlight two issues central to and intertwined in many of Dickinson's poems: the ability to create desire and induce pleasure within the impenetrable circumference of the self. Significantly, both inviolability and the heightening of pleasure are referred to in the poems as products of starvation; for Dickinson, hunger is a paradoxical means of both constructing the boundaries of the self and achieving a sublime self-expansion. While the point of both self-culture and *Bildung* is self-knowledge, Dickinson's renunciation of the exterior world, metaphorized in the poems as food, lead not to a more coherent understanding of the self but, rather, to an ecstatic self-unification that virtually thwarts articulation.

This desire for enclosed self-fusion is exemplified in poem 579, in which hunger provides an impregnable boundary that contains the self. Dickinson speaks of drawing near a "Table" laden with food, after years of starvation; what she finds, however, is that eating causes a painful alienation:

I had been hungry—all the Years—
My Noon had Come—to dine—
I trembling drew the Table near—
And touched the Curious Wine—

'Twas this on Tables I had seen—
When turning, hungry, Home
I looked in Windows, for the Wealth
I could not hope—for Mine—

I did not know the ample Bread—
'Twas so unlike the Crumb
The Birds and I, had often shared
In Nature's—Dining Room—

The Plenty hurt me—'twas so new—
Myself felt ill—and odd—
As Berry—of a Mountain Bush—
Transplanted—to the Road—

Nor was I hungry—so I found
That Hunger—was a way
Of Persons outside Windows—
The Entering—takes away—[7]

Hurt by the ingestion of the "Curious Wine" and the "ample Bread," Dickinson is split: rather than use the conventional pronoun "I" to begin line 14 (the pronoun which she has used without exception to this point in the poem), she uses "Myself," emphasizing the disjunction between the speaker and her self-perception. The image of the "Berry" plucked from its "Mountain Bush"—"transplanted" from its seclusion into traffic with the outside world, "the Road"—further emphasizes the sense of a disoriented splitting of the self. Ultimately, hunger itself disappears when ingestion occurs—not because eating provides satiation, but because, as Vivian Pollak has noted, for Dickinson, "the self has been so completely defined by its starvation that food threatens to destroy it" (113). To violate the boundaries of the self through ingestion is, then, to cause a violent distress that alienates the self from its own ability to feel. The penetration of food into the body cannot satisfy because "the Entering—takes away" hunger itself; and as Dickinson sees it, "Hunger— [is] a way" to construct and protect a unified subjectivity.

Once food has been renounced, what is left to be eaten is hunger itself—and if hunger constitutes the self, then the consumption of hunger becomes a paradoxically productive, unifying act of autoconsumption. In poem 1430, one of many lyrics in which Dickinson essentially spells out her definition of desire, pleasure can be known only through its absence: she writes that "The Banquet of Abstemiousness / Defaces that of Wine—"; that is, satisfaction exists only in the consumption of one's own renunciation, and the "ungrasped" object, kept at a necessary distance, allows for the enthralling "Joy" of "the soul." Poem 773 further portrays the process by which renunciation or deprivation becomes the interior process of self-consumptive growth:

> Deprived of other Banquet,
> I entertained Myself—
> At first—a scant nutrition—
> An insufficient Loaf—
>
> But grown by slender addings
> To so esteemed a size
> 'Tis sumptuous enough for me—
> And almost to suffice
>
> A Robin's famine able—
> Red pilgrim, He and I—
> A Berry from our table
> Reserve for charity—

Here, the self is split into "I" and "Myself," as in 579, only to have the "I" consume "Myself" at an alternative "Banquet" that ultimately satisfies. Indeed, the self cultivates herself here, catalyzing a process of growth that slowly allows for satiation, even to the point at which the excesses of the self can be shared or reserved. This ability to give the self's leftovers away, though, again highlights Dickinson's insistence on the impenetrability of gratification through self-consumption: Dickinson can eat herself, or give herself to others to be eaten, but she does not ingest any nourishment from outside (even the "Berry" she thinks to reserve points back to the "Berry" in 579, which stands in as a symbol for the self).

Poem 383 further elaborates these themes of self-consumption and self-expansion; the interiority of the self becomes the site of limitless supply, as the exterior "Wine" of 1430 becomes a wine fermented within the confines of the self, thus making it fit libation:

> Exhilaration—is within—
> There can no Outer Wine
> So royally intoxicate
> As that diviner Brand

The Soul achieves—Herself—
To drink—or set away
For visitor—Or Sacrament—
'Tis not of Holiday

To stimulate a Man
Who hath the Ample Rhine
Within his Closet—Best you can
Exhale in offering.

Nothing is taken into the self in this poem; what is created within can be consumed, reserved, or emitted, but excitation comes only from an interior source, never from the outside. There is simply no need for penetration by or ingestion of an "Outer" object; aligned with the stimulated man of line 9, Dickinson has not only a limitless supply of self-made "Wine," but a whole *river*—the Rhine itself—welled up inside her "Closet." And, again, she eschews outside religion, for the soul's own wine is "diviner" than that of the church, and holidays (holy days) are unnecessary because of the infinite supply of exhilaration and stimulation within the boundaries of the self.

The theme of self-consumption in 383 pivots on line 5, in which Dickinson's construction "The Soul achieves—Herself" both refers back to the "diviner Brand" of wine created in the self and stands alone as the ultimate statement of self-possessed fulfillment. That is, through refusal, the soul not only produces her own wine but also, in the process, achieves her own *self*. Although John Kucich has persuasively argued (in a different context) that the retreat into an autonomous autoeroticism depends upon a split or dialectic self whose conflicting parts continually chafe against one another to cause a kind of masturbatory friction, I would argue that here, for Dickinson, the opposite is true.[8] In fact, the split self prevents the kind of ecstatic unity that Dickinson seeks; as in 579, for example, an "entering" from the outside rends "I" from "Myself" and causes disorientation. To "achieve" the self is to consume the self and to merge the self's hunger with its own self-generated nourishment. Put another way, the defining hunger of 579, once consumed, becomes the inner wine of 383, which brings about a fusional pleasure in the "achievement" of an enclosed but expansive self-possession.

The construction of the impermeable, unified, and satisfied lyric self further hinges on the imagery of reversal, an anti-teleological move away from a progress model of self-knowledge. As Cristanne Miller has written, "Dickinson's poems characteristically either begin in apparent certainty and move to apparent doubt . . . or begin with a question and end by undercutting the expected answer" (56). Dickinson's renunciatory inversion reverses conventional narrative progression and fosters an obfuscation of meaning: in the sublimity of its expansion through inversion, self-growth affords ecstatic pleasure and eludes intelligibility. In contrast to Dickinson's autoerotic, fused self, both the self-culture project and the traditional bildungsroman trajectory hinge on a self-understanding that, while illimitable, depend upon a split subjectivity, on "the faculty of turning the mind on itself; of recalling its past, and watching its present operations; of learning its various capacities and susceptibilities," as William Ellery Channing writes (355). Indeed, Channing's own description of the *uncultured* self sounds quite a bit like Dickinson's ideal; disparaging the unwillingness of the multitudes to "penetrate into their own nature," Channing remarks, "When [most men] happen to cast a glance inward, they see there only a dark, vague chaos" (356). For Dickinson, unification resists intelligibility inside or out; indeed, the pleasure to be gleaned through acts of self-starvation comes about only in the eradication of such a split, comprehending consciousness. Dickinson's "perversion of volition" here involves a strategy of inversion that combines the fasting girls' self-starvation with the self-reliance of the autoerotic woman. Revising Orson Fowler, Dickinson proposes a lyric self whose abstinence breeds rather than diminishes appetite and pleasure; in creating an enclosed economy in which the self is simultaneously the subject and object of desire, both consumer and consumed, Dickinson obviates the need for exchange with the outside world.

As Margaret Dickie has pointed out, "The brevity of the lyrics [Dickinson] wrote is a form of artistic restraint that relies paradoxically on excess. . . . [T]he lyric speaker suggests a sense of self that is certainly limited and yet remains paradoxically free from the restraints of social viability that will be exerted on the novelistic character" (226). And in shifting focus from Dickinson's poetry of hunger to Elizabeth Stoddard's *The Morgesons,* I argue for the limitations of a nineteenth-century, self-starving lyric "freedom." Like Dickinson, Stoddard's novel experiments with anti-*Bildung* inversions and reversals and emphasizes the difficulty of maintaining self-possession while consuming from an exterior source. But in the social world of *The Morgesons,* a novel whose very title suggests the importance of one's place within an extant, exterior familial structure, Dickinson's autoerotic, impenetrable identity—and the un-equivocal rejection of objects of desire—is impossible.

The younger Morgeson sister, Veronica, whose self-starvation is a way to both construct herself and negate her desires, stands for all that is so interior as to be incomprehensible in *The Morgesons;* her sister, Cassandra, on the other hand, is the dialectic self who tells her own story (Cassandra serves as first-person narrator in the novel) and explores her own emotions. Through the indulgence of her appetite, both literal and metaphoric, however, she exposes herself to potentially objectifying sexual and psychological influences and penetrations. The novel concludes with a partial inversion of identity between the two sisters that, while affording Verry and Cassy a more compassionate view of each other, underscores the impossibility of maintaining a Dickinsonian impregnability and suggests that the reconciliation of duty and volition is possible only through a compromise with the external world of consumption and exchange. Indeed, Stoddard's "crusade against Duty" does not simply succeed in *The Morgesons:* rather, the novel portrays the "perversions of volition" autonomy might require.

Enigmatic and reclusive, Veronica embodies the Dickinsonian tendencies the novel explores and critiques. Using self-starvation to create an impenetrable boundary behind which she can maintain her self-possession, Veronica retreats from exterior objects of desire—a retreat that, like Dickinson's, comes about through negation. While Veronica establishes a sense of self-importance through self-starvation, however—effectively transforming the conventional limitations placed on the Victorian woman into a means of protection from the outside world, a world of sexuality and exposure—her self-enclosure immobilizes her and cannot ultimately shelter her autonomy from the influences and desires of others.

As her nickname suggests (she is called "Verry" throughout much of the novel), Veronica takes things to extremes, but always in the direction of renunciation and denial. Although she is described as "never hungry," she also, at least as a child, "tasted everything, and burnt everything."[9] Her lack of appetite, then, appears to be self-imposed; indeed, her starvation causes her many "long and mysterious illnesses" rather than resulting from them (13). This self-starvation serves several functions for Veronica: through the refusal of food, she both separates herself from her own needs and distinguishes her identity from that of her all-consum-

ing, appetitive sister, Cassandra. Veronica constructs an illegible surface
that thwarts the efforts of others to "read" her; she creates illness and
pain, through which she participates in her own version of self-development. If Cassandra is "possessed" (as Aunt Mercy proclaims in the opening of the novel), then Veronica is the ultimate embodiment of *self*-pos-
session. Her rejection of both exterior objects of desire and desire itself
heightens her sense of power and autonomy.

Asserting that she will "live entirely on toast," Veronica separates herself from her sister, for, as she says, she "supposed [Cassandra] would eat
all sorts of food, as usual" (51). This distinction seems at one with her
wish to separate herself from her own anger, as well, but the act of renouncing almost all food actually appears to heighten Veronica's passions;
she complains, after her austere dinner, that "eating toast does not make
me better-tempered; I feel evil still. You know . . . that my temper is
worse than ever; it is like a tiger's" (52). Likewise, her self-enclosed im-
permeability appears to foster the "genius" that other characters perceive in Veronica. Although her piano playing taps into the emotional
states of others, Veronica remains intact, bounded within an inscrutably
independent self; Cassandra, moved by her playing, remarks, "Strange
girl; her music was so filled with a wild lament that I again fathomed
my desires and my despair. Her eyes wandered toward me, burning with
the fires of her creative power, not with the feelings that stung me to
the quick" (141). Like Dickinson's "Exhilaration . . . within," Veronica's
interior blaze of passionate creativity appears limitless and completely
impervious to exterior forces; Dickinson can exhale, and Veronica can
play, but neither has been influenced from without.

Indeed, only Veronica's "creative power" penetrates her, whereas her
sister repeatedly describes herself as subject to outside influence, to ingestion and penetration; Cassandra exclaims, "Veronica! you were en-
dowed with genius; but while its rays penetrated you, we did not see
them. How could we profit by what you saw and heard, when we were
blind and deaf?" (59). But the powers of vision and hearing ascribed to
Veronica come about only through a characteristically inverted, negative means; when ill, she "made little pellets of cotton which she stuffed
in her ears and nose, so that she might not hear or smell" (56). Her self-
circumscribed vision is emphasized in the view from her window and
in the construction of the window itself; like her "distant," "singular,"
and "*baffling*" eyes, which are no window to her soul, the window in
Veronica's room need never be opened, for she has replaced a pane of
glass with a "wicket" through which she can see but through which

nothing can enter (51, 135). Cassandra, whose room has a view of the limitless expanse of the ocean, asks her sister, "Do you never tire of this limited, monotonous view—of a few uneven fields, squared by grim stone walls?"; Veronica's reply—"If the landscape were wider, I could never learn it"—points to her insistence upon control, as well as to her desire for fixity (135).

Neither a child nor an experienced adult, Veronica attempts to stop time and to arrest narrative progression through the maintenance of her painstakingly drawn limits. Her retreat into herself functions both as a refusal to mature and as a means of becoming incomprehensible to others; that is, she will neither voluntarily enter into the narrative of her own life nor allow others to "read" her. Indeed, even in her own admiration of and fascination with Veronica's impenetrable illegibility, Cassandra is prevented from understanding Veronica's investment in stasis; although Cassandra sees Veronica as mature, her friend Helen asserts that Veronica "will be a child always," for despite the fact that her mysterious "genius" makes her appear to be an adult, "she stopped in the process of maturity long ago" (150). Later in the novel, Veronica herself echoes this interpretation when she confesses, "I never was a child, you know; but I am always trying to find my childhood" (217).

If the genius that separates her from others, and that is intensified by its very boundedness, is a static way of gaining the appearance of maturity, Veronica's illnesses actually contribute to her self-growth. Again, Veronica's identity seems constructed through narrative inversion: she starves herself, which leads to illness, which leads to strength and growth as opposed to frailty and death. Through her "inscrutable disease," Cassandra tells us, "she acquired the fortitude of an Indian; pain could extort no groan from her" (59). Indeed, whereas Cassandra goes away to be schooled and socialized, Veronica "was educated by sickness; her mind fed and grew on pain, and at last mastered it" (59). Veronica's autonomous genius is cultivated through this alternative, inverted mode of nurture and education, but the novel cannot find a place for such "creative power" in the social world. As Cassandra wryly notes, "a woman of genius is but a heavenly lunatic, or an anomaly sphered between the sexes" (242). Less like Dickinson's ecstatic lyric "I" than like Sarah Jacob, wasting away to nothing, Veronica ultimately illuminates not only the allure but the dangers of self-starvation as an identity-preserving strategy.

In contrast to Veronica's static impenetrability, Cassandra is from the outset a divided, penetrated self. The opening line of the novel, "That child . . . is possessed," sets up Cassandra's identity as subject to the entrance of some exterior force (5). The novel's ultimate consumer, Cassandra eats and shops almost incessantly throughout her youth, and her literal consumptions are underscored by her own use of metaphors of appetite: in her narrative, books are "devoured," time "consumed." Her interior dialogues and continual mirror-gazing—and even the first-person narrative itself, which constructs her as both narrator and heroine—emphasize the split subjectivity Cassandra embodies. But this is a self-division that allows for only a conflicted reflexivity and understanding; although Cassandra does gain experience by leaving home on several occasions, and although she indulges her appetites throughout the novel, nonetheless her early transferral from the school of "Mrs. Desire" to the care of the household servant "Temperance" prefigures her regressive self-denial at the end of the novel. Although Susan K. Harris has asserted that "Cassandra's narrative is the record of her survival through self-knowledge, through recognizing her own nature and its imperatives," I would argue that because of the exteriorization of her desires, Cassandra's tale of self-growth ultimately mirrors Veronica's, circling back to confinement (*American Women's Novels* 170). For Cassandra, the imperatives placed upon her are internalized from the outside, but her acceptance of duty plays itself out in the same paradigm of regression and inversion as Veronica's self-imposed starvation. Rather than serving as a revolutionary bildungsroman heroine who gains self-awareness and finds a place for herself through her experiences of growth, Cassandra can only return home, literally scarred by her struggles to at once express her passions and maintain her independence.[10]

While Veronica's illness forms the basis of her inverted narrative of self-growth, Cassandra's growth is patently physical. Indeed, her childhood illness does not put a dent in Cassandra's physical development; she remarks:

> In January I had so bad an ague that I was confined at home a week. But I grew fast in spite of all my discomforts. Aunt Mercy took the tucks out of my skirts, and I burst out where there were no tucks. I assumed a womanly shape.
>
> Stiff as my hands were, and purple as were my arms, I could see that they were plump and well-shaped. I had lost the meagerness of childhood and began to feel a new and delightful affluence. What an appetite I had, too! (46–47)

This awed enjoyment of her own capacities for physical growth and her own burgeoning appetites forms the basis of Cassandra's sense of herself throughout the early part of the novel. Stoddard's frank portrayal of such an appetitive, sensual young woman is entangled with her representation of the dangers of such expansive expression, and just as Cassandra takes pleasure in her body and her desires, she also lacks control over both the contents of her interiority and the boundaries of her identity. She tells us that, as a child, "I was moved and governed by my sensations, which continually changed, and passed away—to come again, and deposit vague ideas which ignorantly haunted me" (14). These sensations of agency themselves cannot be concealed but, rather, are continually expressed; known for her "candor," Cassandra has neither the ability nor, at first, the desire to circumscribe herself as her sister does. She remarks that, in contrast to Veronica's reticent mysteriousness, she herself "concealed nothing; the desires and emotions which are usually kept as a private fund I displayed and exhausted" (58). Dickinson's hoarded, auto-consumptive self here is laid open to exterior influence, as Cassandra continually exposes herself and sates her appetites from the outside.

The construction of Cassandra's identity through her exteriorization is emphasized in her first experience away from home. Construing the significance of her elder daughter's existence only in relation to her own life, Cassandra's mother sends her to the house she herself grew up in, in the hopes that Cassandra thus will "comprehend the influences of [her mother's] early life, and learn some of the lessons she had been taught" (27). That these lessons seem to have more to do with the restraints and constrictions that have made her mother a "self-tormentor" points to the limitations of female education and development in the novel; Cassandra's first foray into the world is actually a regression, and her mirroring of her mother's own (anti)developmental narrative prefigures her acceptance of her mother's role at the end of the novel (17). Cassandra's second experience away from home likewise underscores her susceptibility to exterior influence and, moreover, illuminates the conflicted nature of object-driven desire.

From the moment Cassandra arrives at her cousin Charles Morgeson's house, she falls under his influence; since she has no "private fund" of interiority, she is easily swayed by his power over her: "When in his presence I was so pervaded by it that whether I went contrary to the dictates of his will or not I moved as if under a pivot" (74). Indeed, the "intangible, silent, magnetic feeling" between Charles and Cassandra is the first secret she keeps, the first vestige of her own capacity for interiority—but, of course, the secret is founded on his attraction to her, and thus her experience of her own private emotions is inextricably bound up with Charles's desires. Feeling the influence of his gaze—which, she tells us, she "could not defy or resist" and which "filled my veins with a torrent of fire" (his fiery penetration of her here contrasting with Veronica's self-generated "fires of . . . creative power")—Cassandra confesses to Charles's wife, Alice, that "he influences me so strongly . . . [and] I believe I influence him" (86, 85).

This mutual "influence" ultimately makes Cassandra ill, and it is notably an illness that, unlike Veronica's strengthening afflictions, "made me feel I needed help from without" (85). Indeed, Charles's confession that he loves her causes Cassandra to spit up blood and to ask her friend Helen, "Do you think . . . that I shall ever have consumption?" (110). The exteriorization of desire through the attachment to an object, then, appears to call up the fears that one will *become* an object, that one will be consumed oneself. And Cassandra's sexual desire threatens not only her own health but that of others; acting on her impulse to be near Charles, Cassandra goes for a drive with him that physically scars her, permanently marking her face, and proves fatal for him. This accident propels Cassandra backward, into another regression; the doctor remarks upon her regaining consciousness that she "crawled out of a small hole" (121).

Yet this rebirth of sorts leads not to a furthering of Cassandra's development but, rather, to her return home, where she and Veronica begin to exchange places in the gradual inversion that points toward the novel's troubled conclusion. Upon Cassandra's arrival at her family home, the servant Hepsey remarks that she and Veronica "look something alike now" (128), and although Veronica characteristically disdains such an assertion, Cassandra does begin a Veronica-esque retreat of her own. Once resituated at home, Cassandra says of her room that it, like Veronica's, " 'is the summary of my wants, for it contains me,' " and of her Dickinsonian selection of her own society, she asserts, "The more circumscribed it was, the better I could endure it" (131).[11] By this point, her outspokenness has become taciturnity—she tells Charles's widow, "I am more candid than ever, for I am silent" (153)—and she expresses a wish to leave behind the narrative of her life thus far: "a mad longing sometimes seized me to depart into a new world, which should contain no element of the old, least of all a reminiscence of what my experience had made me" (152).

Just as Cassandra begins to turn inward, Veronica, having become the object of Ben Somers's desire despite her efforts to remain intact and independent of others, begins to eat. The inscrutability of Veronica's surface finally lends itself to misreading, for Ben sees Veronica not as the willful, solipsistic woman she is but, rather, as a "delicate, pure, ignorant soul," a kind of "Angel in the House" who will yield to him (226). Ben's confession that he loves her creates "a new expression in Verry's face—an unsettled, *dispossessed* look; her brows were knitted, yet she smiled over and over again, while she seemed hardly aware that she was eating like an ordinary mortal" (159, emphasis mine). Veronica and Cassandra appear to lose themselves simultaneously, though in ways that mirror their opposition throughout the novel: Veronica, turning outward, no longer possesses herself, and her troubled smiles foreshadow those of the child she will bear to the alcoholic Ben, who "smiles continually, but never cries, never moves, except when it is moved" (252); Cassandra, turning inward to a regressive silence, finds herself empty, "the helm" of her "will" having been "broken" (190).

Even Cassandra's final sojourn in the world outside the Morgeson home, her visit to the Somers household, seems a repetition rather than a new chapter; her sudden romantic interest in Desmond Somers replicates both her desire for the brooding Charles Morgeson and her initial attraction to Desmond's brother, Ben. While Susan K. Harris rightly points out that the attachment between Cassandra and Desmond stems from their mutual acknowledgment that "they share a common history of sexual transgression," the episode at the Somers home nevertheless underscores the increasingly constrained outlets Cassandra finds for passionate expression rather than illuminating the benefits of her maturity (*American Women's Novels* 155). Cassandra takes note of the Somerses' appetites—"They all ate largely," she inwardly remarks—but she herself "declin[es] the gingerbread" and, ultimately, falls ill for the second time in the novel (165, 173).[12] Among the Somerses, Cassandra begins to lose her sense of self, criticizing her own dress as inadequate and suffering the critique of the Somers sisters as well. Attempting to ameliorate this increasing feeling of displacement, she turns to the mirror for affirmation of her existence. "A desire to look in the glass overcame me. I felt unacquainted with myself, and must see what my aspect indicated just then," Cassandra narrates, and she ultimately comes to realize that her dispossession stems primarily from her increasing attraction to Desmond (175). Frowned upon by Mrs. Somers, warned against by Ben, the love Cassandra develops for the alcoholic Desmond becomes a source of both

joy and conflict in her—and, again, is portrayed as a complicated consequence of her passionate nature; as Ben sternly queries, "'Have you so
much passion that you cannot discern the future you offer yourself?'"
(200).

The tension between passion and volition is heightened after Cassandra returns from the Somers household to find her mother dead. Although Veronica is temporarily able to retreat into her room, "the only
one not invaded," Cassandra struggles with her role as her mother's suc-
cessor, which "was imposed upon me" (209). Out by the ocean, Cassandra's appetite for life revives momentarily. "'Have then at life!' my senses
cried. 'We will possess its longing silence, rifle its waiting beauty. We will
rise up in its light and warmth, and cry, "Come, for we wait." Its roar,
its beauty, its madness—we will have—*all*'" (214–15). But this internal
outburst is short-lived, and Cassandra returns to the house to declare to
her aunt, "I will reign, and serve also." Her aunt's reply, "Oh, Cassandra,
can you give up *yourself*?" is met by Cassandra's resigned assertion, "I
must, I suppose" (215). Her "contrary desires" fall subject to "an idea
of responsibility . . . what plain people call Duty" (219), and she finds
herself in a self-willed but inescapable stasis: "I remain this year the
same. No change, no growth or development! The fulfillment of duty
avails me nothing; and self-discipline has passed the necessary point"
(243). Ironically, it is here, alone in her childhood home, that Cassandra
"achieves—Herself": "I was at last left alone in my own house, and I
regained an absolute self-possession, and a sense of occupation I had long
been a stranger to. My ownership oppressed me, almost, there was so
much liberty to realize" (248). But even in this state of self-limit-
ing self-possession, Cassandra faces "the yearning, yawning empty void
within me," and she is "stirred . . . to mad regret and frantic longing.
I stretched out my arms to embrace the presence which my senses
evoked" (250).

A number of critics have read Desmond's appearance at this crucial
moment of tension between autonomy and passion as expressive of the
extent of Cassandra's development; Sandra Zagarell has argued, for example, that "Cassandra's sexuality makes her, like Jane Eyre, one of the
rare nineteenth-century heroines who matures beyond the attractions
of Byronism to attain a love at once equal and complete" ("Repossession" 53). While Desmond and Cassandra's marriage may be that of
equals, it is also the union of two whose self-denial has become the
foundation of their individual identities: now an appropriate object for
the reception of Cassy's longings (having left America to divest himself

of his alcoholic tendencies), Desmond fills the void Cassandra's adherence to duty has created, and Cassandra ends up tied to her family home, her mother's role, and her own need for others. Indeed, Stoddard's resolution seems to insist upon compromise: neither sister manages to maintain the terms they set up for themselves at the beginning of the novel, and both have regressed rather than progressed by its end.

Zagarell's analogy between Cassandra and Jane Eyre is apt: Stoddard's ending fittingly references Brontë's 1847 novel, a text she knew well. Stoddard closes *The Morgesons* with the specter of the alcoholically dissipated Ben Somers, at whose deathbed Cassandra and Desmond watch: "When he sprang from his bed, staggered backwards, and fell dead, we clung together with faint hearts, and mutely questioned each other. 'God is the ruler,' [Desmond] said at last. 'Otherwise let this mad world crush us now'" (252–53). This exclamation encapsulates the novel's ambivalent messages about volition and duty: expressive of a desire to serve a master in a clear hierarchy, to cede power to a divine authority, Desmond's words raise questions about the reconciliation of autonomous identity, the material world, and a highly structured and ordered universe. *Jane Eyre* ends with the zealous words of St. John Rivers, whose devotion to his master, the Lord, both contrasts with and mirrors Jane's final servitude to Rochester. Brontë closes her novel with St. John's letter to Jane: "'My Master,' he says, 'has forewarned me. Daily he announces more distinctly,—"Surely I come quickly!" and hourly I more eagerly respond,—"Amen; even so come, Lord Jesus!" (502). Both novels grapple to the very end with the difficult negotiation between romance and autonomy, and both portray heroines who, on the one hand, have compromised their independence in marriage and, on the other, have developed a self-possession through that very compromise which alters the terms of conventional heterosexual relations.

Given Stoddard's 1856 assertion of her "crusade against Duty," *The Morgesons* may ultimately be read as the portrayal of the limitations imposed on female appetite, development, and self-expression and of the impossibility of exerting volition other than through the manipulation of such limitations. If Veronica stands for an extreme, perversely volitional attempt at independence through self-starving self-enclosure, Cassandra initially inhabits the other extreme. No bildungsroman heroine, Cassandra does not seek self-understanding so much as a way to indulge in emotional, sensual, and sexual expression while maintaining her autonomy. The paradoxical Dickinsonian equation, rejection of object = heightened desire = expansion of self = autoerotic pleasure, breaks down in *The Morgesons;* self-imposed limitation makes Veronica, as Sybil Weir has put it, "a human freak" ("*The Morgesons*" 430), deadened and blind by the end of the novel, while Cassandra can find self-possession and sexual union only through the acceptance of duty itself.

As Brumberg has asserted in *Fasting Girls,* "to live without eating was [for the Victorian fasting girl] to deny one's need for material support or earthly connection" (63). Dickinson participates in a secession from the material, choosing her own form of abstinence, one that undoes both the fasting girls' self-destruction and a Fowleresque obliteration of desire. Viewing both secession and "cure" as dangerous options, however, Stoddard seeks to integrate self-possession and satiation through experiments with literary form and the forms of female appetite themselves. If to do so is to end in compromise, it is also to begin to reimagine the terms by which "material support and earthly connection" may be made compatible with agency and passion. What Stoddard's *The Morgesons* shows us is that nineteenth-century women's "perversions of volition" may have more to do with the perversion of the term *volition* itself than with its extreme implementation.

NOTES

1. From an article dated 3 August 1856.

2. Two years after Sarah Jacob's death from starvation, in his case study *A Complete History of the Case of the Welsh Fasting-Girl,* Robert Fowler (no relation to Orson) reemphasized the theme of perversion: "For a morbid persistence in a perverse determination, the girl . . . of a necessity paid the last penalty demanded by the unerring laws of outraged Nature" (259).

3. Dickinson's words are quoted from *The Letters of Emily Dickinson* (3: 668). In addition to Vivian Pollak and Margaret Dickie, to whom I refer later, both Geoffrey Hartman and Heather Kirk Thomas have identified what might be called an anorexic logic in Dickinson's lyrics. See Hartman, *Criticism in the Wilderness,* and Thomas, "Emily Dickinson's 'Renunciation' and Anorexia Nervosa." Among the more notable discussions of Dickinson's autoerotic aesthetic is Paula Bennett's "'Pomegranate-Flowers': The Phantasmic Productions of Late-Nineteenth-Century Anglo-American Women Poets."

4. Of course, religion also plays an important role in Victorian antimasturbation tracts as well as case histories of the fasting girls. *The Lancet* suggests, for example, that Sarah Jacob had been "unduly stimulated, as well as disordered, by religious reading," a practice that the publication blames, in part, for her

death (416). For an extended discussion of the relation between religion and fasting, see Caroline Walker Bynum, *Holy Feast and Holy Fast,* and Joan Jacobs Brumberg, *Fasting Girls.*

5. See Brumberg, *Fasting Girls,* especially chapters 2–5.

6. Farr is here quoting Susan Dickinson's obituary of Dickinson for the *Springfield Republican* (18 May 1886).

7. All of Dickinson's poems are quoted from *The Poems of Emily Dickinson.*

8. See Kucich, *Repression in Victorian Fiction,* especially his discussion of *Middlemarch* in chapter 2.

9. Stoddard, *The Morgesons* (*The Morgesons and Other Writings,* 13). All further citations of *The Morgesons* will refer to this edition of the text and will appear parenthetically.

10. Although many critics working on *The Morgesons* have wanted to view the novel as a female bildungsroman, and although Stoddard may indeed have had such a convention in mind, I would argue that, in fact, Stoddard inverts the teleological narrativity of the bildungsroman; in so doing, she exposes the limitations of such a novelistic model and, more broadly, highlights the restrictions placed upon women's possibilities for growth and experience. Sybil Weir, in her early and influential article on the novel, has seen Cassandra's narrative trajectory as "the development of a rebellious, ignorant New England girl into a mature, passionate woman"; Susan K. Harris has likewise argued that the novel depicts "a woman's consciousness as she matures from an unruly childhood into responsible adulthood" (Weir, "*The Morgesons*" 428; Harris, "Stoddard's *The Morgesons*" 11). In a somewhat more nuanced interpretation of the novel, Stacy Alaimo discusses the dialogic tension between the novel's bildungromanesque features and what Alaimo sees as a neo-gothic motif. See Alaimo, "Elizabeth Stoddard's *The Morgesons.*"

11. Indeed, even before Charles's death, Cassandra's admiration of Veronica's inscrutable willfulness has gradually become more pronounced; troubled by Charles's pervasive influence, she imagines Veronica as "unyielding" and says of herself, "I seemed to wash like a weed at her base" (85). Seeking a sense of herself separate from Charles, Cassandra remarks to herself, Veronica-like, "In my room . . . I shall find myself again" (110), and after Charles surreptitiously visits her bedroom while she sleeps, she attempts to write to Veronica, as if to invoke her impenetrable presence (99).

12. Julia Stern has posited that the Somers family participates in their own "tragic version of perverse consumption," alcoholism, thus fitting in with the novel's overall focus on "digestive disturbances" that lead to or express "disrupted identification." While Stern and I share an interest in Stoddard's tropic

use of appetite and ingestion, Stern's argument centers on Stoddard's rejection of sentimentalism through the representation of such disruptions of identification. See Stern, "'I Am Cruel Hungry': Dramas of Twisted Appetite and Rejected Identification in Elizabeth Stoddard's *The Morgesons*," also in this collection.

6

Home Coming and Home Leaving

Interrogations of Domesticity in Elizabeth Stoddard's *Harper's* Fiction, 1859–1891

Jaime Osterman Alves

Although she is better known to us as a novelist, Elizabeth Stoddard was also a prolific short-story writer whose career spanned more than four decades, during which some seventy short pieces went to print in periodicals such as the *Atlantic Monthly, Putnam's,* the *Independent, Lippincott's,* and *Hearth and Home.*[1] Her most fertile and longest-running relationship, though, was with *Harper's New Monthly Magazine,* in which, between 1859 and 1891, she published eighteen stories, establishing a literary home for her work and creating a substantial complement to her longer fiction, poetry, and journalistic writings.[2] In all of the *Harper's* stories—and, indeed, throughout her career—Stoddard pursues an interest in isolating and prosecuting the most common tropes of nineteenth-century domestic fiction, such as marriage, female community, and childhood innocence.[3] She viewed as false and saccharine many of her contemporaries' efforts to portray domestic life, and in her newspaper columns she frequently criticized what she took to be their emphases on surfaces and facades, agreeing with a critic from *Putnam's* magazine that "the woman-novels contain puppets instead of characters" and complaining herself that "no one book has been written by a[n American] woman of erudition; no metaphysical tale, novel, or poem; no story that holds in analysis the passions of the human heart."[4] Contrary to those writers, and in fact more like one of the best-known characters from her *own* short fiction—Alicia Raymond of "Collected by a Valetudinarian"—Stoddard was eager to represent through her work "the truth about men and women," to look "thoroughly into the lining of things," and particularly to examine the often hidden and unpleasant aspects of the most intimate domestic relationships (101, 103).[5] As she wrote in an 1860 letter to James Russell Lowell: "At times I have an overwhelming perception of the back side of truth. I see the rough laths behind the fine mortar—the body within its purple and fine linen—the mood of the man and woman in the dark of the light of his or her mind when alone" (qtd. in Matlack, "Literary Career" 185). As her conflation of material, physical structures (buildings, bodies), and ephemeral "mood[s]" or emotions points up, Stoddard's fiction is often centered in the home and organized around deeply personal domestic relationships; nevertheless, it bucks against the proprieties that typically circumscribed nineteenth-century female authors and prevented them from writing explicitly about marital discord, sororal betrayal, or the pleasures of unchecked childhood appetites. Inside the houses of her stories, Stoddard probes the "rough laths behind the fine mortar" to examine the deeply interior motivations and psychologies that can make husbands and wives, parents and children, live together as intimate strangers.

Stoddard's interest in domestic fiction, and her interrogation of domesticity—as a *discourse* rather than as a virtue—is most pointed when she examines the secluded and the shared aspects of life among intimates and thematizes their public and private behaviors. I will consider a broad spectrum of Stoddard's *Harper's* stories, most of them previously unexamined, looking particularly at the ways she used the domestic setting as a locus to explore female conduct, and at how her career-long intervention into domestic discourse complicates and increases our current understanding of domesticity and middle-class women's writing in the nineteenth century. Specifically, Stoddard interrogated the discourse of domesticity by manipulating two main tenets of domestic fiction.[6] First, she played with the convention that material domestic arrangements— the visible layout and accoutrements of the home—accurately and transparently displayed the more ephemeral, intangible aspects of intimate life. As Gillian Brown has observed, this convention suggested that a woman's evident housekeeping style and capability were keys to understanding the operation of her household and especially her sense of agency within that household.[7] I contend that Stoddard disrupts this convention to expose the tyranny it must have exerted over women's lives, and that it certainly exerted over the range of possible plotlines for female authors and female characters. Her own revision of this formula —her assertion that, as Alicia Raymond expresses it, "every flower must have an ugly root . . . that behind or back of all beauty is the black, rough, coarse structure"—suggests Stoddard's desire to disrupt the notion that the home is a private, tidy, and safe haven removed from the messy, fraught, public world and to undercut the symbolic value of the material domestic space in American fiction as a transparent emblem of either domestic harmony or domestic strife ("Collected" 103). In Stoddard's 1867 story "Unexpected Blows," for example, the character Mrs. Shelby so obsessively and skillfully manages the material space and effects of her home that she is able to rearrange furniture, direct the human traffic of her family throughout the house, perceive from her vantage point in the *parlor* that some morsel of food is being overcooked in the *kitchen* (and, accordingly, scold the cook), gauge an injured man's temperature, and wag her finger at him for getting hurt—all at the same time. Still, her ridiculous and manic attention to the administrative details of her house prevents her from noticing more abstract goings-on— namely, that her daughter and the injured stranger are falling in love right under her nose. Clearly, Stoddard devalues her contemporaries' frequent equation of home management with domestic harmony. Throughout her work, she reveals the limitations of the physical domestic environment in representing the more nuanced and subtle relationships between human beings, and she implies that *only* fully realized characters can speak for the complexities of intimate life.[8]

Second and relatedly, Stoddard was keen to dispel the middle-class idea that the home was, for either men or women, a private refuge from the public world. Her chief contribution to domestic discourse is that she contests her culture's divisions between public and private spheres, at least to the extent that those spheres describe a set of physical and ideological boundaries wherein the "public" equals the masculine and active world beyond the home, and the "private" equals the feminine and passive world within it. Uninterested in constructing fictional worlds divided into public and private *spheres* of action, she instead draws characters for whom "public" and "private" are modes of *behavior,* parameters describing the self that a character presents to the world, or withholds from it, in a given situation.[9] The polarized concerns typically associated with either public spaces or private spheres—business versus emotion, for example, or the foreign versus the familiar—collapse and merge in her work, so that physical spaces themselves are inherently dispassionate stages for different kinds of action. Thus, Stoddard rejects as contradictory the republican idea that the home could be both a microcosm for the larger social world *and* a space that is purely private, female, and orderly.[10] If the home is truly like the larger social world, she implies, it must be understood as a gender-neutral space in which character, not location, determines the nature of people's interactions with one another.

In her refusal to portray the home as transparent or separate from the larger social world, Stoddard contests a fundamental principle undergirding nineteenth-century domestic fiction, dismissing the equation between domesticity, safety, and order and introducing the idea that chaos, conflict, secrecy, and duplicity are as plausible within the home as without. And yet, despite her determination to unyoke the home from her culture's fantasy of some nonexistent, purely private and female space, Stoddard nevertheless remains interested in exploring how concepts of "public" and "private" inform (especially) women's relationships to themselves and one another, as well as to their husbands, parents, and children.[11] Seeking neither to rail against nor to defend a vision of society segregated into spheres by gender, Stoddard differentiates hers from her contemporaries' critiques by foregrounding in her stories women's conflicting, *internal* desires to both adopt and reject the social conventions of proper womanhood. Blending the rhetoric of public and private social spheres with her own language about public and private female selves, she authorizes a struggle wherein women possess (at least) two often conflicting identities, a public face and a private face. Resisting the ways that other writers portrayed the dichotomy of public and private as functions of location—rigid, external, and oppressive—Stoddard imagines this binary as contained *within* the individual, and thus more easily manipulated *by* the individual. Stoddard's articulation of her characters' public and private selves grants these women greater control over their own relationships and over the public and private aspects of their lives, diminishing, if not totally dissolving, the degree to which a woman can be restricted by external pressures to a life within the home.

It is fitting that Stoddard's most prolonged investigation of middle-class domestic discourse took place on the pages of *Harper's* magazine. The monthly periodical was begun in 1850 as a "commercial opportunity . . . meant to drum up buyers" (Lapham 58) for books published by the Harper and Brothers firm and was initially distributed as a promotional catalog composed of a few short stories pirated from British magazines alongside numerous advertisements; this latter genre was itself designed almost exclusively for an audience with expendable cash as well as middle-class aspirations toward high culture, fashion, and taste.[12] By December 1859, when *Harper's* printed its first Stoddard story, "Our Christmas Party," the then-decade-old magazine had forsaken a large portion of its advertisements and was dominated by original American fiction. Despite the shift, however, *Harper's* had nevertheless become a prominent vehicle (like the *Atlantic Monthly* and *Godey's Lady's Book*) for many American writers to peddle the myth of public and private spheres, helping to create, consolidate, and promote middle-class values, identity, and domestic ideology. Short fiction and poetry by authors like Harriet Beecher Stowe, Caroline Chesebro', and Louise Chandler Moulton, for example, would continue to help circulate and reify what were, in Nancy Cott's formulation of domestic discourse, "the ideological presumptions, institutional practices, and strongly held habits of mind insisting that the home must be guided by a calm, devoted, and self-abnegating wife and mother: that with her presence, the home would serve—and it had to serve, for social order and individual well-being—as a moral beacon, a restorative haven from the anxieties and adversities of public life and commerce, comforting the hardworking husband and provider for the family, and furnishing a nursery of spiritual and civic values for the children" (xvii).

As Cott has so usefully described it, this discourse of domesticity was "a prime means by which members of the ascendant middle class understood themselves as men and women and presented themselves to the world" (xviii).[13] Of course, not all of the magazine's contributors advocated these ideas: stories by Harriet Prescott Spofford, Alice Cary, Constance Fenimore Woolson, Elizabeth Stuart Phelps, and Stoddard herself added to their culture's ongoing conversation about domesticity in varying registers of dissent. In the late nineteenth century, *Harper's* became a literary battlefield on which was waged the struggle to define both the general parameters and the specific features of idealized middle-class American belief and behavior, with domesticity at its heart.

Thus, even though Stoddard herself did not enjoy tremendous popularity in her own day, her fiction appeared regularly within a favorite and influential literary context, among that of many other contributors whose works we have studied in order to understand, however incompletely, nineteenth-century domestic discourse. Although a few of her *Harper's* stories have garnered scholarly attention and even been anthologized, the majority of Stoddard's short fiction has been consigned to obscurity. I would argue that one reason we have not reckoned with very much of Stoddard's fiction is that our discipline's conceptualization of American women and domesticity has in the past made no room for Stoddard's vision of this relationship.[14] The separate spheres paradigm that, as Cathy Davidson has recently argued, has been for the past twenty-five years both "immediately compelling and [yet] ultimately unconvincing as an explanatory device," has so permeated our critical conversations about nineteenth-century American letters that we have been unable to wrangle with the complexities of a literature that does not fit the narrow model wherein women write about a somewhat transparent private sphere, and men write about a seemingly much more complicated public sphere of experience (444).[15]

However, our discipline has lately launched a new rallying cry, that there be "no more separate spheres!" for nineteenth-century male and female authors, no more forced separation between "public" and "private" lives that were, in fact, complexly intertwined.[16] Gillian Brown's *Domestic Individualism* (1990), to which I have already referred, as well as Lora Romero's *Home Fronts* (1997) and Monika M. Elbert's collection, *Separate Spheres No More: Gender Convergence in American Literature, 1830–1930* (2000), all recognize the need for literary scholarship to take what Linda Kerber has called "an interactive view of [the] social processes" wherein public and private intersect (*Toward an Intellectual History* 171). Recently, critics have returned to fundamental texts like Kerber's *Women of the Republic* (as well as Nina Baym's *Woman's Fiction* and *American Women Writers and the Work of History, 1790–1860*) and found there early germs of thought about separate spheres ideology that suggest this binary model was indeed more "metaphorical" than "actual," more expressive of a desire for codes and rules in a chaotic and changing world than of any real, deep, permanent divisions between male and female life (Baym, *American Women Writers* 11). My goal is to engage that spirit of inquiry, to explore Stoddard's nuanced, resonant, and uniquely voiced short fiction, in order to probe further the complicated notions of domesticity with which she contended.

To best explore Stoddard's revision of domesticity in the *Harper's* stories, I focus first on a small group of the stories that cohere around characters involved in typical domestic plots and settings. Figuratively, the characters are "coming home," converging as they are around familiar domestic tropes such as courtship, marriage, the homestead, and female family ties. The second half of my discussion centers around characters more consciously and deliberately challenging domestic concerns by breaking away from the domestic space and the roles that would seem to inhere in them. These women want to see the world beyond the hearth and to try on new roles and identities; thus, in a manner of speaking, they are "leaving home." There is, of course, some overlap. Rather than creating artificially rigid divisions between stories that take place in the home or outside of it, and thereby repeating the false division between public and private space, I mean for this looser partitioning to foreground the dynamic relationship, the attraction and the repulsion, that Stoddard magnifies between her female characters and her culture's ideas about women's proper relationship to domestic life. By illuminat-

ing the different ways that particular characters negotiate their relationships to both a domestic space and to the roles they are expected to play
therein, the categories of "home coming" and "home leaving" help us
zero in on the interactions that Stoddard arranges between fictional
conventions and social norms, on the one hand, and her female characters' more deeply ambivalent behaviors and attitudes toward domesticity,
on the other.

HOME COMING

Let us consider, for example, Stoddard's treatment of the broad domestic
theme of marital union. Although many of her stories involve courtship
and end with the promise of wedding vows, Stoddard frequently under-
mines her own conventional endings by resolving problems between
lovers too suddenly, by creating highly questionable or overly insular
marriage partnerships (between in-laws or cousins, for example), or by
otherwise making such resolutions and partnerships implausible. In
"The Chimneys," for example, the proud but poor Ruth Bowen twice
rejects the proposals of Ezra Clark, a young man who has repaired the
once-failing farm he inherited from his father and earned a respectable
profit from his efforts. Despite the seeming compatibility that their
similar financial circumstances and upbringing would suggest—for both
of their families struggle to maintain a slippery middle-class status—
Ruth refuses Ezra because she secretly hopes to marry a man more
"genteel," whose "hands were white, his clothes always fashionable"
(731). Indeed, she finds Ezra—along with his slattern mother and those
eponymous chimneys that stand out against the sky to demarcate the
Clarks' ill-furnished and ill-kept house—"hateful," because he seems to
signify a resolute acceptance, so repulsive to Ruth, of being stuck on
society's lower rungs (726). The story's main conflict resides in the tension Stoddard creates between Ruth's longing to claim "equality with
the highest" and Ezra's contrary determination to remain a farmer—to
"twist and screw a profit from the mean acres" he owns—while also
making Ruth his wife (727 and 728, respectively). Throughout much of
the story, there appears to be no hope for reconciliation between this
pair and their antithetical desires.

In the end, however, after detailing at length the reasons Ruth would
continue to hold out for a man of greater wealth and social standing,
Stoddard portrays Ruth quite unexpectedly imagining Ezra as her husband. "Fancies of a well-regulated house for him flitted through her

mind. How much might she accomplish with her ability, industry, and neatness toward making him a prosperous man she could not help reckoning. And what would he not do for her . . . ! She and her mother could turn him round their little fingers if they chose" (732).

It is crucial that Ruth glides easily from imagining a well-regulated house to imagining Ezra as her well-regulated mate. The idea of becoming Ezra's wife is more attractive to Ruth when she thinks of him as malleable, just as easily managed as the house they will inhabit together. Later, meeting by chance on a road between their homes, Ruth and Ezra have a conversation that concludes the story although it does not satisfactorily resolve the tensions Stoddard has been cultivating: " 'Do you feel any different?' he asked at length. She meant to say 'No,' and that she 'never should;' but all at once she felt how lonely the road was; how lonely the world might be, and how deep the 'gloaming' which would surround her. She gave a little gasp and looked up at him. His arm was round her waist like lightning. His shirt-sleeves were rolled up, and barley straws were sticking in his hat, but she returned his kiss" (732). Despite the fact that theirs is "a very unequal match"—that Ruth dreams of fostering in Ezra a gentlemanly appearance, although the man she embraces wears rolled up shirt-sleeves and barley in his hat—Ruth and Ezra do marry, and there their story ends (732).

Stoddard's tale may seem, at first glance, to present an unskilled author's exercise in creating tension, and one that frustratingly abandons that tension rather than bringing about closure or resolution for the reader. Yet as Timothy Morris has rightly perceived, the lack of closure in this and other of Stoddard's stories consistently marks her efforts to comment on the "inadequacy . . . of any fiction to deal with" complicated issues like marriage (39) or "the truth about men and women" more generally. I agree that Stoddard's stories critique the endings that close so many nineteenth-century domestic fictions with pat resolutions unlikely to occur in real life. However, it is equally important to recognize that Stoddard's criticisms and subversions are more than just reactionary and do more than simply point up the ways such fiction *doesn't* work. Indeed, Stoddard also makes her stories operate proactively, striking at the heart of the debate over the purported dichotomy between public and private to reveal *why* such resolutions are as unlikely to satisfy readers as they are to actually happen: the difference between her characters' private motivations and their public actions create too wide a gulf to be bridged, not only in fiction but also in life.

Look, for example, at the two main events that precipitate the sudden and improbable ending of "The Chimneys." First is Ruth's daydream of manipulating Ezra and bending him to her and her mother's will. Second is the difference Stoddard records between what Ruth *meant* to say to Ezra and what she actually *does* express: although Ezra perceives in Ruth the acquiescence he has so long awaited, he does not suspect that she is inwardly still rejecting him and plotting his total transformation. Stoddard's narrative method at the story's conclusion reproduces the disparity between Ruth's secret thoughts and her other, more openly expressed sentiments. Following Ruth and Ezra's kiss, the reader is told (not shown) that "they were married" (732). Thus swinging abruptly from prose that offers the reader a privileged view inside Ruth's mind to prose that thrusts us, all at once, outside of her emotions and even away from the scene of action, Stoddard not only reveals the internal and external sides of this exchange between Ruth and Ezra but also makes us feel the gulf (and the dissatisfaction that there exists such a gulf) between the public and private worlds of her characters.[17]

Too, in this story, Stoddard defeats the equation of tidy houses with tidy hearts and well-managed interior lives. Ruth and her mother may *appear* to be middle class, but they are not. Widowed at thirty, when Ruth was just six years old, Mrs. Bowen had to "cast about . . . for means to live by"; they survive together by taking in sewing and by the neighbors' goodwill handouts. Still, "Mrs. Bowen turned her gifts and money to so good an account that it was difficult to remember their origin always; her pride assimilated what was originally foreign so thoroughly, that no soul would have dared to remind either Ruth or herself of the fact, or played the part of 'Indian Giver' with them." Mrs. Bowen and Ruth, therefore, live in a patchwork house, created from the goods that others have donated, and yet they have gone to such lengths to appear to others as though their own "neatness and good taste" have chosen the goods in their home that they have forgotten the fact that they are truly poor (728).

On the other hand, the Clarks may look disheveled and impoverished, but Ezra's industriousness has secured for himself, his mother, and his future wife quite a good deal of wealth. The Clark homestead "was not a model farm": "Its buildings were without paint and white-wash; tumbling stone-walls and fences of crooked rails divided its ground into cornfields, potato patches and pasture. . . . [Yet the] farm cleared between three and four hundred dollars a year, which was nearly all saved. . . . consequently, [Ezra] was now worth about two thousand dollars" (728). Ezra manages his farm and his money well, but not his own appearance, nor the appearance of his home. Nevertheless, he desires Ruth for her "elegant precision," so unlike his mother's domestic "disorder and confusion," and he is determined to have her (729). After Ruth rejects him upon his first proposal, Ezra asserts himself: "'I am . . . a suitable husband for you. We both earn our living. Our mothers have to labor. I will take care of your mother in her old age. She never need make another shirt; but you would have to work and help me.'" Ruth, mortified, argues that she could "never dream of such a husband as you," and yet we know in the end that she *does* dream of such a husband as he and will likely "assimilate" the idea so thoroughly, as her mother is able to do, that she will forget her initially vehement opposition to taking Ezra as her husband (731). What Stoddard shows us in this match between Ruth and Ezra is how little the material space of one's home can display one's financial acumen or disarray, one's emotional empowerment or vulnerability. Moreover, she implies that it is one thing to impose one's will upon inanimate objects like fences or stone walls and another entirely to impose one's will upon another human being: Ruth may imagine, against all evidence, that she and her mother will "turn him round their little fingers," but Stoddard has shown us that Ezra is a determined individual, not likely to be managed by Ruth or anyone else. The reader, at least, knows that Ruth and Ezra will have a difficult road ahead if they continue to imagine that their spouses are like a home, as easy to divide and conquer as rooms of a house or patches of farmland.

This story comprises an important part of Stoddard's extended critique of the typical nineteenth-century fictional portrayal of married life, wherein marriages governed or arranged according to social ideas about propriety—and especially what is appropriate for women to reveal or disclose to their spouses—will ultimately fail and dissatisfy. As Sandra Zagarell has astutely observed, many of Stoddard's stories "call attention to the cultural work which both heterosexual romance and romance plots perform. They highlight the way romantic love directs women to their 'proper' places in the culture and also the ways in which the plots of fiction translate women's concern with issues such as self-realization, creativity, and power into matters of the heart" (Introduction 27). I would add that Stoddard's interest in the complex relationship between the external and internal sides of married life highlights, too, the ways in which plots of fiction tend to oversimplify and flatten the interior lives of their characters, rejecting the inner contradictions that occur so naturally and so often in real life. In "The Chimneys" as well as "Gull's

Bluff" (1865), "The Inevitable Crisis" (1868), and "The Prescription" (1864), Stoddard portrays marriages whose public faces are unmarred but whose private sides reveal some pretty shaky foundations. Designed to foreground the ways that traditional, unexamined domestic discourse can drive a wedge between women's private thoughts and public actions, these stories all develop two identities for each of their main characters, one visible and one invisible, with the climax of each story estranging these identities from each other. Stoddard leaves the reader to puzzle over how and if these characters might close the gap. In other words, she asks us to deliberate over the validity and strength of marriages that look smooth on the surface but have joined and bound two individuals who seem to know little of themselves and even less of each other.

Other of Stoddard's stories employ tales of female community that similarly urge readers to question the accuracy of this ubiquitous nineteenth-century fictional trope to represent real relationships between women and the so-called female world. While much of nineteenth-century women's fiction does suggest that female relatives and women of like circumstance would provide one another with generous emotional support through life's difficulties, Stoddard frequently engages her female characters in competitive and catty behavior or shows women using their (usually younger and prettier) female relatives as pawns in a game of social and economic ladder-climbing.[18] Creating intimate relationships that are not necessarily *friendships,* Stoddard imagines a female world not only of "love and ritual"—that fine mortar and linen, again—but also of animosity, pettiness, and selfishness.[19] As Carroll Smith-Rosenberg has argued, female-female relationships "existed in a larger world of social relations and social values. . . . To interpret such friendships more fully, one must relate them to the structure of the American family and to the nature of sex-role divisions and of male-female relations, both within the family and in society generally" (54). Now that our understanding of the nature of sex-role divisions, of male-female relations, and of "society generally" have changed with our reappraisal of the spheres, how are we to respond to the nineteenth-century portrayal of relationships among women? How are we to theorize female relationships in fiction now that we can finally imagine women's lives to have been conducted not strictly in the so-called private sphere but in simultaneously public and private spaces, between simultaneously public and private selves?

Stoddard's answer to these questions lies particularly in the development within her stories of duplicitous female characters whose unpleasant private agendas emerge from underneath their more agreeable public faces. Her 1868 story "The Visit," for example, tells of a social call paid by nineteen-year-old Maria and her money-hungry aunt to the aunt's wealthy and eccentric brother-in-law.[20] Aunt Susan is anxious that her dead sister's husband will cease to welcome her into his home unless she is accompanied on her midsummer visit by a young and beautiful marriage prospect for him. Loathe to relinquish the financial and social benefits of remaining within her brother-in-law Mr. Edford's favor and, thus, his social circle, she confesses a desire to make herself "welcome to him, by taking a fresh, attractive girl, my niece Maria," to his house and thus reordering his domestic space (803). Upon their arrival at Edford's house, Maria learns (as does Stoddard's reader) that other pairs of older and younger women have been hatching the same plan as her aunt: a Mrs. Marsh and her daughter Emily are also among the guests at Edford's home, similarly hoping to secure a marriage proposal from the recently widowed man of the house. When Maria realizes that her aunt desires to pawn her off on Mr. Edford, she defiantly declares that she will not be managed like so many household goods (808, also 805). In the end, though, Maria and Mr. Edford do fall in love and decide to marry, both events suggesting Maria's independence and free will since she has first refused her aunt's matchmaking scheme and then established a connection with Edford of her own accord. The tale concludes, however, in a private interview between niece and aunt wherein Maria announces her impending marriage to Edford. Aunt Susan's odd reply— she says only, "Brother Edford is a peculiar man—a very peculiar man" —signals again both her overt and covert motives for marrying off her niece to her brother-in-law and makes clear that the aunt's desire (to please the bizarre Mr. Edford) has outstripped her niece's volition by reinstating Susan's agenda as the primary driving force behind her and Maria's journey (808). Despite the couple's genuine and mutual attraction, they are nonetheless manipulated for Susan's financial gain; her personal and self-serving motives are inextricable from their intimate relationship. Stoddard explores here the sneaking influence women can exert over one another's lives, and to the extent that Susan is successful, Stoddard would seem to lament that there is not *more* of a separation between women in families.

Aunt Susan's relationship to the domestic spaces of this story makes her an especially intriguing and illuminating figure. No hearth-bound matriarch herself, Susan is, instead, a hanger-on, a kind of domestic parasite whom we never see within the context of her own home but who descends upon other people's houses (her sister's, her brother-in-law's) to disrupt and rearrange their very lives. Susan travels to the domestic spaces of her family members as though she is going to market; she is both a consumer of goods (enjoying Brother Edford's luxurious home, meals, and entertainments) and a dealer or merchant, competing with other merchants (like Mrs. Marsh) to sell their wares—in this case, young beauties like Maria and Emily—for profit. And yet, it is crucial to Stoddard's story that Maria and Susan arrive at Brother Edford's during a storm, when all in the house is confusion, and Edford himself lies injured on the floor of his home, recovering after having been thrown by a storm-startled horse. Aunt Susan, the formerly steely and determined deal broker, faints dead away when she sees Edford harmed: perhaps she fears that his injury will get in the way of her matchmaking, or that Maria will not stoop to conquer a disabled and much older suitor. Stoddard does not dwell on the reason for Susan's faint, but we can surely read it as a foreshadowing of her eventual disempowerment in the setting of Edford's home. Indeed, it is hard not to read Susan's swooning as an effect of being overwhelmed by the number of contradictory roles she herself has taken on at Edford's: inside a relative's home, Susan is expected to be emotional, affectionate, and sisterly. Edford's injuries especially demand these responses. However, by her own agenda, Susan is also expecting to play the part of the matchmaker, to be businesslike, competitive, aggressive, and even greedy.

Stoddard suggests that the collapse of boundaries between public and private space that Susan herself insists upon can be devastating to women who do not know or have not learned to control and manage these multiple, even conflicting, identities and roles. Domestic spaces, so often the scenes of both private drama and public (in the sense of "shared") emotional spectacle, require that women learn to partition themselves and so maintain order over the many roles they want to play. Just as she did in her portrayal of married life, Stoddard thus represents even relationships between women in families as an intimacy between strangers. "Female community" may, in fact, be a misnomer for the relationships between the women in most of her stories, although it is clear that Stoddard means for these portraits to represent the bonds of womanhood faithfully, delineating as they do the mercenary motivations that stand alongside more congenial and disinterested bases for female friendship. Even while she adheres to the conventions of domestic fiction that attend so many of her peers' female community plots—having them encourage one another's romantic yearnings (in such stories as "Tuberoses" [1863] and "A Partie Carée" [1862]) or *act* as benefactresses and mentors (as in "Lemorne *versus* Huell" [1863], "Polly Dossett's Rule" [1890], and "A Wheat-field Idyl" [1891])—again and again Stoddard reveals the hidden, rotting beams beneath the polished, pretty mortars of female life.[21] Sisters and friends compete for men; mothers and aunts pimp their daughters and nieces for money and property and thwart their romantic hopes out of jealousy and spite. Relationships in the woman's sphere have their public and private sides, too, and the so-called female world is no more or less able to shelter women from manipulation, greed, or economic concerns than is its male counterpart.

What these tales reveal, ultimately, is Stoddard's ambivalent vision of nineteenth-century domestic discourse. The stories speak to her admiration and respect for the struggles women wage, internally and invisibly, regarding the power of their marriages to shape their identities. Her insistence, furthermore, on revealing all of the insidious negotiations that undergird marriage and the various forms of sisterhood helps her expose the lie in social conventions that idealized the transparency and the supposedly salvific qualities of the private sphere and the female world. Her marriages may seem peaceful on the surface, but they are always arenas for a bitter war—not so much between the sexes but between the public and private thoughts and feelings of husbands and wives. Stoddard asks us not to reconcile private feelings and public behavior so much as to perceive the disparity between them and to recognize, too, the cultural interdictions that disable women from acting as they feel. Her female-female relationships similarly immerse readers in an atmosphere of trust *and* betrayal, of self-sacrifice *and* self-aggrandizement. These mixed messages are part and parcel of Stoddard's revision of domestic fiction, her effort to lay bare the whole truth about intimate life, the "flower" and its "ugly root."

HOME LEAVING

Given what we have seen in her marriages and sororal "friendships," is it any wonder that so many of Stoddard's female characters choose to leave their domestic spaces, wherein are housed so many failing, if true, kinship systems? If, as Nina Baym has argued, " 'home' is not a space" so much as a "system of human relations," what it ultimately means for female characters to *leave* home is that they can escape—or try to escape—systems of human relations like those just described (*Woman's*

Fiction [1978] 49). More than half of Stoddard's *Harper's* stories (ten, to be exact, including some we have already examined) feature girls or women who leave their domestic spaces for a variety of reasons and under a number of different circumstances. As one character observes: "We were all in search of something we lacked at home. Changing the air and situation, we might meet it" ("Love Will Find Out the Way" 567). That "something we lacked" differs from story to story; however, the ten tales can be placed into three rough categories according to what the girl or woman who has left home is seeking. In one handful of stories, for example, Stoddard's female characters depart from home in search of solitude. Moving toward isolated locations where they will have time and space to heal from illness and grief, or to reflect on their own lives without the pressure to look after various family members, the women in "Collected by a Valetudinarian," "The Prescription" (1864), and "Osgood's Predicament" (1863) remove themselves from their regular domestic surroundings and from the system of relationships that crowd in upon them there. In a second possible grouping of stories, including "Lemorne *versus* Huell," "The Inevitable Crisis," "A Wheat-Field Idyl," and "The Visit" (1868), women uproot themselves in search of economic stability or upward mobility. Financially threatened by the positions they find themselves in at home—they are parentless or without work, prospects, or property—each of these women departs from her familiar domestic setting, hoping to secure gainful employment or an inheritance that will stabilize her position in the world.[22] Yet a third group collects a number of picaresque women seeking the excitement and adventure that they could not normally experience at home. Wanting to enlarge their knowledge of the world and to temporarily escape the monotony of their lives, in "Lucy Tavish's Journey" (1867) and "Love Will Find Out the Way" (1882)—two stories we will examine here—as well as a second story titled "The Visit" (1872), Stoddard's heroines travel either alone or in company to places they have never before visited.

Given the particular span of time across which Stoddard penned her *Harper's* tales, it is tempting to seek in these stories a chronological march toward female liberation from the domestic space. Indeed, Stoddard's preoccupation with leaving home is itself a signal of her importance as a writer whose career spanned the larger cultural shift between what we have come to know as the Cult of True Womanhood in the 1850s to the Era of New Womanhood in the 1890s. During this period, American girls' and women's relationships to the domestic space changed utterly, and Stoddard's *Harper's* stories do much to suggest reasons why women abandoned their "proper" place and lit out for a wider or alternate sphere, even if they left home only temporarily (as for school, convalescence, or a brief vacation). Taking place in intimate settings apart from the girls' own homes—for most are borrowed, like the houses of family members being visited for vacation, or those that have been converted to hotels, inns, and places of convalescence—the stories situate female characters in a new relation to themselves and to their very notions of privacy, public life, domesticity, and convention. As such, they can help us understand Stoddard's view of how the discourse of domesticity traveled *with* nineteenth-century females, shaping female behavior inside and outside the home.

As it turns out, a chronological view of the stories does *not* reveal a neat, linear, ever-forward movement away from the domestic constraints of the mid–nineteenth century and toward some more public stage of American female life at the century's end. Rather—and, I believe, just as significantly—it reveals what we might think of as a series or circuitry of roads, leading not *away* from home so much as *between* home and the larger world. The difference is crucial: this latter perspective of home leaving allows for communication and comparison between a woman's own domestic space and a variety of other spaces, giving Stoddard's characters, and us, an occasion to rethink how public and private selves intersect or diverge when the stage upon which a woman finds herself is always, in some sense, not private, not familiar, not her own. Perhaps because their notions of public and private selfhood are so strongly shaped by their domestic identities *inside* their own homes (where they are saddled with the responsibilities of acting always as mothers, wives, and/or sisters), many of Stoddard's female characters find themselves empowered by leaving. Away from the regulatory influence of the parental or conjugal homestead, they have an opportunity to achieve some distance from the social values they would have internalized and must exhibit at home. Those cardinal virtues of True Womanhood that Barbara Welter has so crucially identified as key to the public performance of femaleness—piety, purity, submissiveness or self-sacrifice, and domesticity—can finally be examined as the masks and accessories that they are rather than as facets of an authentic female personality.[23] By extension, being away from home allows Stoddard's females to truly participate in domestic *discourse,* to step momentarily outside of the familiar domestic space in which they are most powerfully influenced and shaped by cultural prescription, and thus to imagine ways they might alter, subvert, or contradict those customs. Home leaving, as we shall see, affords Stoddard's women a distance from their most accustomed and least-examined assumptions about domestic life and social convention. Of course, leaving their own local domestic situations is never an escape from domestic discourse in any broad, general sense but is, instead, a temporary reprieve from the immediate pressures of lived domesticity and, thus, an occasion to engage more deeply and consciously in a process of self-fashioning. Leaving home empowers many of Stoddard's characters with a *choice* either to maintain or to alter their affinities to the larger network of relationships they have come to know.[24]

The stories I examine here center on female characters motivated to travel primarily by their desires for adventure and freedom from their monotonous lives at home. Both "Lucy Tavish's Journey" and "Love Will Find Out the Way" present plucky heroines whose active and willful engagement with the world away from home offers them a potentially more satisfying reward and a deeper reconciliation of public and private selfhood than is experienced by perhaps any other female characters ever to appear in Stoddard's fiction. Still, although they depart from home explicitly to escape the mundane rituals of their lives and to gain firsthand knowledge of a larger world they had only heard or read about, these picaresque women are ultimately attracted again to the homes and domestic scenarios that once repelled them. Having tasted the unaccustomed thrill of freedom, they ultimately come to appreciate and desire the familiar confines of their own homes (this is certainly *more* true of Lucy Tavish, as we shall soon see, than of Ellen Chandon, Lucy's counterpart in "Love") and are, therefore, some of Stoddard's most compelling and provoking characters, fusing their conflicting desires to flee from and remain within the domestic space.

Preparing to settle down to a career and a life in the town where she was born and raised, eighteen-year-old Lucy Tavish wants to see something of the world. Though her family lacks the funds to send Lucy on an extravagant journey, her father manages to scrape up the money for a ticket and traveling clothes and plans to send Lucy by train to visit his estranged brother. The trip will give Lucy her much-sought-after adventure, and it may, too, reunite her father and uncle. Lucy looks forward to a journey that will enable her to convey "information" her friends can only receive "at second-hand" and to build up a store of memories, "the precious treasures of a past not to be repeated" (657). Importantly, she envisions a home-leaving endeavor that will unite and enrich both her private and her public selves: the trip will add to her experience, education, and memory and will amplify her sense of herself as an individual who has left town and seen something of the world. At the same time, such a journey will "elevate her plane above that of her associates and scholars" who cannot afford to travel, giving her the bragging rights and the very public identity of a person who has chosen to leave home, to return, and to tell all about it (657).

Having firmly established Lucy's many reasons for leaving, Stoddard just as steadily articulates the procedure by which the girl's path away from home will ultimately lead her right back where she started. Lucy's journey by train—that movable town—awakens her "to a bewildering sense of an outside world" into which she dreams of asserting herself (660). Lucy is perplexed, however, by the train's deceptive appearance of community, "the sudden, inevitable, and unlooked-for relations . . . whose bonds would [nevertheless] fly asunder at the first glimpse of the destined station" (660). Unable either to perceive a stable community or to articulate a consistent and authentic selfhood that will serve her in the ever-changing social environment of the train, Lucy unavailingly seeks help from other female passengers, whose indifference to her plight makes them seem to her like "veiled crinoline statues" (661). Confused and discomposed for most of her journey, Lucy, it seems, will hardly be able, once she returns home, to assert her claim to the bragging rights she so dearly covets.

In an analogy to the inner tumult she experiences, Lucy's train is derailed by a tornado, and she is thrown headlong into the arms of a man with whom she has recently been chatting. He is able to quickly calm and acclimate her to their surroundings; they fall instantly, passionately in love with each other before he—a doctor, it so happens—valiantly attends to the wounds of the injured passengers. In the end, we are not surprised that this stranger can restore Lucy's sense of the familiar: he turns out to be Dr. John Tavish, Lucy's cousin and the son of the uncle she is headed to meet. "Lucy's mission was accomplished," Stoddard writes in the story's final lines; "She never performed a second journey like that, which ended with her entering her uncle's house as his son John's cousin, and leaving it as his wife" (663). And while Lucy herself does not seem to mind that the world away from home (though not the passage *through*) almost exactly mirrors the home she left, Stoddard would appear to be asking her readers to gauge the value of separate public and private spheres for someone like Lucy, whose own personal aspirations and identity are so bound up in those prefabricated by her social class as to neutralize any potential difference between the two.

Despite leaving home, Lucy Tavish is tethered to a life wherein her

public and private selves are too closely knit to ever afford her any res-
pite from either one. Reinstated once again as Lucy Tavish—daughter,
cousin, and, finally, wife—she has achieved both a public or formal
(Mrs.) and a renewed private identity; yet like the cramped train car she
rides in, "there [would be] no room in it to reflect further" on the difference or the similarity between them (662). Lucy is never able to re-
place the system of human relationships that she finds in her parents'
house with any other or significantly different system of human relationships. In effect, she has not left home at all, and upon her marriage
to John Tavish, we can expect that she never will.[25]

In contrast, Stoddard's "Love Will Find Out the Way" portrays a *real*
home leaving, wherein the young Ellen Chandon is given both a new
social context and a correspondingly novel physical space in which she
can fashion a fresh personal identity. Stoddard is deliberate and explicit
when drawing attention to the many ways that Ellen can be said to leave
home. First, Ellen accompanies her father and sister to Mrs. Bassett's hotel, seeking an "absence of ceremony"—an absence, that is, of middle-
class domestic propriety—which she "hate[s]" but "must practice" at
home (567). Second, Ellen shirks protocol by falling in love with one of
the hotel's "help," Mrs. Bassett's brother, John; the socioeconomic difference between them further enables Ellen to spurn the usual class boundaries that have enforced her sense of identity through an affinity with
her social equals. Ellen is empowered by her new surroundings to dis-
obey her father's particular wishes that she socialize and marry within
her class and to flout social conventions more generally. To magnify the
importance of these surroundings, Stoddard sets the story's climax away
from the hotel, when a sightseeing tour catches Ellen, John, the narrator,
and the hotel's other guests on a hilltop in the middle of a terrifying
electrical storm:

> One prolonged flash of lightning, which ringed and illuminated
> the entire horizon, revealed to us a strange picture. John and Ellen
> stood against a tree. He held her shawl over her head; their faces,
> pale and serene, were turned toward each other; in hers was a rapt
> expression not to be mistaken; her eyes, brilliant and burning, de-
> voured his, asking him for his heart, his life, and he gave them to
> her with a wonderful peace. He bent over her and kissed her lips;
> her hands were clasped about his arm. Then pitch-darkness fell
> again; but we all saw the kiss, and felt it, or was it the electric chain
> of the lightning which bound us in a spell? (572)

Crucial to Ellen and John's love is the support they get from the traveling party, who, as it is expressed by the narrator, all together witness, feel,
and are bound into a new community by this kiss. More stable than the
series of affective ties that are temporarily formed and then broken on
Lucy's train ride in the earlier story, the party on the hilltop provides a
new social context that grounds the forming couple within a simultaneously human and natural setting and that reflects to Ellen her newly
formed vision of herself. She is a woman who asserts her own will,
rather than a girl who succumbs to her father's orders. Furthermore, although she will marry (and, thus, participate in an "approved" female
pursuit), Ellen has chosen a mate based on their mutual love and understanding and according to no one else's wishes.

Through Ellen, Stoddard demonstrates that home leaving is not necessarily a total departure from domestic *discourse* (indeed, the courtship
and marriage plot tether this story to the tradition of domestic fiction).
Rather, with the support of her social group—for that is the function of
the traveling party in this story and, significantly, the critical component
missing from Lucy's train ride—home leaving can help a female character stretch the boundaries of domestic discourse, to distort and misshape
them temporarily, before she inserts herself willfully inside their confining embrace. In other words, home leaving allows Ellen to negotiate
with the "ideological presumptions, institutional practices, and strongly
held habits of mind" that her culture has taught her about domestic life,
and to figure out how that external or public system of beliefs does or
does not meet her own internal knowledge of herself, her private desires, and her most intimate thoughts.

In comparing these two stories, we can perceive Stoddard's more
widely evinced conviction that domestic discourse is, in fact, entirely
malleable and yet too-little malleated. She repeatedly points toward her
culture's tendency to perceive domestic discourse as command: the climactic storms that are key features of both of these stories suggest the
fearsome power and destructiveness, the almost divinely imposed and
naturalized force that, for Stoddard, attend cultural interdictions about
women's domestic roles. Many of the characters view presumptions
about proper female behavior and expectations that women will maintain strict boundaries between public and private selfhood as intractable,
inflexible, and beyond intervention. And yet Stoddard demonstrates, as
well, that women themselves help to reify this perception, although they
might (and in her stories sometimes *do*) effectively challenge it. In her

home-leaving stories, Stoddard advocates that her readers temper their endorsement of domestic virtue through active participation in domestic discourse. She asks her audience to help create a social context that encourages women's vigorous and constant reappraisal of cultural values rather than demanding their obedience to the status quo. She presents a body of work, finally, that sustains and supports a process of female self-fashioning, even if not all of her characters (Lucy Tavish, for one example) are poised to accept that challenge or do not have adequate support systems in place to help them through the ordeal of making the shift. Without explicitly punishing or criticizing those female characters who are unsuccessful in breaking from powerful domestic attractions and restraints, Stoddard's fiction celebrates what attempts women *do* make to individually construct public and private identities within a harmonious whole self—one that includes both the rough laths and fine mortars that compose any living space and, metaphorically, any living person.

But what does Stoddard's particular revision of domestic fiction—her thorough look into the lining of things, and her subsequent appropriation of "public" and "private," not as spheres but as modes of behavior and selfhood—tell us regarding the connections between domestic fiction and domestic discourse? Stoddard's resistance to viewing the home as a transparent index of emotional and intellectual life is not an utter rejection of the home-as-symbol; instead, it is a manipulation of that symbol, a reassignment of meaning that accords with what the homes in her stories can and will display, what they will and will not *do* to shelter and support the characters that people her fiction. For Stoddard, home is most valuable as a locus for examining particular truths about men and women—the ways that they reveal or hide, from one another and themselves, their ability and willingness to live up to the identities they have created for themselves around their culture's exalted vision of domestic intimacy. She reiterates how her contemporaries romanticized the space of the home and idealized, too, the natal, sibling, and marriage relationships that were to unfold there, and she contrasts these notions of home and identity with what she has differently observed as the full, if dramatized, reality of these relationships. Stoddard's stories throw light on both the hidden and the more familiar aspects of domestic discourse—the conversation and the motives behind the conversation—to indicate that a space gets built in, between social prescription and individual longing, which reserves for a woman the right to choose what context most suits her at any given time.

There is ample evidence in her stories that Stoddard fully understood the fearsome impact that traversing (or even collapsing) public and private boundaries might have upon middle-class status and identity. Many of her characters obviously dread, just as her middle-class audience might, the loss of social and financial security they would experience upon losing the distinction between public and private spheres. Despite the potential for her readers' distress (and the possibility of her own subsequent professional failure), Stoddard doggedly interrogated the value of the public/private binary for her culture, for decades weighing its advantages and disadvantages. Her repeated assessment—that this dichotomy is more harmful than helpful, more metaphorical than actual, and that her society would be better off without it—may indicate yet another important reason why Stoddard's fiction found little popular support in her day. George William Curtis, Stoddard's editor throughout her career at *Harper's*, disdainfully attributed the success of other, more fashionable fiction writers to their willing accommodation of the concept of gendered spheres and the supposed separateness of those spheres: "What an intolerable deal of nonsense is talked and written and sung and, above all, preached about women, and their sphere, and what is feminine, and what isn't," he complained, pointing especially to the proliferation of rules, restrictions, and *writing* aimed at governing middle-class women's domestic lives (qtd. in Fischer 27, 30). At the same time, his comment reveals both a personal and a professional preference for writing like Stoddard's and does much to explain how it is that her fiction appeared in *Harper's* at all—in Stoddard's work, Curtis found a singularly weighty counterbalance to the heft of the more standard-fare domestic fiction he felt compelled to print.

Stoddard's version of domesticity, unlike that of her colleagues, reveals the need for women engaged in domestic discourse to actively and honestly *respond* to the social conventions that were outlined in domestic fiction and to confess to themselves both an attraction to and a repugnance for their traditional, housebound roles. To accomplish her goal of prompting others to interrogate both the truthfulness and the usefulness of labels like "public" and "private," Stoddard, as we have seen, often either conflates the two (making a family member's home, for example, into a marriage market and brokerage house) or holds them far apart (as when a character like Ruth Bowen exposes certain of her personal motives for marrying Ezra while hiding other, equally compelling motives from his view). Always blurring what might have once seemed simple and natural categories, Stoddard ultimately forces her readers to evaluate the aptness of public and private distinctions as we try to untangle and sort the behaviors of her characters and the spheres in which they are supposedly operating. Readers who longed for fiction to order and package the world into neat parcels must have found this intensive scrutinizing tiresome. I would posit, however, that this scrutiny lies at the heart of Stoddard's revision of domesticity: she never reaches a definition of domesticity per se, for that might halt the debate she so wants us to undertake. It is only by interrogating the assumptions a culture makes about the roles of its own most critical intimacies—between husbands and wives, parents and children, and all other familial combinations— that these central relationships can be reexamined, revived, and reconstrued.

Focused as they are on courtship, marriage, and female community, Stoddard's home-coming stories demonstrate how the pressure exerted upon women to embrace the public performance of their roles as wives and "sisters" also prevented women from attending to the cultivation and care of their more private identities. Far from being transparent creatures, Stoddard's characters are complex enough to strive toward cultural ideals of womanhood while simultaneously questioning why they are doing so in the first place. It is this complexity that makes Stoddard's women speak so resonantly and urgently to readers in our own time, if they did not in *hers*. In contrast, the home-leaving stories center on characters who have in some sense managed to step outside their system of human relations and who have, therefore, opportunities to begin the process of self-fashioning that Stoddard's home-coming protagonists could only dimly imagine. Making choices to be alone even in company, to support as a virtue female self-absorption, and to prize ambiguity and freedom in their lives, the women in Stoddard's home-leaving tales may not succeed entirely in breaking from domestic constraints; however, they may serve as models for the kinds of female characters we need to search out in other nineteenth-century fictions. In the *Harper's* stories as a body, Stoddard urges her readers, from the nineteenth century and from our own time, to embrace the ways that domestic life is different from (and, perhaps, uglier, rougher-hewn than) what traditional domestic literature has taught us to expect from nineteenth-century women. We may make it her particular and special legacy to prepare our own critical field for further encounters with such richly drawn characters as we, too, look more thoroughly into the lining of things.

NOTES

A number of people deserve my tremendous gratitude for their help and support during the writing and editing of this essay. I would like to thank Emily J. Orlando for her patient and wholehearted readership and for her numerous helpful ideas for revision. I appreciate also Ellen Weinauer and Rob Smith's wonderful editorial guidance, and I am grateful for their kind endorsement of my work. Finally, I want to thank my husband, Steven Victor Osterman Alves, whose support and constant championship has helped me to think through many an argument, refine many a page, and refuel my enthusiasm with the generous and seemingly inexhaustible gift of his own.

1. Although several scholars have written about individual short stories by Stoddard, only one has covered this subject with any breadth. Timothy Morris argues, in his "Elizabeth Stoddard: An Examination of Her Work as Pivot between Exploratory Fiction and the Modern Short Story," that Stoddard is a precursor to the women writers of the 1890s, such as Kate Chopin and Charlotte Perkins Gilman (35). Morris's claim that Stoddard's short fiction serves as a "pivotal point in an as yet largely unwritten history of the development of American modernism" centers around evidence that the stories frequently "explore the contradictions in American culture, presenting the same unresolved issues as later modernist works, but in a multivoiced narrative that presents contradictions without speaking *through* them" (35–36, emphasis in original). Morris's essay is especially valuable for its placement of Stoddard into a recognizable tradition of nineteenth-century feminist authorship that bridges sentimental and modernist fiction and for the ways that it demonstrates Stoddard's formal concerns and skills. However, Morris seems mainly interested in using Stoddard's work as an occasion to explore changes in the genre of the short story over time. In this essay I focus attention instead on Stoddard's preoccupations with the domestic space as a complex sphere in which people acted with "private" and "public" motivations.

I feel it is important to note here, too, that Morris erroneously cites Stoddard's 1860 "My Own Story" as Stoddard's first published fiction (34). Her January 1859 "Our Christmas Party" appeared almost a full year and a half before the May issue of the *Atlantic Monthly* that carried "My Own Story," and it is no more or less autobiographical. Other of Stoddard's stories that appeared during this year seem similarly based on the author's life; see, for example, "Uncle Zeb" in *Saturday Press* (25 Feb. 1860) and "One of the Days of My Life" in *Saturday Press* (precise number of issue unknown).

2. The "Suggestions for Further Reading" section of Lawrence Buell and

Sandra Zagarell's 1997 Penguin edition of *The Morgesons* lists as "significant" the dozen short stories that Stoddard published in *Harper's* between 1862 and 1870 (xxv). While it is true that this dozen constitutes Stoddard's best-written short fiction, and that the period between 1862 and 1870 also constitutes the apex of her literary career, I would like to make a case for reading all of the *Harper's New Monthly Magazine* stories (all future references to this periodical will use the shortened *Harper's*), as well as those published in other venues. Full citation information for all of Stoddard's *Harper's* stories is provided in this volume's list of works cited.

As James H. Matlack's invaluable but unpublished dissertation research indicates, Stoddard also published a large number of short stories in *The Aldine* (sixteen stories, with two under the pseudonym "Betsy Drew" and three under the pseudonym "Elizabeth B. Leonard") and the *Independent* (fifteen stories). She also contributed, although to a lesser degree, to *Hearth and Home* (four stories), *Appleton's Journal* (four stories), and a handful of other periodicals; many of these publications also carried Stoddard's poetry. Stoddard's letters refer, too, to additional writings no one has yet been able to locate; furthermore, since she published several pieces pseudonymously, and because her stories were never collected in one volume in her lifetime, we may never recover the entire body of her short fiction. See especially Matlack's exhaustive "Publication Check-list for Elizabeth Barstow Stoddard" in "The Literary Career of Elizabeth Barstow Stoddard" 625–31.

3. Due to space constraints, this essay cannot linger over Stoddard's fascination with children. Stoddard regularly acknowledged in her fiction conventional attitudes toward the young—particularly the widely held belief that female children are inherently pious and pure—only to delight in defying those conventions. Women who reminisce about their childhood days narrate several of her short pieces, reflecting with longing and nostalgia upon their youthful appetites, their self-absorption, their idleness, and their rebelliousness. See "Our Christmas Party" (Jan. 1859), "Unexpected Blows" (Dec. 1867), and "Love Will Find Out the Way" (Sept. 1882).

The relationship between male characters and the domestic space would present yet another interesting grouping of stories and could promote fruitful classroom discussions about the purported separation between males in the so-called public sphere and females in the private sphere. For Stoddard's stories that detail the lives of men at home and male participation in domestic discourse, see especially "Gull's Bluff" (July 1865), "The Chimneys" (Nov. 1865), "A Partie Carée" (Sept. 1862), and "Osgood's Predicament" (June 1863).

4. In her nonfiction column for the *Daily Alta California* (1854–58), Stoddard sometimes pronounced against what she saw as the tame or insipid writing style

and subject matter of contemporary female writers like Caroline Chesebro' and Ann Stephens, preferring the work of more feminist authors like Elizabeth Browning, George Sand, Margaret Fuller, and Charlotte and Emily Brontë. These citations are from her columns dated 22 October 1854 and 3 December 1855, respectively (Stoddard, *The Morgesons and Other Writings* 322, 314). See also the columns from 2 June 1855, 19 June 1855, and 3 August 1856, all of which are also reproduced in *The Morgesons and Other Writings*.

5. Elizabeth Stoddard, "Collected by a Valetudinarian," *Harper's* Dec. 1870: 96–105. All further parenthetical citations refer to this original printing of Stoddard's story. Stoddard's own journal and private writings provided much of the text for Alicia's diary in "Collected by a Valetudinarian." See "Journal, 1866," in Stoddard, *The Morgesons and Other Writings* 347–57.

6. A great number of scholars have identified what they consider these tenets to be, and not all critics agree on a particular set of defining characteristics. Nevertheless, Nina Baym's *Woman's Fiction* remains an important reference point and springboard.

7. I refer to Brown's *Domestic Individualism*. See especially chapter 1, "Domestic Politics in *Uncle Tom's Cabin*" (13–62), for a discussion of how Harriet Beecher Stowe imagined a transparent relationship between domestic arrangements and "domestic politics."

8. See "Unexpected Blows" (Dec. 1867). See also Stoddard's 1890 story "Polly Dossett's Rule," which is similarly focused on the overbearing home management of Polly Dorsett (the name becomes Dossett under the New England accent of Stoddard's characters).

9. Nina Baym's "Women as Students of History," in her *American Women Writers*, draws this key distinction in asserting that "public and private spheres were metaphorical rather than actual places" and that "public and private were different ways of behaving in the same space" (11).

10. For more about the home as a microcosm of society, see Linda Kerber's *Women of the Republic*, especially chapter 9, "The Republican Mother: Female Political Imagination in the Early Republic" (265–88).

11. I focus on Stoddard's female characters, not because she was solely concerned with the truth about *women*, but because her attention to the ways that women participated in domestic discourse—shaping and responding to the notion of the home as a physical and ideological "space" *primarily* inhabited and controlled by women—is most revealing of the public and private dimensions of the relationships in which that home so centrally figures.

12. In "Hazards of New Fortune: *Harper's Magazine*, Then and Now," Lapham chronicles the rise and continuous success of *Harper's* magazine, from its founding through the end of the twentieth century. Lapham offers here an

overview of *Harper's* long and ever-changing relationship to American political and social life, as well as a detailed account of the ways that the publishers and a succession of editors altered the magazine's format and delivery—including, for example, the institution of the "Editor's Easy Chair" column under George Curtis in 1853 and of *Harper's Weekly* in 1857—to coincide with their personal views and with their perception of the periodical's place in American culture.

According to Lapham's article (and other histories of the magazine), that place was significant. Within the first six months of publication, *Harper's* had more than fifty thousand subscribers, its "clientele" being, in the words of John Fischer, "the governing class of the country—those people in the professions, industry, and public service who largely decided the issues and set the standards of taste for the rest of the population" (xv). Importantly, subscribers hailed from all regions of the United States—a fact that often affected how the magazine positioned itself politically; it remained fairly neutral, for example, on the issue of slavery, declaring equivocally on its back cover in June 1858 that "wise men and true patriots agree upon points far more numerous than those upon which they differ. The object of this magazine will be to unite rather than to separate the views and feelings of the people of different sections of our common country." *Harper's* attempts to be a homogenizing force in American culture certainly seems to apply to political as well as social issues: the predominance of the magazine's domestic fiction and, more specifically, the regular delineation and discussion of "public" and "private" on its pages suggest strongly that the editors of the magazine were conscious of its role as a mouthpiece for the middle class. See Fischer, *Six in the Easy Chair* xv–xix. For further discussion of American periodicals and issues of class, see Buell, "A Narrative Overview of New England's Literary Development" in *New England Literary Culture* (23–55).

13. Many critics have examined the traditions and tropes most common to American women's fiction—indeed, too many to be counted here. See, particularly, Baym's *Woman's Fiction* and Judith Fetterley's introduction to *Provisions: A Reader from Nineteenth-Century American Women,* which make contributions so important to the field that they remain reliable standards, despite their age. Susan K. Harris's *Nineteenth-Century American Women's Novels: Interpretive Strategies* (1990) and, most recently, Karen Tracey's *Plots and Proposals* (2000) have also taken up the task of defining and refining the way we think about and teach nineteenth-century women's writing.

14. In her excellent article on *The Morgesons,* Sandra Zagarell has argued similarly that "Stoddard's place in American literature has remained negligible primarily because readers have never known how to place her" ("Repossession" 45). Zagarell's essay anticipates my own assertions here that the relationship Stoddard draws between "female self-development" and domestic discourse at

once adheres to and "challeng[es the] reigning conventions of her own day" ("Repossession" 45–46).

15. See Cathy Davidson's "Preface: No More Separate Spheres!"

16. See especially Kerber's "Separate Spheres, Female Worlds, Woman's Place: The Rhetoric of Women's History," first published in 1988 and reprinted in *Toward an Intellectual History of Women* (159–99). Also important are Mary Ryan's *The Empire of the Mother,* especially her concluding chapter, "Dismantling the Empire of the Mother," and, more recently, her *Women in Public: Between Banners and Ballots, 1825–1880.*

17. See Buell's "Provincial Gothic: Hawthorne, Stoddard, and Others" in his *New England Literary Culture* (351–70). In his articulation of Stoddard's "provincial vision," Buell sees "always the [author's purposeful] intimation that" the "half-worlds" of her characters are "less than what is capable of being envisioned" (370). Buell's assessment corresponds with my own argument about Stoddard's women's lives being less than they could be. Buell's explicit subject in this essay is the gothic "motif of entrapment within the province" of New England that is so common to—and so wonderfully developed in—Stoddard's (and Hawthorne's) fiction; nevertheless, his formulation that Stoddard's "provincial gothic" takes its "impetus from the awareness of social change but" is "grounded in the premise that institutions and values resist change" applies equally to her interest in the institution of middle-class domesticity as it does to some of the more regionally specific institutions (like Calvinism and witchcraft) that Buell examines in her work (353, 358).

18. Certainly, Stoddard does occasionally portray women who are mutually helpful and kind. In "Collected by a Valetudinarian," for example, Eliza Sinclair is genuinely befriended by Helen Hobson. The two women, both alone and in poor health, seem to mend physically as their friendship develops and their intimacy deepens. In addition to their common health problems, Eliza and Helen also share an admiration for the deceased author, Alicia Raymond (she is, in fact, Helen's cousin); these three women—two sickly and one dead—constitute a kind of female community that flourishes and nurtures its members even though it is itself cut off from any outside nourishment. Ellen Weinauer's excellent article "Alternative Economies: Authorship and Ownership in Elizabeth Stoddard's 'Collected by a Valetudinarian'" argues convincingly that this insular female community closes off these women's access to the larger world—especially the world of commerce—and is ultimately "limiting" and "detrimental" to the writer that Weinauer sees at the center of the story, Alicia Raymond (168). I would argue that it is equally valid to place Eliza, the *other* writing woman, at the center of the story *with Alicia* (for Eliza, after all, does choose to make public the story of her own invalidism within her story about her expe-

riences with Alicia's diary); once we do, we may also be persuaded that Eliza's use of Alicia's diary, as a device that both connects her to and separates her from the larger world, gives her the kind of leverage she needs to construct and maintain both a public and a private self hood. Weinauer's assertion that Stoddard "explores the possibilities of a non-proprietary authorship that can lead to new artist/audience relations; [that] she attenuates the terrors of the marketplace by giving it a new, *familial* form," is, I think, a brilliant assessment, too, of the ways that the "community" of women in this story renegotiates female domesticity and sororal duty to their own individual benefit (168, my emphasis).

In another instance of female camaraderie, "Me and My Son" (1870) details the relationship between a young widow and her dead husband's cousin. The older woman helps the widow emerge from her mourning period and find new love (with the woman's own son, of course); the young widow helps nurse the elder woman back to health when she suddenly falls ill. Similarly, "Tuberoses" (1863) relates the story of a pair of sisters who conspire to set to rights the rather twisted marriage prospects in which they have found themselves entangled. More determined to honor each other's wishes than they are to get married, the sisters hold their suitors at bay until, eventually, the matches they desire can come to fruition. Especially important in these latter stories is the way Stoddard is able to foreground female community without abandoning males and marriage completely. In all of them, Stoddard claims for her female characters a level of intimacy that nourishes and sustains them through some of life's most difficult trials. See "Me and My Son" (July 1870) and "Tuberoses" (Jan. 1863).

19. I refer, of course, to Carroll Smith-Rosenberg's "The Female World of Love and Ritual," in *Disorderly Conduct* (53–76).

20. Elizabeth Stoddard, "The Visit," *Harper's* Nov. 1868. This story should not be confused with one of Stoddard's later *Harper's* stories of the same title; see "The Visit," *Harper's* Nov. 1872.

21. Of these stories, only "Lemorne *versus* Huell" has received any critical attention. One of Stoddard's best-known stories, "Lemorne" has been anthologized widely and has become a marker of Stoddard's skillful use of realism, evidence of her interest in subverting sentimental plotlines, and proof of her determination, almost before her time, to explore female sexuality and sexual imagery. Much has been made, furthermore, of Aunt Eliza's scheme to use her niece, Margaret, as a sexual pawn whose body she will exchange for money and property. Sandra Zagarell and Lawrence Buell have rightly noted that "Lemorne" subverts some of the "formulas of woman's fiction being employed straightforwardly elsewhere in the pages of *Harper's,*" satirically undercutting the happy ending of Margaret's marriage by revealing her shock and cynicism about her

husband's true character (Stoddard, *The Morgesons and Other Writings* 266). John B. Humma additionally argues that Stoddard's use of metaphor, symbolism, and realism throughout the story helps her to foreground sexual and financial power inequities in nineteenth-century marriages ("Realism and Beyond"). However, while each of these critics emphasizes the story's intimate male-female relationships, I would stress the female-female intimacy and dependency that is shared among Eliza, Margaret, and Margaret's mother in this story—a triangulation that speaks as well to Stoddard's interrogation of domestic discourse and the ways that discourse shaped notions of women's familial duty and self-abnegation. It is crucial to note, for example, that Margaret spends two months with her Aunt Eliza because her mother insists: "She thought it wise to cotton to her in every particular, for Aunt Eliza was rich, and we—two lone women—were poor" (537). Thus, although we do well to note Eliza's dishonesty, it does us no service to ignore Margaret's mother's conniving ways. She, too, is guilty of exploiting Margaret under the auspices of "what was expected in my two months' performance" of familial duty—a fact that is not lost on Margaret herself (538).

22. Although "A Wheat-field Idyl" (1891) is perhaps the most poorly organized and poorly written of Stoddard's published stories, it nevertheless importantly enlarges upon her interest in female property ownership and extends that portion of her career across which she explored women's abilities to alter their own economic status. In this late story, characters that initially seem key to the plot are completely dropped out by the middle of the tale; indeed, even the driving force of the story—the economic motive for the trip, in which an aunt and her niece travel to recover some farmland that once belonged to their family—seems forgotten in Stoddard's effort to once again marry off a female protagonist to another unsuitable male. And yet, it does seem significant that Stoddard took pains to write (and *Harper's* editor Curtis to publish) even this inferior piece of writing, especially because it involves two traveling women who, without the help of any male family members, set out to recover a financial investment that they feel rightfully belongs to them. Looking at all the stories mentioned here, we might fruitfully pursue a discussion of the ways that a woman's search to recover property or establish herself financially is enabled by (or even necessitates) her departure from the domestic space.

23. See Welter's pivotal "Cult of True Womanhood: 1820–1860" in *Dimity Convictions* (21–41).

24. For further discussion of American women's opportunities to cultivate an "authentic" individuality in the eighteenth and nineteenth centuries, see Kerber's excellent essay "Can a Woman Be an Individual? The Discourse of Self-Reliance" in her *Toward an Intellectual History of Women* (200–223). Kerber's focus is on the underlying gender assumptions inherent in concepts of Ameri-

can individualism, such as John Winthrop's understanding of the liberated American self that is free because it knows itself to be subject to authority, or, much later, R. W. B. Lewis's identification of stories about Americans in search of autonomy, all of whom are male and are, thus, referred to as American "Adams."

Kerber's essay usefully isolates the types of activities that gave women some room to cultivate their individual selves, and it is not surprising to find that those opportunities present themselves in some sense—albeit a very limited sense—away from the home: she names heightened religiosity, mysticism, and republican motherhood as the three main avenues through which women might have accessed "paths for self-fulfillment and an expression of personal independence" (207). I say that these activities take place in a *limited sense* away from the home because they all require an explicit acknowledgment of and connection to the more "public" world outside a single-family dwelling. Heightened religiosity required a connection to the church and a community of pious observers; mysticism also required a faith in a world beyond this one and demanded concentrated attention to "contemplation and private piety" (208). Even republican motherhood, with its emphasis on interpreting and instilling in one's sons the political ideals of the nation, asked women to look outside their own family's idiosyncratic sense of order and toward a larger national context. These experiences are none so radical as those Stoddard described, wherein women reject altogether, if only temporarily, household duties in order to tend to their own personal needs. Still, one might argue that these smaller steps away from the home that Kerber delineates were important precursors to the activities in which Stoddard's characters engage.

25. The plot device of the girl who physically leaves home and yet is unable to extract herself from the psychologically oppressive ties that bind her there is also a significant feature of Stoddard's 1862 novel, and one which I explore in great depth in my dissertation chapter "The Itinerant Schoolgirl and the Trappings of Home Education: Elizabeth Stoddard's *The Morgesons.*" Cassandra's several journeys in that novel, to schools distant from her parents' home, always land her in the domestic space of another family member, *and* in the romantic embrace of a male relative. The issues raised by such a plot device—especially the suffocating and incestuous relationship that it suggests exists between female education and domesticity—are interrogated more broadly and more fully throughout my dissertation project, "Miss Schooled: American Fictions of Female Education, 1800–1900" (in progress).

3
RACE, RECONSTRUCTION, AND
AMERICAN CITIZENSHIP

7

The "American Sphinx" and the Riddle of National Identity in Elizabeth Stoddard's *Two Men*

Jennifer Putzi

Although all three of Elizabeth Stoddard's novels were either written or published during the Civil War, no one has attempted to read any of these novels as responses to the war or related issues. James Matlack, Stoddard's biographer, goes so far as to say that Stoddard's interest in the war was more personal than political: "Once the war began, her major concern lay with relatives and friends who were in the armed forces, not with the moral or political principles at stake" ("Literary Career" 372). Yet Stoddard's discussion of racial prejudice and miscegenation in her second novel, *Two Men* (1865), demonstrates an interest in some of the most important political controversies of the Civil War era and can hardly be seen as an avoidance of "the moral or political principles at stake" in the war.[1] Using this discussion as my starting point, I would like to further politicize *Two Men*, linking it more firmly to the Civil War era in which it was written and published and simultaneously showing Stoddard to be a much more political writer than has heretofore been acknowledged. Such a politicization of Stoddard's work reveals a complex consideration of Civil War politics and national identity in *Two Men*, one that goes beyond national borders only to question their integrity.

Published in 1865, two months after the surrender of the Confederate army at Appomattox Courthouse, *Two Men* addresses issues of national identity that were brought to the forefront of American politics during the Civil War. The war years irreversibly complicated concepts of American identity that had once seemed beyond question. Who should be a citizen of the United States? What did citizenship mean? And what place did race, gender, class, and region have in these negotiations? As the war ended, it became essential for Americans to decide collectively who was, in fact, American and upon what that identity depended. As James H. Kettner writes, the Reconstruction period comprised "a major effort to resolve problems of allegiance that had long plagued the nation, to bring consistency of principle at last to the concept of American citizenship" (341). The Civil War ultimately "mark[ed] the inauguration of a single American identity" (Norton 7).

Stoddard's discussion of race and her depiction of an interracial relationship between Parke Auster and Charlotte Lang are essential to her participation in this discussion; as Anne Norton explains, "The recognition of the role—and the meaning—of those groups which are peripheral and 'other' to any given polity is essential to the demarcation of that polity's boundaries and to the comprehension of the content of the identity those boundaries define" (7). Yet in the case of *Two Men,* it is important to note that the African American characters are not the only figures whose American identity is called into question. Philippa Luce, Parke's cousin and the heroine of the novel, is also positioned as "half foreign," or of questionable national identity, and her "foreignness" is more than simply metaphorical.[2] Indeed, Philippa is the product of a relationship that crosses international and possibly interracial boundaries. Her alterity is just more difficult to recognize than that of Charlotte Lang, because nineteenth-century Americans and critics of nineteenth-century American literature have regarded American nationality as "a monolithic and self-contained whole, no matter how diverse and conflicted" (Kaplan 15). The "foreign" has been largely ignored in this equation.

In tracing my argument from Charlotte Lang to Philippa Luce, I am guided by critics such as Amy Kaplan and Donald Pease, who argue that American literature must be studied in an international context. According to Kaplan,

> The current paradigm of American studies today, still under intense debate, emphasizes multicultural diversity and scholarly "dissensus" and analyzes American society and culture in terms of internal difference and conflicts, structured around the relations of race, gender, ethnicity, and class. . . . Yet the new pluralistic model of diversity runs the risk of being bound by the old paradigm of unity if it concentrates its gaze only narrowly on the internal lineaments of American culture and leaves national borders intact instead of interrogating their formation. (14–15)

To focus only on the Langs in an interrogation of national identity in *Two Men* is, as Kaplan points out, to leave "national borders intact," even though Stoddard clearly directs her readers (and critics) to do otherwise.

WOLVES IN SHEEP'S CLOTHING

Two Men opens with the marriage of Jason Auster and Sarah Parke. The pair are ill-matched, as Jason is a carpenter who believes in "Socialism, Abolitionism, and Teetotalism" and Sarah is the granddaughter of the aristocratic Squire Parke (3). "The Parke family are next to the Lord, in this country," Jason's friend tells him before their marriage (4). Sarah's reasons for marrying Jason are not clear, but the disappearance of her cousin, Osmond Luce, seems to be a factor. Despite Sarah's love for him, Osmond has willfully distanced himself from the family, emotionally and geographically, exchanging the confines of Crest, a New England coastal town, for the unknown adventures available in South America. "The Squire sent him out in a vessel loaded with merchandise for some southern port; the cargo was sold, and Osmond, taking the proceeds, left the port to go further south. Nothing had been heard of him since the vessel returned" (9).

Sarah and Jason's otherwise sterile marriage produces one child, a son who is named Parke and is raised to identify entirely with his mother and her family. Sarah tells Jason that "he was a Parke, every inch of him, . . . and asked him to notice how much his hands were shaped like her grandfather's" (10). Parke's exclusive claim to the Parke fortune is disrupted, however, when Osmond reappears with a daughter, Philippa, and asks Sarah to take the girl into her home. Sarah begrudgingly does so, yet she makes no effort to hide her disregard for Philippa, especially when she discovers that Philippa is in love with Parke and hopes that the two will marry. The younger generation seems fated to follow in the footsteps of their parents, however, when the arrival of Charlotte Lang in Crest thwarts Philippa's dream.

Based on the "meager . . . details" provided by the captain of the schooner that brings the Langs to Crest, the townspeople suspect that Mrs. Lang is a white man's mistress, liberated from slavery and sent north along with her daughters. While Mrs. Lang's history remains somewhat ambiguous, the gossips of Crest take their clue from her "manners," which are said to reflect "the hut, the boudoir, and the Methodist gatherings of plantation slaves" (111).[3] Both Clarice and Charlotte Lang are beautiful and more sophisticated than their mother, but Charlotte's appearance is particularly striking to those who search unsuccessfully for evidence of her "blackness." Charlotte's complexion, Stoddard writes, is "smooth and opaque, and the curves of her face so beautiful. Her lips were always parted, her wistful light-blue eyes widely opened, and her straight, silky, chestnut hair disordered. She impressed those who saw her with a pitying admiration, a wondering regret, and a mysterious doubt" (112). As a "black" woman who appears to be "white," Charlotte represents a mystery to the people of Crest, one who defies their understanding of race and gender and, above all, sexuality. Charlotte's white skin would seem to demand a certain amount of pity, if not respect. Yet with her "parted" lips, wide eyes, and "disordered" hair, Charlotte seems to be always on the verge of a sexual rendezvous, thus awakening desire in everyone who sees her. Clarice, on the other hand, "had a brilliant swarthy complexion, shining, curly, black hair, large black eyes, with a vindictive sparkle" (112). She inspires "admiration" but no "mysterious doubt," as her appearance clearly reflects her parentage.

Charlotte's "whiteness" prompts her to believe that there is a way in which she can be socially acceptable in Crest. When Parke begins to pursue her, she encourages him, telling her sister that their differences make "no difference whatever to him" (165). Yet Clarice is skeptical: "A little of you will suffice his vanity, you may be sure," she warns Charlotte. Perhaps because of her physical appearance, Clarice understands that racial difference cannot be so easily erased; visible or not, race marks both Clarice and Charlotte as sexually available, existing only for the pleasure of the white men who pursue them. When told by her mother to "attend to the concerns of [her] soul," Clarice asks, "What is the use of my soul to me? No more than my body is. Both are worthless" (166). Clarice's efforts to deter Charlotte from the affair are unsuccessful, as is their mother's attempt to rescue her daughters from the sexual exploitation she presumably experienced as a young female slave.[4]

Although Charlotte claims to believe that Parke's love for her proves the insignificance of difference, she is unable to explain their relationship in any way other than the rhetoric of bondage. "He came after me," she tells Philippa. "I never asked anything of him. I never shall." She continues, "I act according to his wishes. He governs me" (186). Parke also frames their sexual relationship in a similar way, reflecting on "a new and terrible joy in his possession" after their first sexual encounter (161). The relationship with Parke thus renders Charlotte powerless despite her freedom and emphasizes her complete lack of agency, similar to that of a slave resigned to servitude. Resistance and escape in either case are futile. Indeed, the couple's first sexual encounter is haunted by "the baying of dogs along the woody road, the rustling of footsteps among the leaves" (163–64). Parke later tells Philippa that the dogs "sounded like bloodhounds" (160). Thus Charlotte's sexuality, which she fancies she gives freely to Parke, only reduces her to a slave for whom capture and punishment are imminent. Although Parke is her sexual partner, he is also her master, at whose hands she will be punished. Matlack suggests that "the allusion to bloodhounds signals Parke's fear of discovery which he now shares with the fugitive" ("Literary Career" 350). Yet Parke is not nearly as vulnerable as Charlotte; indeed, the repercussions of the relationship are few for him, and he retains his position in society after Charlotte's rather convenient death. For Charlotte, pregnancy and abandonment are ultimately more dangerous than discovery. The allusion to bloodhounds seems much more likely to signify Parke's pursuit of Charlotte and her inability to escape either her history of servitude or her identity as a black woman.

Some critics have recognized Stoddard's treatment of miscegenation in *Two Men* as unique in nineteenth-century American literature. As Matlack notes, Stoddard depicts the interracial relationship between Parke and Charlotte in an objective manner, with a distance that emphasizes the "very normality of . . . the liaison" ("Literary Career" 383). The lovers are not condemned for their attraction to one another, but neither are they made into heroes, larger-than-life figures whose love symbolizes a new social order.[5] As James Kinney observes, however, the relationship functions as a "catalyst" by which all other characters are "tested and judged" (87). The novel as a whole hinges upon this episode of miscegenation, in fact, as well as the presence of Charlotte Lang and her family in the northern coastal town in which *Two Men* is set. Indeed, the Langs illustrate Toni Morrison's assertion that "black people ignite critical moments of discovery or change or emphasis in literature not written by them" (viii). Yet as Morrison also points out, functioning as catalysts or igniting change does not ensure success or even survival for African American figures in nineteenth-century American literature.

Charlotte's inevitable pregnancy certainly does not facilitate escape of any sort, despite Parke's decision to marry her. His intentions are questionable, and even his family remains uncertain as to whether he will run away from the marriage and his responsibilities. Before his commitment can be tested, however, his mother, Sarah, dies, presumably of an illness exacerbated by disappointment and grief, and Charlotte dies in childbirth, along with her infant. While Parke's commitment to Charlotte is debatable at this point, he does insist on burying her in the Parke family cemetery.[6] The gesture elicits mixed responses from the men and women present at the funeral. "All the followers saw that she was to be buried among the Parkes, with his own family. This proud

concession implied more than they could define. . . . The women re-
treated, but with their petty bitterness and hypocrisy, they said to each
other, 'Did you ever see such brass?' and 'Isn't it a pretty thing that the
wolves in sheep's clothing are having it all their own way?' But the men
were silent for a moment; then burst out with 'By Jove, sirs, there's stuff!
Who can blame the girl?'" (216–17).

While the men of the community, at least, excuse Charlotte's transgression, it appears significant that they are only able to do so after she
is dead. Prior to her death, they seem generally to agree with Parke's
friend Sam Rogers, who insists that Parke should not marry Charlotte,
telling him, "Nature is against it—the whole race!" (173). As the women
at the funeral explain, a wolf may triumph while wearing sheep's clothing, but that doesn't make her any less a wolf. Thus, Charlotte's victory
is hardly worth the price she has paid, as it hasn't helped her or her family
in any way. The people of Crest have not really changed their minds
about the Langs or African Americans in general.

Parke's rejection of the Langs is curt and final. When Mrs. Lang im-
plores Parke to stay with them after Charlotte's death, he says, "Yes—till
I go to the grave with her. After that there will be nothing I can do for
you" (214). Clarice understands "that Charlotte would be buried for
good with him, and they also on the day of the funeral" (215). Without
much effort, Parke's uncle, Osmond, convinces Parke to return with him
to Venezuela, where he can ride out the scandal resulting from Charlotte's
death. Of course, Parke, as a wealthy white man, is able to escape Crest,
while Clarice and her mother must remain. "Why shouldn't he leave?"
Clarice asks her mother, expressing a wish that they, too, would leave
Crest and the shameful affair behind them. "No," her mother tells her,
"we should have to take what we are with us, wherever we went."
Clarice responds bitterly, "True, we will stay, and rub in our humiliation,
and keep the brand bright. Ashes are good where the flesh is raw" (215).
The Langs' attempt to begin life anew in the North has failed and,
Mrs. Lang implies, must fail wherever they go. Clarice's response to her
mother reveals an incisive understanding of the way in which American
society shapes this failure by marking black women as, in Hortense J.
Spillers's words, "unprotected female flesh" (68). Unable to claim the
protection afforded white women, black women are thus constantly vulnerable to both physical and sexual abuse. In the case of the Langs, the
cultural meaning of black womanhood appears to be so ingrained that
it is practically inscribed in their skin, inescapable and, ultimately, fatal.
They are no longer slaves, but this "brand" marks Mrs. Lang and her

daughter as outsiders nonetheless, denied citizenship themselves but necessary for the articulation of the rights of others.

THE AMERICAN SPHINX

While there are obvious differences between Charlotte Lang and Philippa Luce, Philippa also strives to leave "what she is" behind her in order to achieve social and familial acceptance. In an early scene, Theresa Bond, Philippa's only intimate female friend, reminds Parke of an earlier occasion upon which Philippa had been called an "American Sphinx" and asks him to "try to guess the riddle she propounds." Parke and his mother agree that there is "nothing erratic in Philippa."

> "Prophets in their own country, Mrs. Auster," Theresa observed carelessly.
> "Philippa does not happen to be in her own country," Sarah replied, with a laugh.
> For once Parke caught and understood an expression of pain in Philippa's face.
> "Philippa," he said, affectionately, "my country is your country, isn't it? You are as much of a Parke as I am." (96–97)

Parke's defense of Philippa reveals the ways in which national identity and familial identity are intertwined in *Two Men*. To belong to the family is to be "in [your] own country," whereas to be an outsider is to be a "foreigner." Charlotte dies in a liminal space between these two extremes—an unwed mother of a stillborn child, who is nonetheless buried in the family cemetery. Given Charlotte's fate, the quest for citizenship would seem to be a dangerous one. As the American sphinx, however, Philippa has a distinct advantage over the ill-fated Charlotte.

According to Sophocles, an inability to answer the riddle of the Sphinx—"What animal has one voice, but goes on four legs in the morning, two legs at noon, and upon three legs in the evening?"— would result in death by strangulation. Of course, the riddle also placed the Sphinx herself at risk; when Oedipus finally answered her riddle, the Sphinx was so distraught that she committed suicide. As the American sphinx, Philippa (re)presents the riddle of American identity presented in the conversation she has with Parke and Sarah. Who is citizen and who is foreigner? How does one become a member of the family/country? As discussed earlier, Charlotte inspires a "mysterious doubt" similar to that of the American sphinx, yet Charlotte's mystery is neatly solved and forgotten with her death. Clearly, Parke and Sarah have come to different conclusions regarding Philippa's citizenship. To allow someone else to solve the riddle, however, may prove fatal for Philippa as well.

In an attempt to assert her right to citizenship, Philippa defines herself through her relationship to her roving and largely ineffective father. "I have absolute faith in my own money," she announces to Sarah, after being criticized as "extravagant." When asked where she learned this, she replies, "From one of the family preceptors—my father, Osmond Luce." "We have hatched a cockatrice!" Sarah tells Jason (53). The image of the cockatrice—a mythic serpent who is hatched by a reptile from a cock's egg—serves to highlight not only the importance of Philippa's father to her sense of identity but the almost complete textual absence of her mother. Although Philippa's childhood is referred to several times in the course of the novel, much about her past remains a mystery precisely because of this absence. Osmond explains that the girl's mother is dead, and Philippa reveals only that she has spent at least part of her childhood in the American South. Philippa's complete silence regarding her mother seems to indicate that she has forgotten her and renounced her past in her effort to identify with her father's family.

The mystery surrounding Philippa's parentage is mirrored in that of Clarice and Charlotte Lang, although in the latter case the father is absent and the girls' identity is established through their relation to their mother. When Clarice insists that Mrs. Lang has "had a white husband," her mother insists that their father's identity is insignificant: "*I* brought you into the world, you are my chil'n—bone of my bone, flesh of my flesh, with all your beauty" (151). As the children of a black woman, Clarice and Charlotte are legally and socially black in the United States and thus are unable to escape their maternal legacy. While Philippa's parental relationship helps establish her right to inherit property, the status of Charlotte and Clarice Lang establishes them as property themselves.[7] This crucial difference ultimately decides their respective fates, but it is important to remember that for much of the novel, Charlotte and Philippa are both positioned as foreigners.

As with the Langs, appearance is essential to determining Philippa's status as "foreigner." When she first appears in Crest, Philippa wears a "brightly-flowered shawl" with "deep fringe" and brings with her a "stuffed macaw" (28, 26). She is described as "a strange-looking . . . girl" with "yellow" hair, and upon her arrival at Sarah's home, Parke tells her, "I don't think you are handsome" (24–25). Although an admirer later decides that her beauty is "tropical," she continues to believe in Parke's assessment of her appearance (58, 42). Yet her father, Osmond Luce, suggests that standards of beauty are cultural and that Philippa would not seem so out of place in another environment:

> "You are a kind of witch, I believe; curious looking, too."
> "I know I am ugly," she answered, coloring painfully.
> "By no means. You have good eyes; witches always have."
> "Yet with diabolical, revengeful yellow hair."
> "Why, girl, what ails you? You are no conjurer, at any rate. The truth is, you are half foreign; in your native town I have seen dozens of girls like you—with a difference." (231–32)

Philippa's "strange" beauty is inexplicable and therefore supernatural, evil, even "diabolical" in a New England setting. In another place, Osmond tells her, she would fit in, but "with a difference," still the child of her father and her mother, a liminal figure. Osmond ultimately confirms Philippa's mixed blood, calling her "half foreign" and raising questions about her national identity.

While Philippa's exact origins remain a mystery, Stoddard clearly suggests that her heroine is linked in one way or another with not only the southern United States but also South America.[8] Given Osmond Luce's adventures in South America—particularly Venezuela—it seems possible that Philippa was born there, the daughter of a Venezuelan woman. Less distinct but even more interesting, perhaps, is the possibility that Philippa may not only have been born in Venezuela but may, in fact, be of mixed race. As Winthrop R. Wright, author of *Café con Leche: Race, Class, and National Image in Venezuela,* writes, "Since the late eighteenth century, travelers to Venezuela repeatedly identified racial mixing as the most striking feature of Venezuelan society" (13). At the end of the colonial era in 1810, 60 percent of Venezuelans "had African origins, with a substantial Indian influence. Indians made up another 15 percent of the inhabitants. So-called whites comprising *peninsulares,* creoles, and Canary Islanders, formed the remaining 25 percent of the population. Of these, some 90 percent were creoles, of somewhat dubious racial origin, many of whom probably had African ancestors" (14). "By all accounts," Wright insists, "racial and cultural mixing affected the inhabitants of Venezuela more than almost any other American society" (21). Racial distinctions in nineteenth-century Venezuela, therefore, were not so clear-cut as they were in the United States and relied more upon skin color than blood. Venezuelans throughout the colonial period and the wars of independence classified people according to a five-category racial system—whites, Indians, blacks, *pardos* (individuals of mixed race), and slaves. As John V. Lombardi notes, "The labels permitted the white elite to control and manage the large numbers of subordinate people produced by the fusion of races that came after conquest and settlement" (48).

Yet this same system allowed for social mobility in a rapidly changing society that placed more emphasis on strength and military experience than money and blood. While white elites held the balance of power and certainly utilized this power to oppress slaves and blacks, some flexibility existed. In fact, a late-eighteenth-century process called the *Gracias al Sacar* "permitted certain worthy *pardos* to acquire the legal status of whites and gain thereby all the rights and privileges of the most favored ethnic group" (Lombardi 57). This process fell out of practice in the nineteenth century, yet the spirit remained, in that *pardos* were allowed a measure of flexibility and opportunity that mixed-race individuals were not in the United States during the same period.[9] According to Wright, "Blacks and *pardos* not infrequently held high positions in federal agencies and military organizations as well, and they certainly formed an important segment of the various bandit factions that operated in the more remote regions of the nation" (10).

Philippa may be the "American sphinx," then, because she is, in fact, an American citizen, yet she represents a racial category unimaginable in the antebellum United States. As a "white" woman whose racial identity is not questioned, she is able to assimilate, albeit with resistance from Sarah. Part of her assimilation, however, is to resist that of Charlotte, another "white" woman who is, paradoxically, not really white. While an awareness of racial politics in the United States makes the people of Crest vigilant about the interloping Langs, they are blind to Philippa's effort to pass—either as northern, American, or simply white. In this sense, it is possible to see Stoddard as writing "beyond white and other" in *Two Men* to create a "narrative of relational positionality" that "moves beyond binary thinking" about race and identity and, most importantly, that considers identity in an international context (Friedman 40). In *Mappings: Feminism and the Cultural Geographies of Encounter,* Susan Stanford Friedman argues that such narratives can allow for the circulation of power "in complicated ways rather than unidirectionally." According to Friedman, late-twentieth-century narratives that feature "contradictory subject positions" also offer "the possibility of connection across racial and ethnic boundaries" (63). This connection is shut down in *Two Men,* however, because like Parke, Philippa needs Charlotte's failure in order to succeed. Rather than facilitating a connection between Philippa and Charlotte, Philippa's "contradictory subject position" causes her to reject Charlotte and benefit from her downfall.

When Philippa first sees Charlotte at the cotillion, she is "amazed at [her] beauty." Yet the sight of Charlotte immediately recalls Philippa's hazy memories of violence against female slaves and prompts a rather detached vision of Charlotte herself being whipped. "She thought of a time, in the twilight region of early childhood, when she had heard the sound of the lash on shoulders as lovely as Charlotte's, perhaps; at any rate, it cut the flesh of her race. Suppose she were tied to a whipping-post at this instant, what would be the tide of feeling? Would it change from the contemptuous coldness now shown to pity and protection?" (144).

Even as she appears to be sympathetic, Philippa is unable to see Charlotte as anything other than a slave, a vulnerable black woman whose skin can be imaginatively marked by any white observer. Philippa's identification of Charlotte with "her race"—African Americans rather than Anglo Americans—negates Charlotte's mixed-race identity, thus recalling Mrs. Lang's insistence that her children have no father. Despite her "silky, chestnut hair" and her "light-blue eyes," Charlotte is nothing but "unprotected female flesh" in Philippa's fantasy, flesh that Clarice will later acknowledge is inescapably imprinted with the cultural memory of slavery and black womanhood. Yet the fantasy also reveals a strange sort of identification between Charlotte and Philippa. As a foreigner and possibly even a woman of color herself, Philippa is by no means secure in her social position. Charlotte's vulnerability recalls Philippa's own, then, and the two bodies may, in fact, be interchangeable in the fantasy. "Suppose she were tied to a whipping-post at this instant," Philippa asks herself. While the "she" in this fantasy seems at first glance to be Charlotte, it is equally possible to read "she" as Philippa herself, outcast in her own home, hungry for "pity and protection."

Philippa's sympathy for the Langs is easily forgotten when she faces the loss of Parke and, thus, her own citizenship. Upon hearing of the affair between Charlotte and Parke, Philippa immediately reverts to calling Charlotte a "slave" (180). Although she had earlier wondered if Charlotte's vulnerability would inspire "pity and protection" from the people of Crest, she shows only contempt for the young woman and "disgust" regarding Charlotte's pregnancy (180). When the two women meet accidentally, Charlotte's beauty infuriates Philippa. Despite "her hair, blown about her face, her languid, wistful eyes, the faint color rising in her cheeks," Philippa is literally overcome with a sense of Charlotte's blackness. "Philippa's eyes," Stoddard writes, "so filled with dazzling beams that crashed down from her brain, that for a moment Charlotte looked a dark, vague shape, whose coming overpowered her with hate and horror" (185). Philippa's jealousy of Charlotte, then, manifests itself as hatred for her blackness—a blackness that is so difficult to see that Philippa must imaginatively create it herself. Yet the "horror" that Philippa feels is no less a reaction to this blackness than it is a reaction to the similarities between the two women. Philippa surely sees herself in Charlotte and understands that Charlotte's fate could be her own.

Philippa manages to avoid Charlotte's fate, at least partly, by giving up Parke and learning to love his father, Jason, after Sarah's death. In Parke's absence, the two establish themselves quite happily in the Parke home, with Philippa's half of the Parke family inheritance. Rather than escaping Crest, as Parke has, Philippa finds herself simultaneously empowered and limited by the boundaries of the town. She tells Jason, "I don't know . . . how much my soul could gather round anything foreign to Crest. When I say Crest, I mean our own surroundings, you know; lately my vision narrows to these walls, our acres, each rock and tree, the sea before the house, the sky over it. Nothing else can contain me" (196). Philippa, the "foreigner" herself, rejects "anything foreign to Crest," thus declaring herself a native of the town. She seems content to be contained by Crest and her surroundings. This containment, however, also suggests a sort of imprisonment, reminiscent of that of the Langs. Neither she nor the Langs share Parke's mobility, nor even that of Jason Auster, whose journeys provide a frame of sorts for the novel.

While the Langs certainly seem contained by Crest, they are not empowered by this containment; containment for them is merely a form of survival. Mrs. Lang and Clarice disappear from *Two Men* after Parke's final visit to them, in which he announces his impending journey to Venezuela. A defeated Clarice tells Parke, "It is like going to the grave again, to part with you, for all that I have hatefully said. You were the link that attached me to a world I do not belong to. Pray that I may die" (243). It is assumed that the Langs remain in Crest, as Mrs. Lang has insisted they must, but their story becomes unnarratable once Parke Auster is removed from it. Philippa's survival after Parke's abandonment becomes the focus of the rest of the novel.

SOUTH AND "FURTHER SOUTH"

With the full support of his family, Parke accompanies his uncle Osmond to Venezuela soon after he buries Charlotte in the family cemetery. As represented in *Two Men,* Venezuela is a land of unrestrained passion and freedom. Osmond, the first to escape the family and journey to South America, leaves because "he must have freedom" (8). When Jason, Sarah's husband and Parke's father, meets Osmond, he compares his own life with that of Osmond, who, "breaking every shackle, like the bold, generous spirit that he was, had made himself free, and followed out his true impulses" (130). Osmond's wayfaring life in South America is clearly without responsibilities, which is why he returns to Crest only to leave Philippa with Sarah and then disappear again. Upon his second return, he finds Parke facing the consequences of his affair with Charlotte Lang and recommends that his nephew adopt the same solution. The novel ends with the two of them on the pampas of Venezuela, "play[ing] the Llanero well" (301). In this hypermasculinized world far from the suffocating influence of Sarah, Philippa, and Charlotte, Stoddard depicts yet another "melodrama of beset manhood," to use Nina Baym's term, in which "the encroaching, constricting, destroying society is represented with particular urgency in the figure of one or more women" (Baym, "Melodramas" 133). In this case, however, Stoddard exposes the melodrama for what it is—an escape from domestic responsibilities and mature emotional commitments to others. She also uses this setting to reiterate the way in which national politics and national identity are always defined within an international context.

The llanos, or the plains of Venezuela, had been the center of the country's cattle-export economy since the seventeenth century. The life of the llanero, or cowboy, was often romanticized in American periodical literature about South America and formed an important part of nineteenth-century Americans' limited knowledge of Venezuela. In an article published in the February 1859 edition of the *Atlantic Monthly,* for example, an anonymous author describes the dress, habits, and homes of "the true Llanero" ("El Llanero" 176). In a passage that may have inspired Stoddard's own representation of llanero life, the author writes,

A Llanero cares little for death. He faces it daily in his lonely converse with thousands of intractable beasts. . . . Content with the wild excitement of his daily round of duty and recreation, with his meal of dried beef and cassava-cake, washed down, it is likely, with a gourdful of guarapo, a species of rum, in comparison with which the New England beverage is innocent and weak, and with the occasional recurrence of some such turbulent festival as that of the branding, he cares nothing for the future, and bestows no thought upon the past. The Llanero may be called a happy man. ("El Llanero" 177)

Their reputation for bravery, violence, and fierce loyalty made the llaneros a valuable asset for any politician or military leader, but they were, for the greater part of the nineteenth century, affiliated with General José Antonio Paez. A Creole who had taken refuge upon the llanos after killing a highwayman, Paez led the llaneros in crucial battles in the Venezuelan wars for independence during the early nineteenth century. The llaneros were at Paez's side in 1830, when he resisted revolutionary leader Simón Bolívar's efforts to consolidate Venezuela, Ecuador, and New Granada into Colombia and declared Venezuela's independence.

Osmond's awareness of the political situation in Venezuela becomes evident when Jason tells Parke that the Venezuelan "Generals of Independence will use up your money."[10] Parke asks how Jason knows about the situation, and Jason asks him, "Do you suppose that I have known nothing of Osmond's career in Venezuela?" (234). Yet Osmond's "career" seems to be more about pleasure than politics. Although he claims to be planning to join Paez's revolutionary armies, Osmond is careful to point out to Parke that he will do so only if Paez "is in retirement." "Would you like to be a mighty cattle-hunter on his pampas?" he asks Parke (226). As revealed at the end of the novel, Parke and Osmond do not go to Venezuela to participate in the controversial wars for independence; they join the llaneros only to gamble, hunt, and break wild horses.

Yet Venezuela functions in *Two Men* as more than an escape valve or exotic historical setting in which Osmond and Parke can play cowboy. Stoddard's references to Venezuela also act as a warning to her readers about the dangers inherent in uncontrolled passion, such as that which led to the wars in South America as well as the American Civil War, during which Stoddard was writing. Throughout the nineteenth century, both Americans and Venezuelans had recognized the parallels between their respective quests for independence. Yet as Judith Ewell points out, "citizens of both countries alternated between a naive belief that they shared political and economic goals and a pessimistic recognition that divergent cultural values and national interests discouraged any alliance. Waves of pessimism frequently accompanied disgusted assessments of the other nation's honor and values" (11). Relations between Venezuela and the United States were best immediately after Venezuelan independence, when Paez assumed power and "epitomize[d] Venezuelan democracy to the United States for the next two decades" (35). After leading the separatist movement in Venezuela in 1830, Paez served as president and unofficial "supreme caudillo" until his exile to the Caribbean and the United States in 1848 (Lombardi 181–82). When exiled, he removed to New York, where he enjoyed the adulation of the American people. The *New York Times,* for example, lauded "the pure and exalted patriotism of Paez" and commended his "steady courage, constancy, and bravery" ("Recall" 6).

Yet when Paez was recalled to Venezuela in 1858 to lead the Conservatives during the Federal Wars (1858–63), the United States, distracted by its own political problems, was not quite so eager to get involved. Toward the end of the Federal Wars, after the Civil War had already begun, the United States was particularly unwilling to support any faction, concerned that any involvement in Venezuela's wars might encourage foreign support of the Confederacy. Judith Ewell points out, "Observers from the United States may have interpreted Venezuelan events during this period through the lens of their own racial fears and concerns for the disintegration of their own union. Surely Venezuela exemplified the lapse into anarchy that would follow a weakening of central authority and the unfettered actions of colored mobs" (52). Thus, the United States's resistance to involvement in Venezuela was a direct reflection not only of a desire to hold the Union together but also of a deep-seated racism and reluctance to address the question of what had to be done in the northern states to facilitate the abolition of slavery and the future success of free blacks. The United States did not officially recognize the Venezuelan government until October 1864 (Ewell 57). Prior to and during the Civil War, the United States consistently resisted the antebellum impression of parallels between the two countries' political histories. Such resistance is clearly evident in a review of *Wild Scenes in South America; or, Life in the Llanos of Venezuela,* a book written by Paez's son, Don Ramon Paez, and published in the United States in 1863. After heralding the book as "the best account of wild herdsman American-Spanish life ever written," the reviewer for the *Continental Monthly* concludes, "The book cannot fail to be extensively read, since it is not only entertaining, but instructive. Its sketches of the *causes* of the continual civil wars in South America are not only explanatory, but may serve as a lesson to us in this country to give ourselves heart and soul to the Union, and to crush out treason and faction by every means in our power. If the rebels and Copperheads triumph, we shall soon see the United States reduced to the frightful anarchy of South America" ("Literary Notices" 632). Obviously, Venezuela is no longer seen as developing along lines parallel to those followed by the United States; rather, this review uses the political situation in Venezuela as a scare tactic directed at northerners whose support of the Union cause is lax or insufficient in some way.

While Stoddard seems not to have shared the *Continental Monthly* reviewer's opinion of "the truly great general Paez," her use of Venezuela in a novel written during the American Civil War would seem to imply that she also regarded the Venezuelan wars for independence as some sort of "lesson to us in this country" (632). Stoddard's position, however, isn't clearly pro-North or pro-South; during the Civil War, she seems to have been a lukewarm Unionist at best. Rather, she applies these political lessons to the lives of her most vulnerable characters—female "foreigners" like Charlotte and Philippa—and reveals the personal dangers of anarchy, especially for women and people of color. When Osmond flippantly asks Philippa to join him in his journey to South America, for example, she "struggle[s] with the phantoms of Liberty and Pleasure which his words had evoked" (230). Yet Philippa finally rejects these phantoms, choosing instead to remain in Crest: "How can I tell," Philippa asks Osmond, "whether I could bear the license of your life? I succumb to tradition and custom because I love them. But if these barriers should be removed, I feel I have that within which could rise, and overtop excess" (230–31). For Philippa, to abandon responsibility and give in to passion would be to deny the traditions and customs of the Parke family, of which she has struggled to be a part. Having defined herself through her paternal family, she cannot throw this identity away for something amorphous and unknown. Her questionable national and racial identity makes adherence to this point even more crucial.

Stoddard's positioning of Venezuela as the site of "Liberty and Pleasure" suggests sexual as well as political dangers awaiting those who expatriate themselves. Philippa's vulnerability to such danger may be suggested by the fate of Charlotte, who gives in to passion, becoming pregnant and, ultimately, dying as a result of her unrestrained affair with Parke. Thus, Philippa chooses to retain the barriers she has erected and avoid "excess." This choice is revealed to be the right one for her because, rather than submitting to an unequal relationship with her cousin

Parke, she eventually learns to love his father, Jason, who has repressed his passion for her for years. Parke would have stifled her, whereas Jason offers to "shelter [her] in the abyss of [his] love, which is as wide and deep as the air" (275). Ultimately, Stoddard advocates a careful balance of "license," on the one hand, and "tradition and custom," on the other, recognizing that the imbalance of the two could have devastating consequences.

The social order is not simply reinforced in *Two Men*. The aristocracy is ousted, and the "foreigners," Jason and Philippa, are left with the family fortune and the ancestral home. The riddle of the "American sphinx" remains unsolved. Despite her questionable regional, national, and possibly even racial identity, Philippa has made Sarah's and Parke's country her own, thus changing the face of America's national identity. If we take this novel as a reflection of Civil War America, as I have claimed Stoddard's references to Venezuela direct us to do, then this conclusion sanctions and even celebrates the societal changes put in motion by the war. Some change, some passion, is positive and even necessary for a society to grow and thrive. Yet this same reflection does not seem to bode well for African Americans, millions of whom were freed by the end of the Civil War. Charlotte Lang's death and the disappearance of her family serve as an uncomfortable reminder that only certain types of "foreigners" are granted citizenship.

NOTES

1. Stoddard apparently worked on *Two Men* throughout the last years of the Civil War. She mentioned the novel in a letter to Edmund Clarence Stedman on 12 July 1863, soon after the Battle of Gettysburg, and it was published just after the surrender of the Confederate army at Appomattox (Stoddard, *The Morgesons and Other Writings* 337).

2. Elizabeth Stoddard, *Two Men* (New York: Johnson, 1971) 232. All further citations of *Two Men* will refer to this edition of the text and will appear parenthetically.

3. Stoddard's biographer, James Matlack, has insisted that Stoddard "created Negro characters free of the usual stereotypes" in *Two Men* ("Literary Career" 381). In the year the novel was published, William Dean Howells also admired Stoddard's realistic approach to the Langs; they were, he claimed, "the most successful creations in the book; they are marvelously well done. . . . We think Mrs. Stoddard succeeds better with these people than with most others in her book, because she keeps them in their place, as the folks at Crest did. They

seldom rise to those heights of epigram on which the other characters tread, and in their simple, vulgar presence one feels a curious relief from the intensity which pursues one throughout the book" ("*Two Men*" 537). Both of these assessments seem a bit too generous, particularly in the case of Mrs. Lang, whom Stoddard describes as "a little, sinewy, gay savage" with the "glitter of negro blood" in her eyes and "the negro modulation in her voice" (111). Although this depiction is problematic, Mrs. Lang is otherwise a quite sympathetic character, one not entirely stereotypical.

4. Although the setting of *Two Men* is ambiguous, the novel certainly takes place prior to the 1850 Fugitive Slave Act, in which runaway slaves would be at risk of recapture in both the North and the South. It is important that Mrs. Lang could expect her daughters to be safe in a northern community like Crest.

5. Stoddard's depiction of the sexual politics of race is closer to that of Harriet Jacobs than it is to that of Lydia Maria Child. That is, she attempts to represent a black woman's sexual negotiations in a more realistic way than any other novelist of her time. As in Jacobs's *Incidents in the Life of a Slave Girl* (1861), the relationships between white men and black women in *Two Men* are primarily about power rather than romance, and they don't lead to a new social order. Child's *A Romance of the Republic* (1867), published two years after *Two Men,* positioned interracial marriage as a utopian solution to racial prejudice in the United States, but both Jacobs and Stoddard clearly demonstrates how far the country was from this sort of solution during and after the Civil War. Rebecca Harding Davis's *Waiting for the Verdict* (1867) is the only other novel of the period to attempt a similarly realistic portrayal of an interracial relationship.

6. Not all critics are so critical of Parke's intentions regarding Charlotte. In his review of the novel, Howells, for example, says that "Parke, whose nature is good and generous, is about to repair his wrong as far as possible by marrying Charlotte Lang, when his mother dies of broken pride—heart she seems to have none—and Charlotte dies in giving birth to his child" ("*Two Men*" 537). In a recent biographical and critical essay, Sandra Harbert Petrulionis takes the same tack, explaining, "Though Parke intends to marry Charlotte, he allows family and social considerations to delay the wedding, and Charlotte dies in childbirth" (400). I am more inclined to see Stoddard as being ambiguous about Parke's real intentions. After Charlotte's death, the insightful Clarice recognizes the limitations of Parke's commitment to Charlotte: "Clarice in her convulsive weeping was conscious of a sentiment of gratitude towards Parke for giving Charlotte the place among the dead of his race that he would have given her had she been his wife. That she would be his wife, had she lived, Clarice had never believed, though aware of his promise" (217).

7. According to the Naturalization Act of 1790, Philippa is an American citizen because her father is a citizen; her mother's citizenship isn't relevant. Charlotte's paternity, on the other hand, is made irrelevant by the fact that her mother is a slave.

8. As Stoddard's 1858 poem "Mercedes" demonstrates, she had already shown an interest in South America and the themes of violence and passion that the region seemed to suggest.

9. This is not to imply that black and/or mixed-race individuals were considered the equal of whites in Venezuelan society. Although the slave trade was eliminated in 1810, slavery existed in Venezuela until 1854. Wealthy whites also managed to structure their society so as to maintain their own economic and social supremacy. As Lombardi writes, "By a complex interlocking network of clients, patrons, and middlemen, plus a sophisticated pattern of family alliances through cousin marriage, this colonial elite created a cohesive and mutually dependent structure capable of maintaining white supremacy within the multi-racial Venezuelan society" (47).

10. This reference, as well as a later one to Paez himself, would seem to position the novel, then, prior to 1830, when Venezuela gained its independence.

8

(Un)Natural Attractions?

Incest and Miscegenation in *Two Men*

Lisa Radinovsky

In 1854, the white supremacist politician and sociologist Henry Hughes published sentiments that would echo in the American press, literature, laws, and courts for decades: "Impurity of races is against the law of nature. . . . The law of nature is the law of God. The same law which forbids consanguinous amalgamation forbids ethnical amalgamation. Both are incestuous. Amalgamation is incest" (qtd. in Sundquist 111). According to David Lawrence Rogers, Hughes's views were representative of "the hysteria that enveloped the discourse of slavery immediately before the Civil War" (166). In the midst of this hysteria, Harvard professor Louis Agassiz made a similar link between interracial relationships and incest: "Viewed from a high moral point of view the production of half breeds is as much a sin against nature, as incest in a civilized community is a sin against purity of character" (qtd. in Sollors 298). While making this curious yet common connection, public figures such as Hughes and Agassiz proclaimed what most white, middle-class Americans had believed for some time: that incest and interracial marriages were unnatural.

Two years after Agassiz made his comments, Elizabeth Stoddard published her second novel, *Two Men* (1865), in which she challenged this belief. Stoddard responded to such views with an epigraph from Ralph Waldo Emerson that valorized a more open view of the natural at the expense of the law: "Nature, as we know her, is no saint. . . . Her darlings—the great, the strong, the beautiful—are not children of our law; do not come out of the Sunday School, nor weigh their food, nor punctually keep the commandments."[1] Nor did Stoddard or most of her characters obey the conventional rules of their time. In *Two Men,* Stoddard rejected traditional marriage plots in favor of unions that unsettled families and crossed social barriers between races and classes. She attacked conventional beliefs about relationships, manhood, womanhood, racial difference, and desire with unusually realistic representations of interracial and incestuous relationships, daring to assert the naturalness of transgressive desire and the prevalence of racism in the North.

Two Men's transgressive tendency is evident in its plot. The two men of the novel's title are Jason Auster and his son, Parke. In the beginning of the novel, Jason brushes aside his youthful beliefs in temperance, abolition, and socialism and marries the egotistical and tyrannical heiress Sarah Parke. When their son, Parke, is nine years old, Sarah's cousin Osmond brings his ten-year-old daughter, Philippa, to live with them, making Jason Philippa's guardian. Philippa develops an adoring devotion to Parke that evolves into a desiring love as they grow up. Jason also falls in love with Philippa, although he does not express that love until after his wife dies. Meanwhile, Parke is attracted to Charlotte Lang, the beautiful, light-skinned daughter of a fugitive slave who has recently moved into town. He seduces her, and she becomes pregnant. Parke's mother, his mistress, Charlotte, and their baby all die nine months later, and Parke leaves the country. Jason and Philippa grow closer, and it is implied that they will marry in the end.[2]

Significantly, the most traditional relationship in *Two Men*—the marriage between Jason and Sarah—is no more successful than the others. Stoddard replaces both that unhappy marriage and a possible storybook (albeit incestuous) romance between the wealthy white heirs, Parke and Philippa, with even less acceptable liaisons: the promise of an incestuous marriage between Philippa and her older cousin, guardian, and foster father, Jason; and an interracial sexual liaison between Parke and Charlotte. In *Two Men,* characters look objectionably "close" and scandalously "far" from their families for their erotic relationships.

In spite of the apparent opposition of the "near" and the "far," the "different" and the "similar," as Werner Sollors explains, there were "at least three different ideological explanations" for the "abundant instances of juxtapositions, comparisons, and conflations between incest and miscegenation" in nineteenth-century America: "a 'pragmatic' state-interventionist, a 'realistic' abolitionist-liberal, and a 'paranoid' proslavery-racialist-fascist trajectory" (287, 314). Racist lawmakers and (other) extremists sought to advance their cause by associating interracial relationships with incest, "one of the most universal taboos in the Western world" (Thorslev 41).[3] Sollors points out that the link between interracial relationships and incest helped "make miscegenation seem 'unnatural' and 'repulsive'" in both legislation and other racist writing (320). On the other hand, Sollors argues, "the liberal-antislavery hypothesis starts

with the 'realistic' argument according to which unrecognized miscegenation may lead to (unknowingly committed) incest" (316–17), as
many antislavery novels demonstrate: many white masters raped their
enslaved daughters, and numerous unknowing or uncaring brothers
were attracted to their sisters.[4] In antebellum literature, the two violations of taboos were most obviously linked under the slave system.

However, none of this explains Stoddard's juxtaposition of the taboos.
While Stoddard did write about women presumed to be fugitive slaves,
she was atypical in setting their story in New England and in depicting
incestuous and interracial relationships that were relatively independent
of both each other and the institution of slavery. Furthermore, she was
unusual in representing both incest and a cross-racial relationship in a
less negative light than most authors of her time. Stoddard's representation of incest, sexual repression, and racism in *Two Men* supported and
stemmed from her general refusal to engage in conventional white,
middle-class intolerance, her work to subvert it, and her insistence that
people be aware of and act on their feelings and desires.

Stoddard's choice of incest as a significant subject for *Two Men* is less
surprising than one might expect. In spite of its taboo status, incest is at
least implicitly an issue in every Stoddard novel. There are undertones
of paternal incest in the relationships between Cassandra and her older
cousin Charles in *The Morgesons* and between the young Virginia and the
middle-aged Argus in *Temple House. Two Men,* in which Stoddard addresses incest most directly (if not strictly literally), was most likely
influenced by both broader cultural anxieties about incest and the subject's prevalence in various types of literature, especially European Romantic poetry and novels.[5]

Stoddard was writing about incest during a time of transition in
popular and legal opinions about such relations. In the first half of the
nineteenth century, regulations against unions between affinal relatives
were overturned, and few marriages between relations more distant than
sibling or parent/child couples were dissolved in court (Grossberg 111–
13). However, beginning in the 1860s or 1870s, and more frequently toward the end of the century, scientific arguments instilled fears about
transmitting hereditary defects, and according to Michael Grossberg,
"the longstanding antipathy to consanguineous unions revived and expanded" (145). While hereditary defects are not an issue for the characters in *Two Men,* since there are no incestuous sexual relations between
close consanguineous relatives, certain court cases (as well as racists' use
of incest to derogate interracial relationships) hint that disapproval of

incest on moral grounds was also on the rise. For example, in 1863, when Stoddard was writing *Two Men,* a Pennsylvania state supreme court decision about an uncle-niece marriage proclaimed "that such connections are destructive of good morals and should not only be frowned upon by the community, but very severely punished" (qtd. in Grossberg 146).

Such negative and fearful attitudes tend to pervade both representations of incest in nineteenth-century American literature and readers' responses to them. James B. Twitchell contends that incest was represented as "uniformly horrible" (196), and American authors did tend to punish incest quite severely.[6] While oblique, contained, or disapproving representations of incest did not exclude an author from respectability or popularity, audiences reacted with outrage to such novels as Herman Melville's *Pierre; or, The Ambiguities* (1852), which emphasizes incestuous desire and concludes with misery and death. According to G. M. Goshgarian, critics declared that Melville's " 'diseased imagination' had boiled over in a 'monstrous,' 'unhealthy,' outrageously 'improper work,' " providing a suggestive sampling of mid-nineteenth-century Americans' attitudes toward the fictional representation of explicitly incestuous desire (ix).

Stoddard's conclusions were more radical than those of most of her American contemporaries: she did not represent incest as evil or condemn it to a disastrous end. Furthermore, with Jason and Philippa, she dared to endorse an incestuous match as the most successful family formation in her novel. Like *Pierre, Two Men* was condemned for its supposed immorality and coarseness,[7] but Stoddard's novel caused less of an outcry, partly because her presentation was less daring than her conclusions: her treatment of incest was less extensive, less explicit, less gloomy, less literal, and hence less troubling than Melville's. She mitigated the "horror" of incest by displacing both the "sibling" and "paternal" attractions from blood siblings or an actual father-daughter pair to more distant relatives: second cousins who were raised as siblings, and first cousins once removed who became guardian and ward and hence were put in the position of father and daughter. Unions between such technically distant cousins, and between adopted siblings and adopted fathers and daughters, garnered concern and criticism toward the end of the nineteenth century, but they may have caused less uneasiness in the mid-1860s.

Metaphorically speaking, however, Philippa and Parke are not just cousins: they are raised by the same "parents," Sarah and Jason, and Parke clearly thinks of himself as Philippa's brother. Only after her childish love matures into desire does Philippa refuse to consider herself Parke's sister. Similarly, Jason is more than Philippa's legal guardian: he takes the place of her biological father during her adolescence and young womanhood.[8] In other words, Stoddard complicated relationships enough that potentially uncomfortable readers could ignore the issue of incest during most of the novel—but not so much that the issue disappeared. Once Jason reveals his desire for Philippa, it is particularly visible. Stoddard did not mitigate the incestuous nature of her characters' desire to the extent that many of her compatriots did.[9]

Philippa is first drawn to the attractive Parke in childhood, when he immediately "engage[s] her affection, and her devotion to him . . . [is] unqualified."[10] The issue of incest first comes up (without ever being named as such) one-third of the way through the novel, when Philippa's devotion to Parke develops into womanly desire. At this point, Parke seems selfish, lazy, and uninterested in Philippa and her pursuits. Even so, Philippa's "life was absorbed in Parke" (67). When her friend Theresa becomes her rival, Philippa's jealousy of Theresa establishes the nature of her love for Parke. Explaining to Theresa why the latter "must not marry him" (94), Philippa insists that she herself "can do more for him than any person in the world. . . . I mean something which your capacity does not include—the care and watchfulness of slow years, without reward—the patience to endure all weakness, indulgence, selfishness—the bond which begins with a white veil, and ends in a white shroud! . . . I would not . . . give in to his own resistance against me. I will compel him finally to *me*" (94). Here, Stoddard sets up and then breaks down a model of True Womanhood: Philippa demonstrates a submissive and self-sacrificing womanliness that Stoddard characterizes as excessive, but Philippa also defies such a recipe for the feminine by insisting that she will compel rather than submit to Parke.[11]

Philippa is allowed only a brief interlude of happiness with Parke. During his mother's illness, he comes to Philippa in his grief. She is "exquisitely alive to the fact that his hair brushe[s] her cheek" as he sits down beside her and lays his head on her shoulder (199). That moonlit night, they share a moment infused with a romantic intensity, as described from Philippa's perspective: "They had never been together as in that moment; it seemed as if he had yielded to her something of himself he was afraid to keep that night. What protection could he feel with her—he had fallen asleep on her shoulder! His fair forehead pressed against her mouth, his soft hair fell on her neck; she wished that he would sleep forever" (200). When he woke up, Parke "stretched out his arms to infold her; [he said,] 'kiss me'" (201). Philippa "bent her head, and they kissed each other. For an instant the life-long hunger of her soul was stayed" (201) by this actively incestuous kiss—but only for an instant.

In spite of this kiss, Parke is so absorbed in himself and his own inclinations that he does not realize that Philippa loves him. Shortly before leaving the country, he tells the housekeeper that he and Philippa "are mutually attached, I hope, but my idea of attachment leaves us perfect freedom still" (236). Parke thinks of Philippa as a sister, but Philippa wishes her brother to be her lover. Philippa's unrequited longing continues to trouble her almost until the end of the novel, but Stoddard implies that her heroine is better off without Parke: the desired consummation could lead to an entire lifetime of the self-immolating endurance Philippa's devotion to Parke has called forth. The contrast between the possibilities for self-possession and selflessness is as strong for Philippa as for Cassandra, who had difficulty retaining her self-possession while expressing her sexual desires in *The Morgesons.* In *Two Men,* Stoddard condemns the sibling relationship to failure, sending Parke out of the country after his mother and Charlotte die. Philippa's strong reaction to Parke's announcement of his impending departure—her insistence that he "shall not go," her "wild fit of crying" and fainting, and her look of "unutterable passion"—finally convinces him that she loves him (239–40). He still insists on going. The plot of this second novel suggests that by 1865 Stoddard was more determined to demonstrate that a woman (here, Philippa) should wait for a lover who would not usurp her self-possession (Jason, rather than Parke), although the loss of an inappropriate mate is no easier for Philippa than it is for Cassandra.

Aside from the incompatibility of Parke's and Philippa's personalities and desires and the danger of Philippa's self-abnegation, the most obvious explanation for the failure of a romantic relationship between Philippa and Parke is his uncontrolled passion for the fugitive slave Charlotte. However, brother-sister incest may also have been too reminiscent of Stoddard's own experience for her to pursue in this novel. Stoddard herself draws attention to the connection between *Two Men* and her relationship with her most beloved brother in her dedication of the 1865 edition of the novel "TO WILSON":

Who will so well remember what I knew
As you, whenever comes the day to part?
We have ascended one wide scale,

With all emotion in its pale;
Girl, boy, woman and man, untrue and true,
Together or apart—with the same heart.

"All emotion in its pale," "untrue and true," and "with the same heart" may be sentimental references to a close relationship with a brother, but these phrases also reflect the unusually intense, even romantic, relationship that seems to have existed between Elizabeth and Wilson Barstow.

Letters provide strong evidence of Stoddard's incestuous attraction to her brother, although it is unclear whether this desire led to sexual relations. Her letters to her friend Margaret Sweat just before and after her December 1852 marriage to Richard Henry Stoddard demonstrate a deep ambivalence about whether to live with her husband or go to California with Wilson, with whom she is also "in love." She admits to two attachments that sound incestuous: "I was in love fifteen years with my Father—now I am in love with Wilson. Happily with the latter I am more independent than with the former—all my life nearly comes of these loves" (23 Dec. [1852]).[12] Stoddard's initial struggle over how to negotiate her marital and sororal relationships hardly demonstrated independence from Wilson. She married Richard Stoddard secretly and lived with Wilson rather than Richard for several months. Two months after her wedding, she finally decided to announce her marriage "in order to avail myself with marital freedom, of Stoddards [sic] protection during Wilson's absence" in California (10 Feb. [1853]).[13] Her husband was a replacement for her brother, yet he seemed to be an inadequate substitute. In the letter that announced her marriage, she admitted, "I would give all I possess and sacrifice all else if I could go with Wilson. I am madly in love with him and my heart weeps blood to lose him." Especially since she did not write about her other brothers' absences in this way, Stoddard sounds much more like Wilson's lover than his sister. Ten years into her marriage (and a year before she began writing *Two Men*), she wrote that no one but Wilson "touches me with the little cares of the heart which are so sweet to women of my temperament. When Wilson is here, he fills the gap—he knows the colors I wear, he feels the inflection of my voice and he gives me flowers!"[14] Wilson occasionally lived with the Stoddards until 1869, when he died.

The Stoddards' friends commented on the strangeness of Elizabeth and Wilson's enduring closeness. An enigmatic letter from James Lorimer Graham to Bayard Taylor in 1866 (the year after *Two Men* came out) may even suggest that Wilson could have fathered Stoddard's third son.

Edwin Lorimer Stoddard, or "Lorry," was born on 11 December 1863 after Stoddard had begun writing *Two Men*. He was named after two of the Stoddards' closest friends: Edwin Booth (the well-known actor) and James Lorimer Graham (whose friends addressed him by his middle name).[15] In the 1866 letter, Graham asked Taylor, "What horrible thought has crossed your mind in regard to the Major Genl [*sic*]? Is Lorrie mis-named after all?"[16] It seems most likely that the "Major Genl" to whom Graham was sarcastically referring was Colonel Wilson Barstow, whom his loving sister respected as if he had a far higher rank.[17] (Such a reference may have been a snide comment on the fact that Wilson's rank did increase suddenly six months before Graham's letter: from major to lieu-tenant colonel and then colonel.)[18] In short, although it is open to vary-ing interpretations, Graham's letter could be read as suggesting that Stoddard's incestuous relationship with her brother had been consum-mated, so that Lorry should have been named "Wilson" after his possi-ble father.[19]

There is some additional evidence in favor of this argument. Wilson was staying with the Stoddards at the likely time of Lorry's conception, recovering from a serious illness (Matlack, "Literary Career" 304). He slept in the Stoddards' matrimonial bed, while Elizabeth claimed to have slept on the couch and Richard slept on the floor. Wilson had displaced his sister's husband. Furthermore, Stoddard's tantalizing but vague reply to a letter about *Two Men* could hint at links between her characters' incestuous desires and her own: the novel "may be all you think it is, but the 'particulars not in the book' are not yet discovered."[20] Decades later, Stoddard explained to fellow writer Lilian Whiting, "Two Men has a special interest for me—I began it, wrote about half and discovered that master Lorimer was also being edited—I stopped till he was well under way in the arms of his wet nurse and finished it."[21] As she began to "edit" this child of perhaps uncertain paternity, she wrote and edited the manuscript of a novel focused on taboo relationships. To Stoddard, her child and his origin were closely connected to the book and its con-struction.

Elizabeth Stoddard's passionate attraction to Wilson was a major issue in her life during the 1850s and 1860s, regardless of whether their rela-tionship was consummated. It is, then, hardly surprising that the possi-bility of sibling incest was introduced in *Two Men*—or that it was re-jected. It may have been too close to the truth to pursue. On the other hand, Stoddard's stronger attraction to her brother than to her father in the 1860s may help to explain why she ended her novel with a representation of paternal incest: it could have been easier to work through a relationship like the one she had gotten over. While I am not arguing for a direct cause-and-effect relationship between Stoddard's feelings for her father and brother, on the one hand, and her portrayal of incest in *Two Men,* on the other, her own incestuous feelings may well have been a factor in her decision to curtail the sibling incest and pursue the paternal incest in *Two Men.*

This was a highly unusual decision. Paternal incest was generally represented—and, apparently, perceived—as even more horrifying than sibling incest. Thorslev goes so far as to claim that idealized sibling incest "is the ultimate expression for the [European] Romantic Movement of the tradition of courtly or 'romantic' love" (49), yet Twitchell points out that even the Romantic poets hesitated to depict *paternal* incest and condemned it as "categorically evil" when they did (114). Sollors makes a similar claim about some abolitionist authors, for whom—"perhaps as a legacy of romanticism"—"sibling incest is positively charged" but paternal incest is "terrible" (319). According to Twitchell, only "disaster and tragedy result" from paternal incest in all but pornographic literature by both British and American writers (103).[22] However, Twitchell suggests that paternal incest could be acceptable and even popular in literature if it was "cocooned in layers of confusion" (113)—perhaps displaced from paternal incest onto uncle-niece or guardian-ward relationships, disguised, and/or represented according to the expectations for an "appropriate" genre—generally, sensationalism or gothicism— and shown to result in the destruction of the villain and, at the least, the chastening of the heroine.[23]

Displaced from biological to adopted relatives, the paternal incest in *Two Men* meets only one of the criteria for acceptability. Paternal incest actually represents the novel's return to comparative tranquillity after the scandal of Charlotte and Parke's interracial liaison and Philippa's disappointment that Parke does not accept her romantic love. Stoddard's representation of paternal incest is not gothic, only occasionally sensational, just barely tinged with bits of sentimentalism, and Romantic to an extent that is limited by a radical, possibly unprecedented, experiment with psychological realism. In the last fifth of her novel, Stoddard allows Jason and Philippa to wrestle with the complexities of defining relationships and negotiating incestuous desire. For example, even after Jason recognizes his romantic attraction to Philippa, he both does and does not regard her as his daughter, as two contrasting quotations within five pages of each other suggest. At one point, Sarah speaks harshly to Philippa, and Jason replies, "Let my daughter alone."[24] But a short time later, he mentions to Philippa that things would have been different "could you really have been my daughter" (195). On the other hand, Philippa indicates that she is troubled by questions of age difference and incest when she insists to Jason, "I see myself, as a young woman, refusing to marry a man much older than herself, with whom she has lived as a relative."[25] Nevertheless, she admits to herself, "For the life of her she could not name the character of the relation; [Jason] never had appeared like a father, and she had never thought of him as a brother" (274). Although Philippa cannot decide whether Jason's attraction to her is incestuous any more than he can decide if she is his daughter, Stoddard upholds the incestuous nature of the attraction by bringing up the closer, more metaphorical relationships of father and brother rather than the technically correct ones of guardian and first cousin once removed.

Rather than hiding it behind "layers of confusion" or punishing it, Stoddard characterizes Jason's attraction to Philippa as "a right between them, which no power could annihilate, for it was not a guilty fact, but an undying truth" (104). Jason both rejects conventional assessments of their relationship and urges Philippa to let go of her socially constructed inhibitions about the unnamed subject of incest. He has already considered the possibility that "if I break through the traditions built round me by the masons who mortar the mass together by plummet and line" —the architects of a conventional moral order—"I shall be deprived of every claim of support from my fellows" (269), but he is willing to endure this. Jason attempts to reduce Philippa's concern about their age difference and status as relatives to an insignificant technicality—"the arithmetic of the subject" (274). He implies that the townspeople will disapprove of both paternal incest and a father's usurpation of his son's potential place in Philippa's affections, but he asks her to reject a conventional view of their relations: "Will you make *father* and *son* a watchword? Let the world do that" (270). It seems that "the world" does disapprove. When a neighbor asks if Philippa will "marry Jason" (260), Philippa exclaims, "Oh the cowardly world, that invents what it contemns [sic]!" (260). When Philippa insists that there are "reasons" why she should "not listen to [Jason], even" (274), he attempts to quell her conventional inhibitions by urging, "Give me your conscience, your will; I can keep them from tormenting you" (275).

As Jason becomes aware of his sexual attraction to Philippa, her touch awakens a long-dormant manhood that Stoddard valorizes as instinctual, physical, and natural: "his heart stopped beating, then bounded forward, and dragged every nerve into the terrible development which made him a *man*. One by one his savage instincts were revealed to him; he knew that he was a natural, free, powerful creature."[26] Earlier in the novel, Jason's soft-spoken lack of ambition and patriarchal power in the ancestral home of his high-born wife set him apart from the nineteenth-century ideal of manhood. Yet as "a husband, a father, and [Philippa's] guardian" (268), Jason fulfilled traditional masculine duties. He insists that these roles kept him in an undeveloped "chrysalis" form (269), but now the incestuous passion that disregards social taboos productively impels him beyond the unfulfilling limitations of conventional manhood. At the same time, he remains a responsible, considerate model of manhood whose comportment contrasts with the egotistical Parke's irresponsible behavior. Jason is praised as "an honor to human nature" (218), and his desire is "not a guilty fact" (104) because he fulfills his obligations to Sarah, Parke, and Philippa by restraining his desire for Philippa until his wife dies and his son leaves the country.

After these events occur, Jason and Philippa are left alone together in their house, with Philippa mourning Parke's absence. Parke was blind to her love for him, and Philippa remains similarly unable to recognize that Jason is "her lover, ardent, resolute, overpowering" (268). When Jason finally declares his love, Philippa resists his entreaties, angrily emphasizing her enduring love for his son and implicitly highlighting the novel's shift from the more acceptable incestuous desire of a sister to the incestuous desire of a father by exclaiming, "Parke! Parke! Parke!" (270). The power dynamics attached to Jason's physical strength and the father-daughter/guardian-ward authority structure begin to lead him away from his self-effacing, considerate behavior: frustrated that Philippa rejects his love, he attempts to "conquer [her] will" (270) and become "master of Paradise" (268), to kiss her while embracing her "by force" (275) rather than allowing her to make her own decisions. Just as Philippa's desire to "compel" Parke to marry her (94) leads her nowhere in her incestuous quest, Jason's moments of tyranny are not allowed to bear fruit. Stoddard emphasizes that both Jason's and Philippa's personalities were "a sacred essence that could not be tampered with," championing self-possession by implicitly opposing Jason's imperious demand, as "he shook her in his embrace," that Philippa give herself to him (275).

Philippa does not immediately give in, but her esteem for Jason does gradually deepen: recognizing "the honor and generosity of his nature," she admits to herself (but not to him) "that she would rather trust him

than any man in the world. The anomaly of her position was most trying—unheard of, and yet she had no thought of ever separating from
him" (277). Caught in an anomalous dilemma based on the vexed questions of kinship, relationships, propriety, and her own resistance and desire, Philippa uneasily juggles conventional taboos and her own ambivalent feelings until Stoddard solves the problems of power imbalance and
threats to self-possession. Out in the woods one day, Jason shoots off his
right hand (whether by accident or not, we never know), providing both
a neat excuse for Philippa to spend time with him and a reversal of
conventional power relations that makes it acceptable for her to fall in
love with him. As she nurses Jason, à la *Jane Eyre,* Philippa's "feelings
changed. . . . Their development was sanctioned by his inability to triumph over them" (288). In a rare mention of this novel in literary criticism, Alfred Habegger implies that *Two Men* differs from "all the other
guardian-ward love stories" in the nineteenth-century United States in
omitting "the coercive pressure" of paternal incest and allowing a true
love to develop ("Precocious Incest" 257).

Stoddard's point is not that power relations should be reversed but
that they should be equalized. As he recovers from his injury, Jason returns to his respectful, considerate attitude toward Philippa. Since Stoddard does not tend to offer her female characters weak men, Jason does
not accept Philippa's love until he has journeyed westward to regain his
health, strength, and self-sufficiency. But he differs from Parke and from
Philippa's father, who have left conventional society for the Venezuelan
pampas by the end of the novel: Jason returns to Philippa and a domestic
life. When he returns, Philippa supports the arm that is missing a hand,
calling it "my burden . . . that I love." When Jason "enclose[s] her with
his other arm," she calls him "my protection, that I love better" (300).
In this egalitarian scene, written in an era that increasingly valued companionate marriage, it is clear that each will support and depend on the
other.[27] Here Stoddard provides a far more affirmative conclusion than
she offered in *The Morgesons* or supplied for Parke's relationships with
Philippa and Charlotte. In this challenge to popular and legal opinions
and socially constructed boundaries, incest does not symbolize what
Thorslev calls "the psychologically dark and irrational, the unconscious
and 'unnatural' desires in the heart of man" (45), but rather the most
rational and natural course toward two lonely characters' emotional regeneration.

Stoddard was less radical—and perhaps less comfortable—in her treatment of an interracial liaison than she was in her treatment of incest; she

was less independent of the conglomeration of racialist perspectives that surrounded her. In 1853, Eva Saks writes, Gobineau introduced the "idea of a pure Aryan race," defining "race" for the first time as "a physical group *within* the human species."[28] Many abolitionists and most proponents of slavery feared that interracial sexual relationships would threaten the so-called purity of the white race, although abolitionists used this as an argument against slavery (since white masters sexually exploited their slaves), while proslavery racists contended that freeing slaves would increase the number of biracial children.[29] Saks argues that laws against interracial sexual affairs and marriage, as well as the enforcement of those laws, became stricter around 1830 or 1840, although extramarital affairs were "generally accepted" by southerners "when occurring between white men and black women" under slavery (43). In Stoddard's home state of Massachusetts—the setting of her novels—abolitionists successfully petitioned to have the ban on interracial marriages overturned in 1843.[30] Still, as Michael Grossberg points out, such legal actions "did little to alleviate the customary barriers to interracial unions"—the strong prejudices against them (349 n. 61).[31] It became difficult—in southern states, illegal—for slave owners to free their slave mistresses and biracial children or to leave them an inheritance. In fact, "many mulatto children after 1850 were seized as slave property" (Kinney 10). All of this encouraged free people of color to leave the South in attempts to maintain their freedom (Kinney 10). This is what the Lang family does in *Two Men*.

Approximately one-third of the way through the novel, we learn that an "elderly planter" from Georgia has sent Mrs. Lang and her daughters, Charlotte and Clarice, to the town of Crest (111). The Langs' status is not definite; one woman calls them fugitive slaves (142), but it is also possible that they have been freed. In any case, this is not a major issue in the novel. The issues are the Langs' status as African Americans facing the racism of northerners in a small New England town and the affair between Parke Auster and Charlotte Lang; these issues constitute the focus of about one-fifth of *Two Men*. Jason rents a house to the Langs, and Parke arranges for them to attend a dance, but other townspeople avoid them. Parke secretly courts Charlotte; apparently at his instigation, their relationship becomes sexual, and she becomes pregnant. Reward, rather than punishment, is initially offered to her as Parke vows to marry Charlotte and share in the shame, but his attendance at his mother's deathbed and the subsequent death of Charlotte and the baby in childbirth forestall his resolution. Parke is too late to marry Charlotte, but he buries her and their baby in the family plot near his mother. Then he leaves town.[32]

Interracial affairs were a common subject in nineteenth-century American literature, but not under the conditions we find in *Two Men*. According to Karen Sánchez-Eppler, "miscegenation provides an essential motif of virtually all antislavery fiction" (32).[33] Stoddard's familiarity with the works of such authors as Lydia Maria Child, Harriet Beecher Stowe, and, especially, John Townsend Trowbridge influenced her depiction of the Lang family. Like Trowbridge's *Neighbor Jackwood* (1857), *Two Men* belongs to a small group of novels written before the late nineteenth century that combine a northern setting with a plot more typical of novels focused on southern slavery: a cross-class, interracial sexual relationship initiated by a wealthy white man who is driven by physical attraction rather than love.[34] Stoddard's novel points to the ways racism supported such exploitation in the North as well as the South, in "freedom" as well as slavery.

When the housekeeper, Elsa, tells Philippa about Parke's affair with Charlotte, Philippa disdainfully refers to Charlotte as "that slave" (180). Elsa replies, "Yes . . . she is Parke's slave, and you know it. But whose slave will be Parke's child, with your blood in its veins?" (180). This is the most emphatic reference to slavery in the novel, as well as the most explicit reference to the idea of blood admixture. Stoddard simultaneously turns the question to the slavery of love and returns it to the issue of chattel slavery and the law decreeing that a child follow the condition of its mother. Elsa's comment literally brings home the problem of slavery: pursuant to the 1850 Fugitive Slave Law, Parke's child—a relative of Philippa's—could have been remanded to slavery if the child had lived and the mother had proven to be a fugitive slave. Without including explicit denunciations of slavery or racism, Stoddard subtly makes their threat real to New Englanders. One of Stoddard's reviewers called *Two Men* (in Stoddard's paraphrase) "the best anti-slave[r]y sermon ever preached" (letter to Whiting).

James Matlack suggests that Stoddard's disgust at the prejudice against the fugitive slave, Eliza, who worked as her servant in her hometown of Mattapoisett, Massachusetts, influenced her treatment of racism ("Literary Career" 314–15, 377).[35] In *Two Men,* Stoddard explains sarcastically that her fictional townspeople's attitudes toward the Langs range from "indignant pride" to "lively curiosity" and careless "indifference" (112). By having Philippa remember witnessing a slave's whipping during her childhood in the South and wonder how she and others would react if

Charlotte were "tied to a whipping-post" now—with the "contemptuous coldness now shown" or impulses of "pity and protection" (144)—
Stoddard also demonstrates the hypocrisy of antislavery northerners
who protest the brutal treatment of slaves but then discriminate against
African Americans in the North. Parke provides another example of
such hypocrisy: while he professes to "pity [Charlotte] from [his] heart"
and accuses "the coarse boobies" of the town of "imbecility" (144) for
failing to treat Charlotte and Clarice "like human beings" (145), he tells
Philippa not to speak to them at a dance and does not publicly endorse
their presence by asking them to dance. Yet he is fascinated by Charlotte's
beauty.

Clarice comments on "the curse" (151) of beauty for biracial women,
and indeed, Charlotte will be the victim of this curse. To some extent,
Charlotte resembles the stereotypically victimized "tragic mulatta" of
nineteenth-century sentimental and sensational fiction: she is beautiful,
modest, and refined; she inspires pity; she dies a tragic death; and the
so-called blackness of her appearance and manners have largely been
obliterated—quite possibly in order to appeal to white readers, but also
to suggest that her mother may have been sexually exploited and to
remind readers that racial boundaries have been crossed and may, indeed,
be rather unclear.[36] Emphasizing the tragic mulatta's purity, the archetype aligned black women characters with the mainstream ideology of
True Womanhood from which African American women had been excluded because of accusations that they were oversexed seducers rather
than victims of white men. However, Stoddard's representation of
Charlotte diverges from the tragic mulatta archetype when Charlotte
gives in to Parke's sexual desire. Rather than being resigned to a melan-
choly life and determined to maintain her purity at all costs, Charlotte
embraces the chance for a better life that Parke offers, and even after her
supposedly shameful sin, she has none of the suicidal tendencies found
in many tragic mulattas.[37]

Both Charlotte's divergence from the tragic mulatta archetype and
the differences between the three Lang women fruitfully complicate
Stoddard's portrayal of African American women. Charlotte's darker-
complected, more cynical younger sister, Clarice, provides a counterpoint to both Charlotte's appearance and her naive hopes for happiness.
Resentful of the townspeople's prejudice, Clarice warns Charlotte that
Parke merely "amuses himself by showing [her] attention," so that a
"little of [her] will suffice his vanity" (166). Stoddard represents Clarice's

suspicion as the rational approach to northern racism, but the more trusting Charlotte disagrees.

Introduced with an appeal to an essentialist understanding of enslaved women, Mrs. Lang is the most stereotypical of the three African American characters in the novel: "The glitter of negro blood was in Mrs. Lang's eyes, and the negro modulation in her voice" (111). She also demonstrates an ingrained racism that leads to undue sympathy for her white oppressor. Singing a plantation song that states, "What [de massa] wants is nebber wrong" (167) after a discussion of Parke's interest in Charlotte, she seems to compare Parke's sexual exploitation of her daughter to slave masters' exploitation of the powerless women they own, suggesting that both are inevitable. On the other hand, she hints that sexual attraction and even extramarital sex are natural for both men and women, regardless of race. Although she is a pious Christian, her feelings about sex might seem to align her with the racist stereotype of lascivious, immoral black women, except that the novel demonstrates that such feelings resemble Stoddard's perspective (as readers of *The Morgesons* will recognize). While Stoddard does not portray any strong, successful African Americans, such as those we see in abolitionist literature, slave narratives, and such later novels as Frances Harper's *Iola Leroy,* the Langs are each more complex than the stereotypes on which they may initially seem to be based.

Their characters are all developed in relation to Parke Auster, whose interest in Charlotte begins to evolve as he chats with her and Clarice at a dance he has organized. He is considered daring for approving of their attendance at the otherwise all-white affair, but instead of publicly developing an honorable relationship, he conducts his affair secretly: he loiters outside the Langs' house, seeks out Charlotte, and invites her to ride in his buggy on deserted roads. Stoddard does not go so far as to describe the act of sexual transgression that arises from this secret courtship. Instead, she foreshadows it and then focuses on its aftermath. Significantly, she represents the emotional and moral implications of the consummation of the relationship very differently for the two participants. In Parke's case, the narrator's judgment is only implicit, and the focus is on Parke's own gradual perception of his sin and the way it will affect his life. His first reaction to his sexual encounter amounts to a bold endorsement of the joys of sex: "his mind was dwelling with rapt fidelity on a new and terrible joy in his possession" (161). When Philippa perceives that he is upset and kisses his cheek (for the first time ever), her caress has a dramatic effect on him: "his sin [fell] into the depths of his soul" (161). Stoddard acknowledges the conventions of her day and demonstrates that Parke has been brought up to believe in them. But Parke still glories in one thought: "he had gained Charlotte" (163). Far more selfish than Jason, he assesses his relationships to women in terms of gain and loss, and initially the gain overrides the sin.

Immediately after consummating the relationship, Parke is able to join unsuspecting friends and family at a tea party, but Charlotte returns home to a "deserted" house (163). (Her mother and sister are at church.) Unlike Parke, Charlotte is not allowed to judge herself or the problems facing her; instead, the narrator breaks in to represent Charlotte as a forlorn figure who crept to bed in the dark:

> Did the angels of Pity and Patience guard that bed? Or waited a demon there, to behold the spectacle of dead chastity in a lovely shrine? Who will summon either to pass judgment upon a drama in which they were neither actors nor spectators!
>
> Ignorant, confiding, weak, poisoned with ancestral blood, none shall judge thee, Charlotte—but God! (163)

Although Stoddard allows for the possibility of *either* angels or a demon, Charlotte is here objectified as a "spectacle" and a "shrine," whereas Parke, sinful as he is, remains a son, a friend, and a cousin. Even while insisting that only God should judge Charlotte, the narrator judges her to be "poisoned with ancestral blood." She both blames Charlotte and offers condescendingly sympathetic, racist excuses for Charlotte's sexual activity.[38]

Especially since Stoddard seldom used this sort of dominant narrative voice to guide readers' opinions in her novels, the oddly archaic, melodramatic, and sentimental language and the conventional tone of the questions and implications here seem suspiciously uncharacteristic of the author. In *The Morgesons,* Stoddard's bold persona Cassandra was in some ways a more sexual being than Charlotte, although she did maintain her virginity until marriage.[39] In *Two Men,* Stoddard contradicts the judgmental portrayal of Charlotte by representing her as "the picture of . . . Innocence" (185) later in the novel. And while several characters demonstrate a tendency to blame Charlotte more than Parke, Stoddard sympathizes with Clarice, Mrs. Lang, and Jason, who save their reproaches for Parke.[40] The incongruity of the judgmental sentence suggests that it could have been a last-minute requirement of Stoddard's editor—a compromise demanded to compensate for her treatment of such a controversial subject. The positioning of the sentence in a separate paragraph, all by itself, may support this argument. But because Stoddard did not remove the sentence from the revised edition of *Two Men,* it is also possible that she voluntarily used it to appease moralistic readers—or that she shared some of her contemporaries' anxiety about racial difference and extramarital sex and was ambivalent about how to represent Charlotte's "sin."[41]

Whatever the reason, Stoddard did not follow her plotting to the potential end of Parke's marriage to Charlotte. Parke's friend Sam voices the kind of opposition Parke faces when he states his intention to marry this African American woman: "Now, by God, Parke, you shall not do it! You must not, cannot do it! Nature is against it—the whole race!" (173). Stoddard shows no sympathy for this outburst, but it is an accurate indication of the greater prejudice against interracial marriage than interracial affairs in mid-nineteenth-century America.[42] So rather than trying to work out a future for Charlotte, Stoddard "resolved" the problem of the controversial relationship that the novel sometimes seems to excuse with the punishment of death in childbirth.

Stillborn children, childhood mortality, and mothers' deaths in childbirth were extremely common in the mid-nineteenth century; by the time she wrote *Two Men,* Stoddard had already lost one of her three sons a few months after his birth and another at age six. In the novel, when Charlotte dies, Parke hopes that their dead child "may turn to a pitying angel" for Charlotte (214). Stoddard thus offers some hope for Charlotte's spirit without expressly sending her to heaven.[43] Especially given this historical precedent and spiritual hope, it is possible to argue that Stoddard was making a realistic point about the *likelihood* of some form of negative ending to an interracial liaison—a likelihood suggested by Sam's outburst. Even so, Charlotte's and the baby's deaths were not the only option in that time of racist claims that amalgamation led to sterility and that the "race" of mulattoes would eventually die out.[44] Charlotte offers another possibility as she tells Philippa, "I wish he would take me, and go with me to the everglades" (187). This sounds like an unusual desire, since most African Americans looking for a better life in mid-nineteenth-century literature fled north to Canada or east to Europe rather than south, but fugitive slaves did actually find refuge with Seminole tribes in the Florida Everglades as well.[45] Nevertheless, Stoddard rejects this alternative conclusion, sending Parke even farther south, to South America, without Charlotte or Philippa. While Stoddard was in certain ways progressive, she was hardly an idealist. Charlotte's and the unnamed baby's deaths represent the most troubling "solution" in her novels.[46] Stoddard offered a much more idealistic picture of an unconventional relationship in Jason and Philippa's successful incest than she provided in her treatment of an interracial relationship.

While her conclusion to this episode is disturbing, it is important to note that Stoddard was critiquing the prejudice that made African American women exploitable and left them with limited choices. Charlotte Lang clearly differs from the African American women in more conventional works by authors such as E. D. E. N. Southworth and Sara Josepha Hale, in which black women characters, according to Hazel Carby, "exist only to confirm their own lack of womanly attributes in contrast to the abundance of virtues" in the white heroine (33). Philippa and the other white women in *Two Men* are neither pious, pure, submissive, and domestic True Women nor Stoddard's ideal women.[47] Charlotte's problem is not that she possesses the "wanton," "rampant," or "uncontrolled" sexuality stereotypically associated with African American women in her time—she does not—but that she is more sexually vulnerable than the more obviously desirous Philippa.[48] The sound of bloodhounds barking as Parke has sex with Charlotte links her probable status as a former slave to her exploitability as a marginally free African American woman in the North whom he feels free to treat with less respect than the white women he knows.

Although Charlotte's affair ends in her death, Stoddard's comparisons of Charlotte's and Philippa's desires constitute an implicit endorsement of women's right to embrace their sexuality—and an intriguing juxtaposition of incestuous and interracial desire, a white woman's sexual repression and a black woman's acceptance of a sexual relationship.[49] Philippa's jealous reaction to the news of Parke's affair with Charlotte provides evidence of her largely repressed passion and contributes to the breakdown of what might seem to be a dichotomous representation of the "good," upper-class white woman versus the "bad," lower–middle-class black woman. As the housekeeper, Elsa, tells Philippa the scandalous news, she implies that Parke's attraction to Charlotte is true to "human nature" (180). When Philippa hears this, she thinks of the world as "a wide, flat, lonely plain, over which she must plod by herself, for she had no 'human nature' like this. An acute vision of Parke's abandonment to a wild, isolated happiness, such as she knew *he* could enjoy, passed before her mind, and for an instant she felt his utter separation from her. But not even this glimpse into the abyss of passion suggested the idea of renouncing him" (180). Against the backdrop of a lonely, dull, unhappy plain, passion is portrayed as wild joy. His happiness with an African American woman may take Parke into an "abyss," yet it is represented as a seductive alternative to loneliness, even for a woman who does not admit to having a passionate nature. Philippa's refusal to face her incestuous passion reflects the conservative nineteenth-century view that middle- and upper-class white women should repress their sexuality— and that white men could turn to African American women or women of a lower class for sex.[50]

Philippa's sexual repression helps prevent the consummation of an incestuous relationship with Parke, but her passion finds an outlet in irrational rage and displaced emotion that make this supposedly pure woman look far less appealing and even, for a time, less honorable than the so-called fallen one. This is evident when Philippa encounters the pregnant Charlotte, who has been picking violets on a country road. Charlotte is here described as "the picture of a sad, lovely Innocence" who speaks "with a childish treble" in her voice (185). Yet "Philippa's eyes so filled with dazzling beams that crashed down from her brain, that for a moment" she perceives Charlotte as "a dark, vague shape, whose coming overpowered her with hate and horror" (185). Born of conventional, racist notions of purity and evil, Philippa's enraged hallucination of a dark monster represents her jealously warped notion of the threat of miscegenation. However, we are clearly not meant to credit this perception of Charlotte, which is completely different from Stoddard's representations of her. Much as she might like to, Philippa cannot continue to view Charlotte in this way either: "when she saw more clearly, and saw the composure with which Charlotte stood before her, an irritation like madness possessed her" (185). She soon has another "maddening vision of a happiness which she had had no part in, and could have no part in with *Parke*" (185). In this scene, it seems as though a conventional woman's repressed incestuous jealousy can be more shocking and sensational than interracial sexual relations and the sexual transgressor herself. Repeated descriptions of Philippa's envious desire undermine her implicit claim to support the ideology of virtuous True Womanhood. While Charlotte embodies "Innocence," Philippa seems to be more obsessed with sex. Philippa will later admit to her father, Osmond, that if the "barriers" formed by "tradition and custom" were removed, she had "that within [her] which could rise, and overtop excess" (231).

Without actually mentioning the subject of which she speaks (sex with

Parke), Philippa tries to insist that she is more virtuous than Charlotte: "'I would have died first,' said Philippa, incoherently, . . . stamping her foot. . . . 'Do you know the misery you have made?'" (185). However, Charlotte replies "earnestly: '*You* would have died. *I* wanted to live'" (185). Stoddard makes it clear that Charlotte gives in to Parke's entreaties because they represent her only chance for friendship and for a life outside the confining walls of her quiet, isolated home. Stoddard also shows that Parke is responsible for initiating and continuing the affair, contrasting Charlotte's retiring modesty in their initial encounters with Parke's willful pursuit. Now Charlotte reminds Philippa, "He came after me, remember. I never asked anything of him" (186). While Charlotte's comments are—in Stoddard's value system—perfectly rational, Philippa's reactions appear deranged.

Stoddard's point here (if not later, when Charlotte dies) seems to be that repressing passion is more destructive than accepting it. In representing Charlotte in a more positive light than Philippa in this single scene in which the two women speak to each other, Stoddard would seem to be opposing stereotypical views of both African American women and premarital sex. When Philippa "sternly" advises Charlotte, "Wish to be dead," Charlotte refuses, declaring that she is "strong enough to bear everything" (187). In the end, she is not, and Charlotte's death in childbirth is reminiscent of the uncharacteristically judgmental passage which claimed that people should not judge Charlotte. The point about the danger of repression—a point repeated later in the novel, when Philippa needs to overcome her inhibitions in order to achieve incestuous happiness with Jason—is much more typically Stoddardian than the judgmental passage. The issue of race seems to have created contradictions for Stoddard, whether in the form of audience expectations, editorial suggestions, or her own ambivalence, and these contradictions weaken her novel's progressive standpoint.

However, race is not a black-and-white issue in *Two Men*. In this novel, Stoddard does not generally use the word "race" in the way it is most commonly used today—the way it was just beginning to be used in the mid–nineteenth century: to refer to people of different skin colors or ethnic heritages.[51] Instead, "race" seems to mean "the human race" in two cases (261), and in other instances to relate to a combination of ancestry and similar personality traits. In this second sense, Sarah's cousin Osmond and her son Parke are "of the same race" (27), and it is implied that Philippa and Jason belong to a different race. When Osmond brings his young daughter, Philippa, to live with Sarah and

Jason early in the novel, Osmond and Parke immediately bond with each other and distance themselves from Philippa and Jason. Observing that Philippa feels left out, Jason reassures her that he "came here to stay once too" (28). Much later, when he proposes marriage to Philippa, Jason tells her, "We are much alike" (271).

They are alike in their "foreignness" and in their difference from Parke, Osmond, and Sarah. As a young woman, Philippa thinks of Jason as "her fellow-alien" (103). Osmond views this man from another town and a lower class as an outsider, and Parke refers to his father, Jason, as "a foreigner" (97). Philippa was born in the slaveholding U.S. South or possibly, as Jennifer Putzi suggests in her essay in this volume, in South America. Sarah says Philippa "has a Southern constitution" (106). Both Sarah and Osmond refer to Philippa as a foreigner (97, 232), although, notably, Parke does not: "my country is your country, isn't it? You are as much of a Parke as I am" (97). Parke's denial of Philippa's foreignness, of her difference in race, may help to explain his willingness to embrace a relationship with Charlotte: although his regard for Charlotte turns out to be destructive, his views of race and difference are more liberal than those of his mother and most of the townspeople.

Throughout the novel, there is considerable emphasis on the Langs', Philippa's, and Jason's difference from others, although the significance of this difference varies. Philippa and Jason are primarily foreigners in their family's eyes; they are obviously highly privileged rather than victims of racism. The Langs, on the other hand, are rejected by the entire town. Osmond calls Philippa "half foreign" (232), which is reminiscent of the idea of being "half black," or "mulatto"—a term that could have been used (loosely) to describe Charlotte Lang, and maybe Philippa. Putzi argues convincingly that Philippa's mother may have been Venezuelan and a woman of color, but Philippa is assumed to be, and treated as, white in the novel—except, perhaps, by Sarah. Her family attributes the blond Philippa's "foreignness" not to any "black blood" but to the fact that she grew up both Catholic and as part of a slaveholding family somewhere to the south.

Yet Philippa and Charlotte have a good deal more in common than one may perceive at first glance: they share both the status of an outsider and an attraction to Parke, the focal point of the issues of both fraternal incest and interracial sex. Both women are treated as obstructions to men's desires and freedom—Parke's and Osmond's. It is suggested that Parke had planned to leave Charlotte after marrying her (if she had lived), and Osmond left Philippa with Jason and Sarah years before because he viewed her as "an obstacle in [his] way of life" (37). There is also some resemblance between the way Sarah treats and views Philippa and the way the townspeople treat and view the Langs, although Sarah does, of course, interact with Philippa and give her a home as well as nursing her through illnesses. But she does so without tenderness: Philippa knows "Sarah hated her" (45). Philippa reflects on "Sarah's perpetual coldness, irritation, and anger" and realizes "how impossible it was for [Philippa] to be considered anything except an intruder and an encumbrance" (199). Sarah's reaction to the idea of Philippa's marrying Parke is also similar to a nineteenth-century racist's reaction to an interracial alliance: " 'Had Philippa been idiot enough to expect to gain Parke?' she thought. If it was so, she would never allow Philippa to dream that such a thing was possible. It was not possible, as far as Parke was concerned, and yet—there was the property, which might be all his again. But no, the idea of that girl being his wife was not to be thought of" (135). She seems to be as unwilling to accept Philippa as her daughter-in-law as she would be to accept Charlotte.

Sarah's treatment of Philippa and the general emphasis on Philippa's foreignness justify a consideration of her incestuous desire for Parke as the desire of an outsider wanting to get in—as close as possible. The incestuous condition of extreme closeness might overcome the outsider's feeling of excessive difference. Yet given Sarah's treatment of Philippa, Stoddard's use of the word "race" in *Two Men,* and Putzi's suggestion that Philippa may be multiracial, it begins to seem that this may be a question of miscegenation as much as incest. So another reason for the failure of fraternal incest in *Two Men* could be that it is too much like the miscegenation that also fails in the novel—and too uncomfortable for Stoddard and her readers. Destroying each segment of the Philippa-Parke-Charlotte triangle, Stoddard rejects the complex interweaving of fraternal incest and miscegenation that both reflects the concerns of her contemporaries and critiques them. She endorses the paternal incest between outsiders, intruders, and foreigners rather than the interracial affair or the questionable incestuous/interracial relationship. Still, while Stoddard was hardly immune to the racism of her time, her empathetic treatment of Jason and his relationship with Philippa suggests sympathy for these outsiders and their nonconformity rather than an endorsement of xenophobia or racism. Although she was unusual in representing paternal incest in this way, Stoddard used incest to challenge conformity as Shelley and other European Romantics did: "to break through the crust of those outworn opinions on which established institutions de-

pend" by portraying incest as "actions which are only crimes of convention." [52]

In the surprising last chapter of *Two Men,* Stoddard turns away from
Jason and Philippa, the two "foreigners" who have settled in the ancestral home, and returns to Parke and Osmond, who appear to be on the
South American plains among a tough group of men. In this chapter,
Parke and Osmond's conversation about Philippa suggests that the Parke
family cycle of incestuous desire will repeat itself. Sarah loved Osmond,
the cousin with whom she grew up, and he left her; when he returned,
she was married to Jason. Philippa loved Parke, the cousin with whom
she grew up, and he left her; when Parke returns, Osmond suggests, he
will find Philippa married to Jason. Stoddard's odd conclusion, which
unsettles the novel's unity by introducing a completely new, decidedly
foreign setting and returning to two characters who seemed to have
disappeared from the plot, may paradoxically serve to unify the novel
in another way: by emphasizing the triple occurrence of incestuous desire and hinting at an interrelationship among those desires as well as a
repetition of them—a repetition of the incest plot for emphasis on that
taboo.

NOTES

1. This is the second of two epigraphs to *Two Men;* both epigraphs are identified only by their author, Ralph Waldo Emerson. This comes from his essay
"Experience."

2. For more detailed plot summaries, which include some interpretations
of *Two Men* that differ from mine, see Matlack, "Literary Career" 341–61 and
Croce, "Phantoms" 227–37.

3. See also Saks, "Representing Miscegenation Law" 53.

4. Cf. Samuels 123–28. A few examples of novels dealing with incest under
slavery are Richard Hildreth's *The Slave; or, Memoirs of Archy Moore* (1836);
Howard Meeks's *The Fanatic; or, The Perils of Peter Pliant, the Poor Pedagogue*
(1846); H. L. Hosmer's *Adela, The Octoroon* (1860); and Martin Delany's *Blake; or,
the Huts of America* (serialized in 1859 and 1861–62).

5. Incest was a notable topic in early American gothics and seduction nov-
els, mid–nineteenth-century American domestic best-sellers, sensational novels,
Edgar Allan Poe's "The Fall of the House of Usher," Nathaniel Hawthorne's
"Alice Doane's Appeal," Herman Melville's *Pierre,* George Gordon, Lord Byron's
Manfred and *Parisina,* various works by Percy Shelley, Emily Brontë's *Wuthering
Heights* (one of Stoddard's favorite novels), other prominent British novels, and

a number of works by American abolitionist authors. Twitchell emphasizes that the "topic of incest" was "a major concern of romanticism" and a significant and "dynamic" theme in American literature, particularly American gothicism (80, 195). Thorslev traces a widespread interest in incest in Germany and England to works by such authors as Schiller, Tieck, Chateaubriand, Lewis, Byron, and Shelley—all of whom Stoddard read.

6. In early American novels, according to Dalke, incest generally resulted in "madness or suicide" (188). "American Romantics," Wilson argues of William Hill Brown, Charles Brockden Brown, Hawthorne, Melville, and Poe, portrayed "incest as self-destructive" (32).

7. See, for example, Stoddard's letters to Whiting and Moulton cited later.

8. For other discussions of nonliteral representations of incest in literature, compare, for example, McGuire and Goetz on Emily Brontë's *Wuthering Heights*. McGuire argues that "for an incest taboo to exist, it is irrelevant whether Cathy and Heathcliff are blood relatives. What is essential is that they were *raised* as brother and sister" (217). Goetz contends that "it is indisputable that Heathcliff's adoptive place in the family turns him into a brother of Catherine" (363).

9. For example, Goshgarian contends that many mid-nineteenth-century domestic novelists portrayed incest in their apparently pious popular novels but displaced and repressed it so thoroughly that they were unaware of it themselves (3–4, 74–75).

10. Stoddard, *Two Men* (New York: Johnson, 1971) 45. Subsequent parenthetical citations will refer to this edition of the novel. The 1901 edition on which the 1971 edition is based includes the revisions Stoddard made for the 1888 edition of her novel. The first edition of *Two Men* was published in 1865.

11. On True Womanhood, see Welter, "The Cult of True Womanhood."

12. Letter from Elizabeth Stoddard to Margaret Sweat, 23 December 1852. Allison-Shelley Collection, Rare Books and Manuscripts, Pennsylvania State U. Libraries. By permission.

13. Letter from Elizabeth Stoddard to Margaret Sweat, 10 February 1853. Allison-Shelley Collection, Rare Books and Manuscripts, Pennsylvania State U. Libraries. By permission.

14. Letter from Elizabeth Stoddard to Edmund Clarence Stedman, 4 September 1862. Edmund Clarence Stedman Papers, Rare Book and Manuscript Library, Columbia University, New York.

15. These namesakes, as well as personal letters, hint that there are actually three plausible candidates for Lorry's father, in addition to Richard Stoddard: Booth, Graham, and Wilson Barstow. See Radinovsky, "Gender Norms" 132–33 n. 18. It is interesting to note that Stoddard's first son, Willy, was named after her brother Wilson.

16. Letter from James Lorimer Graham to Bayard Taylor, 7 November 1866. Harvard (bMS Am 1598 [77–172]). By permission of the Houghton Library, Harvard University.

17. The only major general Stoddard seems likely to have met is Major General John Adams Dix, on whose staff Wilson served during the Civil War. However, he was sixty-five years old in 1863, and I have seen no indication that the forty-year-old Stoddard was attracted to him, or vice versa. (On Dix, see Matlack, "Literary Career" 202.)

18. Some influential friends apparently helped him attain a "triple promotion 'for efficient and meritorious services during the war'" in May 1866; he was promoted to brigadier general in February 1867 (Matlack, "Literary Career" 407, 409).

19. While it could be interpreted as a hint that Wilson might have fathered Lorry, this letter could also imply that Graham thought he or Booth was the father.

20. Letter from Elizabeth Stoddard to Louise Chandler Moulton, 16 December [1865]. Papers of Louise Chandler Moulton, Manuscripts Division, Library of Congress.

21. Letter from Elizabeth Stoddard to Lilian Whiting, 25 June [1888]. Rare Books and Manuscripts Department, Boston Public Library, courtesy of the Trustees of the Boston Public Library.

22. Since American authors generally wrote more hesitantly about any type of incest than the British Romantics did, the difference in representation of sibling versus paternal incest may not appear as great on this side of the Atlantic. However, paternal incest was particularly horrifying to Americans.

23. Cf. Twitchell 150, 154, 212. See also Habegger, *Henry James and the "Woman Business"* 25; Wilson 32–33; and Goshgarian, for example, 78–79. Twitchell claims that the experience of incest was either "uniformly horrible, [and] irrepressibly gothic" in nineteenth-century American literature or sensationalized (196, 212–13). Discussions of incest in the mid–nineteenth century and later tend to focus on these genres.

24. Stoddard, *Two Men* (New York: Bunce and Huntington, 1865) 186. In the revised edition of the novel, Jason says, "Let our girl alone" (191). Only in the 1865 edition does Jason call Philippa his daughter—so that their relationship looks more incestuous in the first edition than in the revision. The revised edition of *Two Men* includes far fewer changes than the revised editions of Stoddard's other two novels, and no major changes at all. On a few occasions, the revision is more positive and conventional, as is the revised edition of *The Morgesons;* the most notable improvements are a few dozen examples of increased clarity or conciseness. While I am generally quoting from the more readily

available revised edition of the novel, my interpretation is based on Stoddard's slightly more radical 1865 edition.

25. Stoddard, *Two Men* (1865) 264. The revised edition omits "much older than herself" (274), deemphasizing the issue of paternal incest.

26. Stoddard, *Two Men* (1865) 103. In the revised edition, Stoddard replaced "savage" and "creature" with "primitive" and "being," respectively (103), slightly deemphasizing the animal nature of Jason's masculine urges.

27. Lystra claims that "historians are arriving at a consensus that the last half of the eighteenth and early part of the nineteenth century were years in which male-female relationships among the native-born middle classes became less patriarchal and more companionate" (228). Rotundo suggests that "loving, companionate marriages were in the minority throughout the [nineteenth] century for middle-class couples, but it seems as well that this minority grew as the century went along," especially "in the last third of the century" (164). Stoddard's letters to her friend Margaret Sweat in the early 1850s, around the time of her marriage, show that she desired and hoped for such a marriage herself, although she was not certain she could attain it.

28. Saks, "Representing Miscegenation Law" 45, referring to *Essai sur l'inégalité des races humaines.*

29. See Skinfill, "Nation and Miscegenation" 67; Sánchez-Eppler, *Touching Liberty* 34; D'Emilio and Freedman, *Intimate Matters* 86–87; Grossberg, *Governing the Hearth* 136–40. Of course, there were also many abolitionists who approved of interracial relationships.

30. Such marriages remained illegal in most southern states and many northern ones (Saks 43).

31. Grossberg quotes from Auguste Carlier's *Marriage in the United States* 87 to show that even where interracial marriage was legal "the force of prejudice is such that no one would dare to brave it. It is not the legal penalty which is feared, but a condemnation a thousand times more terrible" (127).

32. For additional considerations of this episode, see Matlack, "Literary Career" 381–93; Henwood, "Narrative Strategies" 94–120; and Croce, "Phantoms" 243–51. Croce's analysis of Stoddard's treatment of the aftermath of Charlotte and Parke's affair, and of racism in the North, is comparable to mine at several points (245–48), but her approach to the novel is quite different.

33. The word *miscegenation* was coined in 1864, when *amalgamation* was the more popular term (Grossberg 136; Saks 42; Samuels 165 n. 5). Mitchell reminds us that the word *miscegenation* "presupposes the acceptance of race as a scientific concept, something which was acceptable in the 19th century, but is no longer valid today" (128 n. 4). For this reason, I use the word self-consciously and sparingly.

34. As Matlack has argued, *Two Men* probably has more in common with Trowbridge's *Neighbor Jackwood,* which clearly influenced Stoddard, than with any other novel, although the differences between the novels are also striking ("Literary Career" 390–93). On *Neighbor Jackwood,* see also Kinney 76–77.

35. I have been unable to ascertain the terms under which Eliza worked for the Stoddards, but Matlack calls her the Stoddards' "servant-girl" and "maid" ("Literary Career" 377).

36. Sánchez-Eppler argues that the "problem of antislavery fiction is that the very effort to depict goodness in black involves the obliteration of blackness" (31). See also Sollors, "Excursus on the 'Tragic Mulatto'; or, The Fate of a Stereotype" in his *Neither Black Nor White Yet Both* 220–45.

37. Sollors argues persuasively that there is a wide variety of tragic mulatto plots and characters (238–39), but he also acknowledges the importance of two typical figures of "the Mulatto" in nineteenth-century literature, one of which I have alluded to (240). See also Karcher.

38. On the tendency for white authors writing about tragic mulatto figures to blame "black blood" for shortcomings, see Sollors 220–45. Without claiming that *Two Men* is a completely progressive novel, it is worth remembering Sollors's point that "it is possible to think of stereotypical features in progressive literature" (232).

39. Consider, for example, Cassandra's conversation with a specter or devil, in which she strongly denies feeling "remorse and repentance" for her desire for the married Charles (*The Morgesons and Other Writings* 131).

40. Some of the characters' critical attitudes toward Charlotte suggest that the nineteenth-century double standard that demanded more purity from women than from men, and hence reproached women more harshly when they "strayed," was compounded by the racist view of African American women as seducers of white men. (Cf. D'Emilio and Freedman 86 and Welter, "The Cult of True Womanhood" 155.) For generally moral white women who had premarital affairs, social and judicial attitudes were becoming more forgiving by the 1860s: Grossberg argues that "female submission [to sexual intercourse] after a marriage promise was excusable and understandable" (48). He explains that this was part of a mid-nineteenth-century legal trend toward viewing women as weak victims of seducers who deserved legal reparations from men who had made false promises. Although he does not mention race in this discussion, Grossberg must be referring to white women here, because African American women were refused both the legal protection and the status of True Women. Lystra and others have also argued that sex in a loving relationship that was followed by marriage before a child's birth was accepted, even if not approved. But this assumes that both partners are white; I submit that the prejudice against

"miscegenation" multiplies the potential of scandal. However, contemporary reviewers generally sided with Charlotte. Sweetser blamed Parke. Howells both blamed and complimented Parke, referring to his "guilty passion" but saying his "nature is good and generous." (Matlack attributes these unsigned reviews to Sweetser and Howells ["Literary Career" 368, 366].)

41. Also noticing this passage's divergence from Stoddard's usual perspective and narrative voice, Dawn Henwood suggests that at this point "the narrator seems to parody the self-righteous, heavily Christianized discourse that often described 'the fallen woman'" ("Narrative Strategies" 105). But even as she identifies a conscious parody and argued that "the foundations of conventional morality appear to be sabotaged from the very beginning of the excerpt," Henwood also describes "divergent threads of the narrative voice"—"a narrative voice divided against itself" that points to the authorial ambivalence I mention ("Narrative Strategies" 107, 109).

42. Saks points out that the stronger prohibition against marriage as compared with extramarital "fornication" in these cases inverted "traditional moral categories" in order to deny legal sanction and property transmission in the case of interracial affairs (46–47, 54).

43. With a quotation from the German classic *Faust*, Stoddard also implied that Parke, like Faust, is responsible for the evil act of seducing a woman: Charlotte, like Margaret, does sin, but only at the instigation of a more sinful man. Margaret was saved as she accepted responsibility for her actions, so perhaps Charlotte was, too. The *Faust* reference comes up when Parke returns to the Langs' house for the last time after Charlotte's death. He stares into the fire for hours. "What fascination held his eyes to the consuming brands? Did he see Mephistopheles in his scarlet coat and cock's feather, with his eternal grin? Did he hear Margaret cry; 'Day! yes, it is growing day! The last day is breaking in! My wedding-day it was to be'" (242).

44. On these claims, see Sollors 129–35. Sollors asserts, "In the nineteenth and the first half of the twentieth century the belief that Mulattoes were 'feeble' or unable to procreate among themselves, or that their children would be impaired in fertility, had so much political, scientistic, and general intellectual support that it may be called the 'dominant opinion' of the period" (132), although there was considerable debate over this issue. Stoddard is not completely supporting the "dominant opinion," of course, since Mrs. Lang, who is said to have "white blood in her veins" (113), does have two teenage daughters.

45. On the usual destination of literary fugitives, see Sollors 338–39. On the Seminoles, see, for example, Murray "The Unconquered Seminoles."

46. As Sollors points out, "the themes of interracial literature seem to belong

to the category of topics that have generated a particular ambivalence toward endings in writers and critics" (348).

47. Philippa is both conventional—in her devotion to Parke, her obedience, her purity, her weakness, and her fear—and unconventional—in her distaste for domestic tasks, her lack of interest in typically girlish and womanly things, her disapproval of "over-pious" ministers (59), her obstinacy, her general coldness, and her occasional angry or loving passion.

48. On stereotypes of African American women's sexuality, see Carby, *Reconstructing Womanhood* 27; Tate, *Domestic Allegories* 63; and Nelson, *The Word in Black and White* 135.

49. For a somewhat different interpretation of women's relationships to sexuality in *Two Men,* see Habegger, *Henry James and the "Woman Business"* 96–98.

50. On the tendency to blame female slaves' "rampant sexuality" for this, see, for example, Carby 27.

51. The exception occurs when Philippa remembers that she once heard a whip "cut the flesh of [Charlotte's] race" (144).

52. The quotations come from Shelley (last paragraph).

9

Reconstructing *Temple House*

Ellen Weinauer

None of Elizabeth Stoddard's three full-length novels achieved anything like popularity in the author's lifetime, but the last—*Temple House,* published in 1867—seems to have suffered particularly acute neglect. A number of Stoddard's friends and contemporaries viewed this novel as her strongest work to date: Stoddard's husband, Richard Henry Stoddard, believed that *Temple House* was "more powerful" than Stoddard's earlier novels; George Boker called it "Lizzie's best book"; and Edmund Stedman insisted to James Russell Lowell that *Temple House* was "a more artistic and powerful story than its predecessors" (qtd. in Matlack, "Literary Career" 412, 440). But others were not nearly so enthusiastic, and the novel appears to have gone largely unread. While Stoddard's earlier novels had been quite widely reviewed—thanks, in large part, to the indefatigable efforts of Richard Stoddard—according to James Matlack, the only major periodicals to review *Temple House* were *The Nation* and the *New York Tribune.* Nor did the reviews themselves manifest the sort of critical praise garnered by *The Morgesons* (1862) and *Two Men* (1865). While the *Tribune's* George Ripley, one of Stoddard's most consistent supporters, praised Stoddard's "brave sincerity," "mental integrity," and "intense realism," he also criticized the characters for being "pure creations of fancy" and the plot for ending with "great abruptness" and "mystery" (review of *Temple House* [1868] 6). *The Nation's* review was a great deal harsher: "We may as well secure the reader of the story from a possible disappointment by informing him that *Temple House* is a story that has no end," the reviewer proclaimed. "Properly enough, too," he went on, "for it has no plot, and should have no catastrophe. . . . We pay [Stoddard] the compliment of always thinking she was saying something worth hearing, and of trying to comprehend what it was, yet sometimes we understand her . . . simply not at all" (review of *Temple House* [1868] 74).

Such remarks about Stoddard's impenetrability were made frequently in her own day, lending credence to Richard Foster's claim (one echoed by more recent critics such as Lawrence Buell and Sandra Zagarell) that Stoddard was "writing for audiences not yet born" (Foster, "Fiction" 162). But despite obvious changes in literary taste and understanding, the audience for *Temple House* (if not for Stoddard's other work) appears still to be "not yet born." A search of the *MLA Bibliography* turns up nothing—not a single published essay—on the text. Although it is true that a number of dissertations and essays on Stoddard have taken up *Temple House,* either at length or in passing, the assessments of it are, in the main, negative.[1] Ironically, perhaps, instead of being faulted for its ellipticism and resistance to easy comprehension—qualities valorized by recent modes of critical scrutiny—Stoddard's final novel is today criticized for its concessions to mid-nineteenth-century popular tastes. Matlack writes: "Perhaps the most damaging thing to be said about *Temple House* is that it can become almost indistinguishable from the flood of conventional domestic novels of the mid–nineteenth century. The style is distorted and overworked. Elizabeth is not at home with it. Her descriptions become fuzzy and vague, palpitating with some misguided romantic spirit." The "plotting" of the novel, he insists, is "an inventory of sentimental clichés" (439). Buell and Zagarell also note the novel's "greater (though still limited) concessions to lucidity and to popular conventions of plot and character" (xx).[2] But although Buell and Zagarell here treat apparent conventionalism more gently than does Matlack, Zagarell takes her assessment into less neutral and descriptive terrain in noting that *Temple House* is a "melodramatic production" ("Profile" 43) and a "flatly derivative book" ("Repossession" 56 n. 5).[3]

Much could be said about the ways in which this redaction of *Temple House*'s unhappy critical trajectory reveals the paradoxes of Stoddard's own critical reputation—or, perhaps more precisely, reveals the paradoxes and fault lines of the effort to recover Stoddard's work, and the work of other nineteenth-century women writers, for current readers. Stoddard offers us a particularly complex and troubling example of the intransigence of critical categories (whether those categories are in operation in the 1860s or the 1980s) and their resistance to multivalence and multivocality. The ongoing neglect of this novel, judged by many in its own day as inaccessible and frustratingly unconventional and by the few who have read it in ours as too willing to capitulate to convention, allows us to consider the constraints and paradoxes of literary assessment itself. In this regard, one might point out, for example, that efforts to value Stoddard and affirm her place in the "reconstructed" canon on the basis of her *lack* of conventionality and refusal to capitulate to popular taste put the critic, if not the writer, at complex odds with the endeavor to valorize "popular conventions," sentimentalism, and melodrama that has been such a part of the recovery project in which Americanist criticism has been recently engaged.

One of the most significant aspects of this recovery project has been the attempt to acknowledge what Jane Tompkins has called the "cultural work" performed by women's novels in the antebellum and immediate postbellum periods.[4] In particular, critics have become increasingly interested in how novels by nineteenth-century women engaged the social and political debates of the period and worked to reflect, if not to influence, public attitudes toward such matters as slavery and suffrage, domestic economy and the rearing and education of children, temperance, revision of marital and property law, labor reform, and so on. But Stoddard's work fares no better in this interpretive framework; indeed, the framework itself barely seems applicable to Stoddard's fictions, which are frequently set in some undated "past" and which rarely appear to engage, in any explicit way, social or political issues.[5] *Two Men* comes the closest to doing so, and even this novel's exploration of interracial love and racialism north of the Mason-Dixon Line remains on an ostensible level quite detached from immediate historical considerations.[6] In this context, it is hardly surprising that one of the consistencies we can recognize in responses to and assessments of *Temple House,* whether in Stoddard's day or in our own, is the *absence* of any reference to the immediate post–Civil War context in which the book was written and published.

In truth, *Temple House* makes few references to historical events of any sort and no references at all to slavery, the Civil War, or Reconstruction. Set in the fictional town of Kent (closely modeled on Plymouth) at some shadowy moment in the not-so-distant past, the novel tells a story of friendship, desire, and social conventionalism that seems to have little bearing on the deeply traumatic political events of the 1860s.[7] I want to argue, however, that this novel is, in fact, engaged in those events, and that making substantive room for *Temple House* is crucial to an understanding not only of Elizabeth Stoddard's career and place in nineteenth-century (literary) culture but also of some of the divergent ways (ways not perhaps fully accounted for in our operative critical paradigms) in which works of literature reflected and responded to the massive upheavals of life after the Civil War. In particular, I maintain that this novel exists as a meditation on two of the most dynamic, urgent, and intricately connected issues of the postwar period: the meaning of freedom and the nature of national membership.

As Americans, North and South, struggled to recover from and understand the consequences of the bloodiest and most divisive conflict the United States had yet seen, and as, more specifically, the federal government and the states debated the very terms of membership in the American "family," freedom became what Eric Foner calls the nation's new "terrain of conflict" (77). Freedom's "substance," Foner writes, was "open to different and sometimes contradictory interpretations, its content changing for whites as well as blacks in the aftermath of the Civil War" (77). Written in the wake of the passage of the Thirteenth Amendment (1865) and the Civil Rights Act (1866), and amidst debates about the Fourteenth Amendment (passed by Congress in June 1866)—each of which worked to control and contain the "content" of "freedom" and to negotiate expanding definitions of U.S. citizenship—*Temple House* itself explores freedom's content and the kind of (national) "family" that can be established on freedom's foundation.[8] It does so through a complex deployment of gothic tropes—doubling and inversion, fusion and reversal—that expose what Teresa Goddu has called, in her interrogation of American gothic literature, the "historical horrors that make national identity possible yet must be repressed in order to sustain it" (10). Stoddard's exploration of these "historical horrors," her writing of what we might call a national gothic, operates around the contrast between Temple House, an apparently haunted house that is rendered, paradoxically, as a site of liberation and autonomy, and the Forge, an apparently anti-gothic site of domestic comfort and class privilege that is, in fact, a haunted house. Far from being the place of gothic decay, degeneration, and disease that it at first appears, the house that gives the novel its title witnesses the creation of a unified "family" based not on the ties of "blood" and the ideology of industrial development—the foundations of the Forge—but, rather, on principles of desire and jointly realized forms of autonomy, "internal liberty," and "self-possession." In the end, Stoddard's vision of what Frederick Douglass once called the "great national family of America" (qtd. in Foner 27) includes a diverse group of "others": laboring men and upper-class women, "foreigners" and the native-born, Native Americans and African Americans. But if Stoddard holds out Temple House as the site of a nearly utopian community, the novel stages simultaneous and ongoing dramas of power, assimilation, and racialism that trouble this alternative "model nation" and suggest the inescapability of the historical horrors that the narrative sets out to represent. *Temple House* thus functions as a kind of gothic utopia—a narrative that tries to imagine an ideal national household but which registers at the same time the "cultural contradictions" (Goddu 10) that continue to trouble that household and compromise its foundation.

It is particularly striking that Stoddard's work is rarely put in the context of the Civil War and the events of the war decade when we remember that her long fiction spans the early years of the war and the period of early Reconstruction. Stoddard herself invites us to frame her work in a wartime context: "The Morgesons was my Bull Run," she once told Edmund Stedman (qtd. in Buell and Zagarell xix).[9] Buell and Zagarell suggest that, in this remark, Stoddard means to highlight how "the news of the Union's disastrous defeat, ten days after publication, crippled her sales" (xix). Stoddard's remark can surely be read as a reflection on her novel's unsatisfactory fate; but we might also see it as an invitation to consider the complex historical situation—and situatedness—of her text. Yet, again, this invitation has rarely been taken up: tellingly, for example, Stoddard goes completely unmentioned in three recent works about war-decade writing: Kathleen Diffley's *Where My Heart Is Turning Ever* (1992), Elizabeth Young's *Disarming the Nation* (1999), and Lyde Cullen Sizer's *The Political Work of Northern Women Writers and the Civil War* (2000). It is certainly true that Stoddard's fiction bears little apparent resemblance to the work of the writers taken up by Diffley, Young, and Sizer: Louisa May Alcott, Gail Hamilton, Rebecca Harding Davis, Elizabeth Keckley, Frances Harper, Mark Twain, and John W. De Forest, among others. Such writers' explicit rendering of the war and its aftermath puts Stoddard's seeming inattention to or attenuation of wartime and postwar events in sharp relief. I want to insist, however, that Stoddard's work is no less engaged in these events, albeit its engagement is often indirect, its angle of approach oblique. Indeed, one can recognize in the fiction she published throughout the 1860s many of the concerns and thematic patterns identified by Diffley, Young, and Sizer as characteristic of war-decade writing.[10] Sizer's broad explication of the "work" performed by "northern women writers" during and after the Civil War, for example, applies as much to Stoddard as to the other writers under Sizer's scrutiny. That "work," Sizer writes, "was intended to move . . . readers: to shore up traditional ideas, to rearrange them, or to change them altogether. . . . This work was emphatically political—meaning that it participated in the power relations in society—if it was rarely directly partisan: it entered a terrain of national concern, offering an interpretation of the nation's needs and fears" (4–5). This seems a fitting description of *Temple House,* a novel deeply interested in investigating the "power relations of society" and the "needs and fears" of a nation struggling to unify a disparate and much-divided people.

At first glance, though, the "terrain" of *Temple House* hardly seems "of national concern," as a brief rendition of its plot will suggest. Like *Two Men,* the novel focuses on a male protagonist, Argus Gates, who has come to inherit Temple House "by the unexpected will of a distant relative" (14).[11] A retired ship captain who is forty-one when the novel opens, Argus once lived in total isolation at Temple House. Having lost a young wife a few years after their marriage, he interacts only with Mat Sutcliffe, his former first mate, and the wealthy industrialist Cyrus Brande, who owns and operates the Forge, one of the few prospering concerns in Kent, and who helps to manage Argus's business affairs. By the time of the novel's action, however, Argus has broken his isolation. Upon discovering that his long-lost and profligate brother is living in a nearby town, Argus tries to "save" George by bringing him, along with his wife, Roxalana, and daughter, Temple (called "Tempe"), back to Temple House. It is not long before George rejects family and kinship ties: he soon leaves for further adventures (and is eventually acknowledged to be dead), and Temple House is left only to Argus, Roxalana, and Tempe.

It is at this point that the novel opens and that what could be called its action unfolds. The quiet, ostensibly static life at Temple House is broken by several events that bring it into contact with the world outside its walls. First, Tempe marries John Drake, a young man of wealth and standing in Kent. The marriage ends quickly, with John's death in a railway accident; it produces a son, christened (in an interesting denial of paternal lineage) "George Gates" by Roxalana, for whom Tempe feels no affection and whose death at an early age nearly shatters Roxalana and the prospect of life at Temple House itself. Next, Argus is involved in another act of "saving," this time of a man to whom he has no family connection. He and Mat save a "Spaniard," Sebastian, who is the only survivor of a shipwreck that occurs during a terrible storm; Sebastian eventually comes to live at Temple House and to provoke the heretofore passionless Argus into an emotionally powerful and homoerotic friendship.[12] Finally, Virginia Brande, daughter of the owner of the Forge, falls in love with Argus and eventually wins his love in return. Indeed, the final portions of the novel are devoted to the latter heterosexual "romance" plot and to what Richard Foster describes as a "mounting crescendo of irrational emotion" and a "demonic flurry of desires" ("Fiction" 174, 175): Argus discovers his love for Virginia, who finds herself drawn to Sebastian; Sebastian desires Virginia, though he has committed himself to Tempe; both Cyrus Brande and the man to whom he has promised Virginia, Mr. Carfield, lust after Tempe. Ultimately, the lustful (indeed, lecherous) Brande and Carfield are driven from the field. Argus, the novel suggests, will marry Virginia, Sebastian will marry Tempe, and together, as Mat and Argus put it in the novel's final lines, "we shall carry on Temple House" (347).[13]

As we will see, the "carrying on" of Temple House is, in the end, central to Stoddard's postwar vision of national redemption. From the beginning, her novel investigates the meaning of this inherited property and its legacies for all of its inhabitants—an investigation that signals Stoddard's entrance onto what both Foner and Sizer call the "terrain" of national conflict and concern. As Diffley indicates in her exhaustive reading of wartime and postwar narratives published in popular magazines between 1861 and 1876, the metaphor of the nation as "household" was commonly deployed, not only in fiction but in congressional debates and political rhetoric (14); Abraham Lincoln's prewar effort to trope the nation as a "house divided" is perhaps the most famous, but certainly not the only, use of domestic rhetoric to capture the trauma of the (first impending, then ongoing) Civil War and the urgent need of healing and reunification in its aftermath.[14] As Frederick Douglass's invocation of the "great national family" suggests, domestic metaphors also proliferated in the postwar debates regarding constitutional reform and expanding notions of citizenship, particularly as those notions would apply to newly admitted members of the national family—the men, women, and children whose emancipation from slavery was guaranteed by the Thirteenth Amendment. The "rhetoric of home and family," Diffley explains, played a role in "the Congressional debates on the Thirteenth Amendment, which would guarantee personal liberty by changing the 'supreme law' that gave the nation its identity and citizenship its force" (14); nor did such rhetoric disappear in succeeding debates about the 1866 Civil Rights bill and the Fourteenth and Fifteenth Amendments. Thus, Stoddard's titular focus on a "house" does not so much point the text away from national political concerns as it points to the novelist's embeddedness within the conventions of war-decade discourse, and to the novel's engagement of prewar, wartime, and postwar discourses of nation. In the course of the novel, as increasing numbers of individuals identify Temple House as the repository of true "freedom" and seek asylum within its walls, we can, more particularly, recognize Stoddard's effort to interrogate forms of national membership—to look into the role that freedom might play in constituting a national "family" and into the terms on which one might claim kinship in the national "household."

Indeed, so replete is *Temple House* with veiled references to the war-time and postwar scene that it is tempting to read the novel as a political allegory—an allegory precisely of Reconstruction. We have, for example, a man named Brande, a woman named Virginia (repeatedly described in terms of whiteness and blackness),[15] and servants named Martha, Moses, and (in an apparent allusion to *Uncle Tom's Cabin*) Chloe;[16] we have discussions of women being "sold" and servants being "given away," houses that are "temples" and "forges" (metaphorical nation-states), and characters whose names allude to ancient myth and political history (Argus, Cyrus). Always, Stoddard seems to be pointing toward some larger allegorical structure—a structure at which she hints in her epigraphs, among which, amid philosophical and aesthetic meditations on "feeling," "desire," perception, "Life," and the "Book of Nature," we find the following quotation from Johann von Goethe: "Naturalists more frequently get their knowledge by separation and division than by union and combination—more through death than life" (*Temple House* 6).[17] The association of "separation and division" with "death," "union and combination" with "life," is especially apt, of course, to a moment when Americans were tallying up the (physical, economic, emotional) losses of a war generated precisely by "separation" and assessing the terms on which the new Union would be negotiated. It might well appear, then, that, like the war-era women writers taken up by Young, Stoddard is "tak[ing] the idea of 'civil war' as a point of departure to create new allegories of nationhood" (17).

But while it is apparent that Stoddard is engaged, like her female contemporaries, in the urgent national question of how to create a better "Union," a "house" that will be "temple" of life-giving freedom, the metaphors that circulate throughout *Temple House* never operate with the sort of consistency or singularity that allegory demands. Indeed, the text's allusiveness is almost dizzying, the types overabundant. With a character like Cyrus Brande, for example, Stoddard alludes at once to ancient history (Cyrus the Great), to literary history (Nathaniel Hawthorne's "Ethan Brande" and *The House of the Seven Gables*), to the immediate history of the Old South (Brande/brand, Virginia, a house run by servants of color), and to the new industrial order (the economic might of the Forge) emerging in the postwar North. What few historical referents there are push the novel's dating first forward and then back:

references to the nation's westward drift and to the development of the railroads, for example, conflict with other chronological details, such as a character's residence in Carthagena during New Granada's struggles against colonial rule in the early 1800s.[18] Such complexity of reference and temporal sequencing disturbs one-to-one correspondences in the text and (thus) its allegorical function. Whether activated by personal motives (her brother Wilson's involvement in the war and his effort to seek military advancement in the postwar period; her husband's appointment to the Custom House by a Democratic administration) or by aesthetic choice (Stoddard's commitments to what we now recognize as a [proto-] "realist" aesthetic; her consistent ellipticism and stylistic complexity), Stoddard seems to refuse the unidirectionality and fixedness of allegory in favor of a mode that indicates the vexed and shifting dynamics of power, association, and alliance in the post–Civil War milieu.[19] While it does not refuse answers, in short, Stoddard's exploration of national questions reflects her unwillingness to truck in the "stabilizing national allegories" (Young 20) to which many of her contemporaries turned and which might well have appealed to her deeply unsettled readers. While, as we will see, Stoddard's effort to represent the unstable moral terrain of the postbellum "United" States founders on the issue of race (a binary opposition between "white" and "nonwhite" that she seems, finally, unwilling to relinquish and to which she will eventually turn as a stabilizing force), the novel gestures repeatedly toward a shifting world in which such binaries as "North" and "South," "free" and "enslaved," "citizen" and "subject" were increasingly unreliable.

Not surprisingly, the house that gives the novel its title becomes a marker for such unreliability, an emblem of the gap between appearance and reality. Standing as it does "at the end of an almost unused street" (13) in Kent, shut off as it is from sight of sea or village (the house itself is, in the words of one character, "walled in, and fenced in, and treed in" [8]), Temple House seems to be far more bound than free, more like a site of death-dealing "separation and division" than of life-giving "union and combination." Ironically, however, Stoddard makes the house that is perceived by at least one character to be "haunted" (16) a repository of regenerative values. In the model offered by Temple House, the novel suggests, one can perhaps find the antidote to the (gothic) ills that ail the American "family"—ills that Stoddard increasingly comes to associate with the world "fenced out" of Temple House itself. In this inquiry into the prospects of national healing, in other words, Kent (along with Cyrus Brande, the town's most prominent citizen) represents the (gothic) reality from which Americans must escape, Temple House an ironic (if ultimately troubled) emblem of the future.

From its initial depiction in the novel, Kent is associated with dilapidation, decay, and death. "Once a great seaport," Kent has now been "surpass[ed]" by a "hundred younger towns on the Atlantic": "her sails are passing sails, her hulls wrecked hulls rotting in the sand. The old piers have tumbled in, and fallen apart; the black seaweeds are rooted in their own decayed beds on the foundations; and patches of sorrel grow in the gravelly tops. The ware-houses are empty along the water-side; their derricks rattle and swing in the wind, like empty gibbets" (13). Stoddard's vision of a dead or dying seaport, captured most gruesomely in the image of "empty gibbets," seems an obvious echo of the image of Salem earlier offered by Hawthorne, Stoddard's influential precursor (and distant relative), in "The Custom-House" sketch. With its once "bustling" but now "dilapidated wharf"—a wharf that currently "exhibits few or no symptoms of commercial life"—its "decayed wooden warehouses" and "unthrifty grass" (*The Scarlet Letter* 8), Hawthorne's Salem certainly provides an earlier fictional model for the sort of provincial decay, for what Lawrence Buell terms the "New England strangeness," that Stoddard explores both here and elsewhere in her fiction (353). Discussing the connections between Stoddard and Hawthorne, Buell reads both writers in the context of what he calls the "provincial gothic," by which he means "the use of gothic conventions to anatomize the pathology of regional culture" (351).[20] It seems clear that both Hawthorne and Stoddard, echoing her predecessor, draw on gothic metaphors of decay, degeneration, and dying aristocracy—"The old estates are worse than obliterated," writes Stoddard (13)[21]—in order to highlight particular and, in their view, destructive forms of local culture. But, I would argue, something like a "national gothic" is at work in these scenes and texts as well. Insisting on the cultural, historical, and, indeed, national function the gothic serves, Teresa Goddu has recently written that "American gothic literature criticizes America's national myth of new-world innocence by voicing the cultural contradictions that undermine the nation's claim to purity and equality. Showing how these contradictions contest and constitute national identity even as they are denied, the gothic tells of the historical horrors that make national identity possible yet must be repressed in order to sustain it" (10). Following Goddu, I submit that Stoddard, like Hawthorne before her, is interrogating not only the pathologies of region but also the pathologies of nation: the gap between American ideals and American "reality," be-

tween national myth and the actual experience of nation-building, between the freedom the nation promises and the freedom it, in truth,
offers. Writing in the postwar era, Stoddard works, via the gothic, to
uncover the harsh truths that belie America's "national myth of new-
world innocence," the "cultural contradictions" that at once ground and
unsettle American national identity.

To make this discovery, Stoddard once again reverses gothic expectations, taking a site—Cyrus Brande's "Forge"—that exists in apparent
contrast to the "rotting" Kent and the "ruined" Temple House and revealing its own rotten underside. Whereas Kent no longer prospers—
"Commerce has gone elsewhere" (13)—the Forge bustles and thrives, its
prosperity marking its place in an emergent northern-industrial order
and its function as an emblem for the future. A kind of microcosm of
this order and the domestic sphere it was meant to ensure and underwrite, the Forge is described as "quite a settlement: there were shops,
sheds, a row of workmen's houses, and the large house where the family
lived. . . . The house was large, well built, with every modern improvement, and furnished as the houses of rich business men usually are. The
best of everything was in it, in the way of curtains, carpets, and furniture" (42). The ability of "modern" industry to found and "forge" domestic space—to provide the "best of everything" in the home sphere—
is further illustrated later in the novel, in a scene that offers the Forge as
an apparent bastion of domestic comfort and peace. As Brande's daughter, Virginia, plays backgammon with Carfield, her suitor, "the house was
pleasant still with light and warmth, and filled with that silence so attractive at night, when all the paraphernalia of living is perfectly ad-
justed without the accessories of life. The fires were burning, the lamp-
light was steady, the walls, doors, and furniture shone darkly, and the
colors, glaring red and blue by day, were now soft and sombre. With
every hour of quiet, the plants in Virginia's conservatory . . . lived in
deeper dalliance, and sent their perfume through the air in shocks of
delicious sweetness" (206).

From an exterior view, then, the Forge appears to be a domestic paradise, characterized by "pleasant" light, the sweet "perfume" of the flowers, and the warmth of the fire. But while "to the public," as Stoddard
writes, "the machinery which regulated the affairs of the Brandes was
perfect" (42), the reader is granted an interior view that opens a (gothic)
gap between what appears to be and what is and which exposes the
Forge as a counterfeit, a *forgery*. Stoddard's reference to regulating "machinery" links the Forge to key forms of economic development in the

(northern) United States in the postwar period—developments about which *Temple House* seems notably skeptical. In discussing what he calls the "reconstruction of the North," Eric Foner notes that in the years immediately following the Civil War, America witnessed the "triumph" of a "new economy of coal, iron, and steam over a world centered on agriculture and artisanship" (460). "Evidence abounded," Foner writes, "of the consolidation of the capitalist economy: . . . a manufacturing boom, the spread of new forms of industrial organization, the completion of the railroad network, and the opening of the Trans-Mississippi West to mining, lumbering, ranching, and commercial farming" (460).[22]

Temple House reflects and meditates upon such forms of economic development, both in the depiction of the Forge and in other plot details. Upon their marriage, for example, Tempe and John Drake, heir presumptive of entrepreneurial wealth, go on a journey by rail. They "extend" their "tour" for "business reasons," which allows them to "see the rapid growth of some of the Mighty Cities of the West" (68). On their journey, John is killed in a "collision" that "occurred on some Western Railroad" (70). While Tempe repeatedly represents her marriage to wealth and privilege as an "escape" from the poverty of Temple House and an empowering act of social mobility, the novel takes a more cynical approach. That the marriage (which is, in any case, a loveless one, for Tempe at least) "dies" on a "tour" combining domestic rituals (the wedding journey) with "business," that John Drake is killed "on some Western Railroad," and that the marriage ends with no issue (Tempe gives birth to a son, but he is denied his paternal inheritance—he is named after Tempe's father, George Gates—and dies at the age of two) all combine to suggest that, for Stoddard, the "new industrial economy" is no "triumph" and that the domestic order it enables is flawed, even deadly.

Despite its appearances of perfection, flawed, too, is "the machinery which regulated the affairs of the Brandes." Presiding over this machinery is Cyrus Brande, whose Forge represents the kind of northern industrial might and prosperity that was rapidly increasing in the postwar years. (The Forge, we learn, employs two hundred men, many of whom are "English and Scotch workmen" whom Brande has "imported" to the United States [160]; Stoddard's incorporation of this detail reflects the reality of immigration on a vast scale after the war's end.)[23] But while Cyrus—a "great financier" (41)—appears in control of a prospering industrial/domestic "complex," he faces ruin on every front. As was common during this period of wide-scale speculation, wildly fluctuating markets, vast industrial growth, and new forms of corporate finance,

Cyrus finds that one day "his business unexpectedly went wrong; an outside connection failed him, and he lost money"; "the Forge was threatened," and "financial ruin perched over the ledgers in his office" (160). Nor are Cyrus's "troubles" merely financial. His daughter, Virginia, is a "caged bird" (160) who chafes at her position as a virtual prisoner of the Forge and at the duties her father requires her to perform. More troubling still is his wife, Rhoda, whom Cyrus has, in essence, driven mad. A woman who "hated prayers, parties, and to ride in town with the best span," Rhoda Brande feels "torment[ed]" by her "position," but it is a position from which Cyrus will not release her; he "excused her from none of the religious and secular duties which he had imposed upon himself, as a portion of the life he thought necessary to lead" (41). Having initially turned to "drugs and stimulants, to deaden herself against the torments of her position" (41), Rhoda ultimately falls "into a strange condition, which increased her cunning selfishness, and deprived her of reason" (137). Eventually, Cyrus comes to realize that she is "incurably insane" (161) and that a "mad wife sat at his board and slept in his bed" (160).

As she does with the deaths of John Drake and his son, Stoddard, via Cyrus and the world he has "forged," expresses deep skepticism about the promises of industrial development in the postwar period. In the years leading up to the Civil War, rhetoric highlighting the conflict between the (largely northern) ideology of free labor and a slave economy galvanized abolitionist sentiment. For many, the Emancipation Proclamation and the constitutional amendment guaranteeing its promise signaled the triumph of economic freedom and, hence, the triumph of the nation. With "the whole continent opened to free labor and Northern enterprise, . . . the imagination can hardly exaggerate the glory and power of the American republic. Its greatness will overshadow the world," wrote one journalist in 1863 (qtd. in Foner 29). Such a sentiment about economic (re)formation was only to become more pronounced in the early years of Reconstruction, when many looked to "Northern enterprise" and the free-labor principles it allegedly embodied as the keys to national unification, sociopolitical healing, and the genuine achievement of "liberty" promised by the Thirteenth Amendment.

Stoddard's novel, however, takes issue with this view. Registering, perhaps, the ways in which free-labor ideology was being steadily undermined by the consolidation of wealth and capital and the growth of big industry, *Temple House* suggests that no new, "free" nation can be forged by northern industrial power, for such power denies rather than restores autonomy and individual freedom.[24] Like Hawthorne's "Ethan Brand," with whom his name so obviously associates him, Cyrus Brande commits an unpardonable sin, his devotion to commerce leading to exploitation, abuse, and madness. (In response to his financial troubles, notably, Cyrus commits his wife to a mental asylum and "sells" his daughter to a wealthy Englishman.)[25] The novel's representative of northern economic power is, then, a tyrant who essentially enslaves his daughter and his wife to public image, his factory workers and household servants to the labor they perform. Nor is Cyrus himself particularly "free." The antithesis of the primary inhabitants of Temple House—Roxalana and Argus, who are repeatedly associated with notions of "internal liberty" (31), "self-possession," and "self-ownership" (82)—Cyrus is a man who seems to have no "self" to "own." He "lived between two masks," one that "faced the world," the other that "faced—himself" (41). Like another of Hawthorne's sinful men, *The House of the Seven Gables*'s Judge Jaffrey Pyncheon, Brande works hard to maintain his public "mask," to appear always "austere, pious, and reserved" (41).[26] And indeed, it is a mask that rarely cracks. In a passage that captures the prodigious efforts involved in such consistent public maintenance, Stoddard writes, "Through . . . all" the troubles, both economic and domestic, that plague him, Cyrus "carried high his smooth-shaven, long chin; flourished his fine cambric handkerchief,—a furled flag over his knee, or a waving banner in his hand; and kept the pupils of his eyes within their limits" (160). Significantly, Stoddard here associates Cyrus Brande's energetic exertions to maintain his public appearance (captured neatly in the image of Cyrus's "ke[eping] the pupils of his eyes within their limits") with "furled flags" and "waving banners," for the text thereby, and quite directly, connects Cyrus's corruption to the corruption of the nation he salutes. Indeed, Stoddard's syntax renders the connection between Cyrus and the (un)reconstructed nation even more complicated: the sentence allows us to read Cyrus's "fine cambric handkerchief" *as* his flag, *as* his "waving banner." In allowing such a reading, wherein apparently meaningful national emblems collapse into a handkerchief—albeit a "fine cambric" one—Stoddard suggests that, under the order Cyrus forges, the very nation is debased, its symbols rendered mere markers of materialism.

Stoddard's rejection of the social, political, and economic "machinery" over which Cyrus presides is further reflected in the contrast she draws between Cyrus and his namesake, Cyrus the Great. The first Achaemenian emperor of Persia, the historical Cyrus (circa 580–529 B.C.E.) was a formidable conqueror who came to control vast territories throughout the ancient Middle East. But Cyrus the Great has come to be known as much for the tolerance of his rule as for his military skills and political might. In particular, he is remembered for leaving intact the local customs and religious cultures he encountered in conquered lands; for liberating the Jews from slavery in Babylon, allowing them to return to Palestine and authorizing them to rebuild the Temple at Jerusalem; and for inscribing his aims and policies on a decree, the "Cyrus Cylinder," discovered in 1812. Sometimes called the first "Declaration of Human Rights," the cylinder suggests Cyrus the Great's effort to combine political power with cultural tolerance, leading some historians, both ancient and modern, to regard him as an ideal monarch and a very early agent of multiculturalism.[27]

Unlike Cyrus the Great, who forged a stable and apparently benevolent empire out of diverse peoples and cultures, Cyrus Brande, a hypocrite and a tyrant, forges only a deeply unstable "house divided." Describing her father's power over her—he has recently "sold" her to Carfield, her would-be suitor (282)—Virginia Brande figures herself, significantly, as a slave: "I am a slave," she tells Roxalana; "I have the blood and spirit of a slave, and cannot, dare not follow even the imperious dictates of my passion" (233).[28] While we might well be uncomfortable with Stoddard's use of the language of enslavement to describe the situation of a privileged white woman chafing under her father's thumb, we can nonetheless take note of the ways in which Stoddard is referencing larger political structures. In language that echoes intriguingly with wartime and postwar political rhetoric, Virginia later reflects on the conflict between her filial "duty" (to marry the man chosen by her father) and the "sacrifice of inclination" (her desire to marry Argus) that such duty requires. Her meditation results in her determination to "giv[e] up Argus": "To the end," she resolves, "would she live with her father; their house should not be divided because of her conduct" (284). But, of course, the reader is well aware that Virginia's "choice" is both a flawed and a destructive one. Unlike that of Cyrus the Great, this already-divided house denies liberty. The kind of union required by this Cyrus (and by the northern industrial empire he represents) deals death, imprisonment, and madness, not life and growth.

Through an elaborate series of allusions, metaphors, and historical references, then, Stoddard exposes the forgery at the heart of the Forge, the horrors of which reveal the corrosive potential of the new industrial order for which it functions as an exemplar. In contrast with the Forge, ironically, Stoddard sets the ostensibly decaying and "haunted" Temple

House, which becomes, in the course of the novel, a site of functioning community, a newly constituted and regenerating "union." As Virginia herself comes to understand, the divergent ideological foundation upon which Temple House is built enables such a union. In an early visit to Temple House, Virginia recognizes the value of the interior "self-possession" that Argus and Roxalana, in particular, embody: "She comprehended now why they seemed superior to the persons she had lately been intimate with; their outside possessions weighed nothing in comparison to that instinct of self-possession, when well developed!" (82). In this rendering of Temple House, Stoddard reflects on the (manifestly, if not exclusively, American) notion that ownership sustains, even constitutes, the self, the "possessive individualism" that is, as Gillian Brown reminds us, "aligned with market relations such as exchange value, alienability, circulation, and competition" (2).[29] Cyrus devotes himself to, indeed seems to embody, precisely these "market relations"; yet he is depicted as a nonself—a man who "live[s] between two masks." By contrast, Argus and Roxalana seek distance from capitalist forms of exchange and competition: Argus insists that the "ties of property . . . are not for me" (194) and rarely labors, because "he never cared to save, or earn, a dollar" (187);[30] Roxalana is an inveterate recycler who makes petticoats out of "the fragments of worn sails" (31), refuses to buy anything new, and eventually determines not to leave the precincts of Temple House. The fact that these characters are granted a superabundance of selfhood despite their rejection of conventional "market relations" suggests Stoddard's interest in finding an alternative model of personhood, one not harnessed to structures of proprietorship, to the "outside possessions" that, in this novel, undermine rather than ratify selfhood. It is no wonder that, when contemplating the difference between the physical discomforts of Temple House and the luxury of her room at the Forge, Virginia discovers that Temple House "seemed preferable to [her], for freedom was there" (109).

When Virginia finally overcomes her own "yielding" "individuality" (42), breaks from her father, and pledges herself to Argus, then, she makes a choice that bears considerable ideological weight. Stoddard's turn to marriage as an ideological mechanism—a fictional means of working out problems of power, privilege, and (female) autonomy—is not, of course, unusual, either for Stoddard or her (male and female) contemporaries. But in the historical context of Reconstruction, this turn can be seen to have particular significance, as Kathleen Diffley's analysis of the conventions of Civil War fiction suggests. In her study of more than three hundred stories published in popular magazines, Diffley identifies "the Romance" as one of three primary "narrative genres" into which narratives about the Civil War and Reconstruction fall.[31] Diffley's explication of the cultural function of the Romance allows us to complicate a reading of Temple House's apparent conventionalism by returning us to the novel's reconstructive agenda. Not surprisingly, Diffley notes, the "generic promise of the Romance" is "social regeneration through marriage" (119). The stakes of such "regeneration" are high and involve the large-scale transformation of the national (as well as the local) community: Romances, in Diffley's formulation, "customarily asked 'Will I become we?'" (6)—a question whose emphasis on union had clear metaphoric potential for a "reconstructing" nation.

More specifically, Diffley goes on to assert that one of the central "ideological offices of Civil War Romances" is that of "transforming the old homestead of kin into the new homestead of country" (79). To make that transformation, the heroine must "renounce blood for choice" and "local loyalty for national allegiance" (77). It is precisely such a choice that Virginia makes when she is finally able to reject her father's authority over her, relinquishing the ties of "blood" and the kin-based "homestead" that have bound her and choosing, instead, to "live resolutely, with freedom" (267), along with Roxalana, her psychological mentor, and the other inhabitants of Temple House.[32] Stoddard suggests, in keeping with Diffley's "Romance" model, that such a choice can have transformative potential. After Argus tells Roxalana that he means to marry Virginia, she insists on the regenerative function of the alliance, which she locates in the context of a larger community: "Between us all," Roxalana says, "I believe she will be happy. A new happiness in this house, Argus, I never again expected" (327). And while Stoddard turns to a "conventional" form ("Romance") to imagine a new "we" (nation), the "house" she depicts would hardly have been, for her readers, a conventional one. When Roxalana refers to "us all," she means not just those united by the ties of blood or marriage—Virginia, Argus, Roxalana, Tempe—but also the laborer Mat Sutcliffe (an honorary member of the household), a "foreigner" (the Anglo-Spanish Sebastian), and a woman of color (the Native American/African American Chloe). Temple House thus becomes a place where, as Lisa Radinovsky writes, "people who do not conform to white, middle-class Christian standards can congregate" ("Gender Norms" 204)—an emblematic rendition of a new, multiracial "national family" built on the foundations of "internal liberty."

It is here, in working out the parameters of this newly constituted and multiracial family, that Stoddard's novel reveals most fully its engagement in the urgent questions of its day. As Elizabeth Young notes, even before the first shots of the war were fired, the "axis of civil conflict was consistently racial as well as regional, with struggles over black freedom pervading all regions" (16). In 1865, just before the war's end, Frederick Douglass pointed to the long and ongoing centrality of race and "struggles over black freedom" in American political and social discourse: "The American people have always been anxious to know what they shall do with us. . . . Everybody has asked the question, and they learned to ask it early . . . : 'What shall we do with the Negro?' " (qtd. in Chalberg 141). By the spring of 1866, when Stoddard began writing *Temple House,* it was clear that Douglass's question had, in fact, become "everybody's" question. In particular, the nature of citizenship and its meaning for African Americans came under intense scrutiny and acrimonious debate on a federal level. Already more than three million men, women, and children had been emancipated from slavery, their emancipation sealed by the constitutional amendment abolishing slavery in the United States. In April 1866 (just one month before Stoddard began composing *Temple House*), Congress overrode President Andrew Johnson's veto of the Civil Rights Act, which established for the first time the concept of national citizenship—prior to this, a person could be a U.S. citizen only if an individual state first recognized his or her citizenship—and "spelled out rights [citizens] were to enjoy equally without regard to race" (Foner 243). In June 1866, Congress passed the Fourteenth Amendment, intended to "secure citizenship" and "equal rights" for African Americans (Chalberg 77), and sent it to the states for ratification, in direct opposition to Johnson's urging. That year of 1866 would also see the formation of the Ku Klux Klan and race riots in Memphis and New Orleans that resulted in the murder of eighty African Americans and a handful of white radicals. It would indeed appear that, as historian Kenneth Stampp explains, "the central issue of the dialogue [about the nature of Reconstruction] was the place of the free Negro in American society" (87)—and that the dialogue itself was at best fractious and at worst violent, even brutal.

The role of race in the formation of national citizenship certainly appears to be on Stoddard's mind in *Temple House* (the novel), which takes pains to include in the alternative ideological structure that Temple House (the place) represents those who are marked by racial and ethnic otherness. Indeed, we might see in Stoddard's complicated rendition of those "others"—Sebastian and the servant Chloe—the novel's (perhaps unwitting) recognition of the complex and difficult work of Reconstruction. Through these characters and their related yet ultimately divergent stories, we come to the heart of *Temple House*'s gothic utopianism—its desire to imagine a reconstructed, multiracial national community built on the foundations of genuine "freedom," its inability to imagine full membership in such a community for those perceived as "foreigners," regardless of their country of origin. For ultimately, while Temple House may well be a place in which a "diverse group of people . . . can congregate," "congregation" does not occur on equal terms for all.

While, as we will see, Sebastian figures prominently in Stoddard's interrogation of the meanings of national citizenship, it is Chloe whose racial identity most obviously situates her at the center of ante- and postbellum social and political debates. Claiming kin to the nation's two most abject groups, the groups positioned most fully beyond the limits of citizenship, Chloe is the daughter of a "Gay Head Indian" (88) woman and an African American man.[33] While Stoddard places little overt emphasis on Chloe's African American ancestry, the little we know of her personal history aligns Chloe, at least indirectly, with the institution of American slavery and highlights the intersecting forms of disenfranchisement experienced by African Americans and Native Americans in the mid-nineteenth-century United States. Recounting her story in brief to Virginia, she notes that "twenty years ago," when she came to work for the Brandes, "my baby had just died" (141). When Virginia exclaims, "I never knew you were married!" Chloe corrects her in a remark that underscores her own (doubled) powerlessness: "Never was married," she insists; "what was the good of one of the Masapee tribe's marrying?" (141). In this remark, Stoddard, via Chloe, points out the civil disenfranchisement of both African Americans and Native Americans, similarly denied (although through different legal and extralegal mechanisms) rights of citizenship and the protection of American law. Throughout the novel, Chloe's function as an object of trade between the Forge and Temple House underscores her existence outside the bounds of legal protection that citizenship provides. When Rhoda Brande finds Chloe's presence intolerable, Virginia offers Chloe (referred to on occasion as "Brande's Chloe" [152] or "my Chloe" [288]) to Roxalana as a kind of "loan or gift" (150). Later, when Tempe inquires how Chloe's replacement at the Forge is faring, Virginia asks, only halfjokingly, "Will you give me back Chloe again?" (292).

Admittedly and importantly, Chloe repeatedly transgresses the boundaries of her designated, abject position. Most notably, she speaks with "astonish[ing]" freedom to both Cyrus and Virginia about life at the Forge (75). In one instance, she admonishes her ostensible "master" for making Virginia so fully responsible for her mother: "I'm a sinner if she ain't a-waitin' too much on the missis for many visits," she tells Brande (74–75). In another, she tells Virginia: "Let me advise you, Miss Virginny,—don't take on so about your dam worthless mother" (88). In yet another, Brande, cowed by Chloe's power, is "obliged to wink at [her] officiousness in taking the duties of the meal" from Rhoda Brande (110). Stoddard's refusal to consign Chloe to silent suffering, or to punish her for such "transgressions" against her "masters," is, of course, significant. Indeed, Stoddard endorses Chloe's freedom of speech and thought, which she associates repeatedly with her Indian ancestry. In the scene with Virginia, for example, Chloe explains that it is the "Indian" in her that "makes my hair straight" and prompts her to speak (88).[34] Thus, as Radinovsky notes, "In *Temple House,* the independence associated with 'Indians' is honored as a positive alternative model, while Stoddard represents the unnatural restraint of white, middle- and upper-class conventions in a negative light. In spite of her often troubling representations of Chloe's 'Indianness,' and her characters' occasional racism, Stoddard uses Chloe's racial otherness as a repository for positive rebellious fantasies" ("Gender Norms" 205).

In this regard, "race" becomes less a biological category than a state of mind or set of attitudes. In an intriguing remark that she makes to Virginia after coming to live at Temple House, Chloe explains why she has come to feel comfortable with the Gates family: "They are Indians," she declares, "in spite of white skins and learning" (179). Using Chloe as a mouthpiece, Stoddard seems here to liberate notions of "race" from "blood" and to equate "Indianness" with positive models of resistance, transgression, and "internal liberty." Yet even as it attempts thus to denaturalize and "debiologize" race, *Temple House* also reinscribes and renaturalizes it. Chloe herself, for example, repeatedly situates her unruliness as a manifestation of her "bad blood" (88), as emerging from a racial repository (what Stoddard herself refers to as the "Indian demon" [332]) that exists in conflict with the white Christianity to which she has converted: "'Go away, Indian, come again, Christian,'" she tells herself when trying to curb her impulse to act on (rather than simply voice) her anger (244); "'The Indian has got here first this time, . . . but I suppose Chloe will be along, if I wait a few minutes for her,'" she remarks at another point of near-rebellion (328–29). Chloe's gothic self-description, which figures her "Indianness" as separate from—even

as undermining—her "Chloe-ness," suggests deeply complicated attitudes toward racial subjection (does the less recalcitrant "Chloe" embody
white fantasies of compliant and racially nonassertive African Americans?) and a disturbing acceptance of the fractured, divided "selves" produced in a nation bent on racial quantification and categorization. And
even if Chloe's "rebellious fantasies" are rendered positively here, neither they nor the ostensible disturbance of racial categories that Stoddard attempts (but finally fails) to stage have any positive, material impact on Chloe, whose rebellion is notably inscribed within the position
to which the novel's characters—and, it would appear, Stoddard herself—consign her. While Virginia, for example, is able to leave the Forge
and find "freedom," however qualified, at Temple House, Chloe's position remains the same: in either place she is a servant, albeit a transgressive one. Chloe's power is, thus, ultimately contained by the very thing
that defines it: her status as a racially marked "other." Indeed, that containment returns us to Chloe's African American origins, which are virtually displaced by the constant references to her "Indianness." Addressing the "racial organization of emotional labor within the cultural ideal
of domesticity," Elizabeth Young notes how, "in a culture that mandated
civility for middle-class white women, black women could form a conduit for white women's psychic release and a screen onto which they
could project their impulses toward incivility" (35). Often vilified for
her refusal to abide by the codes of "civility" in both her writing and
her personal relations, Stoddard seems to deploy Chloe as a safe repository of rebellion, to use her to open up a space where resistance can be
voiced and at the same time neatly contained by the character's inescapable otherness, her ineffaceable racial difference.[35]

Much like Chloe, the "Spaniard" Sebastian is defined throughout
Temple House by his racial position; and like Chloe, he must in certain
respects transcend that position in order to enter the "temple" of freedom. But unlike Chloe, Sebastian is able, finally, to become a fully en-
franchised member of the Temple House community, suggesting once
again the novel's inability to think beyond America's obsessive, categori-
cal opposition between those who are "white" (read "European") and
those who are "not" (read "African" or "Indian"). The son of a "rich
Spanish woman" and an "English trader who lived in Carthagena many
years," Sebastian Ford is a "Creole" (125) whose mixed-race status allows Stoddard to reflect once again on the meanings of racial identity
and the role race plays in national memberships. Stoddard writes that

Sebastian's father died in Carthagena "in the time of the political troubles which convulsed that portion of South America" (125). Carthagena is a city in what was then New Granada (now Colombia), a Spanish colony that, like most of its counterparts in "that portion of South America," struggled to gain independence in the early nineteenth century.[36] It would appear that Stoddard is referring to this long-running "war for independence," which ended with the return to Spanish rule in 1816, when she refers to the convulsive "political troubles" in Sebastian's homeland. Stoddard leaves ambiguous the question of the Ford family's involvement in the independence struggle, but by situating the family in Carthagena during that struggle, she effectively ties Sebastian to the matter of "freedom" that motivates so many of the other characters in this novel.

It is quite likely, furthermore, that when Stoddard's readers encountered a South American character associated with "political troubles" in 1866, they would have thought as much about contemporary events—namely, the Paraguayan War—as about the independence campaigns. Also known as the "War of the Triple Alliance," the Paraguayan War (1864–70) pitted the forces of Brazil, Argentina, and (eventually) Uruguay against the forces of Paraguay, under the direction of dictator Francisco Solano Lopez. The war was much covered in such periodicals as *Harper's Weekly*—in which, not incidentally, Stoddard's work frequently appeared—in terms that compared it intriguingly (despite the complex, multinational origins of the conflict and the international alliances involved) with the American Civil War.[37] "Notwithstanding the intensity of interest with which we await the development of our own Civil War," a writer for *Harper's* noted, "we can not be indifferent to the more distant conflict in which Brazil is engaged against the South American Republics of Paraguay and Uruguay" ("The War in South America" [8 Apr. 1865]). In *Harper's,* news of the Paraguayan War was frequently set adjacent to columns about wartime events in America or engravings of Civil War battles and actions. Words such as *rebellion, rebels,* and *despotism,* familiar from the Civil War lexicon, circulated throughout the coverage of the Paraguayan War in the periodical's pages. Nor did *Harper's* make any effort to veil its partisanship: "Brazil is a monarchy, but 'it is republicanism itself compared with Paraguay,'" proclaimed the weekly ("The War in South America" [16 Sept. 1865]). Nearly two years later, editors sounded the same theme, noting, "There is nothing in the condition of Paraguay which can command the sympathy of an American, except its military efficiency. The whole region, indeed, is but the *plantation* and camp of Lopez, who is absolute dictator, even to the price of produce" ("Paraguay"; emphasis mine).

While Lopez was marked as the "other" of American democracy— much like the "rebellious" and "despotic" plantation South—the forces allied against him were rendered as practically American. Despite the fact that it was both a monarchy and a slaveholding country, Brazil was "republicanism itself." Bartolomé Mitre, Argentina's president and "Commander-in-Chief of the allied Brazilian, Argentine, and Uruguayan army," became a kind of honorary American: "He belongs to the class of 'self-made men,' like Lincoln, Douglas, and Johnson," intoned *Harper's* in December 1865; "compelled to make his own way from birth," Mitre was now "a member of various scientific societies both in Europe and America" and a "poet of good repute" ("General Bartolome Mitre"). Interestingly, then, *Harper's* exerted itself to assimilate a distant and arguably quite foreign war, to familiarize and simplify a conflict whose shadings are much more complex than the weekly would suggest and use it to offer commentary (however veiled) on the political and military struggle in which the United States was at that time engaged.

The rhetorical and pictorial exertions made by *Harper's* to turn the "otherness" of the war in South America to its own purposes are oddly mirrored in the depictions of Sebastian in *Temple House*. What the treatment of the Paraguayan War in *Harper's* shows is that Latin America (or the parts of Latin America, like Brazil, that manifested affinities with "Europeanized high culture" [Bethell 788]) could change, assimilate, and become "purely" American, joining a cause of a "freedom" that is thereby colored "white." Like the story of the "triple alliance" nations told by *Harper's,* Sebastian's story in *Temple House* is—unlike that of the inassimilable Chloe—in part a story of assimilation and of the whiteness of freedom. Thus, importantly, a large part of what Sebastian seeks prior to his arrival at Temple House is freedom from, precisely, the Spanish heritage represented by his mother. Upon his father's death, Sebastian closes the family business and goes abroad, living, "as Creoles proverbially live," in London and Paris (125). He eventually "return[s] home to tropical luxury," only to find "in his mother's house a Catholic priest of his own age, who was domiciled there, and in her affections." He responds by destroying "all memorial" of his father, except for an "ivory painted miniature, and a locket containing a lock of auburn hair," and leaving "his handsome, violent, brainless mother" forever (125–26). In depicting the conflict between Sebastian and his "beautiful" but "brainless" and apparently vice-ridden mother, Stoddard participates in the culturally prevalent rhetoric that associated Continental "foreignness" (especially in women) with "vice" and uncontrolled sexuality. In this context, we can better understand the horror with which Sebastian greets the knowledge—knowledge kept from him during much of the book—that when Argus and Mat found him in the shipwreck, he was locked in an embrace with a woman whose "hands clutched his temples" and into whose bosom his "face was . . . tightly pressed" (102). On the one hand, Sebastian's horror is that of a man whose life was purchased by the death of his lover; on the other hand, his response marks a profound anxiety about what is figured as a kind of devouring female sexuality: "*There now I have got you, safe enough from her,*" says Mat upon extricating the unconscious Sebastian from his lover's "embrace of death" (102–3).

Given Stoddard's (albeit sometimes hedged) willingness in other texts to acknowledge women's sexual desires and affirm their ability to act on them, her depiction of these desiring and devouring women is at once striking and disturbing, correlating as it does to racialist notions of the "hypersexuality" of "foreign" women and women of color.[38] In any case, it is in the context of such fears of foreignness that we might read the appeal that Sebastian makes to Roxalana when he asks to become "one of the family forever": "Will you have me here without obtaining any knowledge of me? I would have you accept me as if I were born on that night in March" (129). Later, Sebastian suggests that his rebirth has been complete and effective: "I have nothing Spanish about me now," he tells Argus, "I have no other country than the spot you give me, and, absolutely, no other tie outside of it" (227). Sebastian may be wrong that "there is nothing Spanish about me now"—certainly characters continue to refer to his "dark blood" (227) and "swarthy foreign[ness]" (229)—but it would appear that equal membership in the "country" of Temple House seems, at least in part, predicated on his ability to assimilate, to leave (like the virtually "republican" Brazil or the "self-made" and Lincolnesque Mitre) his otherness, his "*Spanishness,*" behind. His ability to do so is a (problematic) "privilege" that the "darker," doubly marked Chloe is not afforded. Indeed, Stoddard leaves clues that allow us to recognize the fundamental separation between Sebastian and Chloe, hinting at Sebastian's possible involvement in the slave trade. We learn that the ship on which he nearly met his death was on its way "from a West Indian port, to a port in the Southern United States" (127); about that ship Mary Sutcliffe, Mat's wife, queries, "What was the cargo, I should like to know? Rum? Slaves? Opium?" (227–28). While Stoddard never explicitly identifies Sebastian's "business," such hints remind us that, however initially "marked" by foreignness, Sebastian occupies a position of economic and social privilege that is denied to the eternally marked and "othered" Chloe.

In the end, the divergence between Sebastian and Chloe suggests both the radical nature of Stoddard's vision for the American future and the limits placed on that vision by culturally assumed models of racial difference and ethnic "otherness." While Chloe might conclude that those with "white skins and learning" can choose to be "Indians" (a loosening of race from biology that mirrors, in reverse, the *Harper's* rendition of Latin Americans shaking off their otherness and embracing the cause of American democracy), the novel finally suggests that they can do so without relinquishing the privileges of whiteness—and that an "Indian" will always be an "Indian," an African always an African. It is thus perhaps all too easy to answer the question Virginia poses to Chloe as she reflects on her feelings of entrapment at the Forge: "Tell me, Chloe, why am I more free with you, poor soul,—than with anybody else?" (87). Ultimately, Stoddard's effort to expose the "historical horrors" and "cultural contradictions" (Goddu 10) that jeopardize the project of Reconstruction—in particular, the racial and economic injustice at that project's core—and to imagine her way out of a "gothic America" and into a truly reconstructed community founders on her inability to imagine one person's freedom without another's (racially designated) abjection. Indeed, it is the novel's failure to escape the confines of this binary—the only one that Stoddard, elsewhere almost relentlessly destabilizing, is unable to unsettle—that, perhaps more than anything else, establishes *Temple House* as a novel of Reconstruction America.

As a way of making final sense of *Temple House's* own failed reconstruction, we might return, paradoxically, to the early and damning review of the novel published in *The Nation,* the review that bitingly declared, "We may as well secure the reader of the story from a possible disappointment by informing him that *Temple House* is a story that has no end." While this remark is deeply, caustically derisive, it is also, to a large extent, accurate: the novel's "ending" does indeed, as James Matlack puts it, leave us "in considerable doubt" about the fates of our characters. Although Argus insists in the last lines of the novel, "Now I shall be married," for example, he does so "rather dreamily" (347), and the marriage remains in the novel's future. And we see a number of shifting alliances in the final pages—a hinted-at marriage between Tempe and Sebastian, desire for Tempe on the part of Cyrus Brande, and, most importantly, declared (and much-discussed) mutual desire between Sebastian and Virginia—that complicate the ending we have long anticipated. If the romance between Argus and Virginia does bear the promise of a "social regeneration" urgently needed in the era of early Reconstruction, then the cloud of uncertainty that surrounds their union might well be understood less as a failure of plot and more as a representational problem—the fundamentally unwriteable nature of a *truly* reconstructed nation. Like the nation it would appear to emblematize, Temple House is a stew of contradictions, a site of complex and shifting dynamics of power, privilege, desire, and racial identity. Like Temple House, the novel that bears its name is, too, a stew of contradictions—a site where cultural complexities and conflicts at once motivate and disturb aesthetic structure.

In a recent essay, Maurice Lee offers a rendition of the problem of allegory in Melville's "Benito Cereno" that is, I think, useful to a reading of *Temple House*. Lee writes of "Benito Cereno" that "there are too many allusions, too many references, to surely determine political analogs, and in this sense the meaning of 'Benito Cereno' is as much sunk in silent depths as drowned in a deluge of discourse" (500). Earlier, I argued that Stoddard's own overabundant allusions and references make it similarly difficult to "determine political analogs" and that we might recognize this as Stoddard's own acknowledgment of the burden of Reconstruction, the politically and morally fraught terrain of the postbellum United States. In 1865, in the brief and heady interlude between Robert E. Lee's surrender and the assassination of Lincoln, James Russell Lowell wrote, "There is something magnificent in having a country to love. . . . I worry a little about reconstruction, but I am inclined to think that matters will very much settle themselves" (qtd. in Chalberg 16). Just a year later, when Stoddard began work on *Temple House,* it was clear that matters would not "settle themselves," that social regeneration would be hard-won, that a harmonious new "union" was increasingly unimaginable amidst a "deluge" of contradictory discourses and their often physically violent displays. Perhaps that is why the novel, dizzyingly allusive and referential throughout, goes silent in the end: it founders on its own speech, as if it acknowledges but cannot overcome its own failures to exorcize the nation's (racial) ghosts. It is perhaps no wonder that *Temple House* "is a story that has no end": in such uncertainty can we recognize that the national story that Stoddard was attempting to write could, quite literally, not yet be finished.

NOTES

I wish to thank Robert McClure Smith and Jonathan Barron for their careful, constructive readings of previous versions of this essay.

1. For exceptions to this critical trend, see dissertations by Radinovsky ("Gender Norms and Genre Forms") and Croce ("Phantoms from an Ancient Loom"), who refers to *Temple House* as "the culmination of [Stoddard's] novelistic career" (263).

2. Buell and Zagarell include Stoddard's *Two Men* in this assessment.

3. Radinovsky offers a useful and nuanced response to Stoddard's use of "popular conventions," describing *Temple House* as a novel that "contain[s] both conventional and melodramatic elements, which are curiously juxtaposed with unconventional features." Her dissertation chapter on *Temple House* makes a substantial case for the ways in which Stoddard "manipulated nineteenth-century readers' expectations by simultaneously utilizing and undermining popular forms and gender norms. Nineteenth-century readers' reactions to the novel's disruption of these familiar forms and norms imply that, at least for them, it was more subversive than conformist" ("Gender Norms" 179).

4. See Tompkins's seminal *Sensational Designs*.

5. Indeed, Stoddard often seemed to lack patience with the participants in such debates. Her response to contemporary events is made most explicitly—and often most bitingly—in the columns she wrote for the *Daily Alta California,* in which she often set herself at odds with the reform-oriented work of her contemporaries, male and female. Here, for example, her expressed commitments to women's individual freedom and intellectual growth ("I am," she announces in an early column, "deeply interested in the development of the woman mind") sit side by side with her rejection of much of the "formula" of organized feminism or other political reform movements (*The Morgesons and Other Writings* 314, 326).

6. For readings of *Two Men* that stress the novel's sociohistorical embeddedness and its meditation on contemporary events and debates, see the essays by Lisa Radinovsky and Jennifer Putzi in this volume.

7. The dating of *Temple House* is complicated. The novel refers to the "rapid growth of some of the Mighty Cities of the West" (68) and to western travel by railroad, which would situate the text in the 1840s at the earliest. Another historical marker in the text, however, would seem to set the story's action in

the 1820s or 1830s. In recounting a (brief) history of the novel's Anglo-Spanish character, Sebastian Ford, Stoddard writes that he "was the son of an English trader who lived in Carthagena many years, and died there in the time of the political troubles which convulsed that portion of South America" (125). It seems likely that the "political troubles" to which Stoddard refers are the struggles against colonial (Spanish) rule in New Granada (now Colombia), which occurred between 1810 and 1816. Upon his father's death, Sebastian takes control of (and soon sells) the family business. Sebastian gives his age as thirty to Roxalana later in the novel. Assuming that Sebastian must have entered his majority by the time his father died, this would date the action of the novel to the late 1820s. Stoddard's vagueness—if not inconsistency—in this regard suggests her lack of interest in writing an explicitly "historical" novel and facilitates the acontextual reading of her work that this essay seeks to counter.

8. According to Matlack, Stoddard began work on *Temple House* in May 1866—just one month before Congress passed the Fourteenth Amendment.

9. The letter to Stedman is undated; Buell and Zagarell place it in the 1880s. See xxiv n. 18.

10. Stoddard's omission from Diffley's work is especially notable, since more than half of the 321 stories Diffley examines were published in periodicals in which Stoddard's work regularly appeared: *Harper's New Monthly Magazine* (60 stories) and *Harper's Weekly* (115 stories). Indeed, Stoddard published an explicit Civil War "romance," a short story titled "Tuberoses," in an 1863 issue of *Harper's Monthly*. I am not faulting Diffley for excluding from her analysis this story or other "war stories" Stoddard may have published; after all, she could hardly be expected to offer explicit commentary on all 321 of her chosen texts. Rather, I wish to note how Stoddard's exclusion from this and like critical studies points to limited ways of understanding "Civil War" writing, ways that compromise our ability to recognize and account for the full range of literary responses to the events of the war decade. Elizabeth Young's reading of the Civil War as a "multivalent cultural symbol as well as literal setting" (17)—her insistence on the war's metaphorical function and its sometimes oblique presence in literary texts—provides perhaps the most capacious avenue into the writing of war and its aftermath. Her analysis is also the least exhaustive ("I do not offer a complete survey of women's Civil War writing," she notes, but rather "a study of selected literary texts" that "illuminat[e] key themes in women's literary relation to the Civil War" [21])—and so Stoddard's absence there seems less glaring.

11. Because I am interested in exploring the ways in which Stoddard is responding to the events of early Reconstruction, I cite throughout this essay the original 1867 edition of *Temple House*. Stoddard revised the novel for republi-

cation in 1888, making some gestures toward both clarity and convention; the 1888 edition was reprinted in 1901 and again in 1971, in the contemporary edition of Stoddard's novels brought forward by critic Richard Foster.

12. For a discussion of the homoerotic relationship between Argus and Sebastian, see Radinovsky, "Gender Norms" 206–14 and Leila Assumpcao Harris 116–21.

13. Like the reviewer for the *Tribune,* James Matlack asserts that the novel ends in problematic "mystery": "the reader," he writes, "is left in considerable doubt as to the conclusion. Sebastian has withheld his claim to Virginia because of his obligation to Argus, which has now been repaid. She shows as much passion for Sebastian, especially in the strained climax, as she does for sturdy old Argus. Which will she marry? What happens to Tempe? Whatever the virtues of understatement, too much is left unresolved at the close of Elizabeth's text" ("Literary Career" 439). As I argue, however, the relative "openness" of Stoddard's ending might be perceived as an acknowledgment of the unfinished work of Reconstruction.

14. Lincoln used the phrase ("A house divided against itself cannot stand") in an 1858 speech to the Republican National Convention (Fehrenbacher 431). For a discussion of the political genealogy of the "house divided" metaphor, see Wald, *Constituting Americans* 53–57. For a discussion of the relation between Lincoln's "rhetoric of house," both here and in other speeches, and the discourses of domesticity, see Young 26–27.

15. Both the narrator and characters within the text, for example, take repeated note of the contrast between Virginia's pale skin and her (voluptuous, ungovernable) hair, "as black as the sky" (99).

16. For another instance of Harriet Beecher Stowe's novel as an intertext for Stoddard, see Julia Stern's essay in this volume.

17. In addition to Goethe, Stoddard includes epigraphs by James Russell Lowell, Johann von Schiller, Bettine Von Arnim (twice), Algernon Swinburne, and Leigh Hunt (twice). By 1901, when the final edition of *Temple House* was published, all but two of the epigraphs (one by Lowell and one by Von Arnim) had been omitted. The fact that Goethe's language of "separation and division," "union and combination" was dropped in later editions suggests the ways in which the 1867 edition responds specifically to contemporary events.

18. See note 7 for a more specific analysis of the novel's dating.

19. While writing *Temple House,* Matlack notes, Stoddard "was concerned about the post-war career of Wilson Barstow," who was seeking a "lucrative political appointment as a suitable reward" for his wartime service ("Literary Career" 407). Stoddard would have had another, and more immediate, reason for treading lightly on political terrain: her husband, a Custom House official in

New York City, was a Democratic appointee. According to Matlack, however, it would be another nine years before Richard Stoddard was removed from office ("Literary Career" 410). For specifics on Wilson Barstow's postwar maneuverings, see Matlack, "Literary Career" 407–11.

20. Buell offers close readings of *The House of the Seven Gables* and *The Morgesons,* examining the ways in which they use the "motif of entrapment within the province" (353) and dramatize the efforts of (especially female) characters to "resist the dead weight of provincial culture that threatens to imprison" them (354). To Buell's interrogation of the use of the gothic to examine the legacies of New England Calvinism and Puritan ideology I would add the effort to understand Stoddard's gothicism in terms of war-decade trauma and America's peculiar and unsettling racial history.

21. See, similarly, Hawthorne's reference to the bygone days of "old King Derby," once called the "father of American commerce with India" (*The Scarlet Letter* 8 n. 229).

22. Foner points out that "by 1873, the nation's industrial production stood 75 percent above its 1865 level, a figure all the more remarkable in view of the South's economic stagnation" (461).

23. Foner notes that, between 1865 and 1873, "3 million immigrants entered the country, nearly all destined for the North and West" (200).

24. Interestingly, Stoddard's suspicion of industrial power sets her in opposition to Radical Republicans who supported northern business enterprise through economic legislation (favorable tariff laws and subsidies, for example). Such legislation came under attack from southern agrarians, Democrats, and Johnsonians, all of whom construed the Radical Republicans as corrupt agents of northern business: "The granting of acts of incorporation, bounties, special privileges, favors, and profligate legislation of every description is shocking," wrote one of Andrew Johnson's supporters (qtd. in Stampp 95). But if Stoddard's rendition of Cyrus and his Forge seems to ally her with such social conservatives, her critique emerges from the quite radical view that such forms of economic power inhibit the selfhood and autonomy of those within its grip. For more on the alliance between Radical Republicans and northern business, see Stampp.

25. Carfield makes this sale explicit, asking Brande—in Virginia's presence— "What was the price of your daughter? . . . I bought *her.* She knows it" (282). Nor does Brande, here or elsewhere, dispute the charge.

26. Stoddard makes quite insistent the parallels between Brande and Pyncheon. Both are powerful in local government and church structures; both manifest tastefully but forcefully their opulence and prosperity; both are "sensual, and cowardly" men (Stoddard, *Temple House* 41) who try to hide from the pub-

lic their lustfulness and prodigious physical desires. One might also recognize echoes between the eventually mad Rhoda and Pyncheon's young wife, who "got her death blow in the honey-moon, and never smiled again, because her husband compelled her to serve him with coffee, every morning, at his bedside, in token of fealty to her liege-lord and master" (*The House of the Seven Gables* [1986] 123).

27. According to Xenophon, for example, Cyrus's "subjects were cherished and cared for as if they were his children, and they reverenced him like a father" (qtd. in Lamb 293). While Xenophon is clearly engaged in an act of (what would later be called) hagiography, even more recent sources present Cyrus the Great in much the same light. According to William Culican, for example, "there can be little doubt that Cyrus' peaceful and benevolent conquest was something new in Mesopotamian history. The populace was neither decimated nor deported, the statues of the city's gods were not degraded" (57). Also see Lamb.

28. In many respects, Rhoda's unruly response to Cyrus reflects an intriguing form of resistance to his authority. In contrast to Rhoda, Virginia largely accepts her father's edicts. A woman whose "individuality" is depicted as "yielding" (42), Virginia accedes to Cyrus's insistence that she minister to (and cloak the increasing instability of) her mother, to his sartorial requirements ("You are too tall to wear stripes," he tells her; "I remark that I dislike that stripe exceedingly"; Virginia responds by going to change the dress [163–64]), and to his insistence that she marry Carfield. Only late in the novel, and through the agency of Sebastian, Mat, and (less so) Argus, is she able to resist.

29. Brown is drawing here from C. B. Macpherson, whose 1962 *The Political Theory of Possessive Individualism* addresses the "proprietary foundations" of selfhood in the liberal-democratic state.

30. According to the terms of his culture—Stoddard's culture—Argus is, essentially, an "anti-man": he seeks to play no role in the public sphere increasingly associated with male wage-earning; he rejects the idea that "productive" labor is necessary, even meaningful. Yet Stoddard allows him to maintain his "internal liberty," suggesting her interest in unyoking the very notion of autonomous personhood from "productive," wage-earning work. Indeed, it is notable that Argus is freed from labor because of a good, nonmonetary, act: it is his saving of Sebastian, which at once echoes and differs from his "saving" of his brother, George, that leads Sebastian to devote his (modest) income to the family at Temple House. Whereas George is "blood kin" to whom Argus seemingly involuntarily turns (Argus cannot understand the "feeling which possessed him" and sends him to George, except perhaps as a response to the "voice of the Temple blood" [23]), Sebastian's "claims" and Argus's answer to them

inhabit the abstract realm of morality. And whereas George ultimately refuses a place at Temple House, Sebastian chooses to make himself a member of the family and to repay the "debts," financial and emotional, that he has incurred. Thus, Stoddard redefines the notion of "free" labor as "work" that is performed without an eye to material gain, that stands outside the system of "productive wage-earning" represented so negatively here by Cyrus Brande.

31. Diffley's other "genres" are "Old Homestead" and "Adventure."

32. Roxalana is perceived as the "central brooding heart" (129) of Temple House, the "object of genuine force" (238) within its precincts. Like Brande, she "ruled the house" (257), committing the family to the "absolute law and bond" of daily tea, for example (12), but as its "contented and comfort-dispensing spirit" (257) rather than its tyrant. Roxalana repeatedly insists on the "use-less[ness]" of "attempt[ing]" to "govern" others. "I never thought that the Lord intended us for weather-cocks, to be veered by the judgment of each other," she tells Argus; "nothing changes my opinion or wishes, after I once know them" (48).

33. It is worth noting that the Civil Rights bill of 1866 named "all persons born in the United States . . . *excluding Indians not taxed*" to be "citizens of the United States" (qtd. in Chalberg 66; my emphasis). Thus, Chloe's racial hybrid-ity makes her a civil hybrid as well—a noncitizen citizen—under the laws in place when Stoddard was writing *Temple House.*

34. For similar passages that equate Chloe's "Indianness" with freedom of speech, see 237, 244.

35. Young offers a description of Stowe's Topsy (who "corporealizes white female rebellion pushed 'downward' through psychic repression, racial differen-tiation, and geographic displacement" [36]) that seems to capture Chloe as well. In this regard, it is not entirely surprising to find Argus remarking on Chloe's physical endowments: "You are a fine woman, Chloe, and belong to a past gen-eration of females possessing hips. . . . I don't know that I object to the turning of the world which brings me Africa, and the lost tribes" (193).

36. Jennifer Putzi makes an excellent case for Stoddard's interest in South America, and in particular for South American independence struggles, in the essay included in this volume.

37. For my purposes, it is less important to understand the origins of the conflict itself than to see how the war is rendered in a periodical in whose pages Stoddard's own work appeared. In this context, it is notable that although *Har-per's* repeatedly presented the war as the result of the depredations of an "in-vading" Paraguay acting under despotic control, commentators (then and now) recognize the war as motivated as much by the "territorial ambitions of both Brazil and Argentina" as by the "foolhardiness and resentment" toward those

countries by Lopez. Lopez's fears of what one historian has called "Paraguayan dismemberment" (Bethell 786) at the hands of an encroaching Brazil were, in any case, realized by the war itself. At war's end, Paraguay had lost between 9 and 19 percent of its total population and 40 percent of its prewar territory (Bakewell 446).

38. Although her interest in *Temple House* lies in what she sees as its ultimately transgressive qualities, Anne-Marie Ford makes a similar point about the ways in which such racialist renderings compromise the novel's progressivism in an unpublished essay on the novel.

Afterword
Will Stoddard Endure?

Lawrence Buell

I'm certain of it—even though the jury is still out. To be sure, few authorial reputations have suffered such hazards and reversals as Elizabeth
Barstow Stoddard's, at least until very recently. Her nineteenth-century
success was inhibited by her refusal to write like a woman novelist, by
her cerebral, elliptical narrative style, by her transitional position between romance and realism, and by the coincidence of her most ambitious—but ostensibly "apolitical"—novels with the American Civil War.
Her novels were republished twice in her old age, and twice again she
fell into oblivion. A 1960s reprint did not thrive, either. First-wave feminist revisionism favored more recognizably plotted women's fiction and
looked askance at a writer who was as astringent toward sorority as she
was toward patriarchy. Since the University of Pennsylvania Press's edition of her works in the mid-1980s, followed by the Penguin edition of
The Morgesons in the 1990s, Stoddard has attracted more critical attention than heretofore, including several doctoral dissertations in which
she figures as sole or significant subject; but the present collection is the
first book-length study.

Will she ever receive what her admirers believe to be her due? What
is her due, anyway?

Perhaps a half-dozen times I have found myself excited by writers
either unknown or out of favor. Among these, only Stoddard, whom I
first read a quarter century ago, provoked me to want to undertake a
comprehensive gathering and selected edition of her work. Had the enthusiasm been mine only, I would have stopped at the samizdat of sourcebook photocopies. But not only did my colleague Sandra Zagarell have
the same "aha" experience, I also found that my best students felt the
same way—not always for the same reasons, of course. This pattern has
continued for the past two decades, during which I have taught Stoddard (with *The Morgesons* usually the centerpiece) at least fifteen times

to perhaps a thousand undergraduate and graduate students—mostly very enthusiastic—at Oberlin, Harvard, and elsewhere.

Is *their* enthusiasm, then, a case of sample bias skewed by the intellectual elitism of the students or by the teacher's overzealous hype? To some extent, perhaps; but these students have been far too diverse and cantankerous a group for a one-size-fits-all explanation. The unequivocal fact of my teaching experience is that Stoddard's work opens up in many directions to readers willing to work patiently with the initial difficulties posed by an elliptical, vignette-oriented style whose element of intensity seems at first strangely disjointed from its satiric dryness and penchant for the oblique. To group her work together with that of Hawthorne, Emerson, Thoreau, Stowe, Jacobs, Dickinson, and Melville has been additionally illuminating—and mutually reinforcing. Nor have I found that Stoddard suffers from such comparisons.

"All men say what to me," Emily Dickinson once told her perplexed "preceptor" Thomas Wentworth Higginson. The upshot is that today her work is read for its unique luminosity, his chiefly as an episode in cultural history—or on account of his relationship with her. As with Dickinson, so too it will eventually be with Elizabeth Stoddard, I believe—her best work, at any rate. It is only a matter of time. Consider, for a moment, the mind that could have chosen as an epigraph (for her second novel, *Two Men*) Emerson's mind-bending remark from "Experience"—"Treat the men and women well. Treat them as if they were real. Perhaps they are." No ordinary writer would have made such a choice. It took an unusual combination of acuity, irony, and chutzpah to risk a motto to which Stoddard *must* have known all readers would say, "What?" Likewise the learnedly allusive telegraphy—"*vestigia retrorsum*" (footsteps backward)—of Cassandra's flashback, in *The Morgesons,* to the bond with Charles that haunts her after his death. In both cases, the reader is put at arm's length as a counterpart to the alienation from the experience being dramatized.

The elegance of these indirections may be caviar to the general. Might it not be best, then, to shield tender undergraduates from Stoddard's fiction, especially since she is not (yet) canonical—as one assigns freshmen "Daisy Miller" rather than *The Golden Bowl*? Yet I myself have found that with minimal preparation, even "naive" readings of Stoddard by motivated younger students can yield exciting results, for both them and for me. They may not fully grasp the strange figures that inhabit Stoddard's imagined worlds, or her narrative rhetoric of staccato glimpses, or her narrative structures of willful unfulfillment; but the sense of something profoundly consequential in the tangled emotional relationships conjoining fascinatingly dysfunctional people, in brilliance coexisting with blindness, in the politics of gender and race, in the collision between "modern" consumption culture and "ancient" abstemiousness, all infused with thrusts of razor wit and laser vision—this they quickly see and find deeply interesting—as I do.

Against my partisanship can be set others', backed by certain statistics. The Penn edition has sold more than seven thousand copies, but the Harvard edition of Harriet Jacobs's *Incidents in the Life of a Slave Girl* has sold hundreds of thousands. The Heath anthology of U.S. literature includes Stoddard, but the Norton no longer does, though it once did. Stoddard's "Lemorne *versus* Huell"—one of her finest tales, of a young woman who thinks she's smart but belatedly realizes that she's nothing more than a pawn in the money/power/marriage game waged between her suitor and her aunt—was added to the Norton in the 1980s but later dropped, so I was told, because market surveys indicated that teachers found it unteachable. Several professional friends I admire with whom I've discussed Stoddard tell me such things as "I really like her work, but I can't seem to teach it" or (perhaps an elaboration of the same point) "I assign Sedgwick (and/or Fanny Fern and/or Louisa May Alcott) rather than Stoddard because the students find them more accessible and they fit my syllabus template better."

Not much can be said in response to complaints about Stoddard's muted affect or about her aesthetic of difficulty as such, except to suggest that most of us probably underrate or dismiss similar troubles students have with difficult writers long since familiar to and beloved by us. The second concern, as to "fit," is the point at which Stoddard's advocates need to strengthen their case. The possibilities are indeed far richer than have yet been shown, at least in print.

Previous studies have begun to situate Stoddard's writing in terms of such narrative-of-development genres as bildungsroman and women's fiction and in relation to gothic and regional traditions. All these are carried further in this collection, as is discussion of Stoddard's writing in relation to nineteenth-century thinking about issues of class, race, and nation—especially with reference to her second novel, *Two Men,* which here for the first time is given really searching critical examination.

Future Stoddard projects will, I hope, take up other important dimensions of her significance as well. She needs to be placed not simply in a U.S. but in a transatlantic context, especially vis-à-vis Charlotte

Brontë (*Villette* as well as *Jane Eyre*), but also in relation to Jane Austen, George Sand, and other admired—but never slavishly imitated—precursors. That Cassandra Morgeson grows up ignorant of her namesake, that "Cassandra" was a signifier of great resonance throughout the transatlantic Victorian world, is infinitely suggestive. In the same vein of subterranean, disruptive cosmopolitanism is the nicknaming of Philippa in *Two Men* as "the American sphinx"—presumably an allusion to Emerson's notoriously enigmatic poem (and to Stoddard's own persona?) as well as to the original—together with the teasing suggestion that the reference will be caught by some but not everybody.

As a practitioner of narrative, quite apart from how one positions her within (inter)national culture(s) and ideologies, Stoddard will repay much closer examination than she has received for her combination of acquiescence to and refusal of mimetic representation, for her desire to break narrative sequences into disjointed pulsations, for her refusal to gratify the expectations of narrative closure her texts set in motion, and for her fascination with patterns of mimetic desire—which, in turn, help explain her fascination with incestuous and quasi-incestuous bonds and with intersubjective phenomena generally.

As this collection begins to make clear, Stoddard's career becomes additionally revealing when connected with the history of authorship and print culture during the nineteenth century. Not only with regard to the thematics of such fictions as "Collected by a Valetudinarian" but also in her repeated remaking of herself as an author, her oscillation between deferral to versus demurral from publishers' expectations and advice from well-meaning mediocre handlers like her husband, Richard, her relations with tastemaker-acquaintances like Stedman and Howells —these make her career a study in balked originality to set beside Dickinson's and Melville's.

Stoddard's fiction, like her biography, is suggestive not only as it relates to the subject of print culture history but also of cultural history more generally. *The Morgesons,* for example, provides a unique window onto the rise of U.S. commodity culture and the rise of immigration in the nineteenth century—particularly tensions between Anglo American New England "natives" and ethnic others. *Two Men* begins to think of "American" issues hemispherically and dramatizes, with what I take to be deliberately strange, discomforting sarcasm, the pettiness and hypocrisy of northern racism.

Although most of Stoddard's genres are discussed in this volume, more remains to be known and shown about her early career as a columnist (both in itself and in relation to other women journalists of the era), her uneven but at best spectacular talent for short fiction, and her sortie into children's literature—*Lolly Dinks's Doings,* which, though certainly no classic, is notable for featuring one of the most repellent youngsters and one of the oddest mother-child relations in the late-Victorian imaginary. This is the anti-Alcott that Alcott herself may well secretly have wished to write.

Altogether, then, the question of Elizabeth Stoddard's critical future strikes me not as a question of whether but of when, and in precisely what directions. I hope this volume will speed the process of retrieval and reevaluation that is bound to come. Meanwhile, I look forward to further study and enjoyment of her work for as long as I continue to read, teach, think.

Works Cited

Abraham, Nicolas, and Maria Torok, *The Shell and The Kernel*. Vol. 1. Ed. and Trans. Nicholas T. Rand. Chicago: U of Chicago P, 1994.

Alaimo, Stacy. "Elizabeth Stoddard's *The Morgesons:* A Feminist Dialogue of Bildung and Descent." *Legacy* 8.1 (1991): 29–37.

Alcott, Louisa May. *Hospital Sketches*. 1863. Boston: Applewood, 1986.

———. *Little Women, 1868–69*. Ed. Elaine Showalter. New York: Penguin, 1989.

Alcott, William A. *The Young Wife, or Duties of a Woman in the Marriage Relation*. Boston: George W. Light, 1838.

Aldrich, Thomas Bailey, Mrs. *Crowding Memories*. Boston: Houghton Mifflin, 1920.

Ammons, Elizabeth. *Conflicting Stories: American Women Writers at the Turn into the Twentieth Century*. New York: Oxford UP, 1991.

Bakewell, Peter. *A History of Latin America: Empires and Sequels*. Malden, MA: Blackwell, 1997.

Bakhtin, Mikhail M. *The Dialogic Imagination: Four Essays by M. M. Bakhtin*. Trans. Caryl Emerson and Michael Holquist. Austin: U of Texas P, 1981.

Barker, Juliet. *The Brontës: A Life in Letters*. Woodstock, NY: Overlook P, 1997.

Battersby, Christine. *Gender and Genius: Towards a Feminist Aesthetics*. Bloomington: Indiana UP, 1989.

Baumgartner, Barbara. "The Unreflecting Mirror: Body, Voice and Identity in *The Morgesons.*" Forthcoming, *ESQ.*

Baym, Nina. *American Women Writers and the Work of History, 1790–1860*. New Brunswick: Rutgers UP, 1995.

———. "Melodramas of Beset Manhood: How Theories of American Fiction Exclude Women Authors." *American Quarterly* 33 (1981): 123–39.

———. *Novels, Readers, and Reviewers: Responses to Fiction in Antebellum America*. Ithaca: Cornell UP, 1984.

———. *Woman's Fiction: A Guide to Novels by and about Women in America, 1820–1870*. Ithaca: Cornell UP, 1978.

———. *Woman's Fiction: A Guide to Novels by and about Women in America, 1820–1870.* 2nd ed. Urbana: U of Illinois P, 1993.

Beecher, Catherine. *The American Women's Home, or Principles of Domestic Science.* New York: J. B. Ford, 1869.

Bennett, Paula, ed. *Nineteenth-Century American Women Poets: An Anthology.* London: Blackwell, 1998.

———. "Not Just Filler and Not Just Sentimental: Women's Poetry in American Victorian Periodicals, 1860–1900." *Periodical Literature in Nineteenth-Century America.* Ed. Kenneth M. Price and Susan Belasco Smith. Charlottesville: UP of Virginia, 1995. 202–79.

———. " 'Pomegranate-Flowers': The Phantasmic Productions of Late-Nineteenth-Century Anglo-American Women Poets." *Solitary Pleasures: The Historical, Literary, and Artistic Discourses of Autoeroticism.* Ed. Paula Bennett and Vernon A. Rosario II. New York: Routledge, 1995. 189–213.

Bethell, Leslie, ed. *From Independence to c. 1870.* Vol. 3 of *The Cambridge History of Latin America.* Cambridge: Cambridge UP, 1985.

Blanchard, Paula. *Margaret Fuller: From Transcendentalism to Revolution.* Reading, MA: Addison-Wesley, 1987.

" 'Boston Culture.' Two or Three Pairs of Blue Stockings." 10 Mar. [no year], Boston. Unidentified newspaper clipping, Louisa May Alcott Papers, Houghton Library, Harvard University, Cambridge.

Bourdieu, Pierre. *The Field of Cultural Production.* Cambridge, MA: Polity P, 1993.

Boyd, Anne E. "From 'Scribblers' to Artists: The Emergence of Women Writers as Artists." Diss. Purdue U, 1999.

Briggs, Asa. *Victorian Things.* London: Penguin, 1990.

Brodhead, Richard H. *The School of Hawthorne.* New York: Oxford UP, 1986.

Brontë, Charlotte. *Jane Eyre.* 1847. New York: Penguin, 1996.

Brooks, Van Wyck. *New England Indian Summer, 1865–1915.* New York: E. P. Dutton, 1940.

Brown, Gillian. *Domestic Individualism: Imagining Self in Nineteenth-Century America.* Berkeley: U of California P, 1990.

Bruche, Hilde. *Eating Disorders: Obesity, Anorexia Nervosa, and the Person Within.* New York: Basic, 1985.

Brumberg, Joan Jacobs. *Fasting Girls: The History of Anorexia Nervosa.* New York: Penguin, 1989.

Budick, Emily Miller. *Engendering Romance: Women Writers and the Hawthorne Tradition, 1850–1990.* New Haven: Yale UP, 1994.

Buell, Lawrence. *New England Literary Culture: From Revolution Through Renaissance.* New York: Cambridge UP, 1986.

Buell, Lawrence, and Sandra A. Zagarell. Biographical and Critical Introduction.

The Morgesons and Other Writings, Published and Unpublished. By Elizabeth Stoddard. Philadelphia: U of Pennsylvania P, 1984. xi–xxv.

Butler, Judith. *Bodies that Matter.* New York: Routledge, 1993.

———. *Gender Trouble: Feminism and the Subversion of Identity.* New York: Routledge, 1990.

Bynum, Caroline Walker. *Holy Feast and Holy Fast: The Religious Significance of Food to Medieval Women.* Berkeley: U of California P, 1987.

Carby, Hazel. *Reconstructing Womanhood: The Emergence of the Afro-American Woman Novelist.* New York: Oxford UP, 1987.

Carlier, Auguste. *Marriage in the United States.* Boston: 1867.

Cary, Richard. *The Genteel Circle: Bayard Taylor and His New York Friends.* Ithaca: Cornell UP, 1952.

Chalberg, John C. *Reconstruction: Opposing Viewpoints.* San Diego: Greenhaven, 1995.

Channing, William Ellery. "Self-Culture." *The Works of William Ellery Channing.* Boston: Crosby, Nichols, 1853.

Cherniavsky, Eva. *That Pale Mother Rising: Sentimental Discourses and the Imitation of Motherhood in Nineteenth-Century America.* Bloomington: Indiana UP, 1995.

Chesnut, Mary. *Mary Chesnut's Civil War.* Ed. C. Vann Woodward. New Haven: Yale UP, 1982.

Child, Lydia Maria. *A Romance of the Republic.* 1867. Ed. Dana D. Nelson. Lexington: U of Kentucky P, 1997.

Clay, Wilfred M. *The Masterless: The Self and Society in Modern America.* Chapel Hill: U of North Carolina P, 1994.

Conrad, Susan Phinney. *Perish the Thought: Intellectual Women in Romantic America, 1830–1860.* New York: Oxford UP, 1976.

Cooper, H. C. "Light or Shadow?" in "Notes and Comments." *North American Review* July 1890: 127–28.

Cott, Nancy. *The Bonds of Womanhood: Women's Sphere in New England, 1780–1835.* 2nd ed. New Haven: Yale UP, 1999.

Crews, Frederick. "Whose American Renaissance?" *New York Review of Books* 27 Oct. 1988: 68–81.

Croce, Ann Jerome. "Phantoms from an Ancient Loom: Elizabeth Barstow Stoddard and the American Novel, 1860–1900." Diss. Brown University, 1988.

———. "A Woman Outside Her Time: Elizabeth Barstow Stoddard (1823–1910) and Nineteenth-Century American Popular Fiction." *Women's Studies: An Interdisciplinary Journal* 19 (1991): 357–69.

Crumbley, Paul. "'As if for you to choose ——': Conflicting Textual Economies in Dickinson's Correspondence with Helen Hunt Jackson." *Women's Studies: An Interdisciplinary Journal* 31 (2002): 743–57.

——. *Inflections of the Pen: Dash and Voice in Emily Dickinson.* Lexington: UP of Kentucky, 1997.

Culican, William. *The Medes and Persians.* London: Thames, 1965.

Cummins, Maria Susanna. *The Lamplighter.* 1854. Ed. Nina Baym. New Brunswick: Rutgers UP, 1988.

Dalke, Anne. "Original Vice: The Political Implications of Incest in the Early American Novel." *Early American Literature* 23 (1988): 188–201.

Davidson, Cathy. "Preface: No More Separate Spheres!" *American Literature* 70 (1998): 443–63.

Davis, Cynthia J. *Bodily and Narrative Forms: The Influence of Medicine on American Literature, 1845–1915.* Stanford: Stanford UP, 2000.

Davis, Rebecca Harding. *Waiting for the Verdict.* 1867. Ed. Donald Dingledine. Albany, NY: New College UP, 1995.

Dean, Sharon L. *Constance Fenimore Woolson.* Knoxville: U of Tennessee P, 1995.

"Death of Mrs. Stoddard." *New York Times* 2 Aug. 1902: 9.

D'Emilio, John, and Estelle B. Freedman. *Intimate Matters: A History of Sexuality in America.* New York: Harper, 1988.

Dickie, Margaret. "Dickinson's Discontinuous Lyric Self." *On Dickinson: The Best from American Literature.* Ed. Edwin H. Cady and Louis J. Budd. Durham: Duke UP, 1990. 537–53.

Dickinson, Emily. *The Letters of Emily Dickinson.* 3 vols. Ed. Thomas H. Johnson and Theodora Ward. Cambridge: Belknap P of Harvard UP, 1958.

——. *The Poems of Emily Dickinson.* 3 vols. Ed. Thomas H. Johnson. Cambridge: Harvard UP, 1951, 1955.

Diffley, Kathleen. *Where My Heart Is Turning Ever: Civil War Stories and Constitutional Reform, 1861–1876.* Athens: U of Georgia P, 1992.

Dixon. Edward H. *Woman and Her Diseases, from the Cradle to the Grave: Adapted Exclusively to Her Instruction in the Physiology of Her System, and All Diseases of Her Critical Periods.* 10th ed. Philadelphia: John E. Potter, 1866.

Dobson, Joanne. *Dickinson and the Strategies of Reticence: The Woman Writer in Nineteenth-Century America.* Bloomington: Indiana UP, 1989.

——. "Reclaiming Sentimental Literature." *American Literature* 69 (1997): 263–88.

Douglas, Ann. *The Feminization of American Culture.* New York: Anchor, 1977.

Dunn, Mary Maples. "Saints and Sisters: Congregational and Quaker Women in the Early Colonial Period." *Women in American Religion.* Ed. Janet Wilson James. Philadelphia: U of Philadelphia P, 1980. 27–46.

Ehrenreich, Barbara, and Deirdre English. *Complaints and Disorders: The Sexual Politics of Sickness.* Old Westbury, NY: Feminist P, 1973.

Elbert, Monika M. Introduction. *Separate Spheres No More: Gender Convergence in American Literature, 1830–1930*. Tuscaloosa: U of Alabama P, 2000. 1–25.

Evans, Augusta Jane. *St. Elmo*. Ed. Diane Roberts. Tuscaloosa: U of Alabama P, 1992.

Ewell, Judith. *Venezuela and the United States: From Monroe's Hemisphere to Petroleum's Empire*. Athens: U of Georgia P, 1996.

Farr, Judith. *The Passion of Emily Dickinson*. Cambridge: Harvard UP, 1992.

Fehrenbacher, Don E., ed. *Abraham Lincoln: Speeches and Writings, 1832–1858*. New York: Library of America, 1989.

"Female Authors." *North American Review* Jan. 1851: 151–77.

Ferenczi, Sandor. *Final Contributions to the Problems and Methods of Psycho-Analysis*. New York: Brunner, 1980.

Fern, Fanny. *Ruth Hall and Other Writings*. Ed. Joyce W. Warren. New Brunswick: Rutgers UP, 1986.

Fetterley, Judith. "Commentary: Nineteenth-Century American Women Writers and the Politics of Recovery." *American Literary History* 6 (1994): 600–11.

———, ed. *Provisions: A Reader from Nineteenth-Century American Women*. Bloomington: Indiana UP, 1985.

Finch, Annie. "The Sentimental Poetess in the World: Metaphor and Subjectivity in Lydia Sigourney's Nature Poetry." *Legacy* 5.2 (1988): 3–18.

Fischer, John. *Six in the Easy Chair*. Urbana: U of Illinois P, 1973.

Foner, Eric. *Reconstruction: America's Unfinished Revolution, 1863–1877*. New York: Harper, 1988.

Foster, Richard. "The Fiction of Elizabeth Stoddard: An American Discovery." *History and Fiction: American Prose in the Nineteenth Century*. Ed. Alfred Weber and Hartmut Grandel. Gottingen: Vandenhoeck and Ruprecht, 1972. 161–93.

———. Introduction. *The Morgesons*. By Elizabeth Stoddard. New York: Johnson, 1971.

Fowler, Orson. *Amativeness: Warning and Advice to Married and Single*. New York: Fowlers and Wells, 1851.

Fowler, Robert. *A Complete History of the Case of the Welsh Fasting-Girl*. London: Henry Renshaw, 1871.

Friedman, Susan Stanford. *Mappings: Feminism and the Cultural Geographies of Encounter*. Princeton: Princeton UP, 1998.

Fuss, Diana. *Identification Papers*. New York: Routledge, 1995.

Gehrman, Jennifer A. "'I am half-sick of shadows': Elizabeth Stuart Phelps's Ladies of Shalott." *Legacy* 14.2 (1977): 123–28.

"General Bartolome Mitre, President of the Argentine Republic." *Harper's Weekly* 2 Dec. 1865: 764–65.

Gilbert, Sandra, and Susan Gubar. *Madwoman in the Attic: The Woman Writer and the Nineteenth-Century Literary Imagination*. New Haven: Yale UP, 1979.

Gilman, Charlotte Perkins. "Why I Wrote the Yellow Wallpaper?" *The Yellow Wallpaper*. Ed. Dale M. Bauer. New York: Bedford, 1988. 348–49.

Glazener, Nancy. *Reading for Realism: The History of a U.S. Literary Institution, 1850–1910*. Durham: Duke UP, 1997.

Glick, Megan. "Written by a Ghost of Their Time: Locating the Civil War in Elizabeth Stoddard's *The Morgesons*." Senior honors thesis, Northwestern U, 2002.

Godbout, Jacques T. *The World of the Gift*. Trans. Donald Winkler. Montreal: McGill-Queen's UP, 1998.

Goddu, Teresa. *Gothic America: Narrative, History, and Nation*. New York: Columbia UP, 1997.

Goetz, William R. "Genealogy and Incest in *Wuthering Heights*." *Studies in the Novel* 14 (1982): 359–76.

Gordon, Jean, and Jan McArthur. "Interior Decorating Advice as Popular Culture: Women's Views Concerning Wall and Window Treatment, 1870–1900." *Making the American Home: Middle-Class Women and Domestic Material Culture 1840–1940*. Ed. Marilyn Ferris Motz and Pat Browne. Bowling Green, OH: Bowling Green State UP, 1988. 105–20.

Goshgarian, G. M. *To Kiss the Chastening Rod: Domestic Fiction and Sexual Ideology in the American Renaissance*. Ithaca: Cornell UP, 1992.

Gray, Janet, ed. *She Wields a Pen: American Women Poets of the Nineteenth Century*. Iowa City: U of Iowa P, 1997.

Griswold, Rufus W. *The Poets and Poetry of America*. New York: J. Miller, 1874.

Grossberg, Michael. *Governing the Hearth: Law and the Family in Nineteenth-Century America*. Chapel Hill: U of North Carolina P, 1985.

Guillory, John. *Cultural Capital: The Problem of Literary Canon Formation*. Chicago: U of Chicago P, 1993.

Habegger, Alfred. *Henry James and the "Woman Business."* Cambridge: Cambridge UP, 1989.

———. "Precocious Incest: First Novels by Louisa May Alcott and Henry James." *Massachusetts Review* 26 (1985): 233–62.

Hager, Christopher. "Aggression and Forbearance: A Political Narratology of the American Novel, 1850–1900." Diss. In progress. Northwestern University.

Harris, Leila Assumpcao. "The Marriage Tradition in the Novels of Elizabeth Stoddard." Diss. Texas Tech University, 1990.

Harris, Susan K. *Nineteenth-Century American Women's Novels: Interpretive Strategies*. Cambridge: Cambridge UP, 1990.

———. "Stoddard's *The Morgesons:* A Contextual Evaluation." *ESQ* 31 (1985): 11–22.

Hartman, Geoffrey. *Criticism in the Wilderness.* New Haven: Yale UP, 1980.

Hawthorne, Julian. "Novelistic Habits and 'The Morgesons.'" *Lippincott's* 44 (1889): 868–71.

Hawthorne, Julian, and Leonard Lemmon. *American Literature, A Text-Book.* Boston: D. C. Heath, 1892.

Hawthorne, Nathaniel. "The Hall of Fantasy." *The Selected Tales and Sketches.* New York: Penguin, 1987: 246–58.

———. *The House of Seven Gables.* 1851. Boston: Houghton Mifflin, 1883.

———. *The House of the Seven Gables.* New York: Penguin, 1986.

———. *Letters: 1853–56. The Centenary Editions of the Works of Nathaniel Hawthorne.* Vol. 17. Ed. Thomas Woodson et al. Columbus: Ohio State UP, 1985.

———. "Night Sketches." *The Selected Tales and Sketches.* New York: Penguin, 1987: 225–31.

———. *The Scarlet Letter.* New York: Penguin Classics, 1986.

———. "A Select Party." *United States Magazine and Democratic Review* July 1844: 33–40.

Hayden, Dolores. *The Grand Domestic Revolution: A History of Feminist Designs for American Homes, Neighborhoods, and Cities.* Cambridge: MIT P, 1981.

Henwood, Dawn. "First-Person Storytelling in Elizabeth Stoddard's *The Morgesons:* Realism, Romance, and the Psychology of the Narrating Self." *ESQ* 41 (1995): 41–63.

———. "Narrative Strategies and Narrative Challenges in the Novels of Elizabeth Stoddard." MA thesis. Dalhousie U, 1992.

Herndl, Diane Price. *Invalid Women: Figuring Feminine Illness in American Fiction and Culture, 1840–1940.* Chapel Hill: U of North Carolina P, 1993.

Howells, William Dean. "First Impressions of Literary New York." *Harper's New Monthly Magazine* June 1895: 62–75.

———. *Literary Friends and Acquaintances.* Ed. David F. Hiatt and Edwin H. Cady. Bloomington: Indiana UP, 1968.

———. Review of *Two Men. Nation* 1 (1865): 537–38.

Humma, John B. "Realism and Beyond: The Imagery of Sex and Sexual Oppression in Elizabeth Stoddard's 'Lemorne *Versus* Huell.'" *South Atlantic Review* 58.1 (1993): 33–47.

Hyde, Lewis. *The Gift: Imagination and the Erotic Life of Property.* New York: Vintage, 1983.

Hynes, Jennifer. "Elizabeth Stoddard." *Dictionary of Literary Biography: Nineteenth-Century American Fiction Writers.* Ed. Kent P. Ljungquist. Detroit: Gale, 1999. 227–32.

Ignatiev, Noel. *How the Irish Became White*. London: Routledge, 1995.

Jackson, Helen Hunt. *Verses*. Boston: Roberts Brothers, 1875.

Jacobs, Harriet A. *Incidents in the Life of a Slave Girl: Written by Herself.* 1861. Ed. Jean Fagan Yellin. Cambridge: Harvard UP, 1987.

James, Henry. *Autobiography*. Ed. Frederick W. Dupee. Princeton: Princeton UP, 1983.

———. *Literary Criticism*. Vol. 1 of *Essays, English and American Writers*. New York, Library of America, 1984.

Kaplan, Amy. " 'Left Alone with America': The Absence of Empire in the Study of American Culture." *Cultures of United States Imperialism*. Ed. Amy Kaplan and Donald Pease. Durham: Duke UP, 1993. 3–21.

Karcher, Carolyn L. "Rape, Murder, and Revenge in 'Slavery's Pleasant Homes': Lydia Maria Child's Antislavery Fiction and the Limits of Genre." *The Culture of Sentiment: Race, Gender, and Sentimentality in Nineteenth-Century America*. Ed. Shirley Samuels. New York: Oxford UP, 1992. 59–61.

Kerber, Linda. *Toward an Intellectual History of Women*. Chapel Hill: U of North Carolina P, 1997.

———. *Women of the Republic: Intellect and Ideology in Revolutionary America*. New York: Norton, 1980.

Kete, Mary Louise. *Sentimental Collaborations: Mourning and Middle-Class Identity in Nineteenth-Century America*. Durham: Duke UP, 2000.

Kettner, James H. *The Development of American Citizenship, 1608–1870*. Chapel Hill: U of North Carolina P, 1978.

Kinney, James. *Amalgamation! Race, Sex and Rhetoric in the Nineteenth-Century American Novel*. Westport, CT: Greenwood P, 1985.

Kolb, Harold H., Jr. "Defining the Canon." *Redefining American Literary History*. Ed. LaVonne Brown Ruoff and Jerry W. Ward Jr. New York: MLA, 1990. 35–51.

Kucich, John. *Repression in Victorian Fiction: Charlotte Brontë, George Eliot, and Charles Dickens*. Berkeley: U of California P, 1987.

Lamb, Harold. *Cyrus the Great*. Garden City: Doubleday, 1960.

Lapham, Lewis. "Hazards of New Fortune: *Harper's Magazine,* Then and Now." *Harper's Magazine* June 2000: 57–72.

Lathrop, George Parsons. "Audacity in Women Novelists." *North American Review* May 1890: 609–17.

Lauter, Paul. *Canons and Contexts*. New York: Oxford UP, 1991.

Lee, Maurice S. "Melville's Subversive Political Philosophy: 'Benito Cereno' and the Fate of Speech." *American Literature* 72 (2000): 495–519.

Lender, Mark Edward, and James Kirby Martin. *Drinking in America: A History*. New York: Free P, 1982.

Leyda, Jay. *The Years and Hours of Emily Dickinson.* 2 vols. New Haven: Yale UP; London: Oxford UP, 1960.

"Literary Notices." *Continental Monthly* May 1863: 630–32.

"El Llanero." *Atlantic Monthly* Feb. 1859: 174–88.

Lombardi, John V. *Venezuela: The Search for Order, the Dream of Progress.* New York: Oxford UP, 1982.

Longfellow, Henry Wadsworth. *The Letters of Henry Wadsworth Longfellow.* Ed. Andrew Hillen. Vol. 6. Cambridge: Belknap P of Harvard UP, 1982.

"The Lounger." *The Critic* Oct. 1902: 299.

Lystra, Karen. *Searching the Heart: Women, Men, and Romantic Love in Nineteenth-Century America.* New York: Oxford UP, 1989.

Macpherson, C. B. *The Political Theory of Possessive Individualism, from Hobbes to Locke.* Oxford: Oxford UP, 1962.

Matlack, James Hendrickson. "Hawthorne and Elizabeth Barstow Stoddard." *New England Quarterly* 50 (1977): 282–93.

———. "The Literary Career of Elizabeth Barstow Stoddard." Diss. Yale University, 1968. Ann Arbor: UMI, 1968.

Matter-Siebel, Sabina. "Subverting the Sentimental: Elizabeth Barstow Stoddard's *The Morgesons.*" *Flip Sides: New Critical Essays in American Literature.* Frankfurt: Peter Lang, 1995. 15–41.

———. "'Untranslated Signs': Narrative Anxiety in First-Person Fiction Written by Nineteenth-Century Women." *Blurred Boundaries: Critical Essays on American Literature, Language, and Culture.* Frankfurt: Peter Lang, 1996. 81–98.

Mattingly, Carol. *Well-Tempered Women: Nineteenth-Century Temperance Rhetoric.* Carbondale: Southern Illinois UP, 1998.

Mauss, Marcel. *The Gift: Forms and Function of Exchange in Archaic Societies.* Trans. Ian Cunnison. Glencoe: Free P, 1954.

McGuire, Kathryn B. "The Incest Taboo in *Wuthering Heights:* A Modern Appraisal." *American Imago* 45 (1988): 217–24.

Melville, Herman. "Hawthorne and His Mosses." 1850. *The Norton Anthology of American Literature.* 3rd ed. Vol. 1. Ed. Nina Baym et al. New York: Norton, 1989.

———. *Moby-Dick.* New York: Norton, 1967.

Miller, Cristanne. *Emily Dickinson: A Poet's Grammar.* Cambridge: Harvard UP, 1987.

Miller, Nancy K. "Arachnologies: The Woman, the Text, and the Critic." *The Poetics of Gender.* Ed. Nancy K. Miller. New York: Columbia UP, 1986: 270–96.

———. *Subject to Change: Reading Feminist Writing.* New York: Columbia UP, 1986.

Mitchell, Domhnall. "Acts of Intercourse: 'Miscegenation' in Three Nineteenth-

Century American Novels." *American Studies in Scandinavia* 27 (1995): 126–41.

Moore, Margaret B. "Elizabeth Barstow Stoddard's 'Immortal Feather.'" *Hawthorne and Women: Engendering and Expanding the Hawthorne Tradition*. Ed. John L. Idol Jr. and Melinda M. Ponder. Boston: U of Massachusetts P, 1999. 121–30.

Review of *The Morgesons*. *Independent* 41 (1889): 23.

Morris, Timothy. *Becoming Canonical in American Poetry*. Urbana: U of Illinois P, 1995.

———. "Elizabeth Stoddard: An Examination of Her Work as Pivot between Exploratory Fiction and the Modern Short Story." *American Women Short Story Writers: A Collection of Critical Essays*. Ed. Julie Brown. New York: Garland, 1995. 33–43.

Morrison, Toni. *Playing in the Dark: Whiteness and the Literary Imagination*. Cambridge: Harvard UP, 1992.

Moss, Mary. "The Novels of Elizabeth Stoddard." *Bookman* May 1902: 260–63.

"Mrs. Stoddard's 'Two Men.'" *Literary World* Dec. 1888: 227.

Murray, Dru J. "The Unconquered Seminoles." *Absolutely Florida Magazine* 1997. 12 Aug. 2001. <http://www.abfla.com/1tocf/seminole/semhistory.html>.

Nelson, Dana. *The Word in Black and White: Reading 'Race' in American Literature, 1638–1867*. New York: Oxford UP, 1992.

Nettels, Elsa. "New England Indigestion and Its Victims." *Disordered Eaters: Texts in Self-Empowerment*. Ed. Lilian R. Furst and Peter W. Graham. University Park: Penn State UP, 1992. 167–84.

Newbury, Michael. *Figuring Authorship in Antebellum America*. Stanford: Stanford UP, 1997.

Norton, Anne. *Alternative Americas: A Reading of Antebellum Political Culture*. Chicago: U of Chicago P, 1986.

"Novels and Novelists." *North American Review* Jan. 1853: 104–24.

"Paraguay." *Harper's Weekly* 20 Apr. 1867: 243.

Pattee, Fred Lewis. *A History of American Literature, With a View to the Fundamental Principles Underlying Its Development*. New York: Silver, Burdett, 1896.

Penner, Louise. "Domesticity and Self-Possession in *The Morgesons* and *Jane Eyre*." *Studies in American Fiction* 27 (1999): 131–48.

Petrino, Elizabeth. *Emily Dickinson and Her Contemporaries*. Hanover: UP of New England, 1998.

Petrulionis, Sandra Harbert. "Elizabeth Drew Barstow Stoddard (1823–1902)." *Nineteenth-Century American Women Writers: A Bio-Bibliographical Critical Sourcebook*. Ed. Denise D. Knight and Emmanuel S. Nelson. Westport, CT: Greenwood P, 1997. 397–405.

Phelps, Elizabeth Stuart. *Chapters from a Life.* Boston: Houghton Mifflin, 1896.

Pollak, Vivian. "Thirst and Starvation in Emily Dickinson's Poetry." *On Dickinson: The Best from American Literature.* Ed. Edwin H. Cady and Louis J. Budd. Durham: Duke UP, 1990. 62–75.

Post-Lauria, Shelia. *Correspondent Colorings: Melville in the Marketplace.* Amherst: U of Massachusetts P, 1996.

Radinovsky, Lisa. "Against All Odds: Elizabeth Stoddard as Obstructed Creator." *Women, Creators of Culture.* Ed. Ekaterini Georgoudaki and Domna Pastourmatzi. Thessalonika: Hellenic Association of American Studies, 1997.

———. "Gender Norms and Genre Forms: Elizabeth Stoddard's Challenges to Convention." Diss. Duke U, 1999. Ann Arbor: UMI, 1999.

"The Recall of General Paez." *New York Times* 6 Oct. 1858: 6.

"Recent American Fiction." *Atlantic Monthly* July 1889: 127–28.

Reynolds, David S. *Beneath the American Renaissance: The Subversive Imagination in the Age of Emerson and Melville.* New York: Knopf, 1988.

Reynolds, Davis S., and Debra J. Rosenthal, eds. *The Serpent in the Cup: Temperance Writing in American Literature.* Amherst: U of Massachusetts P, 1997.

Rich, Adrienne. *On Lies, Secrets, and Silence: Selected Prose, 1966–1978.* New York: Norton, 1979.

Richards, William Cary. *A Day in the New York Crystal Palace, and How to Make the Most of It: Being a Popular Companion to the "Official Catalogue," and a Guide to All the Objects of Special Interest.* New York: Putnam, 1853.

Robertson-Lorant, Laurie. *Melville: A Biography.* New York: Clarkson Potter, 1996.

Rogers, David Lawrence. "The Irony of Idealism: William Faulkner and the South's Construction of the Mulatto." *The Discourse of Slavery: Aphra Behn to Toni Morrison.* Ed. Carl Plasa and Betty J. Ring. London: Routledge, 1994. 166–90.

"A Romance of New Bedford." *New York Times* 15 July 1888: 12.

Romero, Lora. *Home Fronts: Domesticity and Its Critics in the Antebellum United States.* Durham: Duke UP, 1997.

Rorabaugh, W. J. *The Alcoholic Republic: An American Tradition.* New York: Oxford UP, 1979.

Rosaldo, Michelle Zimbalist, and Louise Lamphere. *Women, Culture and Society.* Stanford: Stanford UP, 1977.

Rotundo, E. Anthony. *American Manhood: Transformations in Masculinity from the Revolution to the Modern Era.* New York: Basic-Harper, 1993.

Ruggles, Eleanor. *Prince of Players: Edwin Booth.* Westport, CT: Greenwood P, 1972.

Ryan, Mary. *The Empire of the Mother: American Writing about Domesticity, 1830–1860.* New York: Institute for Research in History and the Haworth P, 1982.

———. *Women in Public: Between Banners and Ballots, 1825–1880.* Baltimore: Johns Hopkins UP, 1990.

Safran, Stephen P. "Asperger Syndrome: The Emerging Challenge to Special Education." *Exceptional Children* 67 (2001): 151–60.

Saks, Eva. "Representing Miscegenation Law." *Raritan* 8.2 (1988): 39–69.

Samuels, Shirley. *Romances of the Republic: Women, the Family, and Violence in the Literature of the Early American Nation.* New York: Oxford UP, 1996.

Sánchez-Eppler, Karen. *Touching Liberty: Abolition, Feminism, and the Politics of the Body.* Berkeley: U of California P, 1993.

Sax, Benjamin. *Images of Identity: Goethe and the Problem of Self-Conception in the Nineteenth Century.* Boston: Peter Lang, 1987.

Scott, Jack, Claudia Clark, and Michael P. Brady, eds. *Students with Autism: Characteristics and Instructional Programming for Special Educators.* San Diego: Singular, 2000.

Sewall, Richard. *The Life of Emily Dickinson.* 2 vols. New York: Farrar, 1974.

Shelley, Percy B. Preface. *Laon and Cythna, or, The Revolution of the Golden City: A Vision of the Nineteenth Century.* By Percy B. Shelley. London: B. McMillan, 1818.

Showalter, Elaine. *The Female Malady: Women, Madness, and English Culture, 1830–1980.* New York: Pantheon, 1985.

Sizer, Lyde Cullen. *The Political Work of Northern Women Writers and the Civil War, 1850–1872.* Chapel Hill: U of North Carolina P, 2000.

Skinfill, Mauri. "Nation and Miscegenation: *Incidents in the Life of a Slave Girl.*" *Arizona Quarterly* 51.2 (1995): 63–79.

Smith, Adam. *The Theory of Moral Sentiments.* 1759. Ed. D. D. Raphael and A. L. Macfie. Indianapolis: Liberty, 1982.

Smith, Barbara Herrnstein. *Contingencies of Value: Alternative Perspectives for Critical Theory.* Cambridge: Harvard UP, 1988.

Smith, Robert McClure. "'A Peculiar Case': Masochistic Subjectivity and Stoddard's *The Morgesons.*" *Arizona Quarterly* 58.3 (2002): 1–27.

Smith-Rosenberg, Carroll. "The Female World of Love and Ritual: Relations between Women in Nineteenth-Century America." *Disorderly Conduct: Visions of Gender in Victorian America.* New York: Oxford UP, 1985. 53–76.

Snow, M. G. "A Gossip about Novels." *Harper's New Monthly Magazine* Apr. 1863: 690–96.

Sollors, Werner. *Neither Black nor White yet Both: Thematic Explorations of Interracial Literature.* New York: Oxford UP, 1997.

Sournia, Jean-Charles. *A History of Alcoholism.* Trans. Nick Hindley and Gareth Stanton. London: Basil Blackwell, 1990.

Spillers, Hortense J. "'Mama's Baby, Papa's Maybe: An American Grammar Book." *diacritics* 17.2 (1987): 65–81.

Stampp, Kenneth M. *The Era of Reconstruction: 1865–1877.* New York: Knopf, 1965.

Stansell, Christine. *City of Women: Sex and Class in New York, 1789–1860.* New York: Knopf, 1986.

Stedman, Edmund Clarence. "A Critical Estimate of Mrs. Stoddard's Novels." Rpt. as "Mrs. Stoddard's Novels" in *Genius and Other Essays.* Port Washington: Kennikat, 1966.

Stedman, Laura, and George M. Gould, eds. *Life and Letters of Edmund Clarence Stedman.* New York: Moffat, Yard, 1910.

Stoddard, Elizabeth. "The Chimneys." *Harper's New Monthly Magazine* Nov. 1865: 721–32.

———. "Collected by a Valetudinarian." *Harper's New Monthly Magazine* Dec. 1870: 96–105.

———. "Collected by a Valetudinarian." *The Morgesons and Other Writings, Published and Unpublished.* Ed. Lawrence Buell and Sandra A. Zagarell. Philadelphia: U of Pennsylvania P, 1984. 285–308.

———. "From a Lady Correspondent." *Daily Alta California* 8 Oct. 1854–28 Feb. 1858.

———. "Gull's Bluff." *Harper's New Monthly Magazine* July 1865: 208–13.

———. "The Inevitable Crisis." *Harper's New Monthly Magazine* Jan. 1868: 248–56.

———. "Journal, 1866." *The Morgesons and Other Writings, Published and Unpublished.* Ed. Lawrence Buell and Sandra A. Zagarell. Philadelphia: U of Pennsylvania P, 1984. 347–58.

———. "My Own Story." *Atlantic Monthly* May 1860: 526–47.

———. "Lemorne *versus* Huell." *Harper's New Monthly Magazine* Mar. 1863: 537–43.

———. "Literary Folk as They Came and Went with Ourselves." *Saturday Evening Post* 30 June 1900: 1222–23.

———. "A Literary Whim." *Appletons' Journal* 14 Oct. 1871: 440–41.

———. "Love Will Find Out the Way." *Harper's New Monthly Magazine* Sept. 1882: 567–76.

———. "Lucy Tavish's Journey." *Harper's New Monthly Magazine* Oct. 1867: 656–63.

———. "Me and My Son." *Harper's New Monthly Magazine* July 1870: 213–21.

——. *The Morgesons.* New York: Penguin, 1997.

——. *The Morgesons and Other Writings, Published and Unpublished.* Ed. Lawrence Buell and Sandra A. Zagarell. Philadelphia: U of Pennsylvania P, 1984.

——. "One of the Days of My Life." *Saturday Press* 1860. N.d., n.pag.

——. "Osgood's Predicament." *Harper's New Monthly Magazine* June 1863: 52–61.

——. "Our Christmas Party." *Harper's New Monthly Magazine* Jan. 1859: 202–5.

——. "A Partie Carée." *Harper's New Monthly Magazine* Sept. 1862: 466–79.

——. *Poems.* Boston: Houghton, 1895.

——. "The Poet's Secret." *Harper's New Monthly Magazine* Jan. 1860: 194.

——. "Polly Dossett's Rule." *Harper's New Monthly Magazine* Jan. 1890: 267–78.

——. Preface to *The Morgesons. The Morgesons and Other Writings, Published and Unpublished.* Ed. Lawrence Buell and Sandra A. Zagarell. Philadelphia: U of Pennsylvania P, 1984. 259–62.

——. "The Prescription." *Harper's New Monthly Magazine* May 1864: 794–800.

——. *Temple House: A Novel.* New York: G. W. Carleton, 1867.

——. "Tuberoses." *Harper's New Monthly Magazine* Jan. 1863: 191–97.

——. *Two Men. A Novel.* New York: Bunce and Huntington, 1865; Rev. ed. New York: Johnson, 1971.

——. "Uncle Zeb." *Saturday Press* 25 Feb 1860: n.pag.

——. "Unexpected Blows." *Harper's New Monthly Magazine* Dec. 1867: 64–74.

——. "The Visit." *Harper's New Monthly Magazine* Nov. 1868: 802–9.

——. "The Visit." *Harper's New Monthly Magazine* Nov. 1872: 860–67.

——. "A Wheat-field Idyl." *Harper's New Monthly Magazine* Sept. 1891: 571–81.

——. [anonymous]. "Woman and Art." *The Aldine* Jan. 1870: 3–4.

——. [Elizabeth B. Leonard]. "Woman in Art—Rosa Bonheur." *The Aldine* July 1872: 145.

Stoddard, Richard Henry. *Recollections, Personal and Literary.* Ed. Ripley Hitchcock. New York: A. S. Barnes, 1903.

Sundquist, Eric J. *Faulkner: The House Divided.* Baltimore: Johns Hopkins UP, 1983.

Sweetser, Charles. "Review of *Two Men,* by Elizabeth Stoddard." *The Round Table* 11 Nov. 1865: 148.

Tate, Claudia. *Domestic Allegories of Political Desire: The Black Heroine's Text at the Turn of the Century.* New York: Oxford UP, 1992.

Taylor, Bayard. *Selected Letters of Bayard Taylor.* Ed. Paul C. Wermuth. Lewisburg: Bucknell UP, 1997.

Taylor, Marie Hansen. *On Two Continents; Memories of Half a Century.* New York: Doubleday, Page, 1905.

Review of *Temple House. Nation* 23 Jan. 1868: 74–75.

Review of *Temple House*. *Nation* 28 Mar. 1889: 272–73.

Review of *Temple House*. *Putnam's* Feb. 1868: 255.

Review of *Temple House*. *New York Tribune* Jan. 1868: 6.

Thomas, Heather Kirk. "Emily Dickinson's 'Renunciation' and Anorexia Nervosa." *American Literature* 60 (1988): 205–25.

Thorslev, Peter L., Jr. "Incest as Romantic Symbol." *Comparative Literature Studies* 2 (1965): 41–58.

Tompkins, Jane. *Sensational Designs: The Cultural Work of American Fiction, 1790–1860*. New York: Oxford UP, 1986.

Tomsich, John. *A Genteel Endeavor: American Culture and Politics in the Gilded Age*. Stanford: Stanford UP, 1971.

Torsney, Cheryl B. *Constance Fenimore Woolson: The Artistry of Grief*. Athens: U of Georgia P, 1989.

Tracey, Karen. *Plots and Proposals: American Women's Fiction, 1850–1890*. Urbana: U of Illinois P, 2000.

Twitchell, James B. *Forbidden Partners: The Incest Taboo in Modern Culture*. New York: Columbia UP, 1987.

Review of *Two Men*. *Nation* 9 Aug. 1888: 118.

Tyrell, Ian R. *Sobering Up: From Temperance to Prohibition in Antebellum America, 1800–1860*. Westport, CT: Greenwood P, 1979.

Review of *Uncle Tom's Cabin*. *North American Review* July 1853: 466–93.

Valverde, Mariana. *Diseases of the Will: Alcohol and the Dilemmas of Freedom*. Cambridge: Cambridge UP, 1998.

Vedder, Henry C. *American Writers of To-Day*. New York: Silver, Burdett, 1894.

Vice, Sue. "Intemperate Climate: Drinking, Sobriety, and the American Literary Myth." *American Literary History* 11 (1999): 699–709.

Von Hallberg, Robert, ed. *Canons*. Chicago: U of Chicago P, 1983.

Wald, Priscilla. *Constituting Americans: Cultural Anxiety and Narrative Form*. Durham: Duke UP, 1995.

Walker, Cheryl. *The Nightingale's Burden: Women Poets and American Culture before 1900*. Bloomington: Indiana UP, 1982.

Walker, Nancy. *Fanny Fern*. New York: Twayne, 1993.

"The War in South America." *Harper's Weekly* 8 Apr. 1865: 221.

"The War in South America." *Harper's Weekly* 16 Sept. 1865: 579.

Warner, Nicholas O. *Spirits of America: Intoxication in Nineteenth-Century American Literature*. Norman: U of Oklahoma P, 1997.

Warner, Susan. *The Wide, Wide World*. 1850. New York: Feminist P, 1987.

Warren, Joyce W., ed. *The (Other) American Traditions: Nineteenth-Century Women Writers*. New Brunswick: Rutgers UP, 1993.

Weimer, Joan Myers. Introduction. *Women Artists, Women Exiles: "Miss Grief" and*

Other Stories. By Constance Fenimore Woolson. New Brunswick: Rutgers UP, 1988. xi–xlviii.

Weinauer, Ellen. "Alternative Economies: Authorship and Ownership in Elizabeth Stoddard's 'Collected by a Valetudinarian.'" *Studies in American Fiction* 25 (1997): 167–82.

Weiner, Annette B. *Inalienable Possessions: The Paradox of Keeping-While-Giving.* Berkeley: U of California P, 1992.

Weir, Sybil. "*The Morgesons:* A Neglected Feminist *Bildungsroman.*" *NEQ* 49 (1976): 427–39.

———. "Our Lady Correspondent: The Achievement of Elizabeth Drew Stoddard." *San Jose Studies* 10.2 (1984): 73–91.

Welter, Barbara. "The Cult of True Womanhood: 1820–1860." *American Quarterly* 18 (1966): 151–74.

———. *Dimity Convictions: The American Woman in the Nineteenth Century.* Athens: Ohio UP, 1976.

Wilentz, Gay. *Healing Narratives: Women Writers Curing Cultural Dis-ease.* New Brunswick: Rutgers UP, 2000.

Williams, Deborah Lindsay. *Not in Sisterhood: Edith Wharton, Willa Cather, Zona Gale, and the Politics of Female Authorship.* New York: Palgrave, 2001.

Wilson, James D. "Incest and American Romantic Fiction." *Studies in the Literary Imagination* 7.1 (1974): 31–50.

Wise, Daniel. *The Young Lady's Counsellor: Or, Outlines and Illustrations of the Sphere, the Duties, and the Dangers of Young Women.* Cincinnati: Hitchcock and Walden, 1869.

Wood, Ann D. "The 'Scribbling Women' and Fanny Fern: Why Women Wrote." *American Quarterly* 23 (1971): 3–24.

Woodman, Lilian (Mrs. Thomas Bailey Aldrich). *Crowding Memories.* Boston: Houghton, 1920.

Woolson, Constance Fenimore. *Women Artists, Women Exiles: "Miss Grief" and Other Stories.* Ed. Joan Meyers Weimer. New Brunswick: Rutgers UP, 1988.

Wright, Winthrop. *Café con Leche: Race, Class, and National Image in Venezuela.* Austin: U of Texas P, 1990.

Young, Elizabeth. *Disarming the Nation: Women's Writing and the American Civil War.* Chicago: U of Chicago P, 1999.

Zagarell, Sandra A. Introduction. *The Chimneys.* By Elizabeth Stoddard. *Legacy* 7.2 (1990): 27–37.

———. "Profile: Elizabeth Drew Barstow Stoddard (1823–1902)." *Legacy* 8.1 (1991): 39–49.

———. "The Repossession of a Heritage: Elizabeth Stoddard's *The Morgesons.*" *Studies in American Fiction* 13 (1985): 45–56.

Contributors

Jaime Osterman Alves is a Ph.D. candidate at the University of Maryland, College Park. Her dissertation, "Miss Schooled: American Fictions of Female Education, 1800–1900," reads narratives of adolescent schoolgirls against historical debates over girls' schooling and shifts in the development of institutionalized education.

Margaret A. Amstutz is a Ph.D. candidate in English and American Literature at Washington University. Her doctoral research focuses on Elizabeth Stoddard's reading of Nathaniel Hawthorne as evidenced in her journalism and fiction. She currently serves as assistant to the president at the University of Georgia.

Lawrence Buell is Powell A. Cabot Professor of American Literature at Harvard University. He is the author of, among other books, *New England Literary Culture* (1986), *The Environmental Imagination* (1995), and *Emerson* (2003), and coeditor with Sandra Zagarell of *The Morgesons and Other Writings, Published and Unpublished,* by Elizabeth Stoddard (1984).

Paul Crumbley is Associate Professor of English and American Studies at Utah State University. He is the author of *Inflections of the Pen: Dash and Voice in Emily Dickinson* (1997) and numerous articles on the poet. He is currently completing a book on Dickinson and politics. Crumbley also serves on the Executive Board of the Emily Dickinson International Society.

Jennifer Putzi teaches American literature and Women's Studies at The College of William and Mary. She has published articles on nineteenth-century American women writers in *Legacy* and *Studies in American Fiction* and is the coeditor of *American Women Prose Writers, 1870–1920*

(2000). She is currently working on a study of the marked body in nineteenth-century American literature.

LISA RADINOVSKY has taught at Duke University, McGill University, John Abbott College, and a Greek language school. She has presented papers on U.S. women writers at conferences throughout the United States and in Greece and published articles in the *Oxford Companion to Women's Writing in the United States,* the *American National Biography,* and other books. Now living in Crete, Greece, she is working on a literary biography of Elizabeth Stoddard.

SUSANNA RYAN is the Woodrow Wilson Postdoctoral Fellow in the Humanities in the English Department at Indiana University. In 2002, she completed her Ph.D. in Victorian literature and culture at the University of Michigan. She is currently revising her dissertation, "Coming to the Whip: Horsemanship and the Politics of Victorian Empathy," for publication as a book.

ROBERT MCCLURE SMITH is Associate Professor of English at Knox College. He is the author of *The Seductions of Emily Dickinson* (1996) and numerous articles on nineteenth-century American literature.

JULIA STERN is Associate Professor of English at Northwestern University. Author of *The Plight of Feeling: Sympathy and Dissent in the Early American Novel* (1997), she is at work on two book manuscripts: "Epic, Miniature, and Mary Chesnut's Civil War" and "Life on the Food Chain: Appetite, Affect, and American Autobiography, 1845–1886."

ELLEN WEINAUER is Associate Professor of English and the Director of the Women's Studies Program at the University of Southern Mississippi. She has published articles on Stoddard, Hawthorne, Melville, and others and is currently at work on a book manuscript, "In the Legal Tomb: Property, Personhood, and the Gothic in Antebellum America."

SANDRA A. ZAGARELL, Professor of English at Oberlin College, is coeditor, with Lawrence Buell, of *The Morgesons and Other Writings, Published and Unpublished,* by Elizabeth Stoddard (1984) Her articles on nineteenth-century American literature include several on Stoddard. She is a senior editor of the *Heath Anthology of American Literature.*

Index